Theology of the Lutheran Confessions

Theology of the Lutheran Confessions

By EDMUND SCHLINK

Translated by

PAUL F. KOEHNEKE AND HERBERT J. A. BOUMAN

FORTRESS PRESS   PHILADELPHIA

This book is a translation of *Theologie der lutherischen Bekenntnisschriften* (3d edition), copyright © 1948 by Chr. Kaiser Verlag in Munich, Germany, and published as the eighth volume in a series entitled "Einführung in die evangelische Theologie."

Copyright © 1961 by Fortress Press

Second printing 1964
Third printing 1967
Fourth printing 1969

First paperback edition 1975
Second printing 1978

Library of Congress Catalog Card Number 61-6757

ISBN 0-8006-1883-1

7439H78   Printed in the United States of America   1-1883

AUTHOR'S PREFACE TO THE
AMERICAN EDITION

This book had its origin in the period of the trials and persecutions to which the Christians in Germany were exposed while the National Socialists were in power. In an entirely new and urgent way this situation called for a courageous and steadfast confession of faith over against the totalitarian state and its world view. Here it became apparent what great assistance and strength for today's act of confessing is provided by the Confessions of the ancient church and of the Reformation. Temptations and heresies take on new forms as history moves, but the Christ who saves us and whom we are called upon to confess remains one and the same. For this reason the confessing act of the individual and the Confession of the church belong together, even though each individual in his own time must use new words to confess the same Christ. The Confession of the church, however, is never merely the confession of contemporaries, that is, of the fellowship of the brethren; it is always also the confession of the fathers. For through all the vicissitudes of the ages and amid all the multiplicity of its current witnesses the church ever remains one and the same. It is the purpose of this book to help clarify the relationship—once again so significant—between the traditional Confession and the confessing act of the moment by unfolding the theology of the Lutheran Confessions in its inner coherence.

During those years of common tribulation the walls between the separated churches also became transparent. Many things which formerly kept the churches apart were demolished by the common foe. All were placed in the same way in the position of having to decide whether they would confess Jesus Christ or deny him. In this situation it became evident that, far from widening the historic splits in Christendom, a concern for the right kind of confessing rather recalls the separated churches to the one Lord from whom alone they receive life. At the same time it became clear that the Lutheran Confession, correctly understood, enhances in a special way the ability to recognize brethren also in the other churches. For all of its statements are concentrated on the Gospel. With all the differences in worship forms and in polity—yes, even in dogmatic formulations—the Lutheran Confessions permit us to recognize anew the one church, if only the Gospel is proclaimed and the sacraments administered in accordance with it. Thus, when we were able after the war to leave the catacombs of the Third Reich and to establish ecumenical relations with the churches around the world, the Reformation Confession proved to be of important assistance. It gave us great encouragement to seek beyond the confessional boundaries the fellowship in faith.

It is my hope that the American edition of this book too will not lead to an anxious and aloof repristination but to a concern for genuine confession in our time and that it will encourage a loving approach to the other churches.

—Edmund Schlink

Heidelberg, September, 1960

TRANSLATOR'S PREFACE

The Lutheran Confessions, or Symbols, represent the result of more than a generation of earnest endeavor on the part of Martin Luther and his followers to give clear and positive expression to their religious convictions. The collection of Lutheran creeds known as the Book of Concord, published in 1580, contains a number of documents of diverse background, authorship, historical setting, and purpose. At least four different groups may be discerned: (1) the three Ecumenical Creeds of the ancient church; (2) the two Catechisms of Luther; (3) the Augsburg Confession, its Apology, and the Smalcald Articles, together with the Treatise on the Power and Primacy of the Pope; (4) the Formula of Concord in its two parts, Epitome and Solid Declaration. Three of these writings are from Luther's pen, namely, the two Catechisms (1529) and the Smalcald Articles (1537); three were composed by Philip Melanchthon, the brilliant scholar and humanist so closely associated with the great Reformer, nameiy, the Augsburg Confession (1530), the Apology (1531), and the Treatise (1537). A number of second-generation Lutheran theologians, notably Jacob Andreae and Martin Chemnitz, were responsible for the series of profound doctrinal declarations set forth in the Formula of Concord (1577).

The Catechisms, of course, serve the constructive purpose of teaching the "young and inexperienced," both children and adults, the "chief parts of Christian doctrine." The Augsburg Confession, the primary statement of the Lutheran faith, is couched in generally mild, conservative language designed to help heal the breach with the Church of Rome. The Apology is Melanchthon's thorough and learned, often sharply worded, defense of the Lutheran position against the exegesis and logic of the Roman Confutation. Six years later the Lutheran princes and estates met at Smalcald to consider their course of action with respect to a general council which Pope Paul III had convoked. Luther was asked by the Saxon elector to prepare the theological guidelines. With his customary vigor the Reformer set down in succession the articles of faith concerning which there was no controversy, those where no concessions could be made, and those that could be discussed with "learned and sensible men." About the same time Melanchthon furnished a careful analysis, based on Scripture and church history, of the question concerning the power and primacy of the pope. Following Luther's death in 1546, some thirty years of intra-Lutheran controversy ensued in which various points of doctrine were debated, now with the Roman, now with the Reformed antithesis in view. The resulting discord was, at last, officially resolved in the Formula of Concord The inclusion of the ancient Ecumenical Creeds in the Lutheran confessional corpus was intended to repudiate the charge of sectarianism against the Lutherans and to demonstrate the genuine catholicity of their teaching.

At first glance there would seem to be little to bind these heterogeneous documents together. In search of a unifying principle we may note that the Lutherans looked upon the Augsburg Confession as basic and central. This was "our Confession," "the Confession of our time," which showed itself to be in perfect agreement with the orthodox Christian faith of all ages. To this Confession all other Lutheran Symbols stood in direct relationship. These declared their function to be one of justifying, defending, expounding, clarifying, and safeguarding the correct understanding of the Augsburg Confession. The Lutherans regarded themselves as "churches of the Augsburg Confession."

But a collection of creeds purporting to set forth the particular orientation of a church body must have more than a formal integration with a specific document. In a number of simultaneously valid creedal statements there must be some single material principle, or central theme, pervading them all.

At this point the question of a theology of the Lutheran Confessions presents itself. Such a systematic study should reveal whether in all their diversity the Lutheran Confessions do indeed bear witness to an underlying unity such as they claim for themselves.

There have been many commentaries, particularly in the homeland of the Reformation, on individual Lutheran confessional writings and even more monographs on individual articles or doctrines. There are extant also various attempts at systematizing the theology of one or the other document. Few, however, are the studies that aim at a comprehensive summary of the genius of Lutheranism. In the year 1940 there appeared the first edition of *Theologie der lutherischen Bekenntnisschriften,* by Professor Edmund Schlink, now of Heidelberg University. The book had grown out of lectures delivered to students of theology at Giessen and Bethel.

The third edition (1948) was the first to come to the translator's attention when, together with Dr. Paul F. Koehneke, long-time instructor at Concordia College, Milwaukee, Wisconsin, and a number of fellow Lutheran pastors, he studied the Lutheran Confessions on the basis of Dr. Schlink's book. All of us developed a high esteem for Schlink's *Theologie* as an aid to increased appreciation of our Lutheran confessional heritage. Dr. Koehneke began to translate the work into English. He died before he could complete the task, but not before he had transmitted the request that the undersigned see the work through to completion. The translator regards it a privilege to be able to do so, especially since in his lectures on the Lutheran Confessions he makes frequent use of Schlink's material. This effort is dedicated to the memory of Dr. Koehneke, genial scholar, theologian, and fatherly friend of young students of theology.

Koehneke's manuscript consisted of the first draft of the book's eight chapters. The present translator made a careful word-for-word revision of this material, added a bibliography and index of subjects, and translated the introduction, the appendix, and a selection of the footnotes. The assistance of the Rev. Kurt Marquardt in checking the translation for accuracy is gratefully acknowledged.

The author's many direct quotations from the Lutheran Confessions are cited according to the magnificent critical edition prepared by eminent German scholars in 1930, the four-hundredth anniversary of the Augsburg Confession, in the so-called *Jubilaeumsausgabe,* which is now in its third edition. The appearance of this *magnum opus,* which prints the original German and Latin texts in parallel columns and furnishes a wealth of critical comments in the historical introductions and footnotes, renders all prior editions obsolete. The quotations in the present volume follow the splendid modern English version prepared by American scholars in 1959, *The Book of Concord, the Confessions of the Evangelical Lutheran Church.*

A word about the method of citing the Confessions: The quotations are referred to by Confession, Article, and paragraph. Thus Ap. IV, 200 means Apology, Article IV, paragraph 200. In the case of the Smalcald Articles, which are divided into three parts, the quotations are given as follows: Part (III), Article (vi), and paragraph (5). Quotations from the Confessions are introduced either by single (') or double (") quotation marks. The former designate quotations from a Latin or German *translation of the original,* whereas the latter indicate quotations from the German or Latin *original itself.* The German originals are Luther's Catechisms, the Smalcald Articles, and the Formula of Concord. The Apology and the Treatise were composed originally in Latin; the German version of the Apology is frequently a rather extensive paraphrase of the Latin original. The Augsburg Confession was prepared originally in both languages; for purposes of citation in this book, however, we are regarding the German version actually presented first to the Diet as the original (see B. of C., p. 24).

It should be stated that while we have omitted in this edition a number of footnotes contained in the original, these omissions are all of a relatively minor nature. None involves extensive comment or discussion by the author. Rather they comprise mostly page references to writings cited in the text, or bibliographies relating to specific topics in the individual chapters. To compensate for these omissions in the footnotes, a comprehensive overview of the literature has been included in topical form at the end of the book. The reader bent on scientific research will want to consult the complete references in the original German text in any case.

Documentation both in the footnotes and in the bibliographies at the back of the book is given largely in the form in which Schlink originally had it; no attempt has been made to supply such detailed facts of publication as are customary in English publications. Since parentheses were used extensively by the author in the original edition, and have here been retained, interpolations by the translator have been set in brackets in this English edition.

—Herbert J. A. Bouman

TABLE OF CONTENTS

ABBREVIATIONS

A.C.	Augsburg Confession
Ap.	Apology
Apost.	the Apostles' Creed
Athan.	the Athanasian Creed
Bek.	*Die Bekenntnisschriften der evangelisch-lutherischen Kirche* (2nd ed.; Göttingen: Vandenhoeck & Ruprecht, 1952).
B. of C.	the Book of Concord, herein cited according to Theodore G. Tappert, ed. (Philadelphia: Muhlenberg Press, 1959).
Con.	Conclusion
Ep.	Epitome
Ep.Comp.Sum.	Comprehensive Summary of the Epitome
F.C.	Formula of Concord
L.C.	Large Catechism
L.C.Pref.	Preface to the Large Catechism
Nic.	the Nicene Creed
Tauf.	Pamphlet on Baptism (Luther's *Taufbuechlein*)
Tr.	Treatise on the Power and Primacy of the Pope
S.A.	Smalcald Articles
S.C.	Small Catechism
S.D.	Solid Declaration
S.D.Sum.Form.	Summary Formulation of the Solid Declaration
WA	*D. Martin Luthers Werke.* Kritische Gesamtausgabe (Weimar, 1883-).

Introduction

THEOLOGY OF THE CONFESSIONS AS PROLEGOMENA TO DOGMATICS

The Confessions may be approached in various ways: We may concern ourselves especially with the history of their origin and development, such as their occasion, preliminary documents, final formulation and recognition, and the path of their dissemination and criticism on the part of the various theologians in the various territories. For example, we could consider the development that led from the Schwabach Articles to the Augsburg Confession, and then the fate of this Confession in its altered and unaltered form. Or, we could consider the original text of the Small Catechism, or the difficult and interesting discussions and theological declarations that led to the Formula of Concord, as well as the arguments surrounding its recognition. In recent years outstanding work has been done with regard to such historical research in the Confessions. We mention only the names of Th. Brieger, J. Ficker, Th. Kolde, W. Gussmann, H. von Schubert, O Albrecht, M. Reu, W. F. Schmidt, and K. Schornbaum. Without this kind of historical investigation no theological study of the Confessions would be possible. However, a study limited to such questions would not yet take the Confessions seriously as confession. It is perhaps not accidental that the wealth of historical studies on the Confessions could not stem the collapse of confessional loyalty on the part of the churches in Germany.

The Confessions may be studied primarily with respect to their contents. What do they teach? What about their modes of expression and thought, their structure and integrating principle? How are their statements and concepts related to the theology of the ancient and late medieval church? To what extent is their content determined by the encounters with the teachings of Zwingli and Calvin and by the controversies among the churches of the Augsburg Confession themselves? In addition, each Confession, depending upon its authorship, must be understood in the light of the theology of

Luther or of Melanchthon, or as the result of complicated over-lappings of diverse theological spheres of influence. This approach too has, from the standpoint of history of dogma and of thought, recently produced a wealth of valuable investigations, as witness the studies of K. Thieme, O. Ritschl, J. Meyer, W. Elert, and H. Sasse, not to forget the notable discussion set in motion by F. Loofs about what the Apology teaches concerning justification. As a matter of fact, no church takes seriously its Confession unless it continues to pene-trate the meaning of the individual concepts of that Confession and the interrelationships of its statements, by means of ever-new research in the area of the history of theology. Yet it must be asserted that this kind of theological concern with the Confessions, that concerns itself in principle with determining what the Confessions say, does not yet do justice to them as a confession.

Confessions in their proper sense will never be taken seriously until they are taken seriously as exposition of the Scriptures, to be specific, as the church's exposition of the Scriptures. Confessions are not free-lancing theological opinions; they are statements of doctrine that must be understood even to their last detail in terms of that exposition of Scripture which is the church's responsibility, entrusted to it in and with the responsibility of proclamation. Con-fessions are primarily expositions of Scripture, more particularly summary presentation of the whole of Scripture, that is, a witness to the heart of Scripture, a witness to the saving Gospel. Resting on Scripture as a whole, the Confessions aim to summarize the multiplicity of statements from Scripture in doctrinal articles directed against the errors of their day and designed for the protection of the correct proclamation then and for all time to come. But exposition of Scripture in which a single member of the church takes his stand against false doctrines cannot yet be called a Confession. As long as Confessions are regarded merely as the writings of Melanchthon or of Luther, along with other writings of Melanchthon or of Luther, they are not yet taken to be Confessions. In the Confessions it is precisely not an individual, but the church which expounds Scripture. Even if the Confessions came from the pen of Melanchthon or of Luther, they no longer belong to these individual members of the church. On the contrary, the teaching church has assumed responsi-bility for them. They are now a sacrifice of praise offered by the whole congregation of believers, who therewith glorify the grace of God in common repentance and in common faith.

This fact, that here the church (not an individual) witnesses to the sum of Scripture (not an incidental exegetical discovery), is the basis for the claim of the Confessions that they are the norm according to which the thinking and speaking of the believers is to be tested and determined. Specifically, they claim to be the obligatory model of all of the church's preaching and teaching. This claim admits of no limits, either of time or of space. At least the Confessions which comprise the Book of Concord make this claim not only with respect to the members of the Lutheran churches, but with respect to the whole Christian church on earth. It is not the "Lutheran" church (this designation is repudiated in the Confessions themselves) but the *una sancta catholica et apostolica ecclesia* which has spoken in the Confessions. They therefore make their claim not only with respect to the time in which they arose, but for all time to come, even until Christ's return. From the beginning the Confessions confronted all people with a comprehensive claim; they confront every man with that same comprehensive claim even today.

Theologically the Confessions have not been taken seriously until one comes to grips with this claim of theirs. In two respects this must be done:

1. We must take cognizance of the claim of the Confessions that they are the church's normative exposition of Scripture.

The unique position of the Confessions over against the writings of individual fathers and brethren must be respected. We must seek and recognize in the multiplicity of their authors and collaborators the consensus of the witnesses, and in the multiplicity of their testimonies the unity of the witness. After all, the one church confesses her one faith through the many tongues of her members. This discovering of the consensus certainly involves knowing how the witnesses differ from one another. And the fact that the Confessions have a unique position over against the other writings of their authors does not absolve us from the duty of interpreting the Confessions in the light of the total theology and thought patterns of their authors. However, this important hermeneutical rule is limited in its application by the unique position of the Confessions as doctrine of the church. This means that, even when they derive from various authors, the Confessions must be explained with reference to one another, because the doctrine of the church has to be interpreted in terms of the doctrine of the church. By elevating the writing of a theologian to the position of a confession, the church places that writing into the context of its recognized creeds in order that from henceforth it will be heard in, and interpreted in terms of, this context, as further attestation of the one biblical witness which the church has borne from the beginning. Hence, within the framework of the Book of Concord the doctrine of the Lord's Supper in the Augsburg Confession must be interpreted no longer merely as an article of *Melanchthon's* theology, but also in terms of its inseparable connection with *Luther's* Catechisms—if the Augsburg Confession is to be taken seriously as a confession.

From this it follows that we may not simply take material from an author's other writings to supplement what seems to be lacking in a Confession, either in statements of doctrine or in the bases given for such statements. There may be a significant reason for these omissions. Perhaps the church intentionally declined to offer these theological opinions as articles of the common faith. Perhaps even the authors themselves did not regard their personal views as *articuli stantis et cadentis ecclesiae*. It is dogmatically significant that certain important articles of the Augsburg Confession are very brief. It is especially significant that the Smalcald Articles and the Small Catechism exercise such great restraint with respect to an unfolding of systematic relationships or motivations that easily suggest themselves on the basis of Luther's views expressed elsewhere. This restraint is no accident. To take the Confessions seriously as doctrine of the church means to segregate them from the remaining literary output of their authors. There is room in their other writings for the authors to say a variety of things in matters of exegesis, history of dogma, and personal polemics. Here space may be given to well-founded theses and to conjectures of the moment, to what is universally valid and to what expresses a personal experience. All of these writings may serve as a commentary, one that is indeed indispensable for a correct understanding of the Confessions, but is not normative as the Confessions are.

To take cognizance of the claim of a Confession means, in addition, to recognize its unique position over against the heresies that occasioned its formulation. A Confession can indeed be understood correctly only by acquaintance with the false teaching against which it is directed, and thus also with the concrete historical circumstances of its origin. Yet we fail to understand a Confession as a confession if we seek in it only a historically conditioned answer to a specific problem of its own time. Surely, if a Confession is an exposition of Holy Scripture and a witness to the one eternal truth, then its claim remains in force even after the concrete heresy to which it first addressed itself has ceased being an issue. Confessions rise above the vicissitudes of heresy, even though they retain the marks of their particular origin as far as their proportions, illustrations, and terminology are concerned. There is a widespread habit of "relativizing" the Confessions by interpreting them as the reaction to a contemporary error, a reaction that is conditioned by its time and therefore valid only for its time. Contrary to such a procedure, we must discover and recognize the confessional statements for what they are—statements designed by the church to bind once for all the proclamation of all subsequent times. This will be done when we single out the positive principles of doctrine from those polemical portions that are directed against dangers which are today no longer so acute. At the same time, we must show, or at least suggest, the implications that grow out of the Confessions for heresies that have since become an issue, e.g., certain modernistic teachings about creation and the law.

oh?

2. We must take a definite stand with respect to the claim of the Confessions that they are the church's normative exposition of Scripture.

This claim is to be affirmed or, if that should not be possible, denied. Neither affirmation nor denial, however, can be left to the arbitrary judgment of the individual. Since the Confessions insist on being recognized as exposition of Scripture, only that response takes them seriously which affirms or rejects them on the basis of Scripture. This presupposes the discovering of the exegetical principles on which the confessional articles rest. In this connection special attention must be given to the Scripture quotations found in the Confessions themselves. Their connection with the articles must be carefully analyzed, both with respect to what the Confessions incorporate of the quoted passages and what they omit. Nor must we overlook the absence of such texts as one might have expected to find.

A legitimate stand with respect to the Confessions is possible only by retracing their exegesis of Scripture. The claim of the Confessions will have to validate itself as their exegesis is measured against Scripture in the very process of expounding the Scripture. *OK* This claim must be judged, however, not only on the basis of the Scripture texts cited in the Confessions, but of all statements of

Scripture. After all, the Confessions claim that they are *summa doctrinae*. A legitimate attitude toward that assertion, therefore, must grow out of a step-by-step investigation of the question whether the confessional statements are scriptural in the sense of representing a concentration of all the varied statements of Scripture. Later on we shall consider the method of this investigation and what is to be done with the results, the judgments concerning the rightness or wrongness—or, more precisely, concerning the compelling necessity or mere admissibility—of the Confessions' exposition of Scripture.

An investigation which in this way comes to grips with the claim of the Confessions—measuring them against Scripture and then presenting their teaching in systematic fashion as the teaching of Scripture—could already in essence be called dogmatics. At any rate, it would become dogmatics in increasing measure, the more it would go beyond the relatively meager exegetical references in the Confessions and present their teachings in a very broad exegetical unfolding of the whole of Scripture, and especially in contradistinction to the heresies that have arisen from the days of the Reformation down to the present.

There is much to be said in favor of giving separate consideration to these two things: taking cognizance of the Confessions' claim and taking a stand with respect to it.

This is desirable, in the first place, because of the manner in which the Lutheran Confessions are frequently used in our day. There is no question but that in recent years they are being listened to again with a surprising intensity. This is true both within the Lutheran state churches and also within the union churches, now that extensive agreement has developed in repudiating the spirit that controlled the union movements of the nineteenth century. (The problem today is not the repudiation of those unions, but how to transcend them.) In the stresses of our time many realize anew that the battle for the preservation of the church's proclamation and for the church's unity cannot possibly be fought on the basis of the individualism of neo-Protestant statements of faith. For that reason people resorted to the Confessions in an emergency, almost as to an arsenal of weapons. Though *in praxi* the church itself had largely given up recognition of the Confessions as normative for all teaching, they were still the legal basis for the church's constitution and were acknowledged as such even by the state. However, in the press of the conflict often only those confessional statements were sought and found that were needed as weapons for the moment. Many sought only for justification of those measures to which they had to resort in a concrete emergency. As a result, the confessional statements were not infrequently abused in a legalistic way; and the weapons furnished in the church's Confessions for battle against the foe were turned against the one who used them. To expect the Confessions to yield concretely binding directives for all concrete situations—as, for example, in matters of church administration—is to paralyze the Christian in his obedience to God. He will be immobilized in those situations concerning which the Confessions do not explicitly speak if he takes their silence for assent to his capitulation in the given situation. Again, he will be severely hampered if he thinks he must take a concrete judgment made by the authors of the Confessions with respect to the emperor or the bishops of their time, and apply it in the same way today. We miss the point of the Confessions and may easily pervert them against their own intention into law, if our renewed concern with them begins with their directives for church activity. The Gospel and the sacraments provide the only proper approach to an understanding of the Confessions. Only the distinction between law and Gospel furnishes the key to a right understanding of the directives for the church's political action. These directives are basically a solemn charge, in the obedience of faith, to make use of the liberty wherewith Christ has made us free. For this reason it is inadvisable to appeal to individual statements of the Confessions without also appealing to their theology as a whole. This, however, means first of all that we must give heed to the claim of the Confessions in its totality.

In this connection we cannot fail to take note of the current situation in the science of biblical and exegetical studies. For decades now in the field of exegesis there has been obvious and significant disagreement concerning every important question of Old or New Testament theology. This is still largely the case, though in a few essential points, at least of New Testament theology, some consensus in exegesis is slowly beginning to emerge. It is too early to tell how much of this consensus will maintain itself and become normative, in terms of method and of content. Important for the matter before us is also the fact that most of the exegetical studies of recent decades have maintained a polemical attitude toward the Confessions of the church. This attitude was justified, on the one hand, by the fact that the Confessions and dogmatics were improperly placed above Scripture, as was customarily done in the period of Orthodoxy. From this procedure exegetical science had indeed to be set free. On the other hand, however, this polemic proceeded without a proper understanding of the task, scope, and limitations that a Confession has by its very nature—already with regard to its thought patterns over against the multiplicity of scriptural statements. Instead, it proceeded largely in the name of a secular claim of free scientific research. The task of teaching the Confessions as exposition of Scripture by means of repeating the exegetical process is, therefore, one for which the groundwork has not really been laid. Even the most recent confessional theology has often evaded this task in a startling way, in that it has frequently been blithely and culpably unconcerned about the rift between exegetical research and dogmatic teaching within one and the same church. This whole situation makes it more difficult to take a proper stand with respect to the claim of the Confessions. It is advisable to work out step by step what this stance should be by way of thorough and painstaking exegesis, beginning with one basic doctrine of the Confessions. Biblical-theological consideration of one doctrine of the Confessions, however, in turn presupposes familiarity with the whole doctrinal corpus of the Confessions. For every part of doctrine is to be understood only from the perspective of the center of the Confessions, the article of justification. For this reason too it seems appropriate to study the over-all doctrine of the Confessions first of all.

Quite apart from the present status of exegesis and the revival of interest in the Confessions, however, it still remains advisable to give separate consideration to these two things: taking cognizance of the doctrine of the Confessions and taking a stand with respect to them. Surely the Confessions as the *voice of the church* are important enough to be heard out first, in what they have to say, before the *individual* Christian lifts his own voice to speak. Since in the Confessions it is the church, not an individual, which is expounding the Scripture for its members, there is every reason for the individual member first to listen as a pupil to the church's instruction. He should do this without offering his own additions, supplementary interpretations, corrections, or criticisms, however well these may be supported by sound exegetical observations. After all, the church is always there before the individual Christian. The church has acted upon him before he himself could act; it has instructed him before he himself was able to believe. The church, it must be remembered, is "the mother that begets and bears every

Christian through the Word of God" (L. C. II, 42). Should we not listen first to the church's exposition of Scripture, since through the Word of God it has given us new birth as children of God? Should we not in preference to all other expositions of Scripture listen with the utmost care to the church's explanation of the Creed, which it confessed over us in our baptism, and in which it follows the Lord's commission in testifying to and explaining the meaning of "in the name of the Father, and of the Son, and of the Holy Ghost"? In the last analysis, all Confessions of the church are nothing more than a fortification built around Baptism, and an explanation of the trinitarian name. Living in the church as those who are borne and nourished by the church, we always have the church's Confession as our point of origin. Should we not, then, to the minutest detail hear how the church in its Confessions explains the Apostles' Creed, which it confessed for us in Baptism? And should we not do this before we offer our own private exposition of Scripture? Yes, should we not from the very outset approach this exposition of Scripture by the Confessions with a confidence in its correctness which exceeds the confidence we give as pupils to this or that member of the church who may be our teacher? More compellingly than any chronological reasons, these considerations impose upon us the obligation first as pupils to take cognizance of the entire claim of the Confessions, before we undertake to become teachers ourselves. And this pertains not only to individual Confessions or their individual articles, but to the Confessions as a doctrinal whole.

This, then, is the task of this theology of the Confessions: In all the humility of hearing and learning to summarize and reproduce the statements of the Confessions in systematic order.

In this connection we designate this systematic presentation of the doctrine of the Book of Concord as "Prolegomena to Dogmatics," and we make it precede the dogmatics which is to follow in this projected series. For the theology of the Confessions is the prolegomenon to dogmatics in a qualified sense, namely, that dogmatics must give consideration to the Confessions before all other commentaries on Scripture. Self-evidently, this "before" is not primarily temporal, but an abiding logical *prius*. This concept of the prolegomena will be more precisely defined at the close of Chapter 1.

If we thus give separate consideration to these two things, taking cognizance of the claim of the Confessions and taking a definite stand with respect to that claim, this in no way implies the liberty of isolating the one from the other. It is impossible either to affirm or to deny this claim theologically without knowing exactly what it contains. Conversely, a knowledge of what the Confessions contain without either a positive or negative response to their claim would not yet be theological knowledge. Only then may a theology of the Confessions be called "Prolegomena to Dogmatics," when the dogmatics keeps in view from the outset a concern with the Confessions. In other words, dogmatics must think the Confessions through to their logical conclusion in the act of critically retracing the Reformation's exegesis of Scripture; the theology of the Confessions must not inadvertently and without further ado be set forth in blind repristination as dogmatics. For this reason this theology of the Confessions consciously paves the way for a response to their claim by devoting the last section of Chapter 1 to the implications that arise for the relationship between Scripture, Confession, and dogmatics from the Lutheran view of the relation between Scripture and Confession. Furthermore, at the end of the book we have added a few biblical-exegetical observations and questions on the foregoing chapters as guidelines for dogmatics. For the rest, this whole presentation would press for a dogmatic decision also in this respect—that here in the introduction we definitely set forth in advance the requirement of coming to grips with the total claim of the Confessions. Only he really does this, however, who allows the Confessions to instruct, judge, and comfort him, and at the same time to compel him to test this claim by the Holy Scriptures.

For various reasons it is no easy matter to present systematically the pronouncements of the Confessions as the *one* doctrine of the church, even apart from the problem of taking a stand with respect to their claim. Indeed, the existing difficulties are so great that, with a necessity rooted in the matter itself, no uncovering of the doctrine of the Confessions as a full-orbed unit will be able to escape the charge of subjectivity in presentation. We refer briefly to a few of the most obvious difficulties:

The Lutheran Confessions do not have one and the same author; consequently they do not have one and the same theological thought pattern. They were not written at the same time, but have their place in the midst of a historical process in which a position was being developed with respect to the Roman church and with respect to the new heresies that were arising at the time of the Reformation. In view of this difficulty, a presentation of the Book of Concord as a doctrinal unit must first of all pay attention to how the Confessions mutually interpret one another. In spite of their large number, they are nonetheless organically related in a kind of family tree in which the numerous interpretations refer back ultimately to relatively few texts. All Confessions of the Reformation age in the Book of Concord aim to be expositions of the ancient trinitarian Creeds; most clearly the two Catechisms aim to be explanations of the Apostles' Creed. The Apology expounds the Augsburg Confession, the two Catechisms interpret each other, and the Formula of Concord, again, wishes to be understood as elucidation of the Augsburg Confession and, beyond that, of all prior Lutheran Confessions.

Not only are the theological thought patterns different in the Lutheran Confessions, but occasionally there are doctrinal statements that contradict one another. Compare, for example, the statements concerning the number of sacraments, or those concerning the pope. Later Confessions serve not only as interpretation, but at times also as correction of earlier ones. In view of this difficulty it will be necessary in presenting the Book of Concord as a doctrinal unit to fix unwavering attention on that which is the center of all the doctrinal statements of the Confessions, namely, the identity of the Gospel to which they all bear witness. Only from the vantage point of this Gospel can the importance of those apparent doctrinal differences be evaluated, whose existence must not be glossed over and evaded by harmonization. On the contrary, viewed from the center, from the proper distinction of law and Gospel, these differences may prove to contribute a great deal to a correct understanding of the Confessions and of their claim (cf., e.g., pp. 265 ff.).

However, even when the Lutheran Confessions are expounded on the basis of their interdependence and in relation to their central theme, the difficulty remains that not all doctrines are in one and the same context of interpretation. Thus, while the doctrine of the sacraments is based on the same Scripture texts in both the Augsburg Confession and the Catechisms, these writings stand in a certain independence side by side as regards their thought patterns and also the extent of their statements. It is well known, for example, what a variety of interpretation seems to be permitted by the cautious formulation of the doctrine of the Lord's Supper in the Augsburg Confession, especially when in explaining the doctrine it is removed from the context of the Book of Concord and is thus isolated. It is evident therefore that, when we set forth the doctrinal statements of the Lutheran Confessions as a unit, we cannot avoid having to make decisions about the point of departure for any given interpretation, decisions which the Confessions do not automatically suggest. In line with this principle, this study will consciously begin its presentation of the doctrine of the sacraments, for example, with Luther's Catechisms, and from this vantage point interpret the statements of the Augsburg Confession and the Apology. For the church of the Augsburg Confession has from the beginning understood its doctrine of the sacraments in the context of *Luther's* theology and not of Melanchthon's peculiarities.

In addition, it is to be noted that to the present day not even the Lutheran churches themselves are agreed as to the extent of the Lutheran Confessions. From the beginning, the Formula of Concord was disputed as a Confession, and to the present day large Lutheran bodies refuse to acknowledge it as such. Thus the Lutheran rally at Hannover in July, 1935, at which the German Lutheran churches established their common confessional basis, indeed recognized the Augsburg Confession, the two Catechisms, and the Smalcald Articles, but not the Formula of Concord. In spite of its disputed status we shall not dispense with it here. For it cannot be denied that the Formula of Concord in many respects represents a model of theological study, indeed of correct exposition of Reformation thinking over against new errors. Think, for example, only of Articles III to VI. To be sure, the Formula of Concord is to be drawn into the discussion only in so far as it appears to furnish a legitimate exposition of the earlier Lutheran Confessions. For we must not lose sight of the fact that the Formula of Concord can and must be a subject of theological interest from an entirely different point of view, namely, that of the question whether in it the task of expounding the earlier Confessions has been exceeded, whether it perhaps departs from the Reformation Confessions in some points and already exhibits the beginnings of the false developments that characterized the later period of Orthodoxy. Inasmuch as this study will hardly concern itself with these questions at all, it will therefore not offer a theology of the Formula of Concord, which by its very nature would have to treat this matter exhaustively. Rather, the Formula of Concord will be drawn in to the extent of its explanatory consensus with the other Confessions.

These few observations alone indicate that the hermeneutical problems that present themselves in the understanding of any text will be considerably increased in connection with so complicated a structure as the Book of Concord. Every attempt at systematizing the Book of Concord as a doctrinal unit is especially vulnerable to the charge of personal prejudice. In view of the procedural difficulties it is, therefore, not at all surprising that for quite some time no such comprehensive task has been undertaken, except perhaps for the rather condensed summaries prepared, e.g., by G. Plitt (*Symbolik* [5th ed.], pp. 75-95) and P. Tschackert (*Die Entstehung der lutherischen und reformierten Kirchenlehre,* pp. 304-372). Nevertheless, in spite of all procedural difficulties the church dare not evade its responsibility of giving ear to the consensus of its Confessions, since it is precisely in their consensus that the Confessions are binding upon the church. Nor may the accusation of subjectivity frighten the church from its duty. Rather, it is well to understand clearly from the start that every individual presentation of the *one* doctrine of the Lutheran Confessions can be no more than *one* voice in the chorus of confessional commentators, and that this need not be objectionable any more than the fact that in the Confessions themselves a whole chorus of witnesses gets to speak directly or indirectly.

To these procedural difficulties with which every theology of the Confessions has to cope, there are added in our case those presented by the limitations of a textbook. As a rule, the scientific theme of a textbook is more comprehensive than the space allotted to the treatment of it. It is inevitable that textbooks often present the results of investigation without being able to repeat in detail the path that has led to these conclusions. So also in this case the presentation and summaries at many places had to be largely thetical, without being able to present thoroughly all the proofs or go into detail with regard to the consideration which has been given to other views. I regret particularly that I could not include a critical introduction to the history of the exposition of the Confessions. The writing of this four-hundred-year history is one of the most intriguing and important tasks of theology, and its undertaking could well lead to a new understanding of the nature and method of the history of theology as distinguished from the humanities. Instead of entering into an explicit discussion with the assimilated recent literature, I had to be content at most points to make passing reference to it. Instead of coming to grips with the older exposition of the Confessions I could only call attention in a bibliography to some of the more significant works.

Other unavoidable limitations of this textbook will be largely compensated for by the fact that it is intended as one of a projected series in which other volumes are expected to deal with such matters as the dogma of the ancient church, the medieval church's understanding of that dogma, the theology of Luther, the history of Old Protestant theology beginning with the theology of Melanchthon, and the distinctive doctrines of the Formula of Concord over against the Reformed Symbols and the teachings of Calvin. Wherever I could anticipate the handling of certain subjects by these other texts I kept my own treatment brief. The historical introductions in the edition of the Confessions on which this study is based (*Die Bekenntnisschriften der evangelisch-lutherischen Kirche* [Goettingen, 1930], pp. XI-XLIV),[1] plus the bibliography given there and at the end of this book, may well serve the purpose of an initial orientation with respect to the genetic history of the individual confessional writings.

Because of the limitations mentioned above, this text can be nothing more than an introduction. By introduction I mean a leading up to the texts of the Confessions, which each must then study for himself. This text is in no sense a substitute for the study of the Confessions in the original languages. (It should be noted that the German translations of the Apology and the Treatise, as well as the Latin versions of the Smalcald Articles, the Catechisms, and the Formula of Concord, must already be regarded and treated as paraphrases and first expositions of the respective originals. This is true especially of the German translation of the Apology by Justus Jonas.) Since I am not dealing explicitly with comparisons with Roman or Reformed doctrine, nor with modernistic Lutheranism of recent decades, I have here purposely refrained from publishing one of those dogmatic compends that had an answer for every question and so, unfortunately, stifled all dogmatic thinking. The topic sentences too, that precede and serve to summarize the attendant confessional statements, are not intended to be exhaustive statements of content, but aids in getting at the systematic line of thought, particularly at the genuine theological dialectic in which is contained the oft-neglected eschatological expectation of the Confessions.

The purpose of this book, therefore, is a modest one and, please God, one of humble service. It will be inadequate, meager, and barren for a romanticizing and esthetic conception of dogmatics, according to which every dogmatician makes a fresh start, as it were, in mental productivity and originality. It will, however, immeasurably enrich and bless every one who, suspicious of the theological originality of the old Adam, submits as a pupil to the discipline of the teaching church and approaches Scripture together with the fathers in a common act of hearing. A subscription to the Lutheran Confessions can hamper exegesis only so long as it remains a formal subscription without penetrating to an understanding of

---

[1] To facilitate reference to the best available original-language edition of the Confessions, it has been thought best in this English edition to refer to the second edition of the *Bekenntnisschriften* (1952) rather than to the first edition (1930) which the author originally used. See *Bek.* in the Table of Abbreviations on page xiii.—Trans.

that which is the heart of the Confessions. But this subscription becomes thoroughly liberating and revealing the moment it is recognized as a liberation through the Gospel, that Gospel which is to be distinguished from the law each day anew and to which, in the act of making this distinction, the Lutheran Confessions bear witness. Therefore, the last word of this introduction must be an expression of gratitude. Granted that only dogmatics proper is able to judge clearly the extent to which the claim of the Confessions can, by retracing their biblical exegesis, be admitted, yet I should like to say already at this point that for me the results of the newer exegesis have not only confirmed the statements of the Confessions to a surprising degree, but that in addition the Confessions have disclosed to me the meaning of Scripture texts and contexts which today are commonly overlooked.

This book grew out of lectures I delivered at the University of Giessen and the Theological School at Bethel before my teaching was abruptly halted in the spring of 1939. With this book in 1940 I greeted my young brethren in the dispersion with whom in the previous years I had been privileged to join in common study of the Word of God. I remember them even now in abiding love and gratitude, especially since many of them have been summoned out of the conflicts of this world and the tentativeness of all *theologia viatorum* unto the theological knowledge of those who have reached the goal.

I

SCRIPTURE AND CONFESSION

1. The sole norm of all teaching in the church is the Holy Scripture of the Old and New Testaments.

The preface to the Augsburg Confession asserts that this Confession is preached and taught "on the basis of divine and holy Scripture" (A.C. Pref., 8). In the concluding statement of the first part of this Confession it is said of the preceding "Articles of Faith and Doctrine" that they agree "with the pure Word of God and Christian truth . . . [they are] grounded clearly on the Holy Scriptures and . . . not contrary or opposed to [the teaching] of the universal Christian church, or even of the Roman church (in so far as the latter's teaching is reflected in the writings of the Fathers)." Accordingly, the Augsburg Confession concludes with the offer: "If anyone should consider that it [this Confession] is lacking in some respect, we are ready to present further information on the basis of the divine Holy Scripture" (A.C. Con., 7). These statements, which presuppose Holy Scripture as the norm of all teaching, bracket all articles of the Augsburg Confession, but at the same time also those of the Apology and of the other Confessions which regard themselves as interpretation of the Augsburg Confession.

Curiously enough, however, the Augsburg Confession does not have a special article on Holy Scripture, and this is true also of the Apology, the Catechisms, and the Smalcald Articles.[1] Even the

---

[1] This accounts for the fact that, in contrast with most other doctrines, little careful study has been given to the confessional doctrine of Scripture, except in the case of the Formula of Concord. That is a mistake, because the absence of a special article on Scripture must not blind us to the fact that the very silence of the Confessions on this point amounts to a doctrinal declaration. Furthermore, in the actual use of Scripture by the Confessions there is implicit not only a doctrine of Scripture, but also principles of interpretation, and even important hermeneutical rules for the exegesis of the Old Testament. By the way, there was in principle no reason why the Confessions might not have included a doctrine of Scripture, not only at the time of the Formula of Concord, but even during the first years of the Reformation. Part III of the Evangelical Declaration of Ansbach, in 1524, very definitely taught that Scrip-

purpose of the three quotations given above is obviously not primarily a declaration about Holy Scripture as being normative, but rather, presupposing its normative character, an affirmation that the Confession is bound by that norm. In the context of the quotations, Scripture itself is so self-evidently presupposed as the norm that its exclusive normative character is not even expressly stated. In fact, formulations are not avoided which might call this into question. For example, what is the significance of the declaration that nothing has been introduced "that is contrary to Holy Scripture *or* the universal Christian church"? (A.C. Con., 5). What does this "or" imply? Is also the church a norm of doctrine? In the immediate connection no clear, unambiguous answer is given. Hence we dare not consider only the relatively rare explicit statements of the Augsburg Confession and the Apology about Holy Scripture, but we must determine the implied doctrine concerning Scripture on the basis of how Scripture is actually used and how other sources of knowledge which might possibly be considered as norms of doctrine are regarded.

We observe, first, the frequency of quotations from Scripture and the importance of their position. Most of the quotations in the Augsburg Confession are from Scripture and they have the character of decisive and conclusive proof. Since they are frequently found at the end of an article they confirm the previously made statements as doctrine. They have been lifted out of the area of merely human questions and opinions, since Scripture has answered the questions and this answer has been received as binding. Since God 'regards a single prophet as an inestimable treasure' (Ap. XII, 66), even a single Bible passage is of decisive significance. But the value of a single quotation rests, in the final analysis, on the fact that it is not an isolated quotation but represents the *oft*-attested teaching of Scripture. This 'strong testimony of *all* the holy prophets may duly be called a decree of the catholic Christian church' (Ap. XX, 2). The confessors know that they are separated from their adversaries not merely by an isolated word of Scripture, but they chide the opponents for 'failing to consider *so many* clear passages which

---

ture is the sole norm established by the Word of God itself, and that in strict trinitarian hermeneutics reason and human wisdom are rejected and the Holy Spirit as the only means of understanding Scripture is asserted. The absence of such an article in the Augsburg Confession is not to be construed as an evasion of the controversial problem of the relation between Scripture and tradition. Rather, it reflects the genuinely Lutheran urgency of coming to grips at once with the *viva vox evangelii* itself, an approach that goes beyond the Ansbach biblicism.

2

clearly state that we are justified by faith and not by works. . . . Do they suppose that the Scripture repeats *this same truth so often* without good reason?' (Ap. IV, 107 f.). Not obscure words of Scripture, but the 'very clear' ones (Ap. II, 50), and again, not single expressions out of context, but the testimonies of which Scripture is "full" (Ap. IV, 102) are the decisive factors. Hence *all* Scripture is the basis of the doctrinal articles.

Next to Scripture the quotations from the church fathers occupy the most prominent position in the Augsburg Confession. Since these voices of the fathers are ordinarily found *after* the Scripture passages, the impression is created that they are consciously accorded an inferior position. Numerous emphatic statements indicate how decisively the church fathers are placed under the norm of Scripture: "There is also great variety among the Fathers. They were men and they could err and be deceived" (Ap. XXIV, 95). "The writings of the holy Fathers show that even they sometimes built stubble on the foundation" (i.e., on "the true knowledge of Christ and faith," I Cor. 3:12; Ap. VII, 20 f.). "It will not do to make articles of faith out of the holy Fathers' words or works. Otherwise what they ate, how they dressed, and what kind of houses they lived in would have to become articles of faith—as has happened in the case of relics." Even the words of St. Augustine are not to be "accepted when they are without the support of the Scriptures" (S.A. II, ii, 14 f.). With a *single* statement of the apostle Peter we may cheerfully oppose thousands of quotations from the church fathers (Ap. XII, 70).

As the history of the church is disallowed as norm of doctrine, so also the measures adopted by the contemporary church: ". . . one should not obey even regularly elected bishops, if they err, or if they teach or command something contrary to the divine Holy Scriptures" (A.C. XXVIII, 28). 'Neither to the pope, nor to the church do we grant the authority to issue decrees contrary to this consensus of the prophets' (Ap. XII, 66). Like tradition and the church fathers, so also all present and future teachers of the church must be evaluated and judged according to Holy Scripture (cf. also Tr. 11, 56).

Beyond all this, all human thought, emotion, and activity is subjected to Scripture with constantly recurring flank attacks on reason and philosophy, on work-righteousness and enthusiasm. The opinion that man can arrive at a true knowledge of divine matters on the basis of human thought and emotion is again and again traced in the most diverse doctrines of the opponents, refuted, and finally made ridiculous. All this is only *"multa fingere,"* to 'invent many things in one's own brain,' which leads only to such opinions as are 'totally unfounded in Scripture and touch neither above nor below' (Ap. XII, 178). Reason cannot even come to a knowledge of original sin, but this "must be believed because of the revelation in the Scriptures" (S.A. III, i, 3). And our feelings cannot even give a clear indication of our thirst for grace: "If you cannot feel the need (the thirst for the sacrament), at least believe the Scriptures. They will not lie to you, and they know your flesh better than you yourself do" (L.C. V, 76).

More strongly than statements of principle about Scripture could do, the actual use of Holy Scripture demonstrates that it is recognized by the Augsburg Confession as the sole norm. What Scripture as a whole teaches must be the teaching of the church. What Scripture does not teach must be rejected as doctrinal pronouncement of the church. Both for the Augsburg Confession and its Apology as well as for the two Catechisms the principle already obtains: "The Word of God shall establish articles of faith and no one else, not even an angel"; "we can discard all human inventions" (S.A. II, ii, 15, 2).

Accordingly, the Formula of Concord teaches nothing new, although it alone of all Lutheran Confessions, fifty years after Augsburg, speaks by way of introduction "Of the Comprehensive Summary, Rule, and Norm, etc." and there confesses that "the prophetic and apostolic writings of the Old and New Testaments are the only rule and norm according to which all doctrines and teachers alike must be appraised and judged" (Ep. Comp. Sum., 1). They are the pure and clear fountain of Israel (S.D. Sum. Form., 3), the only norm, the sole judge, the "only touchstone" (Ep. Comp. Sum., 7). "Other writings and teachers, whatever their names, should not be put on a par with Holy Scripture. Every single one of them should be subordinated to the Scriptures, and should be received in no other way and no further than as witnesses to the fashion in which the doctrine of the prophets and apostles was preserved in post-apostolic times" (Ep. Comp. Sum., 2).

Nevertheless, it remains significant that before the Formula of Concord the Confessions have no special article on Holy Scripture, and that even in the Formula of Concord no statement is made about the extent of the biblical canon, although at that time this was a subject of debate and, at least as far as the Apocrypha are concerned, the canon was given limits differing from those in the Roman church.

We encounter the same, apparently almost disinterested, reticence regarding a detailed doctrine of Scripture when we ask the question, *Why* is Holy Scripture the sole norm of all doctrine?

2. *Holy Scripture is the norm because it is the prophetic and apostolic witness to the Gospel.*

In search of a basis for the normative importance of Holy Scripture we find the expression in the Apology: "The clear Scripture of the Holy Spirit" (Ap. Pref., 9). Furthermore, we are reminded of the questions put to the adversaries about their false traditions and their work-righteousness: "Why does the divine Scripture so frequently forbid the making and the keeping of human regulations? . . . Is it possible that the Holy Spirit warned against them for nothing?" (A.C. XXVIII, 49). 'Do they think that the Holy Spirit does not utter his Word surely and deliberately, or does not know what he is saying?' (Ap. IV, 108).

One should like to ask immediately what it means that the Holy Spirit 'utters his Word.' One should also like to ascertain more accurately whether in these questions of the Augsburg Confession the Holy Sprit is represented as operating through Scripture or as being its author, and, if the latter, in what manner. But no answer is given there to these and many other questions, and the very casualness of such remarks shows plainly that the Confessions are not interested in fixing the significance of Scripture by means of doctrinal statements about its origin. The inspiration of Scripture is indeed presupposed, but there is no detailed doctrine of inspiration. One might think that this silence of the Confessions could be explained by the fact that the doctrine of inspiration was at that time the common theological heritage of the Reformers and of Roman and other opponents, even of Sebastian Frank,[2] for example. When one considers, however, what manifold possibilities in terms of doctrines of inspiration were already present at the time of the Reformation, having been prepared by the Middle Ages, and what far-reaching consequences the decisions in the doctrine of inspiration have for other articles of dogmatics, then this reticence cannot be

---

[2] Frank was at first a supporter of Luther but then became a promoter of mystical idealism and an enemy of all ecclesiastical system, and was opposed by Luther and Melanchthon.—Trans.

accidental, but must be taken seriously as a theological decision. At any rate, the normative position of Scripture is not deduced from doctrinal statements about the divine inspiration of Scripture.

Instead, the Confessions with great force and powerful urgency again and again point to the content and the center of Holy Scripture. "All Scripture should be divided into these two chief doctrines, the law and the promises" (Ap. IV, 5; cf. 102). "These are the two chief works of God in men, to terrify and to justify and quicken the terrified. One or the other of these works is spoken of throughout Scripture. One part is the law, which reveals, denounces, and condemns sin. The other part is the Gospel, that is, the promise of grace granted in Christ. This promise is repeated continually throughout Scripture; first it was given to Adam, later to the patriarchs, then illumined by the prophets, and finally proclaimed and revealed by Christ among the Jews, and spread by the apostles throughout the world" (Ap. XII, 53). Accordingly, the summary of Scripture is law and Gospel, or, to put it another way, the summary of the entire Holy Scripture is the Gospel. The powerful sentence, 'all who believe that through Christ they have a gracious God are made righteous before God without merit by faith,' is in summary 'the principal matter of all epistles, yea, of the entire Scripture' (Ap. IV, 87), and 'entire Scripture' means the sum total of both testaments, not only of the New, but also of the Old Testament. "As Peter says (Acts 10:43), 'To him all the prophets bear witness that every one who believes in him receives forgiveness of sins through his name'" (Ap. XX, 2). If the summary of Scripture is law and Gospel, the Gospel, in turn, is the summary of law and Gospel. The Gospel is the center of all of Scripture, not without the law and yet also in distinction from the law, namely, as God's promise and forgiveness which is to be esteemed a thousandfold more than his demands and judgments (see Chap. IV, 10, pp. 136 f.).[3]

This intense concern with the Gospel suggests that the Gospel is the norm in Scripture and Scripture is the norm for the sake of the Gospel. From this point of view we can understand why none of the Confessions before the Formula of Concord contain a section on Holy Scripture, because not only do individual articles specifically

---

[3] This approach of the Confessions gives expression to Luther's reiterated teaching concerning Christ as Lord and Sum of Holy Scripture. Scripture is the norm inasmuch as it is Gospel, that is, in so far as it "presents Christ." The acting Christ and the Gospel are identical. In this discussion Luther's remarks concerning the relationship of Scripture, Word, and Spirit should also be studied.

treat the Gospel, but in the final analysis all articles in the Confessions are concerned with the Gospel. The assertion that the Gospel is the norm in Scripture and that the Scripture is norm as witness to the Gospel would then have this meaning: Ultimately all articles treat the norm of theological thinking, even though they contain few statements about the normative significance of Scripture.

The occasional hermeneutical directives too—above all, the exegetical practice of the Confessions—favor this understanding of the Gospel as norm in the norm of Holy Scripture. Thus of the doctrine of the forgiveness of sins the Apology says that it 'is of special service for the clear, correct understanding of the entire Holy Scriptures and alone shows the way to the unspeakable treasure and right knowledge of Christ, and alone opens the door to the entire Bible, without which doctrine no poor conscience may have true, constant, and firm consolation, or be able to recognize the riches of Christ's grace' (Ap. IV, 2 f.). Without the knowledge of the Gospel the Bible remains unintelligible and useless. Only from the Gospel do all individual statements of Scripture receive their proper place and meaning. Erasmus, Zwingli, the peasants, and the Enthusiasts had also waged their battle with Bible quotations, as did also the Roman adversaries. By means of Scripture texts employed "in either a philosophical or a Jewish manner" it is possible to abolish the certainty of faith and to exclude Christ as mediator (Ap. IV, 376). Only in the light of the Gospel can we determine which words of Scripture are commands and promises, which words serve to terrify or to comfort, which words are valid for us as God's commandments, and which commandments of the Old Testament have been abolished by Christ. Only by faith in the Gospel can Scripture be interpreted correctly, that is, by receiving the benefits secured for us by the crucified Christ. In the Gospel Scripture has not only its unity but also its simplicity.

The Gospel, moreover, is not a book existing of and for itself, but it is the voice of God addressing us; it is no doctrine of and for itself, but it is proclamation. We do not have the Gospel, but we hear it. We do not know it as we know other concepts, but we receive it anew again and again, spoken to us through the voice of man which proclaims the grace of God and through which God's very voice from heaven resounds among us today. In the most real sense of the term the Gospel is the word of absolution, and *doctrina evangelii* in our Confessions is essentially proclaimed doctrine. Accordingly, in Luther's explanation of the Third Commandment in the Large Catechism the praise of the Word of God does not refer to the book of Holy Scripture, to the Bible as such. "The Word of God is the true holy thing above all holy things. Indeed, it is the only one we Christians acknowledge and have," that is to say, "At whatever time God's Word is taught, preached, heard, read, or pondered, there the person, the day, and the work are sanctified by it" (L.C. I, 91 f.). Not a knowledge about God's Word, but being "guided by God's Word" is required. We meet Scripture as the Word of God only in the act of hearing and learning, of preaching and teaching. "Where the Word is not heard," the devil breaks in. "On the other hand, when we seriously ponder the Word, hear it, and put it to use, such is its power that it never departs without fruit. . . . For these words are not idle or dead, but effective and living" (L.C. I, 100 f.).

God's Word is active as it sanctifies the sinner. But this sanctifying "is nothing else than to bring us to the Lord Christ" (L.C. II, 39). "The work is finished and completed, Christ has acquired and won the treasure for us by his sufferings, death, resurrection, etc. But if the work remained hidden and no one knew of it, it would have been all in vain, all lost. In order that this treasure might not be buried but put to use and enjoyed, God has caused the Word to be published and proclaimed, in which he has given the Holy Spirit to offer and apply to us this treasure of salvation" (L.C. II, 38).

However little and incidentally the Confessions speak about the inspiration of the Bible as a book, they most emphatically and methodically from the Augsburg Confession to the Formula of Concord teach the inspiration of the hearers by the Word of God, that is to say, inspiration through the word of the Gospel. Of course, the two cannot be separated. In both cases it is the Holy Spirit acting through the Word. But the stress of the statements evidently is with the latter. 'Through the Word and the sacraments, as through instruments, the Holy Spirit is given' (A.C. V, 2; cf., e.g., Ap. XXIV, 70). Here "we must hold firmly to the conviction that God gives no one his Spirit or grace except through or with the external Word which comes before." "Whatever is attributed to the Spirit apart from such Word and sacrament is of the devil." Even Moses and all the prophets did not receive the Spirit "apart from or without" the external preceding Word (S.A. III, viii, 3, 10 f.). The operation of the Word is the operation of the Holy Spirit. In this connection the Confessions again and again testify to the Holy Spirit. What Luther describes as a fruit of the Word—that it "awakens

new understanding, new pleasure, and a new spirit of devotion, and
. . . cleanses the heart and its meditations" (L.C. I, 101)—is elsewhere praised as the fruit of the Spirit.

Here one could ask: What, then, is the real norm? Scripture,
or the Gospel, or the preaching? The following considerations must
provide the answer:

The Confessions do not place the norm of the Gospel in opposition to the canon of Scripture; they do not, in contrast to Luther's
familiar expression, employ the Gospel as the criterion and norm in
opposition to some writings of the New Testament, whereby their
canonicity might be rendered doubtful. On the contrary, James,
Hebrews, and Revelation are frequently quoted, and there is even
a noteworthy effort to give an evangelical interpretation of the controversial passage, James 2:21, 24 (Ap. IV, 224, 252; S.D. III,
43). A criticism of the canon of Scripture or even an intracanoni-
cal criticism in the light of the Gospel, though not expressly excluded,
is nowhere undertaken.

Furthermore, the Confessions nowhere attempt to give independent
status to preaching or its edifying results, or to play it off against
Scripture. That would be the enthusiasm of the fanatics "who boast
that they possess the Spirit without and before the Word" and "wish
to distinguish sharply between the spirit and the letter," but at the
same time "do not remain silent but fill the world with their chat-
tering and scribbling, as if the Spirit could not come through the
Scriptures or the spoken word of the apostles, but must come through
their own writings and words" (S.A. III, viii, 3-6). Rather, the
preaching through which the Holy Spirit is given is the "preaching
of the Scriptures."

Thus Scripture, Gospel, and the preaching of the church are connected in the most intimate manner through the identity of their
contents. They have their unity in the Gospel. The sermon must
proclaim the Gospel, and the Gospel is the heart of the Scripture.
In this way the Gospel as witnessed by *Scripture* remains the sole
norm of all Gospel preaching in the church, that is, Gospel as the
prophetic and apostolic witness to the Gospel. The preaching of
the church is based on the preaching of the apostles and prophets
and transmits and bears witness anew to the Gospel which they
preached, that is, exposition of the "prophetic and apostolic writings of the Old and New Testaments" (Ep. Comp. Sum., 1; cf.
S.D. Sum. Form., 3; Ep. Comp. Sum., 2; S.D. Sum. Form., 16).
It is true, the special position of the prophetic and apostolic office

9

over against the subsequent preaching of the church is not further elucidated in the Confessions' remarks about Scripture, yet it becomes evident in the doctrine of the ministry. Since, accordingly, preaching is the Word of God only as proclamation of the Gospel, and since the Gospel is the sole and unique message entrusted to the prophets and apostles, Holy Scripture itself is the sole norm.

If we ask again: Why is Scripture the norm? Why are the prophetic and apostolic Scriptures, why is the prophetic and apostolic Gospel the norm? we receive no further answer to these questions in the Confessions. Even the Formula of Concord does not answer these questions with a doctrine of inspiration (the Holy Spirit is not mentioned at all in the Summary Formulation), but to the claim that Scripture is the norm it merely appends two support-ing Scripture quotations: "Thy Word is a lamp to my feet and a light to my path" (Ps. 119:105) and "Even if an angel from heaven should preach to you a gospel contrary to that which we preached to you, let him be accursed" (Gal. 1:8; cf. Ep. Comp. Sum., 1). However, this proof is obviously not a proof in the ordinary sense, but moves logically in a circle. Why is Scripture the sole norm and guide? Because it says that the Word proclaimed by it is the sole means of salvation! Because God saves through the Word pro-claimed by it. The objection may be raised against the Formula of Concord that in contrast to the earlier Confessions it already shifts to a formal Scripture principle by teaching a "comprehensive sum-mary, rule, and norm" without at once indicating the summary of Scripture, namely, the Gospel. But one will have to concede to the Formula of Concord that its doctrine of Scripture is entirely a doctrine of faith. It has recourse neither to the age of Scripture nor to its dissemination and miraculous preservation, neither to the marvelous offensiveness of its content nor to its incomparable moral effects[4]—or whatever contemporary or subsequent orthodox heter-onomous pillars of support and confirmation may be mentioned. Only by faith in the proclaimed Word of Scripture through which the triune God in Jesus Christ works in us through the Holy Spirit is Scripture presented as the sole norm. Thereby all questions are directed to the living God himself who in the act of proclaiming

[4] The theologians of the period of Orthodoxy classified arguments of this kind as *kriteria interna* and *externa*. This does not yet imply that the recogni-tion of the *autopistia* of Scripture, nor of the fact that the Holy Spirit alone creates the conviction that Scripture is the norm, has disappeared. Cf., e.g., J. Gerhard's emphasis on the witness of the Spirit to the divine address of Scripture, *Loci*, I, 36. However, this recognition becomes progressively weaker in the direction of a formal supranaturalism.

Scripture proves to each individual again and again that Scripture is the norm, that is, a pure fountain of life.

3. The Confession is exposition of Scripture, specifically, a summary of Holy Scripture, namely, a witness to the Gospel.

In the Lutheran Confessions the term "confession" is used in a threefold sense.

In the first place, *confessio* is the confession of sins, and in the articles on confession we have detailed instruction regarding the significance and extent of this confession.

In the second place, *confessio* is mentioned among the good works which follow faith, like the activity of love and the mortification of the flesh. For Christ, "in order to keep the Gospel among men, . . . visibly pits the witness of the saints against the rule of the devil." The confession of the faithful is a weapon of Jesus Christ, just as the dangers, labors, and sermons of the apostles and other teachers of the church are the "battles by which Christ restrained the devil and drove him away from the believers" (Ap. IV, 189 f.). This confession resulting from faith "is done for the praise of God" and public confession of faith before others. Specifically, confession is here the public praise of the grace of God in the words of everyone who has received this grace.

Finally, *confessio* designates a written confession of faith, or creed.

But to this threefold distinction in the meaning of *confessio* it must immediately be added that the existence of a confessional document (its composition, the endorsing signatures, and its validity) is in no case to be separated from the confession of sins and the public grateful acknowledgment of the grace of God. Every Confession is at the same time confession of sins and public testimony. Hence the Augsburg Confession has Ps. 119:46 on its title page: "I will also speak of thy testimonies before kings, and shall not be put to shame." [5]

---

[5] The Confessions thus continue to echo the joyous note of Luther's concept of *confessio*, which not only combines the confession of one's own sin and unworthiness with an overwhelming doxology of the monergism of divine grace, but with the doxology of grace embraces the confession of sin. Cf. E. Vogelsang, "Der confessio-Begriff des jungen Luther (1513-22)," *Lutherjahrbuch*, (Muenchen, 1930). Both in basis and tenor the Augsburg Confession and the Apology are in harmony with Luther's idea of *confessio*. It is, therefore, not correct to say that "there is no bridge between Luther and the Confessions" on this point. H. Kittel, "Das Problem der Confessionalitaet," *Die Erziehung* (1930), p. 3. It is possible to speak of their being diametrically opposed only by divorcing confession as the act of confessing from confession

One feature is common to every act of confession, namely, that it is the response of man to the revelation of God in his Word. For without this revelation man can know neither his sin nor God's grace. The response of man as a rule is not a verbatim repetition of the words of Scripture, but is made in the words of the man hearing the message, thus even in words which are not found in Scripture. So, for example, such concepts as "person," "substance," "nature," are used in the ancient Creeds, and taken over in the Lutheran Confessions even though Scripture does not use them. However, since these terms used in the doctrine of the Trinity obviously become inadequate and fractured, and this happens in principle with all terms used to designate the revealed God, it becomes evident already at this point that the confessing response of man to the Word of God is always merely praise of God, offering up simultaneously a sacrifice of praise with human lips. Confession, accordingly, is always also a declaration of submission on the part of confessing man. And even as man in his *own* words repeats the address of the Word of Scripture, it becomes evident that man actually submits himself.

The essential nature of a confessional *writing* as a document is determined from the outset by the content of its doctrine. This finds expression already in the Confessions' almost total silence on the nature of a confession. But a theology of the Lutheran Confessions is concerned with the doctrinal content of the Confessions as a whole. At this place only the basic relationships shall be indicated in which, according to the Lutheran Confessions, a confession must stand to Scripture, to the church, to doctrine, and to heresy. This undertaking may also be called the theological structure of a confessional document.

a) Confession as exposition of Scripture—Every structural analysis of the Confessions must start with their constantly emphasized expository dependence on Holy Writ. This follows self-evidently from the presentation in the first two theses of this chapter. The Formula of Concord does not teach anything that goes beyond the earlier Confessions when in its introduction concerning "the comprehensive summary, rule, and norm" it expressly states that "the distinction between the Holy Scripture of the Old and New Testaments

as the content of confessing. Neither Luther's nor the Confessions' concept of confession permits this. In this connection we must take note of the problems inherent in a Confession as a consensus of the whole Christian church, as against an individual's act of confessing. These problems concern not only matters of definition but also of ecclesiastical administration.

and all other writings" consists in this: "Holy Scripture remains the only judge, rule, and norm. . . . Other symbols and other writings are not judges like Holy Scripture, but merely witnesses and expositions of the faith, setting forth how at various times the Holy Scriptures were understood in the church of God by contemporaries with reference to controverted articles, and how contrary teachings were rejected and condemned" (Ep. Comp. Sum., 7 f.). But Holy Scripture is the sole norm not only for the Confessions originating in the time of the Reformation. A Confession must *in every case* be exposition of Scripture, that is, the affirmation of man that he has heard God's Word and acknowledges it. The trinitarian first article of the Augsburg Confession is thus taught and defended "in accordance with the decree of the Council of Nicaea" with an appeal to the fact that "the Holy Scriptures testify to it firmly, surely, and irrefutably" (Ap. I, 2). For the Lutheran Confessions the symbols of the ancient church are in principle on the same level in relation to, and dependence on, Holy Scripture as they themselves. The ancient and the Lutheran creeds are equally authoritative as exposition of Scripture.

Being exposition of Scripture, the Confessions also present what is believed and preached in the church of Jesus Christ. After what we heard about the relationship of Scripture and preaching, it should not be surprising that the articles of the Augsburg Confession do not begin with the words "Scripture teaches . . ." but "Our churches teach with great unanimity. . . ." Doctrine, that is, preaching and instruction, precedes the Confession, just as preaching precedes faith. The Confession does not in the first instance determine what is *to be* taught, but sums up what *is* taught in the church. It does not determine what kind of statements the Bible contains, but which statements are made on the basis of the Bible, what kind of call issues from the Bible. This is preaching, and, coming from preaching and leading to further preaching, the Confessions are exposition of Scripture. The fact that the Confessions bear witness to the doctrine of Scripture by confessing what is preached on the basis of Scripture is demonstrated by the kerygmatic, comforting, and hortatory tenor of large sections not only of the Large Catechism, but also of the Apology.

b) Confession as summary of Holy Scripture—We dare by no means stop with the general definition of confession as exposition of Scripture. Rather, the Gospel is an essential component of the very concept of Confession. In the new preface to the Large Catechism Luther scolds many bad preachers that they are "very negligent" and that they "despise both their office and this teaching" (L.C. Longer Pref., 1). They are not concerned about doctrine and doctrinal books, but are "shameful gluttons and servants of their own bellies" who "would make better swineherds and dog-keepers than spiritual guides and pastors" (L.C. Longer Pref., 2). Later Luther says "Now I know beyond a doubt that such lazy-bellies . . . do not understand a single Psalm, much less the entire Scriptures; yet they pretend to know and despise the Catechism, which is a *brief compend and summary of all the Holy Scriptures*" (L.C. Longer Pref., 18). After giving the text of the first three chief parts Luther judges concerning them, ". . . these three parts in which *everything contained in Scripture* is comprehended in short, plain, and simple terms, for the dear fathers or apostles, whoever they were, have thus summed up the doctrine, life, wisdom, and learning which constitute the Christians' conversation, conduct, and concern" (L.C. Shorter Pref., 18, 19). Accordingly, the Formula of Concord declares that we "subscribe Dr. Luther's Small and Large Catechisms as both of them are contained in his printed works. They are 'the layman's Bible' and contain *everything* which Holy Scripture discusses at greater length and *which a Christian must know for his salvation*" (Ep. Comp. Sum., 5). The two Catechisms, then, are to be viewed as a summary of Holy Scripture.

Beyond this, the other Confessions too may be called the summary of Holy Scripture, as they themselves wish to be understood. Self-evidently this term is not to be understood quantitatively. Already the statements given above about the Catechisms would be sense-less if understood quantitatively. We recall that in many statements, for instance, of the Apology, law, and Gospel—that is to say the Gospel as such, the justifying word of redemption—are designated as the total content of Scripture. It is evident, therefore, that the *doctrina fidei* is the proper theme of every Confession, and because of this every Confession is a summary of Holy Scripture. The Augsburg Confession has the first explicit statement of the doctrine of justification; yet it is taught by implication in the three ancient Symbols. "I believe" refers in the second article to the work of Christ, and in the third article to the forgiveness of sins. From the Apostles' Creed on, the Confessions are called confessions of faith, and this not merely as the personal confession of the believers, but because they themselves claim to be "the unanimous, catholic, Christian faith and confessions" or, at the very least, "expositions of the faith" (e.g., Ep. Comp. Sum., 3, 8). Accordingly, the heading of the second chief part in the Small Catechism is "The Creed."

A Confession is not the private expression of a religious nature. Nor does it establish some favorite Bible passage. Nor is it the stressing of Bible passages which are significant only for a specific concrete situation. A Confession is not the expression of the religious experience or guidance of an individual. The truth of a Confession is based expressly on the great number of Bible passages which proclaim this truth; a Confession is the comprehensive exposition of the total Scripture. For a Confession teaches "what a Christian must know for his salvation"; it teaches the Gospel. In this way a Confession as doctrine of Scripture steps out of Scripture and now becomes an approach to Scripture in that the Confession serves as a guide to the discovery of Scripture's content and as an aid in its correct interpretation. For in the labyrinth of the multiplicity of its dark passages and especially of its Old Testament legal demands the Confession helps us to know how much of all this material still applies to the church of Jesus Christ as a divine command and how much has been abolished by him.

From this point of view we may perhaps also understand why the Bible passages added to the individual articles, e.g., of the Augsburg Confession, often seem to be selected so haphazardly. Often they document or elucidate for us a secondary idea in the article, whereas the principal thoughts are left without biblical proof. Often the exegetical proof is missing where it is urgently expected. Again, Bible quotations of apparently minor import are cited as having full weight. The reason for this practice is to be sought in the self-understanding of the Confessions as *doctrina evangelii*. Because the Confessions want to be the summary of the whole Scripture they do not always attempt to give exegetical proof for individual statements. Since they speak from the very heart and center of Scripture, they sometimes are at a loss to quote specific texts for proof of what all of Scripture teaches.

c) Confession as gift of the Holy Spirit—If the Confession is exposition of Scripture, that is, *doctrina evangelii*, a Confession, like all hearing and proclamation of the Gospel, does not result from human ability, but from the operation of the Holy Spirit who is given through Word and sacrament. The human will is incapable of either believing or confessing, of confessing sins or praising the

15

glory of Christ and the grandeur of his merit. The Holy Spirit produces repentance, faith, and confession. Therefore, confession of sins and confession of faith, the fact that we "believe, teach, and confess" (thus the ever-recurring introductory words in the Formula of Concord), are inseparably connected. "No faith is firm that does not show itself in confession" (Ap. IV, 385).

This necessary reference to the Holy Spirit does not place the Confessions on the same plane with Holy Scripture and does not imply a doctrine of a *theopneustia*[6] similar to the inspiration of Scripture. Such an equation is already ruled out by the very fact that the Holy Spirit, in whose power the church confesses, is given through the proclaimed Word of Scripture, that is, through the prophetic and apostolic office; conversely, the Word of Scripture is not given through the church's Confession (not even if the fixing of the canon of Scripture may be called a confession of the church), but only through the divine institution of the prophetic and apostolic office. Even when we speak of the church's Confessions as a gift of the Spirit we must safeguard the pre-eminence of this office over against the ministry of the later church. But if, on the other hand, no mention were made of the fact that faith and confession are possible only through the Holy Spirit, one might think that Confessions could be manufactured according to need and usefulness. Confessions cannot be made; they can only be received as a gift. A Confession is a gift of grace, produced through Word and sacrament.

Both as to content and genesis the Confession as a human act is included in God's trinitarian activity. God seizes us from the outside through the Word, and through the Word he at the same time opens our hearts from within through the Holy Spirit.

[6] Even L. Hutter did not claim an equality when he said, "We have established that the primary author, or the *aitios kurios,* of the Book of Concord was not some man, either theologian or statesman, but God the Holy Spirit himself." *Libri Christianae Concordiae,* Proleg., Chap. I. When he said this he was subordinating this sentence to the *quatenus* of the agreement of the Confessions with Scripture. He was not speaking of an *autopistia* of the Confessions. Carpzov rejected this claim of divine inspiration for the Confessions as being subject to abuse, because, in contrast to the inspiration of the Holy Scriptures, *theopneustia* "concerns not only subject matter, but also the very words and the method of Him who communicates, namely, one not bound by means." *Isagoge* (3rd ed.; 1699), p. 1137. Meanwhile, we shall be able neither to avoid equating Confession with Scripture, nor to make clear the difference between them, if we begin the theological discussion with inspiration rather than with the Gospel whose proclamation God entrusted to the prophets and apostles.

4. The Confession is exposition of Scripture in consensus with the fathers and brethren. Hence it is the doctrine of the church, delimited over against the current heresy.

a) A Confession is not the deed of an individual, but an act of consensus—*Tota Scriptura* and *tota ecclesia* belong together in the Confession. Authors and signers of the Confession want to confess as the entire holy Christian church, as all saints of all time have confessed and are still confessing. The Confession is the voice of the whole church.

This consensus takes several forms: Consensus with the church of the present and with the church of the past, agreement *with the brethren and with the fathers.*

(1) The unanimity with the church of the past fifteen centuries finds expression in the copious patristic quotations which are found scattered through most of the articles of the Confessions, not to speak of the *Catalogus Testimoniorum,* which is added to the Book of Concord by way of an appendix as a "Catalog of Testimonies both of Scripture and of orthodox antiquity." [7] We have already noted with what determination the fathers are subjected to the norm of Holy Scripture. Why, then, bother to quote the church fathers at all? Why not quote only Scripture? The church fathers are quoted because of their consensus in Scripture exposition.[8] The introduction of patristic quotations by means of "similarly," "the same," "not only . . . but also," occurs again and again. Thereby the Lutheran Confessions by no means place the church fathers on a level with Holy Scripture, but they place the fathers' exposition of Scripture next to their own. "For the name spiritual father belongs only to those who govern and guide us by the Word of God" (L.C. I, 158). The patristic quotations are to demonstrate that the doctrine of the Confessions offers nothing new (cf., e.g., A.C. XX, 12: "That no new interpretation is here introduced can be demonstrated from Augustine"). This rejection of the new is not the conservation of ecclesiastical tradition but the rejection of

[7] The "Catalog of Testimonies" is given in English in the *Book of Concord* (St. Louis: Concordia, 1957), pp. 297-307.

[8] Cf. O. Ritschl, *Dogmengeschichte des Protestantismus,* I, 195 ff., for a discussion of the question of traditionalism and of the differences which developed between Luther and Melanchthon concerning the mutual relations of Scripture, doctrine, and church fathers. We may not speak of a formal and basic traditionalism in the Confessions. See also H. J. Holtzmann, *Kanon und Tradition* (Ludwigsburg, 1859), regarding the criticism of these mutual relations in the later history of Protestant theology.

an arbitrary exegesis, and especially is it a distrustful caution regarding the possibility of their own arbitrariness. The church fathers are cited not for their own sake, but for the sake of the church's understanding of Scripture. The church fathers become warning examples through their false exegesis and aids to correct exegesis. Even by means of questionable, yes false, exegesis they serve the purpose of opening the horizon for the manifold exegetical possibilities. If the patristic quotations serve a clarifying purpose for Scripture interpretation by acting through warning and assistance— by means of correct and false exegesis—to uncover the richness of the exegetical possibilities, it is obviously not of decisive importance which father says this or that, but whether he speaks the truth. In spite of certain gradations of esteem enjoyed by individual fathers, they all remain equally subject to Scripture. Occasionally the Confessions also cite the old canons, but only so far as they teach in accordance with Scripture (A.C. XXII, 10).

(2) The unanimity of the church of the present finds expression in the subscriptions to the Confessions. Among the signers were princes, lords, mayors, counselors, and theologians. This means that congregations and larger associations of congregations were also represented. Furthermore, the *consensus fratrum* is expressed by the introductory formula of the Augsburg Confession, "Our churches teach . . ." and in the Formula of Concord, "*We* believe, teach, and confess . . ." What is the significance of "churches"? Are they individual congregations?[9] Or do they refer to the Roman church and the churches presenting their Confession at Augsburg?[10] Or are they perhaps referring to the pastors of the congregations?[11] The question need not be decided here. We shall see later that the different answers suggested are not at their decisive point mutually exclusive. The only point to be made here is that this uncertainty and the possibility of more than one understanding is not accidental. The important thing is not the legally precise fixing of the organ through which the church passes judgment. Without injury to the specific duty of the ministry, the church in principle allows for a

[9] Cf. K. Thieme, *Augsburgische Konfession,* pp. 1 ff; consistent with the above, L. Fendt, *Der Wille der Reformation im Augsburgischen Bekenntnis* (Leipzig, 1929), p. 15, translates: "The congregations on our side teach with full unanimity."

[10] Cf. F. Kattenbusch, "Die Doppelschichtigkeit in Luthers Kirchenbegriff," *Theol. Studien und Krit.* (1927-1928), p. 285. Does the formula perhaps suggest evasiveness *[Leisetreterei]* on the part of Melanchthon?

[11] Cf. the close of the Augsburg Confession: " . . . *confessio nostra . . . et eorum, qui apud nos docent,"* A. C. Con., 6.

considerable latitude of confessing organs. The decisive factor is not which organs or official persons confess, but what they confess, and that they confess in the solidarity of the faith. Hence more is expected of a "general, free, and Christian council" (A.C. Pref., 21) than of the decision of individuals. The judgments of councils are the judgments of the church (Tr. 56).

(3) Finally, this matter of the consensus is to be noted also in the agreement of the several Confessions with one another, and "consensus," like "summary," is to be taken not in a quantitative sense, but from the center of the statements, that is, from the Gospel. It is of fundamental significance that most of the Lutheran Confessions claim in large measure to be exposition of the Augsburg Confession in the face of new misunderstandings and heresies. This is most directly true of the Apology and the Formula of Concord, but even at Smalcald the Augsburg Confession and the Apology were resubscribed, along with Melanchthon's Treatise. The Catechisms, moreover, in their second chief part are an exposition of the ancient Symbols of the church and they make use of ecclesiastical tradition also in other sections.[12]

This twofold and even threefold consensus is the one consensus of the "one holy Christian church." This consensus makes plain that the Confession is not the doctrine of an individual but of the church. Heeding the voice of the fathers and brethren represented a test and a correction of the understanding of Scripture on the part of the individual authors of the church's Confession. Apart from the church, no individual can confess. Indeed, the Holy Spirit who bestows faith and Confession on individuals is the same Spirit who "calls, gathers, enlightens, and sanctifies the whole Christian church on earth and preserves it in union with Jesus Christ in the one true faith" (S.C. II, 6). From the point of view of the consensus the Confessions have greater weight than individual fathers, and, again, the Ecumenical Symbols are relatively more authoritative than the Confessions of the Reformation. Thus the three ancient Symbols are called 'those three catholic and general Creeds, possessed of the *highest* authority' (*illa catholica et generalia summae auctoritatis symbola*). This designation is not applied to the Lutheran Confessions (S.D. Sum. Form., 4). For, in contradistinction to the

---

[12] Kahnis, *Christentum und Luthertum* (Leipzig, 1871), p. 141, says in so many words: "The other Confessions (beside the Augsburg Confession) are Confessions of the second rank, and their significance is restricted to their being authentic Reformation witnesses according to which the Augsburg Confession is to be explained and applied."

Lutheran documents, the ancient Symbols are valid for all of Christendom. Their consensus is more inclusive. All Confessions, however, are equally dependent on Holy Scripture.

From this matter of the *consensus patrum et fratrum* it follows that the Confessions as a rule are Symbols of the unity of the church: ". . . We know that our confession is true, godly, and catholic" (Ap. XIV, 3). The catholicity of the church and of the Confession have an essential connection. This is true because the content of the Confession is faith, and because the unity of the church is the fellowship of the same faith under the Word and in the use of the sacraments. However, although the ancient Symbols included in the Book of Concord are also acknowledged by the Roman church, this common acknowledgment of the same Confession does not guarantee the unity of the church. On the other hand, the unity of the church is not to be recognized only there where the same Confessions are accepted.[13]

b) The occasion of the Confession—Only after it has been determined that the Confession is exposition of Scripture, specifically as witness to the Gospel in oneness with the fathers and brethren, only after it has become clear that the Confession is the work of the Holy Spirit, may we approach the question of the occasion for the act of confessing. Outside of the trinitarian circle only one point is important for the construction of a Confession, namely, its occasion. This cannot yet be an event in nature or a political happening as such. No, Confessions are occasioned by heresies which may, of course, also have a political coloring—heresies, that is, that have invaded the church from within or without and have confused and captured members of the church. As a result of the development and history of heresies the Confession comes into being, fixing the church's doctrine in areas of theological discussion that had hitherto remained dogmatically undecided.

The matter of the occasion is preserved in the Confessions in the very fact that their time of origin is indicated exactly, especially in the "Comprehensive Summary." It is even taken over into the definition of the Confessions: They are "merely witnesses and expositions of the faith, setting forth how at various times the Holy Scriptures were understood in the church of God *by contemporaries* with reference to controverted articles, and how contrary teachings were rejected and condemned" (Ep. Comp. Sum., 8). The historical hour when the heresy invaded the church, or when the

[13] Cf. pp. 202, 206 ff., 220 f.

church became alerted to the heresy, is by no means a source of knowledge for the Confession as is the Word of Scripture; it by no means makes the act of confessing possible as does the operation of the Holy Spirit; it does not even serve as a corrective for the understanding as does the voice of the fathers and brethren. Heresies are nothing more than the occasion, that is, the world's attack in the face of which the church makes plain before all the world that it belongs solely to its Lord and Saviour, Jesus Christ. This stimulus may cause Scripture doctrines to be unfolded by the Confession in a specific direction or through the use of a specific terminology. However, this occasion as such makes no contribution to the real content of the church's doctrine. In contrast to the one-sided historical treatment of the Confessions on the basis of a one-sided concern with them as conditioned by their historical and theological context and an interest only in their morphological significance, which has become the customary approach since the rise of rationalism, we shall do well, above all, to take note of the doctrine of the Confessions, specifically their doctrine as exposition of Scripture. Thus, for instance, the Confession was not honored, nor even brought into view, but rather brushed aside when, referring to the three-hundredth anniversary of the presentation of the Augsburg Confession, Schleiermacher proclaimed that "the real object of our last anniversary celebration was more the act of the presentation of the Confession than the function or content of that document itself." [14]

We must distinguish, on the one hand, between the historical and psychological *motives* that lead to certain Confessions and, on the other, the exegetical *arguments* that determine the Confessions. The former were esteemed far too highly in the days of historicism and up to the present.[15] The latter, however, give exclusive author-

[14] Predigten in bezug auf die *Feier der Uebergabe der Augsburgischen Confession* (Berlin, 1831), pp. IV f.
[15] An overemphasis of the historical situation out of which the Confessions arose is indicated, e.g., by the following statements of Gogarten: "A Confession belongs to its time. Once this time together with its intellectual presuppositions is past, the Confession—which bears witness to the manner in which at that time the Holy Scriptures were understood as the Word of God— ceases to be a Confession. It is now inadequate to accomplish that for which a Confession is required. Since it belongs to the past, it now requires interpretation, yes, translation, for that very reason." *Das Bekenntnis der Kirche* (Jena, 1934), p. 23.
While it is true, as Gogarten rightly emphasizes, that we may in no wise overlook the character of a Confession as event in its confrontation with a specific heresy, yet the present value of the Confession is to be sought, above all, in the consensus of its Scripture interpretation. With respect to the evaluation of the Confessions in the history of Protestant theology since the En-

ity to the Confessions and make of them a weapon in the battle. Both must be carefully distinguished. Heresy is given too much credit if it is regarded as the real cause of the origin of a Confession and as the justification of its existence. A Confession is praise of grace. Heresies come and go, but the Gospel remains.

c) Confession as battle against the devil—To see in heresy nothing more than the work of sinful man would betray a lack of understanding of the essence of heresy and of the attack upon it. It is quite consistent with the relation of a Confession to the Holy Spirit to ascribe heresies in origin and content to the devil 'who stupifies and misleads many a great and wise man in the world by means of dreadful error, heresy, and other kinds of blindness, and plunges men into manifold vices' (Ap. II, 47 ff.). Thus the heresies of work-righteousness are 'doctrines of demons, scattered abroad in the world by Satan in order to suppress the true doctrine of the Gospel, so that none or only a few might be instructed in the nature of law or Gospel, repentance or faith, or the blessings of Christ' (Ap. XII, 141). Luther passes the same judgment on the Enthusiasts: "All this is the old devil and the old serpent who made enthusiasts of Adam and Eve. He led them from the external Word of God to spiritualizing and to their own imaginations" (S.A. III, viii, 5). Every false doctrine is thus traced back to the devil. By these expressions the Confessions are not thinking of "hallucinations of the devil," but they are aware of the real powers of darkness which constantly strive to attack and devour the church. The reality of the devil is directed against the reality of the Holy Spirit, who is God himself. And against the devil the church fights with the weapon of its Confessions. They are the "battles of Christ" against the devil (cf. Ap. IV, 190).

5. Since the Confession is a summary of Holy Scripture, it is the obligatory model for all doctrine in the church.

lightenment, we must say quite generally: The more the significance of a Confession was seen in the event of its frontal-polemic origin, and the less it was seen in the scripturalness of its witness, the more doubtful became not only the unity of the Gospel and the identity of the Holy Spirit, but also the event of the Confession in its peculiarity, namely, the eschatological significance of the act of confession, transcending history and time. The fact that a Confession requires interpretation does not constitute a valid objection to its present value. Gogarten's fine statement applies also to the correct exposition of the Confessions: As it confesses its faith "the church ever again breaks through the walls of truths, of ordinances, of validities which man in search of security seeks to build. The church does this, not to destroy or abolish these truths, ordinances, and validities, but to keep them open for the ultimate truth which alone can preserve them. . . ." *Ibid.*, p. 17.

a) Confession as obligation—Faith in the Gospel involves faith in an eschatological judgment, namely, the merciful divine verdict of deliverance in the final judgment. For the Gospel is at once offer and promise of divine grace. Both are joined together in the concept of *promissio gratiae*. The forgiveness that is now in time received through the Gospel is definitive. The Gospel blesses and saves the sinner not only for a moment, but for all time and eternity. To "believe, teach, and confess" the Gospel therefore signifies an obligation that transcends the initial act of confession. Thus in 1580 the framers of the Formula of Concord professed their allegiance to the Augustana: "By the help of God's grace we, too, intend to persist in this confession until our blessed end and to appear before the judgment seat of our Lord Jesus Christ with joyful and fearless hearts and consciences" (B. of C. Pref., p. 9; cf. S.D. XII, 40).[16]

Believing and confessing the Gospel always implies at once the recognition of the divine commission to preach the Gospel to all the world. But if the Gospel is God's gracious bestowal for time and eternity, then the charge to preach the Gospel is also always the same. It follows that the Confession as *doctrina evangelii* has an obligatory significance for the speaking and acting of the church in all ages. The power by which a Confession binds is the power of the Gospel. And because the Gospel that has been recognized puts the church under obligation, the Confession too—as *doctrina evangelii*—has binding significance for the church's proclamation and action.

Placed under obligation by the proffered promise, the church is bound to its Confession and employs it as "a single, universally accepted, certain, and common form of doctrine which all our Evangelical churches subscribe and from and according to which, because it is drawn from the Word of God, all other writings are to be approved and accepted, judged and regulated" (S.D. Sum. Form., 10).

[16] This eschatological orientation of the Confession is often overlooked, and improperly so. Since Jesus Christ will at the Last Day acknowledge the disciple who confesses him (Matt. 10:32 f.), the true Confession of the church is in itself a veritable eschatological event like the preaching of the Gospel and the outpouring of the Holy Spirit. Cf. G. Bornkamm, "Das Wort Jesu vom Bekennen," *Monatsschrift fuer Pastoraltheologie* (1938), pp. 108 ff. For this reason the church cannot arbitrarily alter its Confession. For the same reason the church does not "have" its Confession as a property of which it may now dispose. Recognizing the Confession as an eschatological event, however, does not exclude but rather includes the proviso which Luther himself expressed in his instruction to the Visitors of Electral Saxony, 1528: ". . . until God the Holy Spirit initiate something better through them or through us." *WA* 26, p. 200, l. 20.

The Confessions are binding for church, school, and home; hence, "from and according to" them all preaching and teaching is to be tested and judged, accepted or rejected. On the basis of the Confessions false teachers are to be condemned, and excommunications are to be carried out. The Confessions, however, also give directions for distinguishing "between needless and unprofitable contentions (which, since they destroy rather than edify, should never be allowed to disturb the church) and necessary controversy (dissension concerning articles of the Creed or the chief parts of our Christian doctrine, when the contrary error must be refuted in order to preserve the truth)" (S.D. Sum. Form., 15). Thus the Confession shows how to distinguish between theological movements within the church, on the one hand, and the separateness of church and heresy on the other. In every case the Confessions exclude the liberty to teach anything and everything, and they make the concept "confessional freedom" impossible as a slogan for the church, inasmuch as such a concept signifies not only freedom with respect to *the* Confession, but also with respect to *every* Confession, namely, freedom *from* confession.

In accordance with the essence of the Gospel, the binding significance of the Confession is in no sense limited to the generation of its origin. The Confession is to serve the purpose that the truth may be *"established* the more distinctly and clearly" in the future too. The Confession is to be "a certain and public testimony, not only to our contemporaries, but also to our posterity of that which *is and should remain* the unanimous understanding and judgment of our churches regarding controverted issues" (S.D. Sum. Form., 16). "In order to preserve the pure doctrine, . . . the true and wholesome doctrine" should be "correctly" presented and "the adversaries who teach otherwise" should be reproved (S.D. Sum. Form., 14), not only in the moment of writing, but also in the future, in line with the Confession. The Formula of Concord itself follows this rule in that it claims to be nothing more than a "general, pure, correct, and definitive restatement and exposition of a number of articles of the Augsburg Confession" (S.D. title page) over against new objections, misunderstandings, and errors. And this was fifty years after the presentation of the Confession at Augsburg.

In this double sense, then, the Confession is obligatory. The Gospel which men have learned to know never bestows and obligates only for the moment, but for all time and eternity. The confessing church knows, besides, that no one is lord over the knowledge of the Gospel, and that therefore no one can presume to regulate the possibility of confessing. The Confession is a gift of the Holy Spirit who produces confession when he pleases.

Not until this is clearly understood may we begin to discuss the meaning of confessional obligation in a legal sense—legal, that is, both in principle and with respect to prevailing church law. Just as we spoke of the Confession first as exposition of Scripture and only then of the significance of the consensus, so in the question of the binding authority of the Confession we must first recognize the binding truth of the *doctrina evangelii,* and only then consider the act of assenting subscription on the part of preachers and governments which—because it was an assent to the Word of divine grace by persons in official capacity—established church law and the obligation in terms of church law.

b) Confession as model under Holy Scripture as norm—In demanding that all doctrine and preaching be "judged and regulated" "from and according to" the Confessions, the Formula of Concord makes use of terms which seem to correspond to the designation of Scripture as "judge" and *"regula."* This suggests that the Confession too be called a norm (cf. B. of C. Pref., p. 10 f.), as actually soon became common practice in the dogmatics of Lutheran Orthodoxy. This would mean that since the Gospel is the norm, the Confession as *doctrina evangelii* is likewise norm of all doctrine and preaching. Since the Gospel is the key to the understanding of Scripture, the Confession too—as *doctrina evangelii*—is able to render important services as a hermeneutical aid. In the Gospel, Scripture and Confession have their unity. The Gospel is the norm in both.

However, the Confessions themselves in ever-new turns of speech designate the Scripture alone as "norm," "judge," "rule," "foundation," "guide." Even though *de facto* doctrine and error are judged "from and according to" the Confessions, and even though the same Gospel is attested in both Scripture and Confession, yet the great, fundamental difference remains: *Holy Scripture* is not the norm because of agreement with the Gospel as witnessed in the Confessions, but the Confessions are authoritative only because of their agreement with the Gospel as witnessed in the Holy Scripture. This relation may not at all be inverted. This difference is so great that the Confessions refrain almost entirely from designating the Confession as a norm. The fundamental distinction remains unblurred: Holy Scripture is the norm as the eternal Word; the Confessions, however, only as witness of "how at various times the

25

Holy Scriptures were understood in the church of God by contemporaries." Holy Scripture as the Word of God teaches the Gospel, but the Confessions are *doctrina evangelii* only as exposition of Scripture. The Word of God is "eternal truth"; the Confessions are "a witness of the truth" (S.D. Sum. Form., 13).

How, then, shall the binding significance of the Confessions for teaching and preaching be maintained? The Confessions are so thoroughly imbued with their subject, the Gospel itself, that they obviously have no special interest in an explicit doctrine concerning the nature of a Confession. Exclusively decisive for them in this respect is the principle that Holy Scripture is the only norm [*unica norma*]. On the other hand, the Formula of Concord, the only Confession to treat explicitly of the nature of a Confession, designates the Confessions as "form and pattern," "summary," and "model" of the church's doctrine. What does this mean? The word *forma* is probably to be understood in terms of the Aristotelian-scholastic tradition, even though the Formula of Concord does not use it in a philosophically precise sense but rather with a denatured meaning. In that case this term implies two things: As the "form" is an object's substantial nature, lifted out of its manifold modes of appearance and grasped conceptually, so the Confession is the *ousia* of the scriptural witness, lifted out of the multiplicity of that witness and "comprehended" in the *doctrina evangelii*. And as the Aristotelian-scholastic *forma* is the entelechy which, as forming principle, actively operates in things, so the Confession is at once the formative and shaping *energeia* for all present and future preaching in the church, even though the Confession—like the sermon—is exposition of Scripture, a renewed witness to the Gospel to which Scripture had first borne witness.

As "summary" of the church's doctrine the Confessions take their place alongside all church doctrine under the Holy Scripture as the judge. On the other hand, as "pattern of doctrine" (S.D. Sum. Form., 10) the Confessions are a step *ahead* of the ranks of all other teaching and preaching. As "doctrine of the church" the Confessions are the model for all teaching and preaching by individual members of the church.

Inferences for Dogmatics

Beginning this study with a presentation of the relation of Scripture and Confession corresponds neither to the structure of the ancient Symbols with which the Book of Concord opens, nor to that of the Augsburg Confession and its Apology, the Smalcald Articles, and the two Catechisms. All of these proceed at once to the matter itself, without giving any thought to the basis, possibility, and nature of a Confession, or even to a special article on Holy Scripture. Our purpose in beginning in a different way was solely to make clear at the outset what part the act of listening to the Confessions must play according to their own statements in the framework of dogmatics. This clarification, which in its particulars is part of dogmatics itself, may be anticipated here by drawing the most important inferences for a dogmatics that is bound by the Confessions. In the main we shall once more follow the order of topic sentences 1 through 5.

1. The sole norm for dogmatics is the Holy Scripture of the Old and New Testaments. All dogmatic statements must be derived from God's revelation in his Word. It will, therefore, not do to base dogmatic sentences, wholly or even in part, on the impressions of nature or of history round about us, or on ideas of reason or intimations of the emotions. On the contrary, all of this manifold material must be subjected to the Word of Scripture. Nor can the witness of God in the works of his creation serve as a source of knowledge for dogmatics,[17] but only the revelation of God in his Word. Hence the task of dogmatics consists in ever anew distinguishing between God's revelation and human religion, God's Word and man's own words.

2. Within Holy Scripture, the Gospel—that is, the promise of forgiveness for the sake of Jesus Christ—is the norm for all dogmatic endeavor. Thus the normative center of Scripture is Jesus Christ, the eternal Word made flesh. Only from this center can the Old and New Testaments be correctly expounded, and only by recognizing this center will the dogmatic assertions be properly founded on Scripture. An exegesis which isolates either the Old or the New Testament fails to recognize God speaking in his incarnate Word. And again, an exegesis that does not proceed in the recognition of the incarnation, the death, and the resurrection of Christ is bound to let the statements of the Old and New Testaments deteriorate into a series of legalistic or libertinistic directives. The center of Scripture, however, is not the Gospel *in abstracto*, but law and Gospel, or, more accurately, the Gospel as distinguished from the law and as definitively superior to the law. Again, the center of

---

[17] Cf. pp. **48 ff.**

Scripture is not Jesus Christ *in abstracto;* it is that Christ who preaches repentance and forgiveness—who judges and saves—but whose proper office is forgiving and saving. Thus the dogmatician is not at liberty to lord it over this normative center of Scripture, to manipulate it as a principle. He must always yield and submit himself again to the center, which is nothing but the living God himself acting in his Word, the God who pardons and judges, demands and bestows. It follows, then, that the decisive task of all dogmatic endeavor is the distinction between law and Gospel in the Word of God. Only he who correctly distinguishes law and Gospel—that is, who remains a pupil in this distinction all his life— will correctly distinguish between God's Word and man's word.

3. As promise, the Gospel is at the same time the bestowal of the forgiveness of sins. The Gospel is not only the message that God forgave sins in the past and will do so again in the future, but it is the Word by which God today forgives the sinner all his sins. This occurs through the preaching of the Gospel and the administration of the sacraments. No proper work in dogmatics can therefore be done apart from preaching and the administration of the sacrament. Dogmatics always proceeds from preaching and the sacraments, and must, in turn, always lead back to them. Dogmatics is derived from preaching, because it is in the act of Gospel preaching that Holy Scripture manifests itself as norm. Dogmatics leads to preaching, because it is never an end in itself and has no value in itself, but its task is to serve the church's preaching—and to instruct, warn, encourage, and support the preacher—by means of an expository summing up of the totality of Scripture statements and a differentiating of them from false doctrine. Beyond this service dogmatics has no task.

4. Natural man cannot believe or know the Gospel except through the Holy Spirit. It is through the Gospel that the Holy Spirit operates and is bestowed on man. Hence the Word of God is not only the objective source of knowledge for all statements about God, but it also bestows the subjective possibility of knowing the revealed God, namely, the Holy Spirit who is active in the Word. The fact that man knows God is thus an act of the triune God, a trinitarian event in which God through Word and Spirit takes hold of the blinded and obstinate man and gives him sight. Having recognized God's Word as the sole norm, dogmatics must be equally single-minded in seeing that *only* by the Holy Spirit can and will the Word of God be known. This is possible in no other way, neither through

the similar natural presuppositions of geography or nationality, nor through the affinity of the historical situation, neither the external similarity in thought patterns nor in the contents of religious and ethical conceptions. Only the Spirit of God makes the understanding of Holy Scripture possible. Dogmatics must see to it that the hermeneutics of the biblical-theological sciences, as well as the theory of knowledge within the field of dogmatic endeavor itself, be and remain strictly trinitarian.

5. Dogmatics is bound by the Confessions as exposition of Scripture. This means again, obligation to Holy Scripture as the sole norm—obligation not so much to a specific exegesis as rather to Scripture itself. Not what men say about Scripture constitutes the sole norm, but what Scripture says to men. A Confession has no binding force apart from the fact that it correctly expounds Scripture. If we were bound to the Confessions simply because they claim to be true interpretation, without being able to see the propriety of this claim on the basis of Scripture, the Confession would be, like tradition in the Roman church, a second norm for dogmatics alongside Scripture. Doctrine cannot be bound to the Confessions in the sense of a *fides implicita,* that is, independent of a clear exegetical understanding of their scripturalness. The truth and binding force of a Confession does not rest simply on its claim—no matter how much that claim may be supported by respected church fathers at various times—but in its actual agreement with Scripture which ever anew discloses itself to exegetical study. The Lutheran Confessions wish to be understood as explanation of the faith—"how at various times the Holy Scriptures were understood in the church of God by contemporaries." For this reason the Confessions must at all times prove themselves the rule and model of the church's doctrine *in the act of Scripture interpretation.* When a church is no longer certain of this proof, or has lost confidence in the clarity of Scripture because of the controversies among various schools of exegesis, together with their methods and results, the church has lost its Confession as that is defined by Lutherans, even though the church may still honor and follow the Lutheran Confessions.

6. Dogmatics is bound by the Confessions as witness to the Gospel in Holy Scripture. This means, again, obligation to the Gospel. The fact that the Confessions regard themselves as *doctrina evangelii* must provide the starting point for both the interpretation of the Confessions and the definition of what confessional obligation means. Not even all Scripture passages are on the same level, much less the

statements in the Confessions. By virtue of a legalistic or libertinistic approach to Holy Scripture it is possible to get lost there as in a maze. The same may happen in the Confessions. The content of the Confessions can be properly interpreted only from their center, the doctrine of justification. This alone enables us to do justice to the claim of the Confessions to be binding doctrine. The accent in nineteenth- and twentieth-century constitutions and consistorial expressions that the Confessions are binding, not in a legal or literal way, but only according to their spirit and sense, were intended mostly as a weakening of their claim in favor of "freedom of inquiry" and resulted in their repeal. "Legal," "literal," and "spirit" are here used in a general and nontheological way. However, what is a legalistic or an evangelical obligation can in no case be determined in a general way, but only on the basis of the content, in an exclusively theological way: Rightly understood, confessional obligation means being bound by the Gospel as witnessed in the Confession. This, in turn, means liberation by means of the Gospel from the killing letter of the divine law. Understanding the concept of confessional obligation on the basis of content does not exclude, but rather includes, an obligation to the very words of the Confession. After all, even the Gospel is the Word that liberates, and in the formula "I forgive you all your sins for the sake of Jesus Christ" every word is also decisive.

7. Dogmatics is bound by the Confessions as the church's exposition of Scripture, as the consensus of the fathers and brethren in exegesis. The Confession is the doctrine of the one, holy church embracing all believers, not the doctrine of an individual, or several individuals, or any school of theology. Therefore, dogmatics must beware of placing the teaching of individual fathers and brethren—whether writings of the young Luther or the *Loci* of Johann Gerhard or theological ideas of Kierkegaard or a theologian of the present—alongside the Confession. Nor is it permissible to refer to the former in the same manner as the latter, or even, without further ado, to pit the former against the latter. The *consensus ecclesiae* dare not be confused with the community of similar theological interests, opinions, or even only thought forms. Dogmatics must also beware of forsaking the church's Confession in the same, perhaps regretful, yet ultimately unconcerned manner as one dissolves a theological friendship or terminates a teacher-pupil relationship. On the contrary, the Confessions are incomparably and uniquely binding beyond all pronouncements which the church's teachers may otherwise make,

and references to the Confessions have more weight in dogmatics than patristic quotations. This does, indeed, not mean that the aspect of the consensus acts as a dead weight for dogmatics, no matter whether it is the consensus of the fathers of the Reformation or of the present day. The Confessions are binding only as the church's consensus in the *correct* understanding of Holy Scripture. It judges both the churchly doctrine of the individual as well as that which is taught in the consensus of the church.

8. The Confessions as rejection of the heresies of their day obligate dogmatics to the task of uncovering and refuting those heresies also that have arisen since the Reformation or after the close of the Book of Concord. To be bound by the Confession necessarily implies for dogmatics the obligation to continue in the act of confessing; for the *con*sensus of the church in the doctrine of the Gospel is and remains until Christ's return a *dis*sensus from the world. A dogmatics that would in an unrelated manner consider only those heresies through which the devil assailed the church centuries ago, but would not be alert to the constantly changing disguises of the devil's destructive purpose in the invention of ever-new heresies, and would not see through the ever-new attacks of the evil powers under ever-new and surprising forms—such a dogmatics would imperceptibly but helplessly fall prey to the attitudes and attacks of this world. Contrary to the Confession is that dogmatics which does not teach the Gospel as witnessed by the Confessions in demarcation against newly arising heresies. Even the most solemn reaffirmation of the Confessions may be a denial of them, if the errors of the day are passed over in silence. Hence no Confession of the church may be regarded as definitive in the sense of precluding the possibility of further Confessions. All the Confessions had their origin in confrontation with errors— this fact is inherent in the very concept of a Confession, as the Confessions themselves and particularly the programmatic introduction to the Formula of Concord expressly declare—and to admit this is to acknowledge that the Book of Concord cannot be regarded as the final and conclusive Confession. At the very least the church, confronted with new heresies, will have to furnish up-to-date and binding interpretations of her official Confessions. But also beyond this we must soberly reckon with the possibility, perhaps even the necessity, of meeting the invasion of new errors with the formulation and validation of new Confessions. "To deny this possibility—and even necessity—would mean to close the history of the Christian

church, not with the day of the Lord, but with that of some man or some event within history, and to deny either the presence of the Holy Spirit in the church, that is to say, the church herself, or the permanent antithesis of the world and its prince over against the church" (F. H. R. Frank, *Theologie der Concordienformel* [Erlangen, 1858-1865], I, 6). A single dogmatician cannot create new Confessions; he cannot even provide binding elucidations of the existing valid Confessions. Only the church, in the consensus of the faithful, can do these things, and it can do them only by the power of the Holy Spirit, who gathers, enlightens, and preserves the church. The dogmatician must, however, by discerning the spirits, alertly prepare, demand, and formulate these decisions of the church.

9. From all this it follows that we must carefully distinguish between a theology of the Lutheran Confessions and a text in dogmatics. If by a theology of the Lutheran Confessions we mean a faithful reproduction of their content in systematic order, this endeavor is not a dogmatics. Again, dogmatics is not simply a repetition or repristination of the Confessions. Two facts must here be considered: (*a*) The Confessions are the model of all church doctrine, including all dogmatic endeavor, which teachers of the church undertake and the results of which they present orally and in writing. As the voice of the church the Confessions have more authority than the voice of an individual. (*b*) On the other hand, the norm for dogmatics is not the Confession, but solely the Holy Scriptures. Dogmatics, like the Confession, must teach the summary of Scripture. Thus, unlike a theology of the Confessions, dogmatics has the ever-new task of measuring the exegesis of the Confessions by the Scriptures through the process of retracing their exegesis, and of teaching the doctrine of the church in the act of expounding the Scripture. Dogmatics will have to give consideration to the development of exegetical science since the Reformation, including its current status. For example, dogmatics may neither overestimate nor overlook the progress of New Testament exegesis based on more exact lexical aids, on the results of textual criticism, the identification of the sources, rabbinical studies, religio-historical researches, etc. The possibility must be conceded from the start that dogmatics may, in the process of exegesis, question some of the confessional formulations. Unlike a theology of the Confessions, dogmatics must, furthermore, review the consensus of the Confessions with the ancient church as well as the consensus of the Reformation age,

develop them further, or even call them into question. In this connection too the results of recent patristic studies and of the history of dogma in general must not be overlooked. Not only are we able to see many an ancient text more clearly due to more reliable information regarding its authenticity, but we may also judge more accurately the theology of some fathers in their own independent context. For example, we may no longer appeal quite so confidently, as did the Reformers, to Augustine in support of their doctrine of justification and of the sacraments. Moreover, dogmatics must consider and indicate also the consensus in which—however obscurely —the church since the Reformation and to the present day has proclaimed the Gospel. Unlike a theology of the Confessions, dogmatics must also expressly take a stand with respect to the heresies which have invaded the church since the Reformation, especially such as at any moment endanger or obscure the Gospel. In the process of uncovering and refuting error, dogmatics must constantly recall the church to its Confession. In addition, dogmatics has not only the right but also the duty to present the church's doctrine by means of a more thorough exegetical support and a more comprehensive systematic order and development than could be done in the Confessions because of their brevity, or because their structure was frequently determined by the opposition.[18]

10. We may therefore designate the theology of the Confessions as the legitimate "Prolegomena to Dogmatics." Since all doctrine of the church is bound by the model of the Confession, every teacher and student of dogmatics is bound to hear the church's Scripture interpretation *before* all other interpretations. In any case, the church is already the given place where we take our first steps in theology by hearing the church's proclamation. Since we live, hear, and pray in the church, we already have our continuous point of departure from the Confession, whether we do so in conscious clarity or in a temporally conditioned lack of clarity. None of us interprets Scripture as an individual but as a member of the church. As we occupy ourselves with the Confessions we must always be conscious of our given place in the church and, with that, of the more or less clear understanding by means of which we ourselves approach Scripture in question or research. The Christian, as one born and instructed by the church, must surrender his own understanding and inquiry to the Word of Scripture for the purpose of being judged and confirmed, answered and rejected by the Lord of

---

[18] Think, e.g., of the structure of the Smalcald Articles.

33

the church. In this way he becomes a teacher. Dogma originates only in the encounter of Scripture with the church, only when Scripture makes its impact upon the church.

This concept of the prolegomena must be secured over against two other points of view:

Here we do not view prolegomena as an integral part of dogmatics. This was the case when John Gerhard began his *Loci theologici* (Jena, 1610-1622) with a *"prooemium de natura theologiae,"* and J. F. Koenig his *Theologia positiva acroamatica* (Rostock, 1665) with *"praecognita theologiae,"* and D. Hollaz his *Examen theologicum acroamaticum* (Rostock and Leipzig, 1707) with *"propaedia theologica."* For here, already in their dogmatic exposition of Scripture, they were dealing with principles pertaining to the content and method of dogmatics, and with Scripture and the relation between faith and doctrine. Recently prolegomena as "a *portion of dogmatics itself"* were treated most extensively by Karl Barth in his *Prolegomena to Dogmatics* (trans. G. T. Thomson, Edinburgh: T. & T. Clark, 1936 and 1957). Barth included the "doctrine of the Word of God" together with the doctrine of the Trinity and, further, sections of Christology. He says that the "syllable 'pro' in the word 'prolegomena' is to be understood figuratively; involved here are not the things that must be said *previously* but the things that must be said first" (p. 45). Over against this view, it may be seen that the theology of the Confessions has its place *before* dogmatics.

On the other hand, we do not regard prolegomena as a universally comprehensible entranceway to dogmatics, in which the dogmatician attempts to demonstrate to the world the justification for—or at least the possibility of—his undertaking, and to deduce principles and insights—or at least points of contact—for his work from the empirical or a priori knowledge possessed by the nonbelievers. Thus Schleiermacher began the introduction to his *Glaubenslehre* with statements borrowed from ethics, philosophy of religion, and apologetics in the belief that "what precedes the explanation of a science cannot be a part of that science itself, and that all statements made here cannot themselves be regarded as dogmatic" (*Der christliche Glaube* [2nd ed.], par. 1, 1). In another way W. Hermann begins his *Dogmatics* (Gotha, 1925) with statements about religion in general, viewed consciously from the standpoint of the general science of religion, and then in Part II treats the "faith concepts of Christianity." In yet an entirely different manner Karl Heim in his theology[19] struggles with the matter of a common ground for conversation between sciences in general and dogmatics, and with the admittedly paradoxical presuppositions for faith in the thinking of an unbeliever. Viewed from the history of doctrine, such endeavors indeed have their ultimate roots in the statements about religion as they are set forth in the prolegomena of the textbooks of the later Orthodox period, especially in their chapters on the natural and the revealed knowledge of God. They differ from the Orthodox, however, in that the latter were concerned at once about the distinction between true and false religion, and these statements were derived expressly from the revelation of God in his Word. Thus, by designating the theology of the Confessions as "prolegomena to Dogmatics," we obviously do not regard them as an approach to dogmatics from outside the doctrine of the church, in the sense of neo-Protestant theology.

The theology of the Confessions is a prolegomenon for dogmatics neither as being an integral part of dogmatics nor as being a secular-scientific entranceway to dogmatics, but as being a part of that way which the Christian must traverse between his Baptism and his speaking in the church's doctrinal office. Before one can be a father he must have been a child and a youth. No one can become a teacher who has not first become a pupil. It is as a pupil instructed by the church's interpretation of Scripture that the theologian must himself interpret Scripture in the church and instruct the church. This pupil status is never at an end. Every teacher remains all his life a child of his mother, the church. The theology of the Confessions is, therefore, not a prolegomenon in a temporal sense, but in principle: even though in the schedule of theological training it may precede dogmatics, yet the Confession of the church remains through all of life the place from which our inquiring and teaching proceeds—a place that was given before we ever did any inquiring or teaching.

It is, of course, not *necessary* that the theology of the Confessions precede dogmatics explicitly as independent prolegomena in the form of a textbook or a lecture course. Placement of the Confession in principle above the doctrine of an individual member of the church will take place within a dogmatics of the church quite apart from that—and not only by means of quotations from the Confessions, but above all through the content of the dogmatic

[19] *Leitfaden der Dogmatik*, I (3rd ed.; Halle, 1923); *Glaube und Denken* (Berlin, 1931; 4th ed., 1938).

statements. In the present moment of church history—coming as it does after a long period of evangelical theology during which dogmatics had become largely a playground for the subjective originality of speculative piety, a period in which Christians generally forgot how to pray through their Catechism—it must be regarded not only as possible, but, beyond that, *advisable,* before we begin to speak, to listen explicitly to the doctrine of the Confessions as a monographic prolegomenon.

II

THE REVELATION OF GOD THE CREATOR

In recent years the criticism has often been voiced that the doctrine of creation has not been clearly and unambiguously explained in the Lutheran Confessions. It is, indeed, noteworthy that there is not even a specific article on creation except in the Catechisms. After presenting the doctrine of the Trinity in Article I, the Augsburg Confession and the Apology immediately proceed to the doctrine of sin, the Smalcald Articles to Christology, and the Formula of Concord starts at once with original sin. The reality of the creation is touched on before the doctrine of sin in the testimony of Article I of the Augsburg Confession to God as the "maker and preserver of all things visible and invisible" (A.C. I, 2)—the Apology even omits this phrase—and in a relative clause Part I of the Smalcald Articles refers to the effect "that Father, Son, and Holy Spirit . . . are one God, who created heaven and earth" (S.A. I, 1). Outside of these references and those in the first article of the Catechisms we find only occasional remarks about the Creator and creation in contexts dealing entirely with other matters.

One might therefore be inclined to speak of a neglect of the doctrine of creation in the Lutheran Confessions, a neglect which is all the more striking in view of the detailed treatment and the very precise formulations of the relationship of sin and grace, of law and Gospel. At the very least, very little emphasis on the doctrine of creation is apparent, and so today there is, even in the Lutheran church, no lack of attempts to emphasize creation more and to make more detailed statements about it than we find in the Confessions. Before attempting, however, to build up such a "theology of creation," as is frequently demanded and as has been undertaken repeatedly, we must seriously ask whether this apparently minor emphasis on the doctrine of creation, and with it the "one-sided" Lutheran equation of Confession and *doctrina evangelii* is not theologically necessary. We must ask whether just this alleged "lack of clarity" and "ambiguity" in the Lutheran doctrine of creation is not an essential feature of the Lutheran Confession. Is it not possible that those people who wish to say more about creation than is stated in the Confessions no longer understand the Gospel?[1]

1. Man is altogether a creature of God, and this purely out of divine goodness.

The Lutheran doctrine of creation is essentially an explanation of the one phrase in the ancient Creeds, "Maker of heaven and earth" (Apost.), or "Maker of heaven and earth, and of all things visible and invisible" (Nic.). Thereby our attention is directed immediately to God and his deed, and the idea is precluded that the creatureliness of created things is a quality of this world which has reality apart from God and his action. God is the Lord who was in eternity before all things and who in the beginning of things called into existence the things that did not exist.

The explanation of these words of the Apostles' Creed in the Catechisms begins with these words: "I believe that God has created me" (S.C. II, 2) and "I hold and believe that I am a creature of God" (L.C. II, 13). This wording at once excludes the thought that God is the Creator only in so far as in the beginning he created the world and man. Rather, we confess that "everything we possess, and everything in heaven and on earth besides, is daily given and sustained by God" (L.C. II, 19). God once was the Creator, and he daily is the Creator. In fact, God not only "is" the Creator, but he actually once did and daily does the work of the Creator. Therefore, in the term "Creator" the *creatio ex nihilo seu immediata* at the beginning of the world and the *creatio continuata* day by day are summarized and unified. Creation today is no less wonderful than creation in the beginning. It is therefore already evident that the problem of the doctrine of creation is by no means confined to the *how* of the original divine creative process, but also includes the *what* of the creative activity of God today amid the fluctuations of catastrophe and renewal within the present-day world: What in this present world is to be acknowledged as "in accordance with creation"? That which is "original"? That which is "natural"? The healthy? The orderly? Is this, at the same time, the good?

For when in explanation of the word "Creator" it is immediately

---

[1] In what follows I have incorporated my study, *Die Verborgenheit Gottes des Schoepfers nach lutherischer Lehre* (Muenchen, 1936).

stated that "I am a creature of God," fallen man is thereby designated as creature, and God is designated as Creator of man even
after the fall. It is impossible to restrict the sentence, "I believe
that God has created me," to Adam, or to the *human race* of which
I am a member, and by virtue of which membership I am also a
creature of God. It is also impossible to refer this sentence only to
my origin and birth. Since God *daily* gives us "everything that we
possess," and since according to Luther's direction we are also to
pray this article *daily,* man is God's creature even in the state of
sin. He not only became a creature of God, but he is ever anew
God's creature. God is our Creator beyond sin and the fall. Thus
the Catechisms do not differentiate between creation and preservation,
nor do the other Confessions make a clear distinction—". . . that
I (namely, man in this world of sin and death) am a creature of
God; that is, that he has given and constantly sustains my body,
soul . . ." (L.C. II, 13). God's creative and preserving activity
are mentioned together again and again, and both are comprehended in the word "Creator." After mentioning the manifold
works of the Creator in giving and sustaining life, Luther in the
Large Catechism concludes by pointing out again that "all this is
comprehended in the word 'Creator' " (L.C. II, 16). Accordingly,
the very concept of creation itself contains the insight that it is by
no means a mere matter of course when God permits his fallen
creature to go on living.

This ego, which in its sin and in spite of its sin is daily preserved
by God, and which is permitted to praise him as the Creator, this
ego is not an abstract, generalized entity, and hence in no case a
transcendental ego or that which because of reason has remained
in fallen man to distinguish him from the beast. Rather, the
creature is the concrete, living man with all his functions—". . .
body, soul, and life, my members great and small, all the faculties
of my mind, my reason and understanding, and so forth; my food
and drink, clothing, means of support, wife and child, servants,
house and home, etc. Besides, he makes all creation help provide
the comforts and necessities of life. . . . Moreover, he gives all
physical and temporal blessings—good government, peace, security"
(L.C. II, 13 ff.). These last two gifts, which go beyond the explanation of the Small Catechism, plainly characterize once more the
creative activity of God as preservation in a fallen world. At the
same time it becomes clear that we believe in God not only as
the Creator of man in general, but of the concrete individual person.

No function of man is excepted. Indeed, the long list of things in which man is the creature of God—the list which Luther compiled and to which we could add—is expressly left unfinished when it is stated "that none of us has his life of himself, or anything that has here been mentioned or can be mentioned, nor can he by himself preserve any of them, however small and unimportant" (L.C. II, 16). Did God, then, create sinful man? No. But man even in sin and in spite of sin is altogether God's creature.

Luther gratefully glorifies this act of God the Creator: "All this he does out of his pure, fatherly, and divine goodness and mercy, without any merit or worthiness on my part" (S.C. II, 2). "All this he does out of pure love and goodness, without our merit . . ." (L.C. II, 17). God gives and does these things "so that we may sense and see in them his fatherly heart and his boundless love toward us" (L.C. II, 23). In this connection it is striking that with all this emphasis on the unmerited character of this love the term "grace" is not used. Nor do the Lutheran Confessions elsewhere speak of a "grace of creation" corresponding to the grace of forgiveness.

2. *Every man is altogether a sinner and under the wrath of God.*

Man as a sinner is 'without fear of God, . . . without trust in God, and . . . concupiscent' (A.C. II, 1). This lack of the fear of God and of trust in God is by no means merely a deficiency, but it is the reality of the creature's active rebellion against the Creator, "hating his judgment and fleeing it, being angry at him, despairing of his grace, trusting in temporal things, etc."—'fleeing God as a tyrant, hating and grumbling against his will; again, not daring to entrust ourselves to God's goodness, but rather always putting more reliance on money, property, and friends' (Ap. II, 8). The sinner hates God instead of fearing him, he is angry with him instead of loving him, and he despairs instead of trusting in God. The reality of the enmity against God is, again, not merely a sinful deed, but it is sinful craving, lust, and desire. "When we use the term 'concupiscence,' we do not mean only its acts or fruits, but the continual inclination of nature" (Ap. II, 3). Concupiscence is a corruption of the physical constitution and also 'an evil lust and inclination, according to which we, in spite of the best and highest faculites and the light of reason, nevertheless are carnally inclined and minded against God' (Ap. II, 25). Concupiscence "pursues carnal ends contrary to the Word of God (that is, not only the desires of the body but also carnal wisdom and righteousness in which it trusts while it despises God)" (Ap. II, 26).

Men are sinners, such as "are full of evil lusts and inclinations from their mothers' wombs and are unable by nature to have true fear of God and true faith in God" (A.C. II, 1). Sin is not merely the reality of individual deeds, but of all thoughts, words, and deeds of man, both of the evil as well as of the so-called good ones. Thus 'man sins truly even when he performs noble, beautiful, and precious deeds, such as the world values highly' (Ap. IV, 33). Sin is not merely the deed of individual people, but it is a reality for all men. "Here no one is godly" (S.A. III, iii, 3). "Men are all liars" (Ps. 116:11; Ap. II, 34). "For we are all under sin" (Ap. IV, 75). Sin is a reality for every human being at every moment "from his mother's womb." For being a sinner means not only "not to have true fear of God, no true faith in God," but to be "*unable* by nature to have true fear of God and true faith in God" (A.C. II, 1); "*lack of ability* to trust, fear, or love God" (Ap. II, 26). Thus since the fall sin is the inescapable necessity of every human being from birth; it is his enslavement and his prison.

Sin is real because original sin is a reality; sin and original sin are interchangeable concepts. "Of Original Sin" it is taught "that since the fall of Adam all men who are born according to the course of nature (that is, all men except the Virgin-born Son of God) are conceived and born in sin" (A.C. II, 1). The concept 'original sin' clearly presupposes and includes the fact of the fall and of man's original state, but this presupposition is not further explained, and statements about the pristine state and the manner of the fall are scanty.[2] The whole weight of the numerous doctrinal declarations about original sin is forthwith concentrated on *our* sin. As in the doctrine of creation, so also in the doctrine of original sin the thought is at once focused on us—there on God's goodness toward us; here on our malice against God. *We,* as doers of sin, are the object of the doctrine of sin.[3] It is striking, furthermore,

---

[2] So scanty, in fact, that J. Mueller (*Die christliche Lehre von der Suende* [5th ed.; Breslau, 1867], II, 560) claimed to be able to prove that the Augsburg Confession and the Apology contain no definition "that would exclude the assumption of a cause of our inborn sinfulness going beyond the fall of Adam (namely, a prehistoric fall)."

[3] Emil Brunner, in objecting to the "ecclesiastical," specifically the Lutheran, doctrine of sin, maintains that "sin is and remains an act. The doctrine of the church which, through the idea of inherited sin, has slipped into the physical sphere has overlooked this permanent quality of the actuality of sin or at least—through its physical emphasis—has obscured it."

that the Confessions do not further elucidate the *how* of the connection between Adam's sin and our sin. Thus, for example, they do not develop a doctrine of the imputation of Adam's sin to his progeny.[4] To be sure, they teach that original sin "is transmitted through our carnal conception and birth out of sinful seed from our father and mother" (S.D. I, 7; see also 11, 27 f.). But this does not explain the sin of the progeny biologically, nor does it

This objection is not valid, because the Confessions nowhere speak of an original sin that is not real in the frightful actuality of hatred against God, of flight from God's judgment, of disobedience to the double command of love. The concepts of being a sinner and of committing sin are peculiarly interwoven. Brunner's criticism of the church's doctrine of the fall tends in the same direction, namely, that the weight of our actual sinful decision and, hence, of our responsibility and guilt, is transferred to a "kind of legendary figure," namely, Adam. According to this doctrine, we human beings since Adam would have to "take over the responsibility for guilt, for something in which we have actually no part." Olive Wyon (trans.), Emil Brunner's *Man in Revolt* (Philadelphia: The Westminster Press, 1947), pp. 114, 148 ff. But this very thing the Lutheran doctrine has denied in the strongest terms. Since Adam, every man is a sinner and therefore himself guilty, because every man is a sinner in that he commits sin, and in that he is a sinner he commits sin. *Peccatum* and *peccatum originis* belong together. It is true, the word "inherited" sin seems to support Brunner's recurring charge of a derailment of the Lutheran doctrine in the direction of the physico-biological. A careful scrutiny of the Confessions reveals, however, that in using the term "inherited" [*Erbsuende*], they have no interest in the physical aspects as such. Rather, they use this term to make statements about the *whole* man, that is, about the sin of the whole human race. It is not the biological relationship of men and the succession of generations that is labeled original sin, but the reality of the sin of all those people biologically related. The matter concerns "the rationally imperceptible fact that all human existence, involved biologically through conception and birth in the succession of generations . . . is at all times and in all details an existence that from the outset provokes God, yields to the devil, and realizes itself in being dead before and for God. The mystery of how this happens is more concealed than revealed by the term 'hereditary' sin, which sounds biological but is not so intended. Yes, by this terminology the irrationality of an existence chained to sin is not abandoned, but rather safeguarded." G. Niemeier, "Die Lehre von der Suende und Erbsuende in den Bek. der Ev—Luth. Kirche," *Ev. Theol.* (1938), p. 195; cf. *ibid.,* n. 11.

[4] Koellner, in his confessionally derived "System der Lutherischen theologischen Dogmatik" (*Symbolik,* I, 610 ff.), indeed teaches as an assertion of the Confessions that "the guilt of Adam was imputed also to his descendants, and this is one chief reason why they may expect nothing but damnation." "Original sin . . . is the other cause." (*Ibid.,* 630). But this can only be understood as reading into the Confessions the later theological opinions of Lutheran Orthodoxy. (Koellner unfortunately is guilty of this quite often.) Vilmar rightly points out that an *imputatio culpae et poenae primorum parentum,* though taught in the old Protestant dogmatics, "is not found in our Symbols." A. F. C. Vilmar, *Dogmatik* (reprint of 1st ed.; Guetersloh, 1937), I, 371. It still remains questionable whether Vilmar's opinion is correct that this doctrine has its basis in the dubious mingling of *culpa* and *reatus* in the Apology and the Formula of Concord, or whether this failure to distinguish these terms is not rather theologically necessary and highly meaningful.

view sexuality as the essence of sin.[5] Rather, the fact of the universal relationship of all men in sin is established to be equally as comprehensive as is the community of creatures. The community of all men, of all their deeds, and of all their inclinations is, ever since Adam's fall, the community in sin.

Accordingly, original sin is a "deep . . . corruption of nature" (S.A. III, i, 3), 'the rapidly spreading hereditary plague' (Ap. II, 8), the "abominable and dreadful inherited disease which has corrupted our entire nature" (S.D. I, 5).[6] The "abiding deficiency in an unrenewed human nature" (Ap. II, 31) must in no way be minimized in its extent. Sin is not a mere defect, 'a failing or imposed load, or burden' (Ap. II, 5), not only "a simple, insignificant, external spot or blemish, merely splashed on" (S.D. I, 21), by no means only a partial corruption, but "a deep, wicked, abominable, bottomless, inscrutable, and inexpressible corruption of his entire nature in all its powers, especially of the highest and foremost powers of the soul in mind, heart, and will" (S.D. I, 11). Therefore, he who is willing to acknowledge sin only as an act is told in no uncertain terms that "original sin is not a sin which man commits; it inheres in the nature, substance, and essence of man in such a way that even if no evil thought would ever arise in the heart of corrupted man, no idle word were spoken, or no wicked act or deed took place, nevertheless man's nature is corrupted through original sin" (Ep. I, 21), and "his nature and person" are as with "a spiritual leprosy . . . thoroughly and entirely poisoned and corrupted" (S.D. I, 6). Nothing in man is excepted from this corruption, neither in

---

[5] It is wrong to say with E. Gerstenmaier (*Die Kirche und die Schoepfung* [Berlin, 1938], p. 127) that "the old negation of the sensual-sexual" is here asserting itself.

[6] We must beware of introducing into the nature concept of the anthropological statements of the Confessions the modern understanding which contrasts nature and spirit, or nature and person, and assigns the nature concept in anthropology to the realm of the biologico-physical. In the terminology of the Confessions nature and person are not contrasted in this way, but they may even be equated: "Nature *or* person" (S.D. I, 6), " 'nature-sin' *or* 'person-sin' " (S.D. I, 5) are interchangeable terms. In agreement with biblical anthropology the theological interest is here centered in the *total* man, and thus neither in his physical nature apart from his personal decision, nor in man's responsible decision apart from his corporeality. The nature concept of the Confessions embraces body and soul, biological *physis* and personal responsibility, and the confessional concept of person embraces soul and body, personal responsibility, and biological *physis*. Speaking of the total corruption of the human person or nature in this sense, this anthropology, then, corresponds to the expectation of the new creation at the Last Day, namely, the bodily resurrection of the believer unto eternal life. Conversely, placing person and nature in antithesis must lead to an attenuation of the biblical eschatology and an approach to the humanistic body-soul theory.

his body nor in his soul, neither in his deeds nor in his thoughts or inclinations. "The fruits of this sin are all the subsequent evil deeds which are forbidden in the Ten Commandments" (S.A. III, i, 2).

Even though fallen man cannot but sin, this sin is *guilt*, nevertheless; "is *truly* sin"—sin which condemns "to the eternal wrath of God" (A.C. II, 2). Even though sin is inherited sin, 'what a grievous mortal guilt original sin is in the sight of God!' (Ap. II, 45). Original sin is original *guilt, "culpa originis"* (A.C. XXIV, 25). Not for one moment is concupiscence ever an *"adiaphoron,"* 'neither good nor bad' (Ap. II, 41 f.), but it is *poena et peccatum,* at once penalty and guilt (Ap. II, 47), it is the punishment inflicted on Adam's children for Adam's deed, and yet it never ceases to be the sin and guilt of Adam's children. Guilt and not being able to do otherwise, guilt and ignorance, responsibility and nature are not mutually exclusive in the doctrine of sin. In numerous statements any rationalizing of these dreadful paradoxes is expressly declined (cf., e.g., Ap. II, 1, 38, 42).

Thus we all stand under the angry God who 'wants to punish sin in so dreadful a manner with both temporal and eternal penalties' (Ap. IV, 129). "There (Gen. 3) human nature is subjected not only to death and other physical ills, but also to the rule of the devil" (Ap. II, 46), who keeps all men under his tyrannical rule, smites them with blindness, and seduces to vice. Through Adam's disobedience, i.e., through God's wrath because of Adam's disobedience, all men are "subject to death and the devil" (S.A. III, i, 1). Thus all of us are " 'by nature the children of wrath,' of death, and of damnation" (S.D. I, 6). Over against the wrath of God man with all his works is 'like a little feather tossed aside by a hurricane' (Ap. IV, 47). 'When the heart feels God's wrath, all joking and playful thoughts are gone' (Ap. IV, 20).

3. *The whole man is a creature and totally corrupt at the same time.*

Man in this time is therefore, on the one hand, a creature and, on the other, a sinner; a creature in his whole nature of body and soul, and "thoroughly and entirely poisoned and corrupted" "in the sight of God" as by "a spiritual leprosy" (S.D. I, 6). Every day his reason is given to him by his Creator, and yet it is corrupt through and through; given to him by God, and yet unable to decide in favor of the good. Daily God gives man life, and yet a a sinner he is dead. Thus man as a creature receives divine love, while as a sinner he is under the wrath of God.

The Lutheran Confessions do not attempt to evade this terrible dualism of the human situation, but they face the issue. However, not only is man's situation terrifying, but also the creative activity of God is here acutely threatened by the suspicion that God is the author of sin. The Confessions do not evade the issue by restricting God's creative activity to the pristine state, nor by restricting sin to the individual act or to a part of human nature in order to exclude the person of man or any human possibility from corruption. There is no doubt that the same features of man recur whether we view him in his creatureliness *or* in his corruption. No part of man is mentioned which, subtracting corruption from his creatureliness, could remain as a positive residue. Lutheran teaching does not go beyond this point that man is a creature and a sinner at the same time, and it formulates this *simul* by giving *glory to God*. This is the theme of Article I of the Formula of Concord in its attempt to settle the Flacian controversy. What is the result?

a) Man's nature "even after the Fall . . . is and remains a creature of God" (Ep. I, 2). "Scripture testifies not only that God created human nature before the fall, but also that after the fall human nature is God's creature and handiwork" (S.D. I, 34).

b) Original sin is "so deep a corruption" of human nature "that nothing sound or uncorrupted has survived in man's body or soul, in his inward or outward powers" (Ep. I, 8).

c) The distinction between creatureliness and sin "is as great as the difference between God's work and the devil's work" (Ep. I, 2). Along this line the following distinctions are made:

"corrupted nature"	"the corruption which is in the nature" (Ep. I, 7)
nature as "essence"	nature as "quality" (Ep. I, 22)
"our nature as it is created and preserved by God and in which sin dwells"	"original sin itself which dwells in the nature" (S.D. I, 33)
"our corrupted nature or substance or being"	"original sin" (e.g., S.D. I, 48)
"substantia"	*"accidens"* (S.D. I, 54 ff.).[7]

45

The basic stress is always on creatureliness. This creatureliness includes man *in statu integritatis et in statu corruptionis et in statu gloriae.*

d) At the same time it is evident that this is merely a conceptual distinction, in no case an empirical one. While the Formula of Concord distinguishes creatureliness and sin as concepts and even says that this distinction "is clearly set forth" (Ep. I, 7), it declares at the same time "that no one except God alone can separate the corruption of our nature from the nature itself" (Ep. I, 10). Therefore in this age of sin and death it is expressly and definitively forbidden to attempt to delimit empirically in fallen man what is creation and what is sin, or, even more, what is still original creation and what is already corruption. Every quantitative definition of what is creation and what is sin is absolutely eliminated.

e) The differentiation of these concepts *substantia* and *accidens* serves only "to set forth the distinction between God's handiwork, our nature in spite of its being corrupted, and the devil's handiwork, the sin which inheres in . . . God's handiwork" (S.D. I, 61). The heavier stress—so far as content is concerned—which is given to the former term means simply that honor is to be given to God and not to man or to the devil, that God and not the devil or man himself is to be acknowledged as the Lord. For the creatureliness of man derives from God, but sin comes alone from man and from the prince of this world (A.C. XIX; cf., e.g., S.A. III, i, 1). God is not "the creator or author of sin" (S.D. I, 40). The devil, on the

---

[7] We are justified in asking whether it was proper to introduce into the discussion of the relationship between creation and sin a thought pattern so freighted and ambiguous in the history of philosophy. Might not rather a great deal of misunderstanding and confusion have been avoided by omitting the concepts *substantia* and *accidens*? However, this question is not dogmatically decisive. We must rather ask, first of all, what content the Formula of Concord gives to these terms and whether thereby the church's doctrine of creation and sin has been surrendered to philosophy. Since all theological terms are ultimately derived from secular language, not their etymology is decisive, but the way in which these terms transcend their secular meaning and are given a new meaning in the service of witnessing to God's revelation. It is evident that the Flacian controversy was concerned about theologically transcending the philosophical concepts. By attacking Strigel's designation of sin as *accidens* Flacius was attacking an underestimation of original sin in the sense of the Aristotelian concept of *accidens*. Cf. Frank, I, 67 ff. Again, by declining the Flacian designation of sin as *substantia* the Formula of Concord showed itself equally afraid of an unscriptural understanding of *substantia*. This would, as a matter of fact, have resulted in a sort of Manichaeanism. When, finally, the Formula of Concord, without agreeing with Strigel, designated creatureliness as *substantia* and original sin as *accidens*, it gave these terms a meaning completely different from that used in Aristotelian scholastic language; the theme of the theological statements has transcended and reshaped the philosophical concepts.

other hand, is in no way a creator (A.C. I, 5 rejects Manichaean-ism). When in this conceptual distinction creatureliness is granted the primacy, God the "Almighty Creator" is thereby awarded the primacy.

f) However, by designating the corruption as "*accidens,*" original sin is by no means "minimized" (S.D. I, 61). This is clearly evidenced in the doctrine of the image of God. Of fallen man the Confessions do not teach that he is in the image of God and at the same time not in the image of God. The image of God and the loss of the image are not placed in dialectical antithesis, like creatureli-ness and corruption. Rather, the fact that fallen man is at the same time wholly a creature and wholly corrupt is given this unambiguous significance: He has lost the image of God. There is predicated of him "a complete lack or absence of the original concreated right-eousness of paradise or of the image of God according to which man was originally created in truth, holiness, and righteousness" (S.D. I, 10). "So original righteousness was intended to involve not only a balanced physical constitution, but these gifts as well: a surer knowledge of God, fear of God, trust in God, or at least the inclination and power to do these things. This the Scripture shows when it says that man was created in the image of God and after his likeness (Gen. 1:27). What else is this than that a wisdom and righteousness was implanted in man that would grasp God and reflect him, that is, that man received his gifts like the knowledge of God, fear of God, and trust in God?" (Ap. II, 17 f.). But fallen man has lost the image of God. Only when we are regenerated are we " 'changed into his likeness'; that is, we acquire the true knowl-edge of God" (Ap. IV, 351).[8]

All this means: Creatureliness and corruption mutually cover one another in the empirical observation of human reality. If we were able empirically to observe our creatureliness, we could surely not observe our corruption. And if we were able to recognize our cor-

---

[8] This strongly unequivocal doctrine of the image of God and its total loss was not maintained by the dogmaticians of Lutheran Orthodoxy, but they soon spoke of the *reliquiae* and *residua* which were said to have survived the fall. See, for example, J. Gerhard, *Loci,* VIII; more restrained, C. Dieterici, *Institutiones Catecheticae,* pp. 230 ff. Cf. F. K. Schumann, "imago Dei," *Festschrift fuer G. Krueger* (Giessen, 1932), pp. 167 ff.; *Vom Geheimnis der Schoepfung* (Guetersloh, 1937), pp. 37 f.; and E. Schlink, "Gottes Ebenbild als Gesetz und Evangelium," in *Der alte und der neue Mensch* (Muenchen, 1942).

ruption, we would surely not see our creatureliness. But the conditions in the protases are themselves contrary to fact. To be sure, man imagines again and again that he can see creation in some phases of life and corruption in the opposite phases! But seeing this in individual phases, e.g., in that which is healthy, only the expression of creation, and the expression of corruption in what is sick, man has really recognized neither creatureliness nor the corruption of sin. For every man is altogether both, creature and sinner, at the same time.[9]

4. Accordingly, neither God's goodness nor God's wrath, neither man's creatureliness nor his corruption, can be recognized from the natural reality of man.

This topic sentence means to say that *God* is hidden from the empirical observation of human reality. He is completely hidden behind the *simul* of creatureliness and corruption. Neither God the Creator nor God the exacting Lawgiver, neither God's love nor God's wrath can be recognized in this fallen world.[10]

In view of what has been said, the Lutheran Confessions are entirely consistent in denying natural man the ability to know God, as they do frequently. Besides the characteristics mentioned in the previous section, the *"ignoratio Dei"* is directly named as the essence of original sin. Among the "more serious faults of human nature" are mentioned "ignoring God, despising Him . . ." ('This is our true and supreme misery that we are all born in such a way that we do not know, see, or notice God and the works of God, but despise God . . .', Ap. II, 8). Original sin "involves such faults as ignorance of God, contempt of God, lack of the fear of God and

---

[9] For a recent critique of Formula of Concord, I, see Gerstenmaier, *op. cit.,* p. 137. But the claim made there is not valid, namely, that it is Flacian heresy not to distinguish clearly between being a sinner and committing sin. If this were true the entire doctrine of sin in the Confessions would be Flacian heresy. "Where this distinction is not made, the simple result of such an application of the judgment, in itself correct, that man is and remains a sinner, would be that *everything* this sinner does is sin without any distinction." The inference here attacked by Gerstenmaier is drawn without scruple by the Confessions, including the anti-Flacian Formula of Concord. Nor is it refuted by their references to the *justitia civilis*. This conclusion in no wise questions the creatureliness of man, except perhaps for one who has forsaken the nonperceptible dialectic of "creature and sinner at the same time."

[10] Cf. F. Blanke, *Der verborgene Gott bei Luther* (Berlin, 1928), p. 10: "God's hiddenness does not begin only in the area of the Christian experience of salvation, but already in creation. The Creator is himself the hidden God." The revelation of God the Creator is treated correctly only when the hiddenness of God is treated at the same time, and vice versa.

of trust in him, inability to love him" (Ap. II, 14). To define sin correctly we must include the loss of "the knowledge of God" (Ap. II, 23). Before we heard God's Word "we were entirely of the devil, knowing nothing of God and of Christ" (L.C. II, 52). Fallen man knows nothing either of God's love or of God's wrath; for, as long as the human heart is at rest, it "does not feel God's wrath or judgment" (Ap. IV, 9). The heart will be snatched out of this state of ease, i.e., it will be hurled into spiritual agony, only through God's law in the Word. Furthermore, man by his own powers is incapable of obtaining any knowledge of God, either when face to face with nature or when confronted with the revealed Word of God. Hence original sin signifies ignorance of God in the most comprehensive sense of the term.

At first glance this seems to be contradicted when it is occasionally said of "man's reason or natural intellect" in a subordinate clause, ". . . although man's reason or natural intellect still has a dim spark of the knowledge that there is a God, as well as of the teaching of the law (Rom. 1:19 ff.)" (S.D. II, 9; cf. V, 22). A similar thought is hidden in the expressions concerning the loss of the *notitia Dei certior* of paradise (Ap. II, 17), where already the German text, however, passes over the problem of the comparative. How do the Confessions arrive at equating this "spark" of the knowledge of God with ignorance of God?

This question occupied the Confessions surprisingly little. They give no direct answer. The problem involved in the natural knowledge of God is treated in the Confessions as so unimportant and insignificant that apparently no need of harmonizing the opposing formulations was felt. Only indirectly can we seek to attain clarity in the matter, by a conclusion of analogy. For further clarification we consider the propositions about the natural knowledge of the law:

a) ". . . to some extent human reason naturally understands the law (it has the same judgment written in the mind by God)." 'Natural law, which agrees with the law of Moses or the Ten Commandments, is innate and written in the hearts of all men, and accordingly reason can to some extent grasp and understand the Ten Commandments' (Ap. IV, 7). "The Ten Commandments . . . are inscribed in the hearts of all men. No human wisdom can comprehend the Creed" (L.C. II, 67). How are such statements to be harmonized with the natural "ignorance of God," with the many statements of the Confessions that reason is blind and impotent in all divine matters? The Apology itself (Ap. IV, 7 f.) gives the answer with a twofold qualification.

b) "But the Decalogue does not only require external works that reason can somehow perform. It also requires other works far beyond the reach of reason, like true fear of God, true love of God, true prayer to God, true conviction that God hears prayer, and the expectation of God's help in death and all afflictions" (Ap. IV, 8). That is, the First Commandment, which demands true fear of God and true love of God, is "far beyond the reach of reason"; but the reach of reason (in contrast to the law revealed in the Word) is restricted to the external civic works, that is, to the commandments of the second table (cf. Ap. IV, 131). Here there are certain correspondences (cf. Ap. XVI, 3 ff.). In the sense of *pars pro toto* we can also speak of a natural knowledge of the Ten Commandments, but reason by its own powers does not recognize the commandments of natural law as the commandments of *God,* just as natural man in his worship does not serve God but an idol (L.C. I, 17 ff.). It is especially true of the first table that it is "far beyond the senses and understanding of all creatures" (Ap. IV, 131).

c) Natural man does not clearly understand the Ten Commandments, furthermore, inasmuch as the natural knowledge of the law does not see that the commandments cannot be fulfilled. By the law (in its natural understanding) "they seek forgiveness of sins and justification" (Ap. IV, 7). 'For all human reason and wisdom cannot but hold that we must become righteous by the law and that a person externally observing the law is holy and righteous' (Ap. IV, 159). This perversion is often stressed as indicative of the thinking of natural man and of reason concerning the law: "Our opponents concentrate on the commandments of the second table, which contain the civil righteousness that reason understands. Content with this, they think that they satisfy the law of God. Meanwhile they do not see the first table, which commands us to love God . . ." (Ap. IV, 34; cf. also, e.g., II, 16). Hence the natural knowledge of the law, like the Roman Catholic doctrine of works, is not only without any significance for salvation, but, on the contrary, since it does not even attain to the knowledge of divine wrath, it leads to the intensification and to the pinnacle of enmity against God. If the Confessions place Roman work-righteousness on the same plane with the behavior of natural man which results from his rational knowledge of the law, must the latter not also be asked this question: Does not this bury Christ completely? Not only of work-righteous-

ness in the sphere of the church, but of the moral activity of fallen
man in general we are permitted to say that 'they again put Christ
into the grave and invent something different, as though we had
access (to God) through our works' (Ap. IV, 81). For work-
righteousness belongs to the nature of the corrupted creature; it is
the essence of natural religion.

Natural man, then, knows God's *law* "to some extent" (Ap. IV,
7 f.), but he misunderstands it in its decisive aspect, namely, as the
law of *God*. And in the very performance of occasional works of
the law he blasphemes God, because he thinks he is justified thereby.
Since men refuse to confess their sins to God, this judgment applies:
". . . they neither see nor read the sentence of the law written in
their hearts" (Ap. XII, 48).

By analogy, then, we may say of the natural knowledge of God
in general:

a) Man has a "dim spark of the *knowledge that there is a God*"
(S.D. II, 9).

b) This knowledge, however, is only "a dim spark," an indefinite
and general knowing.

c) As soon as man tries to take this vague knowing seriously
and to put it into practice concretely by calling God by name and
devising a ritual for him, he only falls more deeply into sin with his
natural obedience to the law and does not come to God but to idols.[11]
It is true on the one hand that "there has never been a people so
wicked that it did not establish and maintain some sort of worship,"
but it is true without exception, on the other hand, that "everyone
has set up a god of his own, to which he looked for blessings, help,
and comfort" (L.C. I, 17). Thus men come to Jupiter, Hercules,
etc. "The truth is that their trust is false and wrong; for it is not
founded upon the one God. . . . Accordingly the heathen actually
fashion their fancies and dreams about God into an idol and entrust
themselves to an empty nothing" (L.C. I, 18 f.).

Thus natural man knows that there is a God but not who God is,
and so he does not know God the Creator. He knows in part what
is demanded but not who demands it, and therefore he does not
recognize God's wrath. He knows neither God nor his own reality;

[11] Even though the rich and manifold earthly gifts of God the Creator, as
enumerated by both Catechisms in detail, provide *signa* which daily point the
believer to God's fatherly care, this is, in fact, "something different from natural religion which sees in the world of the senses a sufficient basis for our
knowledge of God." J. Meyer, *Hist. Kommentar*, p. 282. These gifts do not
bestow faith in God's fatherly goodness, but they are a corroborating witness
for him who by faith has already come to know it.

the innate internal uncleanness of human nature is not seen by him, and "this cannot be adjudged except from the Word of God" (Ap. II, 13; cf. 34). "This hereditary sin is so deep a corruption of nature that reason cannot understand it. It must be believed because of the revelation in the Scriptures" (S.A. III, i, 3; cf. also Ep. I, 9; S.D. I, 8). Original sin is "ultimately the worst damage . . . , that we shall not only endure God's eternal wrath and death but that we do not even realize what we are suffering" (S.D. I, 62). Thereby our creatureliness too is hidden from the natural knowledge.

5. The law comprises the divine commandments written in Scripture; only under the law can God's wrath be recognized. The Gospel is the assurance of forgiveness for Christ's sake; only in the Gospel can God's grace be recognized.

The Confessions again and again call the Ten Commandments, and thereby the Word of Scripture, the source of our knowledge of the doctrine of the law of God. It was by no means only for the sake of children that Luther in the Small Catechism taught 'Christian Ethics' in the explanation of the Ten Commandments. At least he would not have had to show this consideration in the Large Catechism.

"Here, then, we have the Ten Commandments, a summary of divine teaching on what we are to do to make our whole life pleasing to God. They are the true fountain from which all good works must spring, the true channel through which all good works must flow. Apart from these Ten Commandments no deed, no conduct can be good or pleasing to God, no matter how great or precious it may be in the eyes of the world" (L.C. I, 311). "This much is certain: anyone who knows the Ten Commandments perfectly knows the entire Scriptures. In all affairs and circumstances he can counsel, help, comfort, judge, and make decisions in both spiritual and temporal matters. He is qualified to sit in judgment upon all doctrines, estates, persons, laws, and everything else in the world" (L.C. Longer Pref., 17). It is not only the Gospel of Jesus Christ, but even the "Ten Commandments, the Creed, and the Lord's Prayer [which] are not spun out of any man's imagination but revealed and given by God himself" (L.C. IV, 6). Hence the doctrine of the law is revealed theology; otherwise the Ten Commandments would not be regarded as normative in so comprehensive a manner. Thus it is taught that 'strictly speaking, the law is a divinely *revealed* doctrine' (Ep. V, 3); it is "a divine doctrine which reveals the righteousness and immutable will of God" (S.D. V, 17; cf. VI, 15). Since the doctrine of the law is revealed theology, it is in its essence doctrine of Scripture. God's law comprises "the commandments of the Decalogue, wherever they appear in the Scriptures" (Ap. IV, 6). This applies not only to the First Commandment. To be sure, the First Commandment is "like the clasp or the hoop of a wreath that binds the end to the beginning and holds everything together" (L.C. I, Con., 326; cf. also 324, 329), but, as may readily be seen in an analysis of the First Part, the First Commandment is "clasp and hoop, chief source and fountainhead" of the other nine commandments, not of just any imaginable moral order. The glory and praise bestowed on the commandments of the second table (cf., e.g., the explanation of the Fourth and Sixth Commandments) in Luther's Large Catechism is the encomium of the "great, good, and holy work" which is "utterly despised and brushed aside, and no one recognizes it as God's command, or as a holy, divine word and precept" (L.C. I, 112). The First Commandment—indeed the double commandment of love—is the summary of the similarly revealed divine will in the nine remaining specific commandments.

Only through the divine commandment revealed in the Word do the ordinances of this world receive normative significance. They do not have such significance in themselves (e.g., on the basis of their distribution, their utility, their preservatory effect, etc.), just as water as such is plain water and has no sacramental significance in itself. "In the same way we speak about the parental estate and civil authority. If we regard these persons with reference to their noses, eyes, skin and hair, flesh and bones, they look no different from Turks and heathen. . . . But because the commandment is added, 'You shall honor father and mother,' I see another man, adorned and clothed with the majesty and glory of God. The commandment, I say, is the golden chain about his neck, yes, the crown on his head, which shows me how and why I should honor this particular flesh and blood" (L.C. IV, 20; cf. 38, 61).[12] According to these words from Luther's teaching on Baptism, the ordinances are related to the law as the elements are related to the word of the sacrament. These are not mere chance remarks, however; the underlying principle is used for a theological decision also in cases where the use of natural data as theological arguments might seem obvious, as, for instance, in the doctrine of marriage. The Apology indeed

[12] Cf. pp. 236 f.

concludes from the indestructibility of the natural concreated inclination between man and woman that marriage cannot be abrogated (Ap. XXIII, 7). But marriage is recognized as created by God on the basis of Gen. 1, not on the basis of empirical impressions. Similarly, the Apology mentions 'natural appetite' and 'burning' as reasons for permitting marriage; but the ground of knowledge for recognizing God's commandment is here not the appetite of sinful man, but the word of Scripture, I Cor. 7:9 (Ap. XXIII, 17). Only after Scripture has spoken may rational and empirical considerations be introduced; also, such ordinances as, e.g., government, are in responsible decision placed under commandments which do not directly deal with them, e.g., the Fourth Commandment. Only after Scripture has spoken are there, even though rarely, considerations arguing on the basis of natural law (Ap. XXIII, 11 f.). Thus the basic problem of Lutheran ethics is not "commandment and ordinances," but "God's law and God's commandment," or "law and liberty." Attempts at substituting ordinances for the law, or equating law and empirical ordinances, are romanticizing attacks on the Lutheran doctrine of the corrupted creation and, at the same time, antinomian attempts to flee from the Word of God.[13]

The law produces either open rebellion, or work-righteousness, or knowledge of sin, terror, and despair (S.A. III, ii); in every case, however, it intensifies the enmity against God. By demanding obedience from corrupted and enslaved man, an obedience which he is utterly unable to render, the law is the revelation of God's wrath. "The law always accuses us and thus always shows us an angry God" (Ap. IV, 295). The law "is the thunder-bolt by means of

[13] It is surprising for our time that the Confessions say nothing about the nation as God's ordinance and refer to the German nation only in the Preface, but not in the doctrinal articles. It may be debated to what extent a national question already existed at that time, and, if so, to what extent this silence of the Confessions represents a conscious doctrinal decision, namely, as attesting the silence of Scripture. But from what we have determined it is certain that the empirical fact of national ordinances and the establishment of the principles governing national ordinances at certain periods of history do not yet substantiate theological statements concerning the nation as a divine ordinance, nor are they able to supplement and transmute the theology of government, as was frequently demanded in recent years. The doctrine of government as God's creation and ordinance is expressly derived from Scripture passages concerning government, not from the fact of government and even less out of its self-understanding. A doctrine of the nation as a divine ordinance would likewise in principle have to be founded on Scripture. If this cannot be done in the desired sense it must not be done at all. The empirical ordinances of this world cannot establish the doctrine of the church. Rather must the doctrine of the church ask Scripture whether and in what sense such ordinances are confirmed as God's ordinance by God's Word.

which God with one blow destroys both open sinners and false saints. He allows no one to justify himself. He drives all together into terror and despair" (S.A. III, iii, 2). Again, "where the law exercises its office alone, without the addition of the Gospel, there is only death and hell" (S.A. III, iii, 7).

Thus the theological problem begins for us human beings, who are at once creature and sinner, only after we have been confronted by the Word of God. Not only the theological solutions, but also the theological problems arise only under the Word of God. For I recognize my sins only from the Word of God: ". . . sin terrifies consciences; this happens through the law, which shows God's wrath against sin" (Ap. IV, 79). Only the Word of God reveals our reality as being sinners *and* creatures: the reality of being under the wrath of God, the wrath of the Creator. We cannot now appear before God with the reminder that he has created us and that we are still his creatures every day. The fact that we, though sinners, are still God's creatures does not excuse us, but burdens and accuses us. As a sinner I stand under the wrath of God. I must live—yes, even after dying I must continue to exist and can by no means escape the necessity of continued existence. This fact under the law is not joy, but curse and judgment. Whoever is under the law and so under God's wrath cannot extol God's creative activity as love and goodness.

Therefore the decisive theme of all theology, not only of certain moments of church history but at all times, day by day, must be: Sin and grace, law and Gospel, judgment and forgiveness, God's wrath and God's mercy.

The Gospel is the message of the work of Christ. Now Christ's work is both law—yes, his cross is the most dreadful declaration of divine wrath (cf. S.D. V, 12)—and Gospel. But his proper office is the Gospel; and Christ's work becomes Gospel in that it does not remain with him, but is imputed by God to the sinner without any merit, by grace alone. Jesus Christ takes the sinner's place and God accounts the sinner righteous like his only-begotten Son. The Gospel permits us to believe this, and by this faith we become righteous for Christ's sake. What is decisive, therefore, is not the co-existence of God's wrath and God's mercy, of sin and grace, but the victory of mercy over wrath, the victory of grace over sin and condemnation. Therefore, according to the Lutheran Confessions, the summary of Scripture—and therefore also the content of the Lutheran Confessions themselves—is not only law and promises (*lex et promissiones,* e.g., Ap. IV, 5, 102), but simply the *promissio* of the Gospel (e.g., Ap. IV, 87, 2 f.).

Since the questions asked at the beginning of this chapter are in principle answered the moment it has become clear that *the* theme of all theology must be the Gospel, we need now merely draw some conclusions from what has been said.

6. Recognition of the Creator-goodness of God is possible only by faith in the Gospel.

The line of thought presented in the preceding theses 4 and 5 is to be summarized as follows: (4) Apart from God's Word, man is found in culpable ignorance of God. He "does not feel the wrath . . . of God" (Ap. IV, 9); (5) Under the law, man recognizes and senses only God's wrath. Only by faith in the Gospel does he recognize God's goodness; "only then does he become an object that can be loved," 'a lovely, blessed sight' (Ap. IV, 129).

From this follows the truth that the recognition of the Creator-goodness of God is possible only in the knowledge of his grace. Luther's praise of the "fatherly and divine goodness and mercy" of the Creator is praise flowing from faith in Jesus Christ.[14] If this were not true, how could man glorify the peculiar divine goodness which preserves him as a sinner and dying person and which preserves his existence even though he should wish to put an end to his existence in death? The peculiarity of divine creation and preservation *in* sin and death is maintained solely in view of the Son and his church: God "created us for this very purpose, to redeem and sanctify us. Moreover, having bestowed upon us everything

---

[14] "God the Father" in the first article was understood by Luther not by analogy with earthly begetting as synonymous with "Creator." "Luther never put the idea of creation into the concept 'Father,' but rather he views 'Father' in contrast to 'Judge.' " J. Meyer, *Hist. Kommentar,* p. 274. Therefore *Christ* is for us "not only the means of knowing the paternal love of God, but also the true basis for our real status as God's children." Meyer rightly declares that "the comfort derived from the thought that God is the Creator . . . rests in the last analysis on the thought that God is the Father." *Ibid.,* pp. 274, 277. Not for one moment may the explanation of the first article forget the fact that here God the Creator is acknowledged as the Father—not only as the eternal Father of the only-begotten Son, but through him also as our Father. This necessarily implies that God the Creator cannot be known apart from the Gospel. For "Creator" and "Father" are so intimately connected in the first article that the Creator cannot be known without the Father, nor the Father without the Creator. This applies in principle and independently of the question whether the first article places the major emphasis on the Father concept or the Creator concept. Even though in the Catechisms Christ is not expressly mentioned in the explanation of the first article, he is not lost sight of.

in heaven and on earth, he has given us his Son and his Holy Spirit, through whom he brings us to himself. . . . We could never come to recognize the Father's favor and grace were it not for the Lord Christ, who is a mirror of the Father's heart. Apart from him we see nothing but an angry and terrible Judge" (L.C. II, 64 f.). But if God has created man for redemption and sanctification, then he also deals daily with man as the Creator for the same purpose. He preserves the sinner as his creature for the sake of forgiveness. He preserves the fallen world for the sake of the new creation. His love to the creature is always and only a love based on the sacrifice of his Son.

Thus the Gospel too treats of God the Creator. The general truth is: ". . . one cannot deal with God or grasp him, except through the Word" (Ap. IV, 67). And this means specifically: "Whoever knows that in Christ he has a gracious God, truly knows God (*"is vere novit Deum"*), calls upon him, and is not, like the heathen, without God" (A.C. XX, 24). Through the Holy Spirit 'we learn to know how securely and blindly all men live, how they do not fear God, in short, do not believe that God has created heaven, earth, and all creatures, sustains our breath and life and all creation every hour, and protects them against Satan. . . . But when we now hear the Word and the Gospel and come to know Christ by faith, we receive the Holy Spirit, so that we may know God truly, fear him, and believe him' (Ap. IV, 135). Not only the goodness of the Creator, but also the Creator himself is 'truly' recognized only through faith in justification for Christ's sake. Since in its very essence the Lutheran Confession is *doctrina evangelii,* we may say that all of the Lutheran Confession treats of God the Creator.

Therefore the brevity of the Lutheran doctrine of creation is no weakness, and the apparently unsystematic dispersion of the individual statements is not a lack of system. On the contrary, the apparent incompleteness and the lack of emphasis on the doctrine of creation proves itself to be a theological necessity. As we saw, the decision in the doctrine of creation must be made in the doctrine of justification.

What little the Confessions teach concerning man's creatureliness is, when we know about our sin and believe in Jesus Christ, so immeasurably much that we can never finish learning it. Even though we should spell it out day after day, still we would not comprehend that we are altogether—all people and the whole world—creatures of God. To grasp the fact that God is our Creator and remains our

Creator in spite of sin and guilt—this surpasses all the happiness and the gratitude of which we are capable. Hence it cannot be called a deficiency that the Catechisms, which alone treat the doctrine of creation in a special article, do this *after* the doctrine of sin. It is precisely at this point that the goodness of the Creator is most loudly glorified, and precisely at this point the permission that we may call ourselves creatures becomes an inconceivably rich gift.

7. *To confess God the Creator means at the same time to confess the cross of Jesus Christ.*

If thus the whole Lutheran Confession, that is to say, the doctrine of the Gospel itself, treats of God the Creator, the reverse may also be said: The doctrine of creation also treats of Jesus Christ as the Creator and of the *Creator Spiritus Sanctus*.

Thus in Lutheran teaching Jesus Christ too may and must be confessed as "our Lord, Creator, and Redeemer" (S.D. VII, 45). Jesus Christ is not only our Redeemer but he is also our Creator, and the fact that this assertion is made in the doctrine of the Lord's Supper makes it plain that, even as the One who goes toward the cross and as the crucified One, Christ is our Creator. Thus the Creator is offered to us and received by us in the Lord's Supper.

However, meeting the Creator under the cross is taught not only in an individual statement, as the foregoing, but any access whatever to the knowledge of the Creator is to be found under the cross. By the very fact of being told that the specific human being is a creature of God, we are cast into great distress and incited to violent rebellion. When the church teaches every Christian to confess: "I believe that God has created me and all that exists; that he has given me and still sustains my body and soul, all my limbs and senses, my reason and all the faculties of my mind, together with food and clothing, etc.," it in fact expects every Christian daily to take up the cross of Jesus Christ. For we must not understand the explanation of the first article to mean that everybody can omit what does not suit him, but everyone is to say, "I believe this," be he sick or well, poor or rich, insecure or secure. The cripple is to believe that God has given him all limbs and still preserves them; the psychopath, that he has received and still receives from God reason and all senses; the beggar, that he lacks nothing. And, in the words of the first article, we may and should believe this, just as under the cross of

Christ we may and should believe in his divine sonship and his glory —just as we are sure by faith that we live even while dying.

It therefore is not easier to know God's creation than his redemption. The more we know Jesus Christ the more we shall know God the Creator also. As we do not know Christ without the cross, so we do not know the Creator without the cross. To be asked to believe in the Creator is as offensive as to believe in the cross of Christ. For God the Creator is not only hidden in a general way under the empirically visible reality of man, of human nature and history, but in a very concrete way God is hidden in Jesus Christ and thus under the cross.

8. *To confess God the Creator means at the same time to confess the Holy Spirit, who makes us alive.*

As the church confesses Jesus Christ as the Creator, it also prays, "Come, Holy Spirit!" and thus confesses the Creator-Spirit.

This truth too is not to be viewed in the isolation of occasional formulations, but the whole confession of the Holy Spirit and his work is a confession of the Creator. For only in the third article does it become possible to say more about the creatureliness of man than the little that has been said up to that point. We have heard that the whole man is creature and completely corrupt, and the Formula of Concord adds, "No one except God alone can separate the corruption of our nature from the nature itself" (Ep. I, 10). "This will take place wholly by way of death, in the resurrection. Then the nature which we now bear will arise and live forever without original sin and completely separated and removed from it." The possibility of a concrete (not merely conceptual) separation of created nature from the corruption of nature is exclusively God's eschatological possibility. ". . . concerning the doctrine of the resurrection Scripture testifies that precisely the substance of this our flesh, but without sin, shall rise, and that in eternal life we shall have and keep precisely this soul, although without sin" (S.D. I, 46). Then the corruption will be completely severed from the creature. Then our creatureliness will be knowable not only in faith, but visibly and concretely. Then the image of God, which man through the fall has lost "completely" (S.D. I, 10), and to which he must be regenerated through faith (Ap. IV, 351), will be completely restored. Because the resurrection is acknowledged as a work of the Holy Spirit, and because all activity of the Holy

Spirit aims at the resurrection and the new creation, the doctrine of creation finds its continuation and completion in the third article. And, conversely, the church, in preaching "the resurrection and life everlasting" in the third article, is at the same time teaching and preaching the first article. When the cripple confesses that God has given him "all limbs and senses, my reason and all faculties of my mind . . . and still sustains" them, he is confessing the Creator-Spirit who will give the new body and who makes this eschatological fact, now invisible to human eyes, more sure and more present than the mutilated visible reality of this world of sin and death.

To sum up, whoever wishes to teach and preach the *uncorrupted* creation must preach the return of Christ—the return of the second Adam, the new man with the spiritual body.

9. When we confess God the Creator we necessarily confess the triune God.

The content of the preceding theses 5 through 8, together with thesis 1, is summarized in Article I of the Augsburg Confession, which confesses the triune God as Creator in this manner: ". . . God the Father, God the Son, God the Holy Spirit. All three are one divine essence, eternal, without division, without end, of infinite power, wisdom, and goodness, one Creator and preserver of all things visible and invisible." Likewise the Smalcald Articles: "That Father, Son, and Holy Spirit, three distinct persons in one divine essence and nature, are one God, who created heaven and earth, etc." (S.A. I, i). This confession regarding the triune God does not exclude the statement that God the Father is the "Maker of heaven and earth" and that God's only Son is he "by whom all things were made" (Nic.). But the Son would not be "of one substance with the Father" and the Holy Spirit would not properly "together with the Father and the Son [be] worshiped and glorified" (Nic.), if in the Father's *opus proprium* the Father, the Son, and the Holy Spirit were not also active together. This confession concerning the triune Creator, Father, Son, and Holy Spirit, follows also from the formulation in the Athanasian Creed which is expressly taken over in the Book of Concord: "What the Father is, that is the Son and that is the Holy Spirit: the Father is uncreated, the Son is uncreated, and the Holy Spirit is uncreated" (Athan. 7, 8). "Likewise the Father is almighty, the Son is almighty, and the Holy

Spirit is almighty, and yet there are not three who are almighty, but there is one who is almighty" (Athan. 13, 14).

This excludes the possibility of "building up" the second or the third article on the first. All three articles have to do with the triune God, and there is no other access to God than the revelation of the triune God.[15] It is not possible to build a stairway leading to him on the basis of earthly data. Nor can the doctrine of creation be utilized as such a stairway. If in the doctrine of the triune God we maintain a sequence such as is followed in the three articles, we do it only because we human beings cannot express the divine unity of the three divine persons in one word, but only in the succession of several words. Attempts at making the doctrine and preaching of the Creator a universally intelligible preliminary step to the doctrine of redemption necessarily indicate that we are no longer speaking of God the Creator. For the Creator is the triune God, Father, Son, and Holy Spirit. Without the Son and the Holy Spirit the Father is *not* known as "creator and preserver of all things visible and invisible" (A.C. I, 3). "In these three articles God Himself has revealed and opened to us the most profound depths of his fatherly heart" (L.C. II, 64).

Thus the line of thought in this chapter demonstrates that the three Symbols of the ancient church and, with them, the ancient doctrine of the Trinity, are not placed at the beginning of the Book of Concord merely as an act of dead formalism. The statements of the Lutheran Confessions concerning the Creator receive mean-

---

[15] If the question is debated whether the first article must be the basis of the second, or vice versa, the point at issue cannot be to reject "the attempts to base faith in the Creator on faith in the Redeemer and redemption" as "conforming neither to the Gospel nor to Reformation theology." W. Luetgert, *Schoepfung und Offenbarung* (Guetersloh, 1934), p. 52 and frequently. In any case this question requires a twofold answer, such as Th. Harnack has at least suggested in his explanation of the Small Catechism: The first article has "its entire center of gravity only in connection with the second and third; so much so that only by way of faith in God the Redeemer can we come to genuine living faith in the creation and preservation and, conversely, that faith in God the Creator, which also is found only within revealed religion, is already a preparatory start of faith in Him as the Redeemer." *Katechetik*, II, 152. We would, of course, have to ask what is meant by "preparatory start" and "revealed religion." Still, the idea of preparatory revelation and preparatory knowledge of God is obviously transcended by basing faith in the Creator on faith in the Redeemer, as expressed in the first half of the sentence. Harnack adds with emphasis that the love of God the Creator "can be known only in the presupposition of faith in Christ." "Therefore all three articles are the content of the Christian belief in redemption." See pp. 152 f. Certainly the theological support of the articles by each other can only be a reciprocal and a reversible one, for they all rest on the revelation of the triune God in his incarnate Word.

ing only from the doctrine of the Trinity and are conceived and formulated with this doctrine as the basis. At the same time it follows that God the Creator can be known only in Jesus Christ, the incarnate Son, the Redeemer. "But neither could we know anything of Christ, had it not been revealed by the Holy Spirit" (L.C. II, 65). In other words, the triune God reveals himself in the Gospel through which he grants us the merit of Christ and gives us the Holy Spirit who in us takes hold of Christ's work.

In preparation for the following chapters we at this stage go one step farther:

10. The doctrine of the Trinity is the basis for all statements of the Lutheran Confessions.

This must be said with all definiteness over against the manifold attempts of neo-Protestantism to give a new interpretation of the ancient church's doctrine of the Trinity as contained in the Confessions, or to explain it away from the Confessions.[16] No article in the Confessions can be understood apart from the doctrine of the Trinity. We must rather establish the following points:

Not only are the three ancient trinitarian Symbols placed in the Book of Concord ahead of the Confessions of the Reformation, but also in the Confessions the doctrine of the Trinity precedes the other articles, namely, in Article I of the Augsburg Confession, the Apology, and the Smalcald Articles. Thus Article I of the Augsburg

---

[16] A. Ritschl, in agreement with old Roman insinuations, was of the opinion that Luther and Melanchthon retained the ancient doctrine of the Trinity only because it was part of the juridical basis of the Roman Empire according to the code of Justinian. This "correctness of their stand within the boundaries of Christendom which obtained for the Roman Empire made it possible for the rulers and governments to tolerate and protect them and make common cause with them." John S. Black (trans.), *A Critical History of the Christian Doctrine of Justification and Reconciliation* (Edinburgh: Edmonston and Douglas, 1874), p. 127. Thus A. Harnack maintained that there was "no bridge" that led from justifying faith to the ancient doctrine of the Trinity; furthermore, that Luther had left an "unspeakable confusion" behind with regard to its meaning, and he proceeded to give Luther's doctrine of God a modalistic turn. *Dogmengeschichte* (5th ed.), III, 874. K. Thieme, on the other hand, in spite of correct polemics against Ritschl and Harnack, felt called upon to discover a "naive Ditheism" and "Tritheism" in the writings of Luther and Melanchthon, or at least feared that their doctrine must lead to that by inference. *Augsburgische Konfession*, p. 174; cf. pp. 144 ff.

Even though the doctrine of the Trinity in the ancient church is not regarded as Melanchthonian soft-pedaling or as civil or ecclesiastical political maneuvering, neo-Protestantism is at least convinced that this doctrine had for the Reformers a significance belonging only "to the periphery of their theological thinking that was concentrated in the Gospel of justification by grace." E.g., H. H. Wendt, *Die Augsburgische Konfession*, p. 27.

Confession teaches that "there is one divine essence, which is called and which is truly God, and that there are three persons in this one divine essence, equal in power and alike eternal: God the Father, God the Son, God the Holy Spirit. All three are one divine essence, eternal, without division, without end, of infinite power, wisdom, and goodness. . . ." In this statement the unity of God is the starting point and the terminus; moreover, it is affirmed in the naming of the 'three persons in this one divine essence': *'God* the Father, *God* the Son, *God* the Holy Spirit'. (The threefold use of the name of God cannot be understood tritheistically as neo-Protestants interpret it, but only as knowledge of the *"distinctae personae ejusdem essentiae divinae"*, Ap. I, 1). The "one divine essence" is designated as God himself (*"et appellatur et est Deus"*). In the Smalcald Articles too the emphasis of the trinitarian declaration is on the confession of the unity of God: "That Father, Son, and Holy Spirit, three distinct persons in one divine essence and nature, are [following the German original of the Confession, Schlink's quotation of it retains here the singular verb *ist*] one God, who created heaven and earth" (S.A. I, 1). Father, Son, and Holy Spirit "is," not "are," the one God.

At the same time the three persons are not dissolved into manifestations or modes of revelation of the one God, but they are confessed as *"distinctae personae,"* distinct not only as to the three works of the one God in creation, redemption, and sanctification, but distinct from eternity also internally, distinct in God himself. Thus the Smalcald Articles teach the intratrinitarian relationship: "That the Father was begotten by no one, the Son was begotten by the Father, and the Holy Spirit proceeded from the Father and the Son." In order to prevent a misunderstanding which might equate *persona* with *hupostasis* or *substantia*—and especially to prevent the equation of *persona* with *prosopon,* mask, form, or mode of manifestation—the Augsburg Confession safeguards the correct understanding by using the old definition: "The word 'person' is to be understood as the Fathers employed the term in this connection, not as a part or a property of another but as that which exists of itself" (A.C. I, 4). In these relatively few trinitarian doctrinal statements of the Confessions we may note as a special feature at most the Augustinian concentration of the ancient doctrine in its emphasis on the divine unity, which already appears in the Athanasian Creed. However, the vigor of the trinitarian concern is underscored by the specific identification and condemnation of a wide variety of ancient antitrinitarians in the Augsburg Confession (A.C. I, 5 f.) and by the condemnation of the antitrinitarians of the age of the Reformation in the Formula of Concord (F.C. XII).

The doctrine of the Trinity, however, is taught not only in the terminology of the ancient church, but also in other words. The second chief part of the Small Catechism does not use the terms "trinity," "essence," "person," and in the same section of the Large Catechism the term "trinity" is not used. Nevertheless, the essential unity of God the Father, the Son, and the Holy Spirit is by no means denied in the second chief part of both Catechisms, but is safeguarded once for all through the preceding first chief part: The one God beside whom you may "have no other gods," whose name you must "not take in vain," whom we should "fear and love" in all the commandments, this one God is the Creator, the Redeemer, and the Sanctifier, whom we confess in the second chief part. Furthermore, the essential equality and unity of God the Father and his only Son is acknowledged in the word "Lord." The explanation of the second article in the Small Catechism reaches its climax in the confession: "Jesus Christ . . . is my Lord." The "substance" of this article, according to the Large Catechism, is the lordship of Jesus Christ (L.C. II, 26). The same word, in capital letters, is found in the Conclusion of the Ten Commandments: "I the LORD your God am a jealous God." Jesus Christ, as Luther sings, is "of Sabaoth Lord, and there's no other God." As the Lord he is "a mirror of the Father's heart" and as the mirror and image of God he is God the Lord (L.C. II, 65). He is "true God, begotten of the Father from eternity" (S.C. II, 4). Again, the Holy Spirit is not a created spirit like the "spirit of man, heavenly spirits, and the evil spirit," but "God's Spirit" (L.C. II, 36).

But the distinction of the three persons is clearly indicated also by the juxtaposition of the three articles and their individual statements. It is true both that God the Father "has given us his Son and his Holy Spirit, through whom he brings us to himself" (L.C. II, 64), and "as the Father is called Creator, the Son is called Redeemer, so on account of his work the Holy Spirit must be called Sanctifier, the One who makes holy" (L.C. II, 36). Though the Holy Spirit is "God's Spirit" and the Son is "begotten of the Father from eternity," they are not subordinated to God the Father, but God Father, Son, and Holy Spirit are confessed in the distinguishing juxtaposition of the three articles, "in three articles, according to the three persons of the Godhead" (L.C. II, 6). Not only the Son but also the Holy Spirit is strongly presented in his own activity alongside the Father. The Spirit decidedly is not merely a divine power. All distinctions of the persons remain in this parenthesis: "*One* God and one faith, but three persons, and therefore three articles or confessions" (L.C. II, 7).

Consequently, Luther's direction to the head of the family as to how he should teach the members of his household to bless themselves in the name of the triune God by saying, "In the name of God, the Father, the Son, and the Holy Spirit. Amen," is not a dead relic of antiquated doctrine, nor a fossilized custom. Besides, that the Catechisms teach the doctrine of the Trinity is practically asserted simply by the paradoxical spectacle of the neo-Protestant interpreters who accused the Catechisms of both modalistic and tritheistic tendencies. The ancient doctrine of the Trinity will always produce these two misconceptions among its opponents.

The doctrine of the Trinity is thus the basis of the Lutheran Confessions and it determines the structure of all their doctrinal statements. Just look back at the doctrine of the relationship between Scripture and Confession: The authority of Holy Scripture as the Word of God consists in the reality of the Gospel, i.e., the work of Christ for us, and in the reality of the Holy Spirit who enlightens us through the Gospel and who once enlightened the prophets and apostles. The binding significance of the Confession as the norm and model of all teaching in the church is again motivated by the Gospel, i.e., in the work of Christ which Scripture says was done for us, and in the activity of the Holy Spirit who produces the Confession after he has created the church. Similarly it will become evident that the doctrine of justification is trinitarian in its strictest sense, which is further emphasized by the fact that reconciliation and justification are inextricably interwoven, yes, are in part identified in their concepts. The work of Jesus Christ would be worthless for us if he were not God's Son and as such very God, and our faith would be merely a new work of self-righteousness if in it God's Spirit and therefore God himself were not active, by whose power alone we can lay hold of the work of Christ. We have a gracious God as the triune God, or we have no gracious God. The structure of all doctrinal articles in the Confessions is trinitarian. But nothing speaks more compellingly for the importance of a dogma than that it is not merely repeated, but that it is the center of all thinking.

Nevertheless, in the Confessions the doctrine of the Trinity is evidently quoted as a presupposition rather than developed and proved dogmatically. After all, it is taken over as a finished and settled doctrine. This fact, however, should not prevent us from recognizing two decisive contributions of the Confessions to the doctrine of the Trinity as proclaimed by the ancient church:

a) They emphatically point out that the triune God is not yet recognized when we acknowledge the "unity of the divine essence," "the three persons in this one divine essence" (A.C. I, 1 f.), but do not acknowledge the *works* of these three persons in creation, redemption, and sanctification. ". . . the entire *essence* of God, his *will,* and his *work"* belong together (L.C. II, 63). I confess the works of the triune God only when I believe "that *I* am a creature of God" (L.C. II, 13), that Jesus Christ "is *my* LORD" (S.C. II; L.C. II, 27), that "the Holy Spirit makes *me* holy" (L.C. II, 40). 'Jesus Christ the Lord' means not only that he is equal in essence with God, "true God, begotten of the Father from eternity," but also "that he has redeemed me from sin, from the devil, from death, and from all evil" (L.C. II, 27). The doctrine of the immanent Trinity dare not be separated from the economic Trinity, nor the doctrine of the *opera trinitatis ad intra* from the *opera trinitatis ad extra*. In reality the triune God is known only by that man who confesses him as the Lord who daily performs his creative, redemptive, and sanctifying activity on the confessing man himself.

b) The triune God is not yet known if he is presented without the distinction of law and Gospel. In the Roman church the dreadful fact had become evident that, in spite of the preservation of the orthodox doctrine of the Trinity, God was *not* known any more, since the Gospel had been lost. But to know God's essence means to know "the most profound depths of his fatherly heart, and his sheer, unutterable love" (L.C. II, 64). To know God's love means to receive his gracious love. However, the love of God the Creator, Redeemer, and Sanctifier is not given through the demands of the law but through the gift of the Gospel. The triune God, therefore, is known only in the distinction of law and Gospel, that is, by faith in the Gospel. The train of thought in this chapter has shown that the Creator is known only in the Gospel. The same holds true of knowing God the Sanctifier, for the Holy Spirit is given only through the Gospel. Of every knowledge of God the statement applies: "Thus the entire Holy Trinity, God the Father, Son, and Holy Spirit, directs all men to Christ as to the book of life" (S.D. XI, 66).

III

LAW AND GOSPEL

(PART ONE)

1. God's law comprises the Ten Commandments as recorded in Holy Scripture.

Basic for the article on justification in the Apology is the following definition of the law: "By 'law' in this discussion we mean the commandments of the Decalogue, wherever they appear in the Scriptures. For the present we are saying nothing about the ceremonial and civil laws of Moses" (Ap. IV, 6). This definition says at the very outset that no true statements can be made about the law of God without faith in the Gospel.

These sentences indicate in the first place that in all discussions of law and Gospel we must speak of God's law only as God's revealed Word. The starting point for the doctrine of the law is not given in the natural knowledge of the law but only in the Word of Holy Scripture. Holy Scripture witnesses to the law as God's revealed Word. Even though the "ceremonial and civil laws"—i.e., the laws governing the religious exercises and community life of Israel—are presented in the Word of Scripture as God's revealed law, nothing shall be said of these "for the present." "For the present" ['*Hier*' (*in praesentia*)] means not simply in the year 1530 or in Article IV of the Apology, it signifies also the 'place' of the church of Jesus Christ in general. Since the time of Christ the divine ceremonial and civil laws of the Old Testament, revealed in the Word, are no longer to be preached to men as demands of God. The Old Testament ceremonial law was "necessary for the time being" (Ap. XV, 32). And we are to be silent about these laws, not only in so far as they are found in Scripture in addition to the Ten Commandments, but also in so far as they are found in the Old Testament Decalogue itself. In this silence the distinction of law and Gospel in the Word of Scripture is already put into effect, and without this distinction the law of God cannot be known.

In what respect does this silence indicate a correct understanding of the Gospel? The answer to this question is given particularly in Article XXIV of the Apology,[1] especially with reference to the Old Testament laws of sacrifice. The guilt offerings of the Old Covenant "meant that a victim was to come to reconcile God and make satisfaction for our sins, so that men might know that God does not want our righteousness but the merits of another (namely, of Christ) to reconcile him to us" (Ap. XXIV, 23). Hence it is true that 'the guilt offering in the law was not the true sacrifice to atone for sin, but another sacrifice must come, namely, the death of Christ' (*ibid.,* German version). The guilt offerings in the law 'were merely signs and types of the real propitiation,' 'but there has been only one true propitiatory sacrifice or offering for sin in the world, namely, the death of Christ' (Ap. XXIV, 22). Therefore we may say: '. . . in the Law the slaying of oxen and sheep signified both the death of Christ and the preaching of the Gospel, whereby the Old Adam should be daily mortified and the new and eternal life be begun in us' (Ap. XXIV, 34). And the daily sacrifice (Num. 28) in all three parts "symbolizes not only the ceremony but the proclamation of the Gospel" (Ap. XXIV, 36). Just so the Levitical priesthood was a "picture (*imago*) of Christ's priesthood" (Ap. XXIV, 53). With respect to the ceremonial laws it may be said quite generally that 'the whole law of Moses is a shadow and figure of Christ and the New Testament, and therefore Christ is portrayed in that law' (Ap. XXIV, 36).

In these and many other statements the Old Testament sacrifice and the sacrifice of Christ, as well as Old Testament ceremony and the preaching of the Gospel, are not equated but clearly distinguished by the terms "sign," "type," "image," "figure," "picture," "shadow." This distinction, based on an understanding of the historical nature of the events connected with the revelation of God at Mount Sinai and *later* in the incarnation of his Son, is expressly maintained

---

[1] The extremely relevant Old Testament expositions of this article have been strangely neglected in the existing literature over against the contribution of this article to the doctrine of the sacraments. However, they not only have basic significance for the doctrine of the law, but beyond that they contain the elements of an Old Testament hermeneutics. Cf. the still-important work of L. Diestel, *Geschichte des Alten Testamentes in der christlichen Kirche* (Jena, 1869). See also H. H. Wolf, "Das Verhaeltnis von altem und neuem Testament nach den lutherischen Bekenntnisschriften," *Jahrb. d. Theol. Schule* (Bethel 1948), pp. 67 ff.

also by the use of many verbs in the future tense. In spite of the most intimate relationship between the Old Testament sacrifices and Christ's sacrifice as to their significance, they are not identified.

Nevertheless, there are other statements in this article which point to an identity beyond that of a mere correspondence of meaning. Reference is made to the "church of God" in the midst of Baal-worshiping Israel and of Judah (Ap. XXIV, 98), and it is expressly stated that the saints of the Old Covenant were justified through faith in Christ in the same manner as the saints of the New Covenant. 'For the patriarchs and saints in the Old Testament were also justified and reconciled to God by faith in the promise of the coming Christ, through whom salvation and grace were promised, just as we in the New Testament obtain grace by faith in the Christ who has been manifested. For all believers from the beginning believed that there would be a sacrifice and payment for sin, namely Christ, who was to come as promised' (Ap. XXIV, 55). Already in the Old Testament they 'knew that our works could not pay so great a debt. Therefore they received forgiveness of sins, grace, and salvation without any merit, and through faith in the divine promise, the Gospel of Christ, they were saved in the same manner as we or the saints in the New Testament' (Ap. IV, 57). Such Old Testament faith did not merely point forward to New Testament faith, but the believers there believed 'just as we do in the New Testament.' Justification there is not merely a type of future justification, but both are one and the same. Then as now it takes place "by faith in the promise of the forgiveness of sins" (Ap. XXIV, 55). This faith and this justification were preached to the saints of the Old Covenant not only by means of the messianic prophecies, but also by means of the Mosaic ceremonial law, for its priesthood and sacrifices were instituted by God 'solely to signify the future true sacrifice, Christ alone' (Ap. XXIV, 54). In this respect the Old Testament ceremonial law is already the office and preaching of the Gospel.

This dialectic of the future and the present of the Gospel in the Old Testament is the same as the dialectic of the formula *propter Christum venturum*. It appears thoroughly paradoxical to say at the same time that Christ's sacrifice was *future* in the Old Testament, and that *because of* the sacrifice of Christ forgiveness of sins was received in the Old Testament (Ap. XXIV, 55)—to say at the same time that the Old Testament promises that Christ *will* come, and that it promises *for his sake* forgiveness of sins, justification, and eternal life (Ap. IV, 5). Yet we may and must speak thus, for God is faithful and his promise is true. Therefore we must reckon with a divine promise as with a fact, and the divine future is as real and sure as is ordinarily only the past. Therefore the ceremony's pointing forward to the coming Christ is already the proclamation of the gift of him who has come.

However, the identity of forgiveness and faith in the Old and the New Covenants does not remove the difference between sign and reality, but the "signs," "figures," "types" fade away and prove to be mere shadows in the moment when the reality they signify, the *res significata,* itself is revealed (Ap. XXIV, 37). This happens in the moment of the incarnation and sacrifice of Jesus Christ. 'The guilt offerings in the law had to cease when the Gospel was revealed and the true sacrifice was accomplished' (Ap. XXIV, 23). 'They were merely signs and types of the true propitiation.' Since the promise has been fulfilled, the demands of the ceremonies by means of which God had sketchily outlined the promised work of redemption are no longer valid as demands. The church must now maintain 'that in the New Testament the sacrifices of the law of Moses are abolished, and that there are wholly pure sacrifices without spot, namely faith in God, thanksgiving, praise of God, preaching of the Gospel, the cross and the trials of the saints, and the like' (Ap. XXIV, 30). Anyone who after Christ's completed sacrifice would still wish to offer up the sacrifices demanded in the law of Moses would be establishing human ordinances against God's Word. Though the Mosaic laws of sacrifice were revealed by God, they are since Christ's death nothing more than human traditions as soon as they are practiced by men or are taught as demands of God. Thus in many and at times almost contemptuous expressions Moses, human ordinances, and human reason are mentioned in one breath and are no longer distinguished: "St. Paul contended mightily against the law of Moses *and* against human tradition" (A.C. XXVI, 5). The ceremonies have been abrogated, "whether of Moses *or* of another" (A.C. XXVI, 28). "Far away from human reason, far away from Moses, we must turn our eyes to Christ!" (Ap. IV, 296).

The Apology uses this line of reasoning not only to prove that in the doctrine of the law the church must pass over the Mosaic laws of sacrifice. By analogy it becomes necessary also to seek in Christ the reason why we must pass over the civil laws of Moses, since, on the one hand, these must be understood as pointing to the office of Christ as judge and king and since, on the other hand, they have been nullified by God—not only by the revelation of Jesus Christ the King, but also by the rejection and dispersion of the people of Israel for whose order they were intended. The Confessions do not take up the civil laws in detail. But they do point out that the laws of the sacrifices also had a significance for the national constitution of Israel, for the *iustitia legis* of the Israelite commonwealth (Ap. XXIV, 21, 24). Since the ceremonial laws thus were themselves at the same time civil law, the civil law is abrogated with them. This abrogation is evidenced by the fact that the Confessions refer to the ceremonial and civil laws almost exclusively in polemical contexts, when they are misused exegetically by opponents who want to use them as biblical proof for false doctrine. In the proper doctrine of the Confessions they are hardly mentioned at all. And so it becomes clear at this point also that the ceremonial and civil law on the one hand, and God's permanently valid demand on the other, cannot be distributed neatly and casuistically among Old Testament texts. As the Decalogue also contains ceremonial and civil law, so, conversely, every Old Testament ceremonial and civil law—even though it is no longer valid literally as a demand for the church of Jesus Christ—also embraces the First Commandment, for "the entire Scriptures have proclaimed and presented this commandment everywhere" (L.C. I, 325).

If, then, God's law is correctly understood only when we know the Gospel, i.e., the work of Christ, it follows that the rediscovery of the Gospel is also the rediscovery of the divine law. It would be an erroneous possibility to try to know the law of God in truth *apart from the Word of Scripture* (see above, pp. 49 ff.). It would also be an erroneous possibility—and this is even more important— for natural man to try to know the law of God *in the Word of Scripture,* namely, in the multiplicity of its legal prescriptions. Apart from the Holy Spirit, apart from faith in the Gospel, man will lose his way in the Bible just as much as when he attempts to base a system of ethics on conscience, reason, natural order, utility, etc. The necessary result, on the one hand, is only Roman legalism, which still teaches Old Testament ceremonies as divine law and uses them exegetically as a basis for the priesthood, for masses, etc., and, on the other hand, the religious fanaticism of theologians and peasants who by an appeal to the Mosaic law wanted to introduce the jubilee year. Legalism and religious fanaticism, being closely related, result from ignorance of the law—i.e., from ignorance of the Gospel, really—and their attack is at least as dangerous to the church as the natural ethics of the heathen. One can correctly understand the second part of the Augsburg Confession and the Apology, which treat of the correction of abuses, only if one realizes that with the rediscovered Gospel the rediscovery of the law and its divine glory has been given too. The Augsburg Confession not only knows that in former times among the opponents the *Gospel* "was not heard in preaching"; it also states rightly that concerning the *Ten Commandments,* and the estates and works commanded by God, "little was taught in former times, when for the most part sermons were concerned with childish and useless works, like rosaries, the cult of saints, monasticism, pilgrimages, appointed fasts, holy days, brotherhoods, etc." (A.C. XX, 2 ff.). The basis and criterion for the abolition of all such "useless works" is both the rediscovered Gospel, which is denied by these works, and also the rediscovered divine law. To faith in Christ the glory of the Ten Commandments is evident. The believer sees "how highly these Ten Commandments are to be exalted and extolled above all orders, commands, and works which are taught and practiced apart from them. Here we can fling out the challenge: Let all wise men and saints step forward and produce, if they can, any work like that which God in these commandments so earnestly requires" (L.C. Con., I, 333). And the believer praises not only the First Commandment but also the individual commandments of the second table in all their concreteness (cf., e.g., the explanation of the Fourth and Sixth Commandments in the Large Catechism). To state this concretely, the true works are those 'expressed in the Ten Commandments' (Ap. XII, 145).

However, Christ has by no means eliminated only the ceremonial and civil laws that were given in the Mosaic law *in addition to* the Decalogue, but also the ceremonial and civil laws *in* the Decalogue, and they are no longer to be taught by the church as God's law. The church no longer demands the remembrance of the Sabbath Day, but the sanctifying of the holy day; it adds immediately that in no case ". . . the appointment of Sunday in place of the Sabbath" should be regarded "as a necessary institution" (A.C. XXVIII, 58). ". . . the Holy Scriptures have abrogated the Sabbath and teach that after the revelation of the Gospel all ceremonies of the old law may be omitted" (A.C. XXVIII, 59). Every day is to be sanctified; Sunday was designated *by the church* in the freedom of faith solely in the interests of the common worship (A.C. XXVIII, 60; L.C. I, 84 ff.). This elimination of the ceremonial law has its effects on the understanding of all commandments of the Decalogue.

In any case the church can teach the Ten Commandments as God's law in no other way than as coming from the completed propitiatory sacrifice of Jesus Christ.

This means too that the church can no longer go back behind Christ's exposition of the Ten Commandments. In the Sermon on the Mount "Christ takes the law into his own hands and explains it spiritually" (Ep. V, 8). Since the Sermon on the Mount, all commandments have been unfolded. Especially has it become evident since then that none of them can any longer be restricted to individual deeds. Desire and action, thought, word, and deed, the whole inner heart and all its outward deeds are under the demand and judgment of the commandments. This is so evident that the Ninth and Tenth Commandments seem almost superfluous, given quite exclusively to the Jews, adding specifically to the other commandments: "Thou shalt not *covet* . . ." (L.C. I, 293 ff.). Thus, if the church in its preaching of the law cannot go back behind the preaching and death of Jesus Christ, neither can the church in explaining the Decalogue dispense with the admonitions of the apostles who preached the Christ who has come. Accordingly the words of the Lord and the words of the apostles are added to the Decalogue as norms in eliminating human traditions.

The law demands perfect obedience, true fear of God, and true love of God and neighbor. The first table—actually the First Commandment—is *"aeterna lex,"* the 'highest, holiest, greatest, most important commandment, far exceeding all human and angelic understanding, pertaining to the highest divine service, to the Deity itself and the honor of the eternal majesty, where God commands that we should with all our heart regard him as our God, fear and love him' (Ap. IV, 131). The First Commandment not only ranks *above* all other commandments, but "we should fear and love God" is also commanded *in* all other commandments. The First Commandment is not only the "first and chief commandment, from which all others proceed," but it is also the hoop which runs through the wreath of the commandments. In each commandment the First is repeated; "for example, in the Second Commandment we are told to fear God and not take his name in vain by cursing, lying, deceiving, and other kinds of corruption and wickedness, but to use his name properly by calling upon him in prayer, praise, and thanksgiving, which spring from that love and trust which the First Commandment requires" (L.C. Con., I, 326; cf. 324). "Thus you see how the First Commandment is the chief source and fountainhead from which all the others proceed; again, to it they all return and upon it they depend, so that end and beginning are all linked and bound together" (L.C. Con., I, 329).[2] Thus we love God only when we love our neighbor, and we love our neighbor only when we "fear, love, and trust in God above all things." This love is demanded as obedience to the concrete commandments of both tables.

Even though the church cannot teach the Ten Commandments as though it were still living in the Old Covenant, even though the Confessions are therefore peculiarly uninterested in the Exodus (the corresponding word of the Decalogue is missing in the Catechisms), in Mount Sinai, even in the person of Moses, it is nevertheless true that the very Ten Commandments revealed on Sinai are taught in the Confessions as the law of God, and according to their direction are to be taught in the church continually. Though the church teaches the Ten Commandments correctly only in the knowledge of the Gospel and in connection with the demands of Jesus and the admonitions of the apostles, this still does not change the Ten Commandments; but, as commandments that have been kept, their demands finally become fully evident. They are and remain the law, "the immutable will of God according to which a man is to conduct himself in this life" (S.D. VI, 15; cf. V, 17), they are the "divine, eternal law" (S.D. II, 50; cf. Ap. IV, 131).

2. On the part of corrupted man the law of God produces open rebellion, work-righteousness, or despair; the sinner cannot obey the law of God.

The response of corrupted man to the revelation of the law is threefold:

a) "Some, who hate the law because it forbids what they desire to do and commands what they are unwilling to do, are made worse thereby. Accordingly, in so far as they are not restrained by punishment, they act against the law even more than before" (S.A. III, ii, 2). This is the response of the open rebellion of passions and of ridicule.

b) "Others become blind and presumptuous, imagining that they

---

[2] The fact that all commandments are bracketed by the First Commandment is demonstrated in the structure of the first chief part of the Catechisms, where the commandments are inserted between the text and the epilogue of the First Commandment.

can and do keep the law by their own powers. . . . Hypocrites and false saints are produced in this way" (S.A. III, ii, 3). How does such "imagining" originate? These people rebel against God's law by changing its demands and accommodating them to their own capacity. This is done both by eliminations in the Decalogue and also by additions. Especially the First Commandment is eliminated; they "look at the second table and political works; about the first table they care nothing, as though it were irrelevant" (Ap. IV, 131; cf. 35). When the first table is segregated, the commandments of the second table are changed also. Works of obedience to the isolated second table are something entirely different from the obedience which *God* demands in the second table. They are merely *externa opera civilia—politica—honesta,* which in their outward appearance correspond to the works demanded by the law and which serve the preservation of civil life. But the works which belong to the "essence" of the law are "the impulses of the heart toward God," which are commanded in the first table (Ap. IV, 130). The segregated second table is then changed still more and supplemented by existing or desirable laws pertaining to civil or political order. The second table is further supplemented by demands through which man establishes ceremonial and civil prescriptions of the Mosaic law which had been abrogated; or he uses them at least as a model and point of contact. In place of the first table and, accordingly, of the entire Decalogue, man thus places the inventions of his natural religion, whose essence consists in beguiling men with an illusion of fellowship and peace with God apart from the atonement procured by Christ's blood. Thus, not only civil decency and political utility, but also celibacy, fasting, alms, rosaries, pilgrimages, etc. 'are preferred to the true works expressed in God's commandments. In this way the law is obscured in two ways: one, because satisfaction is thought to be rendered God's law by means of external works; the other, because wretched human traditions are regarded as better than the works commanded by God' (Ap. XII, 145). Thus the "saints" together with the decent people, the "pious" together with Philistines and heroes turn against the law of God, falsifying it secretly but praising it publicly. This work-righteousness is opposed by the Confessions more caustically than all open revolt and profligacy.

c) "However, the chief function or power of the law is to make original sin manifest and show man to what utter depths his nature has fallen and how corrupt it has become. So the law must tell

75

man that he neither has nor cares for God, or that he worships strange gods—something that he would not have believed before without a knowledge of the law. Thus he is terror-stricken and humbled, becomes despondent and despairing, anxiously desires help, but does not know where to find it" (S.A. III, ii, 4). The third effect of the law is the despair of the sinner in his sin, the *"terrores conscientiae,"* the *"conscientiae perterrefactae."* This experience of the anxieties of the terrified conscience is again and again mentioned in all the Confessions: 'But when a conscience is properly aware of its sin and misery, all joking, all playful thoughts vanish and the situation becomes one of utmost gravity; here no heart or conscience can be pacified or appeased, but rather it seeks all sorts of works and more works and longs for solid ground underfoot. But such terrified consciences surely feel that nothing can be merited either of condignity or of congruity, and so they quickly sink into fear and despair' (Ap. IV, 20).

Now, whether the law produces open rebellion, work-righteousness, or despair, in every case it produces enmity in the sinner against God. This is obviously true of the open rebellion against the law. In the case of work-righteousness too no further elucidation is necessary. But does the law produce enmity against God also when it hurls man into the terrors of conscience, yes, even when it shows man, and confronts him with, his sin? Is the very knowledge of sin, sin? The answer is: The man thus terrified and haunted "begins to be alienated from God, to murmur, etc. This is what is meant by Rom. 4:15, 'The law brings wrath,' and Rom. 5:20, 'Law came in to increase the trespass'" (S.A. III, ii, 4 f.; cf. also Ap. IV, 36 and 312). Despair under God's law is not a good work, is no basis for forgiveness. It too is sin, and in it sin is unfolded, since now man, instead of loving God, flees from him in fear and terror. Therefore even the knowledge of sin under the law as such is of very doubtful value, since men "fail to learn the *true* nature of sin from the law" (Ep. V, 8). There is a knowledge of sin which is not contrition and repentance; for repentance is never without faith in forgiveness. Repentance is the despair of one who is comforted, the dying of one who sees divine mercy. But the despair of Judas remained without comfort. In his case the law alone performed its function.

In every case, then, the law of God produces the unfolding of sin, unless the Gospel has made the sinner righteous. Therefore the Confessions do not discuss the reasons why God's law produces rebellion in one case, work-righteousness in another, and despair in a third. For it is certain that "without Christ and without the Holy Spirit we cannot keep the law" (Ap. IV, 135; cf. also 35 ff.). "It is false, too, and a reproach to Christ, (when it is taught) that men who keep the commandments of God outside a state of grace [*ohne den heiligen Geist*—Schlink's rendering] do not sin" (Ap. IV, 28).

In this threefold and yet so frightfully identical effect of the law the culpable enslavement of the human "will" is manifested. Here it becomes evident that "man possesses some measure of freedom of the will which enables him to live an outwardly honorable life and to make choices among the things that reason comprehends. But without the grace, help, and activity of the Holy Spirit man is not capable of making himself acceptable to God, of fearing God and believing in God with his whole heart, or of expelling inborn evil lusts from his heart" (A.C. XVIII, 1 f.). The human will is able, *"aliquo modo,"* "to obey rulers and parents. Externally, it can choose to keep hands from murder, adultery, or theft." Thus 'in some measure our free will is capable of living honorably or dishonorably, and this is what Holy Scripture calls the righteousness of the law or of the flesh' (Ap. XVIII, 4 f.; cf. the possibilities for the will as enumerated by Andreae in his original draft of S.D. II, *Bek.* pp. 868 f.). But as a result of man's evil lust and the devil's temptations this civil righteousness is much rarer and much more imperfect than is commonly supposed. Above all, however, because of the lack of obedience to the First Commandment, it is not only imperfect, but altogether sin.

This does not exclude the fact that in the area of civil righteousness good and evil, obedient and disobedient, honorable and dishonorable may be distinguished. Yet disobedient and obedient, evil and good, dishonorable and honorable, civil disorder and civil righteousness are at the same time sin in the presence of God.[3] Through political righteousness and civil decency God preserves man *in* sin and *in* guilt and *under* the spell of death. The *justitia*

---

[3] This is affirmed again and again so incisively and definitively that it is impossible to use the distinction of good and evil within the *justitia civilis* of natural man as the occasion for basing theological ethics on the natural knowledge of the law and the natural works of the law. Theological ethics dare not say anything apart from the first table about God's commands and the distinction of good and evil. This distinction in the *justitia civilis* serves to make the demands of the first table all the more radical, that is, a challenge of *all* human activity. Otherwise this distinction serves to acknowledge the preserving activity of God the Creator. Cf. pp. 228 f. and 276 ff.

civilis of which man is capable is, in the sight of God, neither good nor a cause for pardon. Therefore the extent of this enslavement of the will dare not be underestimated, as is done when the Reformation concept of "will" is interpreted psychologically in accordance with present usage, perhaps by distinguishing emotion, volition, and intellect. As the Latin *arbitrium* has the connotation of a judicial sentence in which judgment and power, sentence and force are interwoven, so the *servum arbitrium* in this connection is the enslavement of the free determination of judgment and action, of knowledge and volition.

3. Through the law God reveals his terrifying wrath against the sinner.

God's law magnifies sin and causes sin to unfold, but it does not free from sin. It indeed produces a certain degree of order in earthly life, but it does not lead out of sin and death. It indeed leads to despair, but despair need not yet be contrition. God's law accuses, judges, condemns, and punishes, but it does not help. Rather, even though the sinner is unable to obey the law, he is summoned and judged by the law. Though "to a certain extent" he can do only a few external works of the law, his whole "nature or person is under the accusation and condemnation of the law of God" (S.D. I, 6). Since God by the revelation of the law thus seems to give the sinner a chance and yet takes away every chance, the law is the revelation of God's wrath.[4]

"The law *always* accuses us, it always shows that God is wrathful." 'The law shows *only* God's wrath and sternness; the law accuses us and shows how God wants to punish sin so terribly with both temporal and eternal punishment' (Ap. IV, 128; cf. also 295 and elsewhere). Both terms, "always" and "only", occur repeatedly in the statements about the law. "But where the law exercises its office alone, without the addition of the Gospel, there is only death and hell, and man must despair like Saul and Judas. As St. Paul says, the law slays through sin" (S.A. III, iii, 7). The revelation of the *lex sola* is God's wrath, and its gift is death. "Therefore men cannot keep the law by their own strength, and they are *all* under sin and subject to eternal wrath and death" (Ap. IV, 40). Each human is a child of divine wrath, whether he knows it or not.

[4] Lennart Pinomaa, *Der Zorn Gottes in der Theologie Luthers* (Helsinki, 1938).

But if man in his despair under the law recognizes God's wrath, this is then not merely knowledge, but the innermost terror. Since God through his law 'terrifies and attacks us as if he would cast us from himself in eternal disfavor into eternal death, the poor, weak nature must lose heart and courage and must ever tremble before such great wrath, which so fearfully terrifies and punishes. . . .' (Ap. IV, 37). Then man not only fears the wrath of God, but he also "experiences" and "feels" this wrath. Again and again this *"sentire"* is ascribed to the trembling and terrified consciences. Only 'the inexperienced' do not know 'what a burden sin is, what a torment it is to feel God's wrath.' The conscience is distracted and the heart writhes in the dust. Man's death is the counterpart of God's wrath. Where the "thunderbolt" of God, the "hammer" of the law "with one blow destroys" man, there is "true sorrow of the heart, suffering and pain of death," ". . . *sensus mortis*" (S.A. III, iii, 2). In this way the frightened conscience "experiences" (*experitur*) in its own dreadful experience that the attempts at overcoming the misery of sin in a speculative way are empty dreams and vain activities. In this 'experiment' of religious experience— religious experience, however, is the experience of the *wrath* of God—man collapses. Face to face with the wrath of God, all human merit or work is only 'a little feather in a hurricane' (Ap. IV, 47).

4. God's only Son became man, rendered complete obedience under the law, and died on the cross. Thus he endured the divine wrath.[5]

Opposite our sin and God's wrath stands Jesus Christ, who is "true God and true man, who was truly born, suffered, was crucified, died, and was buried" (A.C. III, 2). In this statement Christ's preaching, Christ's miracles, yes, Christ's life between birth and cross are not mentioned, except for his suffering. The Apology too with impressive one-sidedness again and again points to the death of Christ. The same peculiar silence regarding the public activity of Jesus is found in the Catechism, corresponding to the same situation in the Apostles' Creed. The redemption was accomplished in this manner: He "became man, conceived and born

[5] See especially A. C. III. Ap. III, S. A. I and II, S. C. and L. C. Second Article, and F. C. VIII. Beyond this the work of Christ is so thoroughly in the center of all statements in the Confessions that here, as in the doctrine of justification, we cannot limit ourselves to individual articles of the Confessions.

without sin of the Holy Spirit and the Virgin, that he might become Lord over sin; moreover, he suffered, died, and was buried that he might make satisfaction for me and pay what I owed, not with silver and gold but with his own precious blood" (L.C. II, 31). But is the life and activity of the Lord between his birth and his arrest really passed over, if one considers that "suffering" is mentioned? Is it not possible that in this way his whole life with all its activity is described as suffering?

Going beyond this simple statement, the Formula of Concord speaks of Christ's obedience, "which as God and man he rendered to his heavenly Father into death itself" (Ep. III, 3). The sinner is adopted into sonship "solely through the merit of the *total obedience,* the bitter suffering, the death, and the resurrection of Christ our Lord, whose obedience is reckoned to us as righteousness" (S.D. III, 9). The series "obedience, suffering, death, and resurrection" seems at first to suggest the understanding of a succession in time. But at the same time the whole way of Jesus until death is described as obedience. In his entire life he rendered "total obedience" to God "by doing and suffering, in life and in death" (S.D. III, 15). The work of the incarnate Son is obedience, pure and simple, a "sole, total, and perfect obedience" (S.D. III, 55). This obedience to God, however, is not mentioned merely in a general way, but it is obedience to the law of God. The Son was voluntarily placed under the same law and has by this obedience "satisfied" the same law (S.D. III, 15), which God gave to his people in the revelation of his commandments through Moses.[6]

This obedience, this death, is the deed of one of us and yet also the deed of one who is entirely different. For the obedience of every man could at best be nothing more than civil decency, which remains in sin. Whatever good the sinner does can only be sin. The death of every other man can only be the consummation of the wrath of God which man has himself incurred. Obedience to the law comes into being only when one who is good does good. Only when an innocent man suffers death is death imposed as undeserved punishment. Only the Son of God accomplished an obedience which is not sin, and only he suffered a death that he did not deserve. The Lord of the law is made under the law to

[6] For this reason one can indeed say: "The fact that the Formula of Concord drew the *obedientia activa* into the atoning work of Christ . . . was no departure from the confessional doctrine taught hitherto, but rather a not inconsistent expansion of the same." Tschackert, *Entstehung,* p. 325; similarly Frank, II, 36; cf. 27 ff. for the concept of *obedientia activa.*

fulfill it. The Lord of life goes into death to conquer it. Therefore, not only Jesus' death and not only his activity and his suffering are obedience to the law of God, but his incarnation itself means "made under the law."

Since the sinless Christ obeys the law which was given to the sinner, his entire obedience is also a suffering from his birth to the cross. And since his suffering comes not only from men, but reaches its most appalling climax in the God-forsakenness on the cross, this suffering and death is also obedience to the law through which God expresses his anger and kills. Therefore Jesus' death is his work in its full dimension.

The doctrine of the obedient death of Jesus Christ is, then, under no circumstances to be separated from the ancient doctrine of the two natures as its premise. Accordingly, the Augsburg Confession asserts that "the two natures, divine and human, are so inseparably united in one person that there is one Christ, true God and true man" (A.C. III, 2; cf. the express references to the decree of the Council of Chalcedon of 451 at the beginning of the Catalog of Testimonies, *Bek.*, p. 1104). Like the doctrine of the Trinity, the doctrine of the two natures is taken over by the Confessions where the concepts of the ancient church are utilized, (and it is in terms of them that the assertion of the Small Catechism must be understood, namely, that Jesus Christ is "true God, begotten of the Father from eternity, and also true man, born of the Virgin Mary." The doctrine of the two natures is the implicit presupposition of all christological statements in the Confessions; it is particularly the necessary premise for the doctrine of substitution in all its consoling severity. To sunder the work of Christ from the person of Christ would necessarily mean that neither the love of God nor the sin of man is recognized. Therefore the Formula of Concord teaches nothing new over against the Augsburg Confession when it unfolds the connection between person and work as follows: "For even though Christ had been conceived by the Holy Spirit without sin and had been born and had in his human nature alone fulfilled all righteousness but had not been true, eternal God, the obedience and passion of the human nature could not be reckoned to us as righteousness. Likewise, if the Son of God had not become man, the divine nature alone could not have been our righteousness. Therefore we believe, teach, and confess that the total obedience of Christ's total person, which he rendered to his heavenly Father even to the most ignominious death of the cross, is reckoned to us as righteousness. For neither the obedience nor the passion of the human nature alone, without the divine nature, could render satisfaction to the eternal and almighty God for the sins of all the world. Likewise, the deity alone, without the humanity, could not mediate between God and us" (S.D. III, 56).[7]

Accordingly, Christ's virgin birth too becomes important from the point of view of his obedience and death. If it is decisive that the "sinless Christ" underwent "the punishment of sin" and "became a sacrifice for us" (Ap. IV, 179), then we dare not teach only "that since the fall of Adam all men who are born according to the course of nature are conceived and born in sin. That is, all men are full of evil lust and inclinations from the mother's womb" (A.C., II, 1), but we must add that Jesus Christ, the sinless Son of God, "was conceived by the Holy Spirit, born of the Virgin Mary" (Apost.).

It is impossible to see in the ancient Christology of the Confessions merely an obsolete remnant of the tradition of the history of dogma and a piece of soft-pedaling. If the Confessions at first show no interest in presenting a detailed monographical treatment of the doctrine of the two natures, they were moved by the consideration that in their discussions with Roman theology they could take this for granted. Besides, it had become evident that an isolated doctrine of the two natures does not protect people from falling into heresy and despair, unless it is immediately added that the incarnate Son of God "is *my Lord,* who has *redeemed* me, a lost and condemned creature, *delivered* me and *freed* me from all sins, from death, and from the power of the devil" (S.C. II, 4). Just as knowing about the immanent Trinity is not yet a knowledge of God, so also knowing about the one divine Person and the two natures of Jesus Christ is not yet a knowledge of Christ. "This is what it means to know Christ, namely, to know his benefits" [*Hoc est Christum cognoscere, beneficia eius cognoscere*]—this sentence of Melanchthon,[8] so much abused by neo-Protestantism and falsely turned against the ancient Christology, serves as a fundamental principle in the Confessions too (Ap. IV, 101). To know the benefits of Christ is to receive these benefits; it is the reality of the act of the incarnate Son of God for me and upon me. Christ is known as little in a mere contemplation of his life on earth as in an abstract

[7] For the peculiarities of the Christology of the Formula of Concord cf. pp. 188 ff.

[8] Charles Leander Hill (trans.), *The "Loci Communes" of Philip Melanchthon* (Boston: Meador, 1944), p. 68.

doctrine of the two natures. "The remembrance of Christ" [*Meminisse Christum*] is something quite different from watching a play; it cannot be accomplished by mere spectators, but "it is rather the remembrance of Christ's blessings and the acceptance of them by faith, so that they make us alive" [*sed est meminisse beneficia Christi, eaque fide accipere, ut per ea vivificemur*] (Ap. XXIV, 72). Since Christ's work is known only by him to whom it is imputed by grace, the Confessions are not interested in a strict dogmatic distinction between reconciliation and justification. The complete reconciliation is not only the presupposition of justification, but in the justification of the sinner reconciliation with God takes place. Justification *is* reconciliation (Ap. IV, 158; cf. S.D. III, 25). In other words, the doctrine of the two natures also, like the doctrine of the Trinity, dare not be taught independently of the distinction of law and Gospel. The triune God and his only-begotten, incarnate Son is to be known only in the distinction of law and Gospel, i.e., by faith in the Gospel. To know Christ is to make use of Christ; to make use of Christ is to receive forgiveness for Christ's sake.

Christ's obedient suffering and death is his merit. It is the only merit of the whole human race, for he alone did not need to be subject to the law of sin and death. No other human deed deserves this name. His merits (*"merita Christi,"* e.g., Ap. IV, 53) are *the* merit.

This deed of Jesus Christ is at the same time God's deed.[9] Not for a moment dare the essential unity of the suffering Son of God and of God the Father be overlooked. If Christ is the incarnate Second Person of the Godhead, then God himself is active in his

---

[9] This must be remembered even when the affirmation is made over against the Confessions' doctrine of the atonement that according to New Testament statements "the love of God for us sinners manifested itself in its greatest power in bringing about the death of Christ for our salvation, hence the saving death of Christ did not establish that love or make possible its reference to sinners." H. H. Wendt, *Augsburg Konfession*, p. 33. As a matter of fact, the doctrine of the atonement in the Confessions contains noteworthy shifts in emphasis over against the New Testament statements. But calling attention to matters of this kind—as the school of Ritschl particularly liked to do—leads necessarily to distortions and extravagant objections, if the Reformation's premise of the doctrine of the two natures is no longer shared. For this premise assures at the outset that Christ's deed is God's deed. Therefore also the love of God is not only the effect of the death of Jesus Christ which appeases God's wrath, but it is already the premise: Christ "was *given* for us to make satisfaction for the sins of the world and has been *appointed* as the mediator and the propitiator" (Ap. IV, 40, *et al.*). The recognition of the unity of essence existing between God the Father and Jesus Christ is the circle within which the differences between the New Testament and the Lutheran doctrine of atonement exist.

incarnation and in his suffering. God the Father sends and God the Son obeys. God the Father gives up and God the Son permits himself to be given up. God the Father sent his beloved Son into the flesh, put him under the law, and placed the burden of his wrath on him. God the Father forsook his only Son on the cross and let him die, before he raised him from the dead and exalted him. This is the deed of the same God who has revealed himself through the law. But even though the Son was put under the law, his being sent occurred without the law and independently of the law. For the law proclaims the fact that God punishes and kills the sinner. But the incarnation and death of Jesus Christ proclaim that God gives up his sinless Son and punishes him in order that the sinner might go unpunished and live.

5. By his suffering and death Jesus Christ has atoned for all sins and has appeased God's wrath.

Article III of the Augsburg Confession continues: "Christ . . . truly born, suffered was crucified, died, and was buried, in order to be a sacrifice not only for original sin but also for all other sins and to propitiate God's wrath" (Latin version: '. . . that he might reconcile the Father to us and be a sacrifice. . . . ' A. C. III, 2 f.). By his suffering and death Christ influences the Father to abandon his wrath against the sinner. But from this it may not be inferred that Christ alone is the reconciler, and not God the Father. Already the doctrine of the two natures excludes this alternative. Nor is it permissible to conclude that only God has been reconciled by Christ. For it is also true, of Christ that he 'suffered and died to reconcile us to the Father' (Ap. III). The reconciliation of God with us is also our reconciliation with God. But the statements about the reconciling influence of the Son on the angry Father preponderate.

Jesus Christ is the sacrifice, the sacrificial lamb that was slain (*hostia, victima, sacrificium*). His death is "the sufferings and blood of the innocent Lamb of God who takes away the sin of the world" (S.A. III, iii, 38). Jesus Christ is the high priest who with his pleading intercedes for us before God (Ap. IV, 332). The priest and the sacrifice God ' "has put forward as an expiation" or a propitiator' (Ap. IV, 82, quoting Rom. 3:25). Thus Jesus Christ is the mediator, being at once priest and sacrifice and mercy-seat. He is the one reconciler and mediator, "the only saviour, the only highpriest, advocate, and intercessor before God." For Scripture places the one Christ before our eyes as 'mediator, propitiation, highpriest, and intercessor' (A.C. XXI, 2).

Jesus Christ is the highest and only "treasure." His merit 'is the treasure, for that which pays the debt of the whole world's sin must needs be a treasure and precious security' (Ap. IV, 53). As when "one pays a debt for one's friend, the debtor is freed by the merit of another as though it were his own. Thus the merits of Christ are bestowed on us" (Ap. XXI, 19). Christ "suffered, died, and was buried that he might make satisfaction for me and pay what I owed, not with silver and gold, but with his own precious blood" (L.C. II, 31). If Christ's merit is this treasure, then also Christ himself is the 'treasure . . . by which our sins have been paid for' "the price for our sins" (Ap. IV, 57). He himself is the forfeit, the price, the ransom. However, he is not only the treasure that was given and paid for our sins, but also a "treasure which God gives us . . . , a treasure comprehended and offered to us in the Word and received by faith" (L.C. IV, 37). And just as Christ is priest and sacrifice at the same time, so he is also the ransomer and the ransom at the same time. The act of ransoming is so much *the* work of Christ, that in the confession of him, God's only-begotten Son our Lord, "the little word 'Lord' simply means the same as Redeemer" (*"Salvator seu redemptor,"* L.C. II, 31).

Thus Jesus Christ by his death has reconciled and propitiated the wrath of God and 'has made satisfaction for our sins' (*sua morte pro nostris peccatis satisfecit,* A.C. IV, 2). By his death he has appeased God (*placatio*) and has redeemed us (*redemptio*). These terms and others describe the redemptive work of Jesus Christ. They are all most closely connected. After all, his sacrifice is a propitiatory sacrifice, and his blood is the ransom price. In accordance with the usage of the time *versoehnen* and *versuehnen* are not clearly differentiated in spite of the distinction between *reconciliare* and *propitiare*. However, the Confessions are not much concerned about a nice distinction and an isolation of the various terms—a comparison of the Latin and German texts makes this especially clear—but precisely by using all of them together they bear witness to the work of Christ. In fact, none of the terms mentioned can be correctly understood if *isolated*.

But no matter which terms are used to designate the atonement, all have this common denominator that they acknowledge the obedient death of Jesus Christ to be a *substitutionary* death. He bore *our* punishment and he paid *our* debt. He bore the punishment which God inflicts on us sinners. He took upon himself the debt which we owe God and he paid it.

Thereby all statements about the atoning work of Jesus Christ are brought into relation to the law of God: "The law condemns all men, but by undergoing the punishment of sin and becoming a sacrifice for us, the sinless Christ took away the right of the law to accuse and condemn those who believe in him" (Ap. IV, 179). The blood that Jesus offers for the sins of the world is demanded by the law. The ransom is the payment of the debt for which men are liable because of the demands of the law. Therefore it may also be said that Jesus Christ "satisfied the law for us and paid for our sin" (S.D. III, 15). Satisfaction for sin is satisfaction of the law; it is the suffering of the punishment which the law has set for the sinner. The appeasement of God's wrath too is the appeasement of the very same wrath which the law displays and which reveals itself through the law. Thereby it becomes completely evident that the law can be understood neither as a statute above God nor as an immanent rule of this world. The obedience of Christ to the law is obedience to God the Father, and Christ's obedience to the Father is also obedience to the law. To satisfy God is at the same time to satisfy the law of God. As the law cannot be preached without Christ, so Christ's work cannot be preached without the law.

Jesus Christ, then, is the mediator not in the sense of a general bridging of the gap between God and man, between Creator and creature, between the infinite and the finite, between eternity and time; but very concretely he is the mediator between the angry God and the sinner, and to that extent the mediator between God and man, between Creator and creature. He is "the mediator who reconciles the Father," 'the mediator and propitiation through whom the Father is reconciled' (A.C. XX, 9). He is the 'mediator and propitiator, and for his sake alone the Father becomes reconciled to us,' ". . . the propitiator, through whom the Father is reconciled to us" (Ap. IV, 80). As here "propitiator" is rendered *"Mittler und Versoehner,"* and in other places *"Mittler"* is rendered *"mediator et propitiatorium,"* so Jesus Christ is mediator and propitiator at the same time; he is mediator as the propitiator, and propitiator as the mediator. As such he is shepherd and head of his church, the advocate of his people with God.

The significance of this single propitiatory death of Christ is all-inclusive. His merits are 'a treasure and precious pledge whereby the *whole* world's sins are paid for' (Ap. IV, 53). 'Since the whole world became guilty, he took away the sin of the *whole* world' (Ap. IV, 103). He was a sacrifice "not only for original sin but also for all other sins" (A.C. III, 3). Christ made satisfaction for all actual sins and for every corruptness of nature. "The death of Christ, furthermore, is a satisfaction not only for guilt but also for eternal death" (Ap. XII, 140). He made satisfaction for all the guilt and all the punishments of all men. Christ was given to us "to destroy the rule of the devil, sin, and death" (Ap. II, 50).

"The whole world" and "Christ alone" are set in contrast to each other, as are "all sins" and "the unique sacrifice." The totality of the effect and the uniqueness and singleness of the deed belong together with the same necessity as God the Creator of all things and God the only-begotten Son. The *particulae exclusivae* are set forth and defended with great vehemence against every kind of tampering. "Christ alone," "none other but Christ," "the single sacrifice of Christ," and the all-inclusive significance of *"satis"* are extolled in ever-new turns of speech. *"Unicum esse sacrificium Christi"* means negatively ". . . for the sins of others . . . there is *no other* such sacrifice *left* in the New Testament except the one sacrifice of Christ on the cross" (Ap. XXIV, 56). Since Christ alone is the mediator and propitiator, the use of these terms in the plural already constitutes a dishonoring of Christ. Nor are the saints in any way whatever mediators, neither mediators who intercede for us nor mediators who redeem us (Ap. XXI, 14 f.). He alone 'is to be prayed to, and he has promised to hear our prayers' (A.C. XXI, 3). With holy vehemence and jealousy the Confessions watch over these concepts "only," "one," "unique," and glorify Jesus as *the* Lord. Even the doctrine of sin and of man's enslaved will thus becomes a doxology of the exclusive merit of Jesus Christ by establishing beyond a doubt that no one was obedient to God except his only-begotten Son.

But the totality of the effect and the uniqueness of the deed together constitute the honor and glory of Christ. The glory of Christ consists in this—that the only obedience rendered to God by the human race is the obedience of the incarnate Son of God, that the only death that was not well-merited punishment for the dying person is and remains his death, and that his obedience and death is the only merit of all mankind. Christ's honor, however, is not a uniqueness which he preserves in and for himself, but it is the very uniqueness of his self-surrender and his sacrifice for the sins of the whole world. It is his glory that he, as the only one, truly sacrificed himself and that with his completed sacrifice he *offers* himself to all sinners for forgiveness and life eternal. To acknowledge Christ's glory, therefore, means to receive Christ, to eat and drink him. Thus understood, the glory of Christ is the theme of all Lutheran Confessions.[10] In the focus of all statements is not the glory which God has for himself, but the glory of Christ which manifests itself in his sacrifice for men and in his self-giving. The only permissible *theologia gloriae* is, therefore, the *theologia gloriae Christi*, i.e., the *theologia crucis*.

6. To the act of reconciliation corrupt man responds by reviling the honor of Jesus Christ through the works of the law; the sinner cannot know what makes for his welfare.

Man's response to the incarnation and obedience of the Son of God not only *was* the crucifixion; it *is* the crucifixion. Men do not want to "use him as the only Mediator." They are constantly occupied with crucifying him anew and with reburying him (Ap. IV, 81). Or, in other words, they "obscure the glory and the blessings of Christ" (Ap. IV, 3), they 'deprecate the glory of Christ's Passion' (A.C. XXIV, 24).

Thus they indeed use the name of Christ, but they mingle his words with the words of *Weltanschauung* and of philosophy and seek to prove that 'the word of Christ harmonized well with the sayings of Socrates and Zeno, as though Christ had come for the purpose of giving good laws and commandments whereby we might merit the remission of sins' (Ap. IV, 15).

Or they indeed speak of Christ's merit, of grace and faith, but they understand grace as merely the first beginning (*prima gratia*), which gives man help and the inclination to love God more easily (*habitus dilectionis*) and thus to merit life eternal for themselves. Since, however, they thereby make salvation dependent on Christ's merit *and* man's achievement, "the people conceal Christ from us and bury him again" (Ap. IV, 18; cf. 81). A synergistic use of the merit of Christ is already a total denial of it. The relatively kindest judgment of these theologians is that they dream, they imagine, they entertain the motion, "they cling to the fiction . . . that

---

[10] Quite properly L. Hutterus in his *Concordia Concors* at the close of the Prolegomena summarizes the Confessions in the following prayer: *"Tu CHRISTE nobis adesto: Tua enim agitur Gloria atque veritas: Nostra vero salus. AMEN."*

we have an access through our own works" (Ap. IV, 81). But at the same time it becomes plain that this pious liquidation of Christ is more horrible than open mockery and open ridicule.

Thus men respond to the revelation of Jesus Christ by reviling him through the works of the law. "They claim to keep the law, though this glory properly belongs to Christ. In opposition to the judgment of God they set a trust in their own works" (Ap. IV, 146). These works of the law done by men are certainly not the works which God's law demands of men. If they were, the people would know that they are not keeping God's law. The works of the law with which the sinner responds are rather deeds by which he distorts God's revealed law. In the place of the sacrifice of Christ man places the works of civil decency and of pious extraordinariness (fasting, celibacy, etc.). In the place of forgiveness for Christ's sake man places the works of his moral improvement; in the place of the righteousness of God, the righteousness acknowledged by other men and by himself. As once Christ was crucified by an ordered process of civil justice, so now civil righteousness and human piety remain his enemies without and within the church.

Accordingly, work-righteousness is a reviling of the glory of Christ, 'a horrible blasphemy,' a lack of a feeling of shame (Ap. XX, 4). These works are called works of the law because God's law produces no other works than such as transgress that very law. Therefore, not only the works of the law, but also the law itself stands in opposition to the merit of Christ. The opinion that a man is pleasing to God "because of his own *keeping* of the law" is identical with the error that we have a gracious God 'for the *sake* of the *law*' (Ap. IV, 165).

As in connection with the threefold response of men to the law of God, so here too we may not stop with the fact that man resists, but we must continue: No sinner *is able* by his own power to receive Christ and to extol his merit. To be sure, every man "can talk about God and express" his "worship of him in outward works" (Ap. XVIII, 4). Every man can also "hear the Gospel, meditate on it to a certain degree, and can even talk about it" (S.D. II, 24). Knowing about Jesus' life, words, miracles, and death is by no means beyond the power of the *servum arbitrium*. Even the devils "believe the history of Christ's suffering and his resurrection from the dead" (A.C. XX, 23). Thus corrupt man without the aid of the Holy Spirit may even speculate about Christ's being the Son of God; why should he not also be able to reproduce the doctrine of the two natures correctly, yes, why not even promote Christian doctrine? But all this is not yet to know the work of Christ.

"But what is the knowledge of Christ except to know Christ's blessings . . . ? And to know these blessings is rightly and truly to believe in Christ" (Ap. IV, 101). But what is faith in Christ except receiving the merits of Christ? However, "without the grace, help, and activity of the Holy Spirit man is not capable . . . of believing" (A.C. XVIII, 2); '. . . we say that free will and reason can do nothing in spiritual matters, namely, to believe God truly, to be truly confident that God is with us, answers our prayers, forgives our sins, etc.' (Ap. XVIII, 7). In this connection St. Paul is repeatedly quoted: "The unspiritual man does not receive the gifts of the Spirit of God, for they are folly to him, and he is not able to understand them" (I Cor. 2:14; cf. also Ep. II, 2; S.D. II, 10, 12). It is, therefore, entirely logical for the Formula of Concord to reject not only the gross error that man by his own powers could convert himself and believe the Gospel (Ep. II, 9), but also the more subtle error "that man by virtue of his own powers could make a beginning of his conversion but could not complete it without the grace of the Holy Spirit" (Ep. II, 10). Explicitly rejected is even the error that the will of man, after the Holy Spirit has made a beginning, would be able in the smallest measure "to help, to cooperate, to prepare . . . for grace, . . . to apprehend and accept it, and to believe the Gospel" (Ep. II, 11). The formula, "God draws, but draws the person who is willing" [Deus trahit, sed volentem trahit] is rejected even though the fathers used it (Ep. II, 16; S.D. II, 86).

As corrupt man falsifies God's law by his work-righteousness, so he also falsifies the Gospel. Work-righteousness is the enemy of law and Gospel, of every word of God. Thus the sinner can neither obey the law nor believe the Gospel. He does not recognize the Gospel as the word of mercy nor, consequently, the Decalogue as God's eternal law in its glory. "For this reason the Holy Scriptures compare the heart of the unregenerated man to a hard stone which resists rather than yields in any way to human touch, or to an unhewn timber, to a wild, unbroken animal" (S.D. II, 19, 20 ff.).

7. God pronounces the sinner righteous for Christ's sake apart from the law by grace.

God for Christ's sake forgives the sins of this "wild animal," who revolts against Moses and Christ. God does not forgive for the sake of man's works, for all of man's works are sin; nor for the sake of man's love (e.g., Ap. IV, 77), for also the sinner's love is hatred against God's commandment and mercy. God does not forgive for the sake of human merits, for such merits are nonexistent, and where they are claimed sin reaches its apex. But neither does God forgive because of man's despair nor because of the savageness of his contradiction, nor because of the emptiness of his civil righteousness. Despair and the experience of God's wrath remain sin too. Here there is no preference of one sin above the other. God forgives sin only because of the merit of Jesus Christ, i.e., by grace alone. Just as the sending of the Son into this world was an act of incomprehensible divine grace, so also the forgiveness for Christ's sake is pronounced to the sinner by grace alone.

By forgiving the sins of the sinner God justifies him. By receiving "forgiveness of sins" the sinner receives "righteousness before God" (A.C. IV, 1). Forgiveness of sins and justification are not only repeatedly used side by side, but they are also interchanged promiscuously.[11] It is stated not only that "the forgive-

---

[11] This fact must be the starting point for the exposition of the much-debated doctrine of justification in the Apology. Only from this viewpoint is the unique unconcern intelligible with which the Apology designates justification either as a being declared righteous or as regeneration. The real theme of Ap. IV is not the problem of the real or the ideal *justificatio,* but *sola fide propter Christum.* Cf. the analysis of the structure of Ap. IV by H. Engelland, *Melanchthon,* pp. 559 ff. Whoever begins with the question whether justification is a forensic judgment *or* a renewing act, whether the justified one is acknowledged as righteous *or* is renewed with new thoughts and impulses, will find only unclear answers in Ap. IV (this is evident from the long and singularly undecisive oscillation of the debate concerning Ap. IV). The theme is the word which justifies, its only basis (*propter Christum*), and the rejection of all human presuppositions (*sola fide*). This is indicated also by the constantly recurring equation of justification and forgiveness. In most careful dogmatic delimitation the interest in Ap. IV rests in securing the *sola fide propter Christum* by means of the detailed discussion of the *particulae exclusivae.* Over against this, relatively little attention is paid to a dogmatic-conceptual clarification of the distinction of the effects produced by the justifying Word of God. Overwhelmed by the wealth of the gifts of grace which are bestowed by the word of forgiveness, the church in Ap. IV acknowledges this wealth as artlessly and joyously as children receiving gifts, without attempting to analyze the gift in detail or even to preserve a certain order in describing it. The decisive factor remains that all these gifts are gifts of *grace* and that they are all received only for Christ's sake through faith. In expounding Ap. IV we must be careful not to abridge the wealth of the effects of the Gospel by way of a false attempt to establish at this point more exact definitions than are actually given. "Thus the doctrine of justification embraces the fullness of the gift of the Gospel precisely because it shows what the word of forgiveness involves. But this *fullness* brings *tensions* with it; these produce the problems of the doctrine as it is mirrored in the complicated discussion concerning the doctrine of justification in the Apology. We would abridge, yes, perhaps entirely miss the understanding, if we would see only the one or the other tension, and this altogether, if we would then resolve the tension and take

ness of sins is supremely necessary in justification," but also that "forgiveness of sins is the same as justification" (Ap. IV, 75 f.). Both forgiveness of sins and justification have their basis in the same way only in the obedient death of Jesus Christ. God gives forgiveness and justification in the same way not because of human works of love or merits or satisfactions, not because of theological knowledge, not even because of the human act of confession (*"confessio ex opere operato,"* Ap. IV, 383 f.), but only by grace.

We may also put it this way: Forgiveness and justification are given without the law. If works and justification are opposites, then also the word of God which demands the work of man, and the forgiving word which justifies the sinner, are opposites. ' "This righteousness of God is manifested without the law" (Rom. 3:21), i.e., the remission of sins is offered gratis' (Ap. IV, 41). Neither works nor the law can "free us from sin or justify us" (Ap. IV, 40). "If the forgiveness of sins depended upon our merits, and if reconciliation were by the law, it would be useless. For since we do not keep the law, it would follow that we would never obtain the promise of reconciliation" (Ap. IV, 42).

If the forgiveness of sins is justification, then justification above all means the act of pronouncing righteous. The word through which God forgives sins is at the same time the judgment by which God declares the sinner righteous. The work and merit of Jesus Christ for the sake of which God forgives sins is at the same time the righteousness of Christ which God imputes and grants to the sinner. As forgiveness of sins is nonimputation of sins for Christ's sake (*"peccatum non imputatur,"* Ap. II, 40), so justification is the imputation of Christ's righteousness. As the sinner receives forgiveness not because of his own works, but because of the work of another, namely, the Son of God, so the sinner is declared righteous because of a foreign righteousness. Thus "justify," as the explanation of Rom. 5:1 shows, is used "in a judicial way (*forensi consuetudine*) to mean 'to absolve a guilty man and pronounce him righteous,' and to do so on account of someone else's righteousness, namely, Christ's, which is communicated to us through faith. Since in this passage our righteousness is the imputation of someone else's righteousness, we must speak of righteousness in a different way

note of only one side of the picture." H. E. Weber, *Grosser Katechismus,* I, 1, p. 70. If the investigation of the doctrine of justification must begin with the word of forgiveness, then this means that the doctrine of justification must not be isolated but discussed within the framework of the doctrine of law and Gospel.

here from the philosophical or judicial investigation of a man's own righteousness" (Ap. IV, 305 f.).[12] Justification by God and by human courts have in common that they are both a judgment and the pronouncement of a judgment. The difference between the two is that a human court may in justice acquit only the innocently accused; God, however, declares the guilty guiltless, the sinner righteous. In the place of the guilty sinner God, having made his Son to be sin for us in our stead, looks upon his guiltless Son. 'As when a good friend pays a debt for another, the debtor is freed by the payment of another, as though it were his own payment. Thus the merit of Christ is bestowed on us and imputed to us, when we believe in him, just as though his merit were ours, so that also his righteousness and his merit are imputed to us, and his merit becomes our own' (Ap. XXI, 19).

Since justification is effected only for Christ's sake, it is never a partial justification. To claim that it is incomplete and is in need of supplementation would be blaspheming the honor of Christ. If Christ's righteousness is bestowed on the sinner, he is *entirely* righteous. For "justification is not the approval of a particular act, but of the total person" (Ap. IV, 222). It must be maintained that "God will and does account us *altogether* righteous and holy for the sake of Christ, our mediator. Although the sin in our flesh has not been completely removed or eradicated, he will not count or consider it. . . . The *whole* man, in respect both of his person and of his works, shall be accounted and shall be righteous and holy through the pure grace and mercy which have been poured out upon us so abundantly in Christ" (S.A. III, xiii, 1, 2). Because God looks upon Christ instead of the sinner and awards Christ's righteousness to the sinner, the whole man is righteous and holy, i.e., he is hidden in Christ. If after we have received forgiveness of sins "we have a gracious God who cares about us" (Ap. IV, 141), —if it is true that we "have a reconciled God" (Ap. IV, 196),

---

[12] F. Loofs denied that, according to the doctrine of the Apology, justification is an *actus forensis,* and supported this, among other things, by saying that this forensic concept was rare in the Apology and that in part it had no connection with the doctrine of justification proper, in part it had been deleted in the octavo edition of 1531. *Die Bedeutung der Rechtfertigungslehre der Apologie,* pp. 622 ff. Over against this K. Thieme and others have correctly pointed out that the expressions *"justum reputari," "Deo acceptum esse," "coram Deo," "justitia Christi aliena"* in essence also speak for justification as an *actus forensis.* Yes, Thieme will admit only the forensic concept in Ap. IV, since here *"justum reputari"* is the dominant meaning of *justificari. Die Rechtfertigungslehre der Apologie,* p. 383. However, in spite of the correctness of many of his objections to Loofs, we cannot stop here.

i.e., that God no longer imputes any of our sins to us—then this means that we as justified people are altogether God's own and are well pleasing to him. If it is true that we do not "have" half a God, but the triune God himself, then it is all the more true that God does not "have" us only halfway, but altogether. For only because God has us entirely as his own in Jesus Christ do we "have" him.

That justification must be understood from the viewpoint of pronouncing righteous—even in the much-disputed passages of the Apology—the Confessions confirm by the many statements which expressly mention God's "imputing," "declaring righteous," "esteeming righteous," "pronouncing righteous," (*imputare, reputare, pronuntiare*) etc., and, furthermore, by the consistent equation and interchange of justification and forgiveness of sins, by the definition of the Gospel as the promise of forgiveness, and then also by the simultaneous stress on the zeal for the glory of Christ and on the insistence that the justified sinner is altogether righteous and holy, in spite of his being altogether a sinner, and not yet rid of sins even though he has been renewed.

If the sinner is declared righteous by God, he is not only regarded as righteous; he *is* righteous. If he is "accounted" altogether righteous and holy for Christ's sake, then he also *is* altogether righteous and holy (S.A. III, xiii, 1). As believers we are not only *called* the children of God, we *are* God's children. '. . . eternal life belongs to those whom God esteems righteous, and when they have been esteemed righteous they have become, by that act, the children of God and co-heirs of Christ' (Ap. IV, 333). Justification "makes us sons of God, . . . it also makes us co-heirs with Christ" (Ap. IV, 196; cf. 356). God's justifying verdict is never "merely" a verdict; this verdict posits a reality. Since God's verdict is true, the justified man is truly righteous. Since God's verdict is real, the righteousness of the justified man is more real than all the sins of which he himself and other people may be aware. It would be a denial of the truth and reality of the thoughts and words of God in which he imputes and bestows, if pronouncing righteous were not at the same time designated as making righteous, and if the nonimputation of sin were not also called regeneration.[13] To obtain

[13] As a matter of fact, it must be said as plainly as possible: To be declared righteous is the same as to be made righteous, and vice versa. *"Justum effici, regenerari, vivificari"* are other terms for *"justum reputari, remissionem accipere, Deo acceptum esse,"* but one and the same event takes place. This observation is the achievement of Eichhorn and Thieme (this is actually sup-

forgiveness of sins, or to be justified, 'that means that an unrighteous person has been made pious, holy, and reborn' (Ap. IV, 117). Justification is thus defined in a twofold way: To be justified means both "to make unrighteous men righteous or to regenerate them" (*ex injustis justos effici seu regenerari*), and also "to be pronounced or accounted righteous" (*justos pronuntiari seu reputari*, Ap. IV, 72).[14] Neither of these definitions may be omitted. However, the "making righteous" must be understood exclusively in the light of the "pronouncing righteous"; the "pronouncing righteous" is not to be understood in the light of the "making righteous." For all extended discussions start with the forgiveness of sins and return to the forgiveness of sins, "that faith alone makes a righteous man out of an unrighteous man, that is, that it receives the forgiveness of sins" (Ap. IV, 72).

8. The sinner is justified without the deeds of the law by faith alone.

As God does not justify the sinner because of his works but by grace for Christ's sake, so the sinner receives justification not through his works but through faith alone. Faith by grace receives the remission of sins because it "sets against God's wrath not our merits of love, but Christ the mediator and propitiator" (Ap. IV, 46). This means "by faith alone" (*sola fide*). "If they dislike the exclusive particle 'alone,' let them remove the other exclusive terms from Paul, too, like 'freely,' 'not of works,' 'it is a gift,' etc." For these also exclude every human motivation and accomplishment (Ap. IV, 73). By grace alone, not by works—that is the theme of the entire doctrine of justification. In the light of this statement the further distinctions concerning faith must be understood which are given negatively and positively.

The faith here spoken of "is not that possessed by the devil and the ungodly, who also believe the history of Christ's suffering and

---

ported also by the comparison which Eichhorn made between the Latin and the German texts of the Apology. A. Eichhorn, *Die Rechtfertigungslehre der Apologie* [1887], pp. 477 ff.). This must be maintained against all attempts to distinguish declaring righteous and making righteous in Ap. IV in content or in time as two separate acts of God, or even to base the declaring righteous on the making righteous. It is indeed impossible, for the sake of the logical correctness of identifying 'making righteous' and 'declaring righteous,' to isolate the *motus spirituales*, the renewal of the heart and its drives, from regeneration, as Eichhorn and Thieme have done in Ap. IV. Cf. pp. 105 ff., especially 108 f.

[14] For further comments cf. p. 115, n. 5.

resurrection from the dead, but we mean such true faith as believes that we receive grace and forgiveness of sin through Christ." True faith 'believes not only the history but also the effect of the history' (A.C. XX, 23). Faith is "no mere historical knowledge, but the firm acceptance of God's offer," the certainty or the certain and firm trust in the heart, when with my whole heart I regard the promise of God as certain and true, through which there are offered me without my merit the forgiveness of sin, grace, and all blessing, through Christ the mediator' (Ap. IV, 48). This faith is always *fides specialis,* the faith by which each individual "believes that his sins are forgiven because of Christ" (Ap. IV, 45). Whoever believes merely in a general way that God exists, etc. (Ap. XII, 60) does not believe at all.

With all these delimitations faith is designated as receiving, obtaining, grasping (*accipere, apprehendere*). It is not man who is active here but God in his free mercy. If faith were only knowledge it would still be a human deed beside other human deeds. If faith were the knowledge about a one-time event that happened in the past or is now happening only to others, but not to oneself, it would still be possible to use this knowledge to assert oneself and to follow one's own course of action undisturbed as before.

"To avoid the impression that it is merely knowledge, we will add that to have faith means to want and to accept (*velle et accipere*) the promised offer . . ." (Ap. IV, 48), it is "a desire to accept and grasp" (*velle accipere seu apprehendere,* Ap. IV, 227). As "the terrors of sin and death are not merely thoughts in the intellect, but are also a horrible turmoil in the will as it feels God's judgment; just so faith is not merely knowledge in the intellect but also trust in the will, that is, to desire and to accept" (Ap. IV, 304). What does "will" mean here? Justus Jonas translates ". . . *est velle et accipere* . . .": 'Faith is that my whole heart takes to itself this treasure,' and he adds emphatically: 'And is not my doing, not my granting or giving, not my working or preparing, but that the heart comforts itself and is altogether confident that God bestows on us and gives us, and not we him, that God showers on us the full treasure of grace in Christ' (Ap. IV, 48). Here the act of volition is not a deed of man, but it is the longing desire and wish which is aroused and appeased by the promise. When we as believers rely entirely on God's grace, when we say to God: 'Because Thou hast promised the forgiveness of sins, I will cling to this promise, and thus I rest courageously on the gracious assurance' (Ap. IV, 60), then this daring reliance and clinging is the extent of our activity.[15]

Although these expressions embrace the totality of human activity and although, by referring to the "will," the complete psychic experience of emotion, volition, and thought is indicated and claimed for the concept "faith," still this alone is to be expressed: that the whole man with all his acts and thoughts, his emotions and his will, becomes a recipient in faith, and that he and his yearning will receive a gift, 'that his whole heart takes to itself this treasure.' *"Velle"* in the concept of faith does not indicate a more precise psychological delineation of faith, but signifies the surrender and abandonment of the *psyche* to the gracious activity of God. *"Velle,"* as bracketed with knowing, consenting, daring, relying, etc., does not safeguard the peculiarity of a specific psychic process, but it does safeguard the divine permission for the sinner to believe the promise, no matter what may distress him, be it the agony of despair, the distress of decision, or the torment of doubt. These statements about faith warn against limiting the reception in any way; but rather faith as willing, knowing, daring, etc., signifies precisely that the total man becomes a recipient. By using apparently psychological terms all accomplishments are in fact excluded, all sinners are invited, and every sinner is told that he has been completely surrendered to the grace of God and that he may expect and receive everything from this grace.[16]

If faith and works are thus contrasted, so also are faith and law in opposition to each other. The works that are excluded are man's response to the law. If the law reveals God's wrath, the believer sets the merit of Jesus Christ against the wrath and, hence, against the law of God. 'Therefore this propitiator will benefit us in this way, when by faith we apprehend the Word, through which mercy is promised, and the same against God's wrath and judgment' (Ap. IV, 82). When the sinner under the law feels God's wrath in the fearful disturbance of his soul, he, in the very midst of this feeling, by faith hurdles his feelings and goes to the promise which is given in Christ. The experience of God's wrath is also a work of the

---

[15] Even in the statement that faith sets against (*opponit*) "God's wrath . . . Christ the mediator and propitiator," the activity of this opposition is at the same time the complete passivity of reception. As faith "sets against," it accepts "the forgiveness of sins" (Ap. IV, 46).

[16] That faith is not defined as a psychological phenomenon, e.g., by the degree of awareness of the *notitia*, is supported by the fact that faith in Christ is viewed as identical in both Old and New Testaments (Ap. IV, 59; cf. p. 69).

law and, therefore, a work of man and, as such, sin. Therefore faith is not placed over against the feeling of wrath as a feeling of grace. Justifying faith is not a "feeling" (in reference to justification *sentire* has a different meaning than in reference to God's wrath; cf., e.g., Ap. IV, 163, 211, 214 ff.). But "faith is conceived *in* the terrors of a conscience that feels God's wrath against our sins" (Ap. IV, 142). In the midst of the anguish of conscience and in spite of the anguish of conscience the sinner is permitted to believe that he has peace with God. While he feels death and God's terrible wrath he is permitted to believe that God loves him and that he is acceptable to God for Christ's sake. Were faith to demand the *feeling* of the divine grace and were the doctrine of justification to require the *experientia* of the propitious God, then this doctrine would be the perpetuation of despair under God's law.

In summary this means: Faith is confidence (*fiducia*), that is, "assurance that God is gracious to us," "confidence in God and in the fulfillment of his promises" (A.C. XX, 26, 25), 'the certainty, or the certain and firm trust in the heart, when with my whole heart I regard the promise of God as certain and true, through which there are offered me without my merit the forgiveness of sin, grace, and all blessing, through Christ the mediator' (Ap. IV, 48). This conception of faith as confidence deflects our view entirely from man's introspection and from reflections on the question whether he is a believer. He is directed exclusively to him in whom we are permitted to believe, i.e., to him who gives himself to the sinner by grace.[17] Therefore we must reject the notion that the sinner is justified by faith *and* works (A.C. XX, 6), or that faith, as the beginning of good works, is also only the beginning or the preparation of justification (Ap. IV, 71). If in the doctrine of justification faith is mentioned alongside of works, then faith also is understood as an activity; then confidence, daring, reliance, etc., are human activities and dispositions. Faith as confidence, however, 'neither brings nor gives God the Lord any work, or any merit, but relies solely on pure grace and knows of no way to be comforted or to trust, than by mercy alone' (Ap. IV, 44). Everything in faith is the work of Jesus Christ. Therefore the classic formula reads: Men are justified "for Christ's sake, through faith" (*"propter*

---

[17] As surely as faith is not only *notitia,* so also it is not a *fiducia* that could be separated from *notitia.* It was a mistake for neo-Protestantism to claim to speak of faith in the sense of the Reformers by emphasizing the aspects of trust, confidence, daring, etc., but referring them to other contents of faith.

Christum per fidem," A.C. IV, 1), but the formula may not be inverted—"for the sake of faith through Christ."

The Confessions say not only that God imputes Christ's right eousness to the sinner, but also that "God will regard and reckon this faith as righteousness" (A.C. IV, 3). "It is faith, therefore, that God declares to be righteousness; he adds that it is accounted freely . . ." (Ap. IV, 89). Faith is "the very righteousness by which we are accounted righteous before God" (Ap. IV, 86). But is not Christ alone our righteousness?

Furthermore, the Confessions teach not only that God justifies the sinner, but repeated reference is made also to justifying faith. The heading of Ap. IV, 61 ff. reads: "Faith in Christ justifies." This section teaches that faith "receives the forgiveness of sins, justifies, and quickens . . ." (Ap. IV, 62). For Luther too it is "clear and certain that faith alone justifies us" (S.A. II, i, 4). Does not God alone justify?

Finally and most puzzling of all is the occasional formula *"propter fidem." "Because* of faith" the imperfection and impurity of our observance of the law are not imputed (Ap. IV, 177; cf. 189). Is not the statement "for *Christ's* sake" the only correct one? May we say more than *"through* faith"? Is not man, then, given credit for something decisive, and is not something demanded of him which he cannot accomplish at all? In the above formulations does not faith appear, after all, as an accomplishment beside the work of Christ, and thereby as its substitute?

But if we look at these formulations once more in their contexts, we shall see the very opposite.

God imputes to the sinners as righteousness "faith, when we believe that Christ suffered for us and that for his sake our sin is forgiven and righteousness and eternal life are given to us" (A.C. IV, 2). Faith is imputed as righteousness, that is, Christ, who has suffered for us, is imputed as righteousness. "Faith is the very righteousness" precisely does not mean that faith is "a work worthy in itself." But faith receives the promise of God to be propitious for Christ's sake and faith knows that God made Christ our wisdom, our righteousness and sanctification and redemption (Ap. IV, 86).

Hence, in the references to "justifying faith" that faith is meant which trusts the promise of Christ "that for his sake we have the forgiveness of sins" (Ap. IV, 62). For no other reason but that Christ is the mediator must we "defend the proposition, 'faith justifies' " (Ap. IV, 69). In like manner the statement from the Smalcald Articles quoted above is immediately preceded by the acknowledgment of the redeeming work of Jesus Christ in his blood. By it we are justified (S.A. II, i, 1-3).

Therefore, justification *propter fidem* is also mentioned precisely because of the awareness that "we are accounted righteous because of Christ, not because of the law or our works" (Ap. IV, 177).

All of these formulations, which at first glance appear so dubious, thus express all the more strikingly and exclusively that faith is not a deed of man, but is reception of the gracious deed of God. For in these formulations faith is used interchangeably both with Christ, as the righteousness and the ground of justification, and with God, as the one who justifies. 'Christ' and 'faith' are interchanged, because faith lives from him in whom it believes and is all things through Christ but nothing without him. Christ and faith are so intimately united that *propter fidem* may be said for *propter Christum,* and *per Christum* for *per fidem.* "It is faith therefore that frees men through the blood of Christ" (Ap. IV, 103; cf. also 83). "For these two belong together, faith and God," and nothing can separate them (L.C. I, 3). God's deed of mercy is at once cause and content of faith. We may speak of faith as is done in all these formulations because this definition is strictly maintained: ". . . at every mention of faith we are also thinking of its object, the promised mercy. For faith does not justify or save because it is a good work in itself, but only because it accepts the promised mercy" (Ap. IV, 55 f.; cf. 53 f.).

Accordingly, faith as confident reception is not an achievement of man.[18] If faith were to be understood in this way, one would

---

[18] This only *seems* to be contradicted by the beginning of the L. C. I: ". . . the trust and faith of the heart alone make both God and an idol. If your faith and trust are right, then your God is the true God. On the other hand, if your trust is false and wrong, then you have not the true God. For these two belong together, faith and God." From A. Ritschl to G. Wobbermin these statements have been much overloaded dogmatically and often abused. From these words of the Large Catechism it is not possible either to deduce Wobbermin's "religio-psychological circle," or to maintain that here is to be found the beginning of the process of making religion worldly, or of desupranaturalizing it." Heitmueller; cf. the survey of the newer interpretations and their critique by K. Thieme, *Augsburgische Konfession,* pp. 98 ff. Rather, to understand these words correctly we must note that they are here speaking not of the triune God exclusively, but in a transcending formulation of God and idol, of true faith and false religion. "A god is that to which we look for all good . . ." is a very general definition; just as general is the closing statement of the paragraph: "That to which your heart clings and entrusts itself is, I say, really your God." To the extent that these general statements speak of the relationship of "the true faith" to "the one true God," we must not overlook the

have to say immediately that faith is not a receiving, but merely a permitting something to happen to us. But this "permitting" too is no achievement of man. It is not we who permit God in his mercy to reach out for us or in his grace to operate in us. Rather, faith is the astonished realization that God does it, yes, that he did it long ago, long before we ourselves could permit it to happen to us, namely, in the death of his Son on the cross.

Therefore the insistence on the *"sola fide"* is identical with the jealousy and passion which keeps an eye on the *"solus Christus."* Because the obedient suffering and death of Jesus Christ, the incarnate Son of God, is the only and sole merit of the whole human race, we are saved "by faith alone." Only by faith in Christ do we really also recognize our sin; for under the law the knowledge of sin always remains dubious (Ap. II, 15; Ep. V, 8).

9. He who believes is free from the law. Faith is the work of the Holy Spirit.

The believer is free from the law through Jesus Christ, in whom he believes, and through the Holy Spirit, who creates faith in him.

The believer is free from the law, since he is justified not by the deeds of the law but by grace. The believer is free from the law, since God accounts him obedient for the sake of the obedience of Jesus Christ and since the law has no further claim against one who is obedient. He is free from the curse of the law, because the law has no more accusation against him and no further occasion to judge him. Finally, freedom from the law means that the believer begins to do his works not in response to the law, but in the power of Jesus Christ. "He is the end of the law (Rom. 10:4), and he himself says, 'Apart from me you can do nothing' " (Ap. IV, 372). It is precisely as the end of the law that Christ is the Saviour of the corrupt human nature (Ap. IV, 30). Because he bore the punishment innocently, the law has been deprived of the possibility of accusing and judging. Because he innocently bore the wrath of God, that wrath as revealed by the law has been appeased. But if the law has no more claims on Jesus Christ, it has none either

fact that according to the testimony of the Large Catechism faith is the work of God in man, and therefore faith and God are interchangeable concepts, just as in the Augsburg Confession and the Apology faith and Christ are interchanged. The true faith "makes" God, namely, the giver of "all good." Only for the believer is God the helper in every need; he is wrathful and hostile to the unbeliever. Cf. also K. Barth, *Church Dogmatics*, I, 266 ff.

on those who believe in him. "Paul teaches this when he says in Gal. 3:13, 'Christ redeemed us from the curse of the law, being made a curse for us.' That is, the law condemns all men, but by undergoing the punishment of sin and becoming a sacrifice for us, the sinless Christ took away the right of the law to accuse and condemn those who believe in him, because he himself is their propitiation, for whose sake they are now accounted righteous. But when they are accounted righteous, the law cannot accuse or condemn them, even though they have not really satisfied the law" (Ap. IV, 179).

The basis of this freedom of the believers is the Holy Spirit along with Christ. Faith is 'a strong, powerful work of the Holy Spirit' (Ap. IV, 99). The Holy Spirit kindles and produces faith and he preserves it day by day to the end through the Word (A.C. V, 2; S.D. II, 16). Faith is not the response of men to God's law, and it is not the obedience of man to the commandment through which God commands him to believe in him and love him. Faith is not a work of the law; it is not man's work at all. The believer is free from the law, for he becomes believing and obedient without the deeds of the law through the Holy Spirit who is given to him not by the law, but only by the Gospel.

10. The Gospel is the word of forgiveness through which God justifies the sinner for Christ's sake.

That which has been presented in theses 4 through 9 in the succession of theological concepts is simultaneously attested, recognized, given, and received in one indivisible act through the Gospel.

The Gospel, as is explained repeatedly, is "the promise that sins are forgiven freely for Christ's sake" (Ap. IV, 120). This could also be stated thus: The Gospel is, "strictly speaking, the promise of forgiveness of sins and justification because of Christ" (Ap. IV, 43). And as the promise of forgiveness, the Gospel is also the 'assurance of the grace promised in Christ' (*"promissio gratiae in Christo promissae,"* Ap. IV, 388).[19] *"Promissio,"* however, not only signifies "promise" with a view to the coming Last Judgment and the acquittal pronounced there, but it also means assurance

[19] In such definitions of the Gospel it is noteworthy that Christ is almost always expressly mentioned, but not always faith. Since the concept of faith is missing in numerous summarizing definitions of the Gospel, this very absence again insures the significance of "faith justifies," that is, *Christ* is our righteousness, *God* justifies us for Christ's sake.

now. The Gospel is not only a promise of forgiveness, but is itself already forgiveness; not only the announcement of the divine deed of grace, but itself the deed of divine grace. God's rich grace is bestowed "through the spoken word, by which the forgiveness of sins (the peculiar office of the Gospel) is preached to the whole world" (S.A. III, iv). The Gospel is the word "which teaches that we have a gracious God, not by our own merits but by the merit of Christ, when we believe this" (A.C. V, 3; cf., also e.g., Ap. XXVII, 11). This means not only that the Gospel teaches God's grace, but this very teaching is also a bestowal. For through the Gospel the gracious God himself speaks and acts. (Ap. XII, 40).

Again, "Gospel" does not merely mean the proclamation of a historical fact, a reminder of the merit secured by Christ in the past; rather, in the Gospel this merit is a present reality. It is true, "the work is finished and completed, Christ has acquired and won the treasure for us by his sufferings, death, and resurrection, etc." Therefore, indeed, no one "could ever know anything of Christ, or believe in him, and take him as our Lord, unless these were first offered to us and bestowed on our hearts through the preaching of the Gospel by the Holy Spirit" (L.C. II, 38). However, the Gospel does not merely teach Christ's merit; rather, Christ's merit is the treasure in the Gospel which is given by the Gospel. "In order that this treasure might not be buried but put to use and enjoyed, God has caused the Word to be published and proclaimed" (*ibid.*). The whole Gospel, the divine promise of the forgiveness of sins, and the whole Christ dare not be torn apart. Through the Gospel the sinner is made contemporaneous with the death of Jesus Christ on the cross. By the Gospel he is reconciled, even though the work of reconciliation was already finished in Christ's death on the cross. The reconciliation is not only the basis for justification laid long ago in the historical event, but "justification is reconciliation for Christ's sake" (Ap. IV, 158).[20]

But of what help to us is this great treasure if nobody can appropriate it? We are much too blind and deaf even to recognize the treasure! The Gospel not only requires us to hear, but also

---

[20] This equation does not mean, as A. Ritschl suggested, that "the doctrine of the atonement of Christ" received "the position of an auxiliary doctrine," "which has its significance in the fact that it explains the alleged exclusive dependence of justification on faith." *Rechtfertigung und Versoehnung* (3rd ed.), I, 140. Rather, justification is the event of the one-time act of reconciliation today; it is becoming contemporaneous with the atoning suffering and death of Christ through Word and sacrament in the act of reception.

gives us the ability to hear; it not only offers the treasure of the benefits of Christ, but it also places it in our hearts. For the Holy Spirit operates through the Gospel, illuminating us and changing recalcitrant men into recipients. 'Through the Word the Holy Spirit is given' (A.C. V, 2) and "faith is conceived by the Word" (Ap. IV, 73). In the Word God "has given the Holy Spirit to offer and apply to us this treasure of salvation (i.e., the suffering and death of Christ)" (L.C. II, 38). "To obtain such faith God instituted the office of the ministry, that is, provided the Gospel and the sacraments. Through these, as through means, he gives the Holy Spirit, who works faith, when and where he pleases, in those who hear the Gospel" (A.C. V, 1 f.).

The Gospel is the message of Christ's work, the assurance of forgiveness, the means by which faith is created, and, beyond this, the power which renews the old man and produces new obedience out of corruption. Very properly, therefore, Article V of the Augsburg Confession ("The Office of the Ministry"), being the first one to define the Gospel, stands between the articles concerning justification and new obedience.

Thus the sinner has in the Gospel 'a sure, firm, and eternal consolation against sin, the devil, death, and hell. Everything else is a foundation of sand and will not survive attack' (Ap. IV, 85). Not through the law, but through the word of forgiveness it takes place that 'our heart is comforted and lifted up through the divine promise which is offered us for Christ's sake' (Ap. IV, 81; cf. 44). The law terrifies; the Gospel comforts and cheers the terrified person. The law beats a man down; the Gospel raises him up and strengthens him. The law accuses and condemns; the Gospel pardons and bestows. The law punishes and kills; the Gospel makes free and alive. 'Nor would it be possible for any saint, however great and exalted he is, to remain and stand his ground against the accusations of the divine law, against the great power of the devil, against the terror of death, and, finally, against despair and the anguish of hell, if he would not grasp the divine promises of the Gospel, as a tree or branch in the great flood, in the strong, violent stream, amid the waves and billows of the anguish of death; if he did not by faith cling to the Word which proclaims grace, and thus obtain eternal life without any works, without the law, from pure grace' (Ap. IV; cf. *Bek.*, p. 224). '. . . this word: Dear man, Christ died for you!—this has revived and refreshed in trouble and has alone given peace and comfort' (Ap. IV; cf. *Bek.*, p. 164).

IV

LAW AND GOSPEL

(PART TWO)

1. Faith is not only an act of receiving, but also a renewing power in the heart, and it cannot exist together with sin. Justification is not only the imputation of the work of Christ, but also regeneration, and it cannot remain without new obedience.

We must now expound the richness of the gift which is bestowed on the sinner with the Gospel. Neither the richness of the gift, however, nor the temptation which arises from the doctrine of this treasure for the sinner will be properly understood unless in the following sections what was said in the previous chapter about justification and faith is kept in view every moment. Knowing about justification as imputation of the merit of Christ and about faith as pure acceptance, we must now continue:

'But since we speak of a faith that is not an idle thought, but such a new light, life, and power in the heart as renew the heart, mind, and spirit, namely a new light and work of the Holy Spirit, everyone knows that we are not speaking of a faith with which mortal sin is joined, such as our opponents talk about' (Ap. IV, 64).

Faith, then, is also life and a renewing power in the heart, 'a strong, powerful work of the Holy Spirit, which changes the heart' (Ap. IV, 99). " 'Faith is a vital, deliberate trust in God's grace, so certain that it would die a thousand times for it. And such confidence and knowledge of divine grace makes us joyous, mettlesome, and merry toward God and all creatures. This the Holy Spirit works by faith, and therefore without any coercion a man is willing and desirous to do good to everyone, to serve everyone, to suffer everything for the love of God and to his glory, who has been so gracious to him. It is therefore as impossible to separate works from faith as it is to separate heat and light from fire' " (S.D. IV,

12). These and many other statements teach not only that faith receives cheerfulness, courage, and good works, that it 'brings peace and joy and eternal life to hearts and consciences' (Ap. IV, 100), but also that faith cannot exist without them at all.

This thought is developed by way of many negative statements: "On the contrary we teach that those who still take pleasure in their sins and continue in a sinful life do not believe. For where there is no terror of God's wrath there is no faith" (A.C. XX, Editio princeps, *Bek.*, pp. 82 f.). "Receiving the forgiveness of sins for a heart terrified and fleeing from sin, therefore, such a faith does not remain in those who obey their lusts, nor does it exist together with mortal sin" ('Faith cannot exist in those who still live carnally in the world and follow the will of Satan and of the flesh,' Ap. IV, 143). If sin "rules," if it gains "the upper hand in such a way that sin is committed," if it "does what it wishes, the Holy Spirit and faith are not present" (S.A. III, iii, 44). "We should not imagine a kind of faith in this connection that could coexist and co-persist with a wicked intention to sin and to act contrary to one's conscience" (Ep. III, 11).

Justification, renewal, and good works are bracketed in the same way as faith, renewal, and good works. If it is true that the believing sinner receives forgiveness and that faith does not sin, then, similarly, justification is effected not only without works by grace alone, but it is also taught that justification cannot be without renewal and good works.

It was already pointed out that, according to the Apology, justification is not only forgiveness and the imputation of righteousness but also a making righteous and a regeneration. For the sinner whom God declares righteous is righteous before God in God's judgment and, therefore, in truth and reality, even though he himself and all the world see nothing of his renewal and righteousness. However, the Lutheran Confessions do not permit us to stop with this interpretation of making righteous and of regeneration. The statement *"ex injustis justos effici"* is rendered in the German text of the Apology with 'to be converted or regenerated' (Ap. IV, 72), 'to be changed from a sinner to a pious man and to be born again by the Holy Spirit' (Ap. IV, 78), 'unrighteous men become righteous, holy . . .' (Ap. IV, 117). Luther answers the question as to "how one is justified before God," by stating first that ". . . by faith (as St. Peter says) we get a new and clean heart . . ." (S.A. III, xiii, 1). With these statements about justification as making righteous and as regeneration,[1] justification, as shall be shown in detail in the following, is no longer taught merely as a reality in the judgment of God, but as a change of man, as a change of man also in man's judgment. As faith 'renews and changes the heart' (Ap. IV, 125), so justification is also regeneration, that is, renewal and transformation of the sinner.

But if justification is not without renewal, it is also not without the good works of new obedience. In ever-new formulations, justification and new obedience are joined together. Justification cannot be separated from new obedience, if we really take the statement regarding justifying faith seriously: "When through faith the Holy Spirit is given, the heart is moved to do good works" (A.C. XX, 29). The justifying word of forgiveness and the new obedience are joined together especially in the relation of cause and effect: '. . . love certainly follows faith, because those who believe receive the Holy Spirit; therefore they begin to become friendly to the law and to obey it' (Ap. XII, 82). This 'follows' which connects justification and new obedience is not merely a possible, but a necessary result. Faith, forgiveness, the reception of the Spirit are *"certainly"* followed by love, by pleasure in the law, and by the new obedience. "Certain," "necessary," "should," "must" (*certe, necesse est, debet, oportet*) are the concepts which make this connection inseparable. It is taught that "such faith should produce good fruits and good works, and that we must do all such works . . ." (A.C. VI, 1). Thus it is valid not only to say, "After we have been justified and regenerated by faith, therefore, we begin to fear and love God, to pray . . . ," but also in an *exclusive* and *necessary* 'together' it is maintained that 'it is impossible for true faith, which consoles the heart and receives the forgiveness of sins, to exist without the love of God' (Ap. IV, 141). But the love of God is not only God's love to us; in this connection it is also our love, the love of the beloved, to God.

[1] It is to the abiding credit of F. Loofs to have demonstrated that the view of justification which had become customary on the basis of the Formula of Concord does not apply in the Apology. Actually, justification in Ap. IV must be understood not only in a forensic sense, but also as regeneration, particularly as renewal of the heart and will. To be sure, from this important insight we may not deduce a devaluation of the *actus forensis* in Ap. IV, as F. Loofs then proceeds to do. Neither does it follow from the acknowledgment of this insight that we must agree with Loofs' distinction of *justum effici* and *justum reputari*, as though the latter involved the entire life, the former only the *modus conversionis*. On the contrary, both concepts, as Eichhorn has correctly shown, are frequently interchanged without following a specific principle. The subject of careful distinction in Ap. IV is *propter Christum sola fide,* not the relationship of ideal and effective *justificatio.*

2. Regeneration is the renewal of the heart toward a free decision of the will for God in joyous assent to the law of God. The regenerated man is in the law, not under the law.

Regeneration is the Holy Spirit's renewal of the dead into life in Jesus Christ. This makes regeneration a reality which, though imperceptible in human experience, must be believed on the basis of the Gospel alone. This follows at once from the doctrine of Baptism as the washing of regeneration: In Baptism we are regenerated, even though with our physical eyes we can see in ourselves only the old man. This follows too, for instance, when the doctrine of regeneration as the beginning of life eternal is proved exegetically by quoting II Cor. 5:2, "We long to put on our heavenly dwelling, so that by putting it on we may not be found naked" (Ap. IV, 352). If regeneration is thus understood as putting on the resurrection body—and the resurrection from the dead is really the central concern in Baptism—then regeneration as being present is also future. It must therefore be believed in the same manner as the justification of the sinner. This must be maintained most emphatically over against the erroneous arguments of Lutheran theologians of the past century who based their doctrine on religious experience.

But we dare not stop at this point and consider the doctrine of regeneration to be nothing more than a mere doctrine of belief in regeneration. Even though regeneration is contained in faith in the Gospel and accordingly must itself be apprehended again and again by faith alone, the gift of regeneration is extolled in terms which extend into the area of things already visible in this life—statements about the effects by means of which regeneration changes the soul of man. "For this purpose we are reborn and receive the Holy Spirit, that this new life might have new works and new impulses (i.e., new motions, inclinations), the fear and love of God, hatred of lust, etc." (Ap. IV, 349). Since faith "produces a new life in our hearts, it must also produce spiritual impulses in our hearts. What these impulses are, the prophet shows when he says (Jer. 31:33), 'I will put my law upon their hearts.' After we have been justified and regenerated by faith, therefore, we begin to fear and love God, to pray and expect help from him, to thank and praise him, and to submit to him in our afflictions. Then we also begin to love our neighbor because our hearts have spiritual and holy impulses" (Ap. IV, 125). God creates a new heart for man "that man's darkened reason becomes an enlightened one and his resisting will becomes an obedient will" (S.D. II, 60). All functions of the heart are to be mentioned here, and none is to be excluded from renewal. This renewal is "a change" which involves "activities and emotions in the intellect, will, and heart" (S.D. II, 70).

Regeneration is the liberation of the enslaved human "will." In the place of the *servum arbitrium* of the sinners, God through the Holy Spirit produces the *arbitrium liberatum* of his children. He makes the unwilling will willing. He changes the enemy of the divine Word into its friend and changes opponents of God's actions into "an instrument and means of God the Holy Spirit" (Ep. II, 18). Now man is "able" to hear the Word of God, he can not only hear it externally; he can also understand the things of the Spirit of God. Now he is "able" to "assent to [God's Word] and accept it" (S.D. II, 67), rather than by external works or open hostility only to distort and ridicule it. Now it becomes possible that man's will not only "lays hold on grace, but also co-operates with the Holy Spirit in the works that follow," and this "in all the works which the Holy Spirit performs through us" (Ep. II, 18, 17). This "co-operation" is of a peculiar kind; it is not "as though the converted man co-operates alongside the Holy Spirit, the way two horses draw a wagon together" (S.D. II, 66). This "ability" of the *arbitrium liberatum* is evidently a very peculiar ability. This ability is not mine, but God with his great ability has become Lord over me. I have this free will not by my having it, but by my believing that God has me. Nevertheless, it is I who now "even though . . . still . . . in great weakness" (S.D. II, 65) am "able" to hear and obey God. A riddle for me myself, this miracle of grace![2]

Now the regenerated man faces God's law as an altogether different person than he was before his regeneration. ". . . those who have been regenerated by faith receive the Holy Spirit and . . . their impulses agree with God's law" (*motus consentientes legi Dei,* Ap. IV, 175). They 'begin . . . to love the law and to obey it' (Ap. XII, 82). They do not fear the law in the distraction of their consciences, in despair and distress. Nor do they resist God's commandments as the old man does, but joyfully give their assent to

---

[2] We must agree with Paul Althaus: "This new Ego, as surely as it is not an abstraction but a here and now reality of the concrete man . . . , is never simply identical with the empirical man. Until death, there will always remain also "flesh," the old man. The sign of the Holy Spirit's presence in man is therefore not the unity of a completely renewed Ego which now need simply run its course as self-evidently as a process in nature, but the sign of the Spirit's presence is precisely the duality, the conflict between the Spirit and man, as far as he is flesh." *Der Geist der luth. Ethik,* p. 29.

them. Nor do they distort God's law and tear it down, as the work-righteousness of natural man does, but they establish it with their consent by faith ("when Paul says that the law is established through faith," Ap. IV, 175, quoting Rom. 3:31). However, they do not establish the law by again moving under the law from which Christ has made them free, but they establish it because God's law has become the reality of their life. "But when a person is born anew by the Spirit of God and is liberated from the law (that is, when he is free from this driver and is driven by the Spirit of Christ), he lives according to the immutable will of God as it is comprehended in the law and . . . does everything from a free and merry spirit" (S.D. VI, 17).

The regenerated man lives *in* the law, no longer *under* the law. ". . . the children of God live in the law and walk according to the law of God. In his epistles St. Paul calls it the law of Christ and the law of the mind. Thus God's children are 'not under the law, but under grace' (Rom. 7:23; 8:1, 14)" (Ep. VI, 6). The regenerated man lives in the law, for he lives in the Holy Spirit, who is fulfilling the promise: "I will put my law in their inward parts" (Jer. 31:33; cf. Ap. IV, 123). The activity of the Holy Spirit is in harmony with the law. To be sure, the mode of activity of these two is entirely different: The Holy Spirit operates in the sinner; the law stands above the sinner and in opposition to him. The effect of both too is diametrically opposite: The Holy Spirit produces good works; the law causes sin to grow in the sinner. "The law of the mind" is not a demand, but a realized demand. The law of the Spirit comprises the works and fruits of the Spirit, and his law is a gift. The law in which the believer lives is the product of the Spirit of God in the believers who have been liberated from the law through Christ. In spite of all these differences, however, God's law in the Decalogue and God's activity through the Holy Spirit have this content in common—that the Holy Spirit bestows the same gifts which the law demands. The law forbids murder, adultery, etc., and the Holy Spirit, likewise, does not produce murder and adultery, but gentleness and chastity.

To the extent of the sinner's rebirth the law loses its terror. The law as the revelation of wrath becomes God's kindly, fatherly directive. The curse is changed into an aid. The demand becomes admonition, which is exhortation and comfort at the same time. Now both the law and the doer of the law can be praised in the words of psalms 1 and 119: " 'Blessed is the man whose delight is in the law of the Lord, and on his law he meditates day and night' " (S.D. VI, 4). Having been comforted by the Gospel, the regenerated man can now know the law as a comfort, and in gratitude and joy he can teach the commandments of the law, as it is done in the Large Catechism: "You should rejoice heartily and thank God that he has chosen and fitted you to perform a task so precious and pleasing to him" (L.C. I, 117). The believers are able to "say with a joyful heart in his presence: 'Now I know that this work is well pleasing to Thee' " (L.C. I, 118). "Should not the heart leap and melt with joy when it can go to work and do what is commanded . . . ?" (L.C. I, 120). "If this truth could be impressed upon the poor people, a servant girl would dance for joy and praise and thank God; and with her careful work, for which she receives sustenance and wages, she would gain a treasure such as all who pass for the greatest saints do not have" (L.C. I, 145). Such eulogy of the law, however, is by no means restricted to one specific commandment of the Decalogue, but Luther would have all Ten Commandments "highly . . . exalted and extolled." We should "prize and value them above all other teachings as the greatest treasure God has given us" (L.C. I, 333). In what respect is God's law the greatest treasure for the regenerate? The Ten Commandments are a treasure because for him whom they can no longer condemn they become a reflection of the glory of the Gospel. The "thou shalt not" of the law has now become "thou needest sin no more," and "thou shalt" has become "thou mayest."

3. The new obedience consists in good works of obedience to the law of God. It is not a work of the law, but the fruit of the Holy Spirit.

The new obedience of the believer is the obedience of Jesus Christ which God imputes to the sinner by grace. The good works of the new obedience are the works of Christ that have been imputed by grace. New obedience, accordingly, is a verdict of God which imputes to the sinner precisely that which he did not do, nor ever was able to do. In this verdict and by this verdict the new obedience is a reality. Without this verdict, however, all good works remain sin. Like justification and regeneration, so also new obedience is a reality that must be believed. It may be believed on the basis of the Gospel, the message of the obedience, suffering, and death of the Son of God.

111

However, here too—as in the section on regeneration—we dare not stop at this point and understand the statements about the new obedience only as statements about faith in the imputed obedience of Christ. The good works of the new obedience are a reality not only in the verdict of divine imputation, but also in human action, that is, in concrete human action. The good works are works of concrete obedience, just as God's law establishes concrete demands. "New obedience" never means *in abstracto* to fear and to love God, but *in concreto* love of divine worship, use of the Word of God, zeal in prayer, hatred of blasphemy, etc. The First Commandment would lose its significance if it were isolated from the concrete precepts of the first table. New obedience, moreover, does not refer *in abstracto* to the commandments of the first table, but it becomes a reality in that now the parents are respected, marriage is kept pure, and lies and machinations are put away, etc. God is feared and loved only in concrete obedience to his concrete commandments. God is loved only in love to the neighbor, as the second table concretely defines that love.

Thus regeneration means that man can now do works which formerly were impossible for him. He is now free from obligations which his own decision never mastered. He is now master of vices which formerly conquered him again and again. "For Christ conquered the devil and gave us his promise and the Holy Spirit, so that with the help of God we, too, might conquer" (Ap. IV, 139). And the new obedience of the regenerated is obedience to the same law, the same Ten Commandments, through which God judges and punishes the sinner. Therewith the doctrine of the new obedience too enters the area of what is visible to the human eye in the life of the individual and of the congregation. New obedience is no longer taught merely as a reality that is to be believed, when in concrete reference to the Ten Commandments it is stated that 'one must keep the law, and every believer begins to keep it, and he increases the longer the more in the love and fear of God, and this is what it means to keep God's law. And when we speak of keeping the law and of good works, we include both, the good heart inside, and the works outside' (Ap. IV, 136). Good works are no longer only something demanded, nor only something imputed, but they become a reality as deeds of the believers themselves.

Even though the new obedience is obedience to God's law, the good works are not deeds of the law but fruits of the Spirit; they are not products of the Ten Commandments, but of the Gospel.

The frequently used *debet, oportet, necesse,* and *certe,* by which justifying faith and good works are joined, are to be understood in a twofold sense. "Good works must follow faith" can mean, "Good works will surely and always spring from faith," or, secondly, "Good works should and must be done by the believer." The one means, "Good works are God's gift"; the other, "Good works are God's demand." When the Confessions testify to the reality of the new obedience, they mean to say above all that good works are the fruits proceeding from justifying faith and regeneration. They are man's deeds, and yet they are not man's achievements. For man here does what the Holy Spirit does in him. It is characteristic of the new obedience that "without any coercion a man is willing and desirous to do good to everyone, to serve everyone, to suffer everything for the love of God and to his glory, who has been so gracious to him" (S.D. IV, 12). The good works of the regenerate are done "from a free and merry spirit. These works are, strictly speaking, not works of the law, but works and fruits of the Spirit" (S.D. VI, 17).

By his obedience the believer responds not to a "thou shalt" or "thou must," but to a "thou mayest." His works are not extorted by demands but are given by grace. They are not a response to the law but to the Gospel; that is, they are the result and gift of the Gospel. For we never attain to obedience by staring at the law, but only by looking to and receiving the merit of Jesus Christ. Only in Christ is "thou shalt" changed into "thou mayest," and only through him does what cannot be kept and what is coerced become a glad assent and deed.

4. Like justification, so also regeneration and new obedience are gifts of God's grace.

Justification and sanctification are gifts of God, not the work of men. As man's own work both justification and sanctification would, after all, be the self-righteousness of civil uprightness, and hence blasphemy. Both are God's gifts, given for Christ's sake through the Word of the Gospel. Both are the work of the Holy Spirit through Word and sacrament. Like freedom from the law, so also the new obedience to God's law is God's grace.

If justification, regeneration, and new obedience are produced by the Holy Spirit, then light is shed on the peculiar temporal concepts by means of which the statements of the doctrine of justification and of sanctification are co-ordinated, especially the concepts of succession: Good works must follow faith, etc. To understand these numerous statements we must start with the definitions which indicate the relationship of faith and Spirit, as well as regeneration and Spirit—definitions which are strikingly reversible.

On the one hand, it is taught repeatedly and very distinctly that faith is not a human thought and a human work, but the work of the Holy Spirit in man who himself is not able to believe.[3] But this statement is contrasted with another which declares that "we receive the forgiveness of sins and the Holy Spirit by faith alone" (Ap. IV, 86). ". . . faith brings the Holy Spirit and produces a new life in our hearts" (Ap. IV, 125). Faith is at the same time the work of the Holy Spirit and it receives the Holy Spirit. The Holy Spirit leads to faith, and faith leads to the Holy Spirit. Both statements belong so closely together that in the Latin and the German texts they are used interchangeably and can be bracketed together: Faith is *"res accipiens spiritum sanctum et justificans nos"* [a thing that *receives* the Holy Spirit and justifies us], *"ein stark kraeftig Werk des Heiligen Geistes, das die Herzen veraendert"* [a strong powerful *work* of the Holy Spirit which changes hearts] (Ap. IV, 99).

Expressions concerning Spirit and regeneration likewise demonstrate that the definitions indicating relationships can be interchanged. On the one hand, it is true that the Holy Spirit 'creates new light and eternal life, and eternal righteousness in us' (Ap. IV, 132). On the other hand, 'those who have been regenerated . . . receive the Holy Spirit' (Ap. IV, 175; cf. XII, 82). Here too it is correct to say that regeneration is the product of the Holy Spirit, and the regenerated man receives the Holy Spirit. The regenerated man comes from renewal and goes into renewal. Here too both ideas are placed side by side in the most intimate connection: The Latin text, *"renati accipimus spiritum sanctum"* [having been regenerated, we receive the Holy Spirit], is rendered in German: ". . . *wir neu geboren werden durch den Heiligen Geist"* [we are regenerated by the Holy Spirit] (Ap. IV, 126).

These two-sided definitions of relationship are maintained and no attempt is made to reduce the one logically to the other. The Holy Spirit is confessed as the cause and the goal of reception, but one statement is not suppressed because of the other, nor subordinated to it. In this way the element of time—which is also contained in the concepts of operation and result—is eliminated,

[3] Cf. pp. 89 f., 102, 104.

not only with respect to the relationship of the Holy Spirit and faith, or of the Holy Spirit and regeneration, but also logically and necessarily with respect to the relationship of faith and regeneration, and, beyond this, of justification and sanctification generally. As a result of the above-mentioned statements about the Holy Spirit as cause and goal of faith and regeneration, the development of a series which connects faith and works by means of temporal concepts of cause and effect has been deprived of its temporal cogency. Such assertions prove to be primarily a serial development of theological explication, but not a development of the Christian life. The succession is essentially the succession of pedagogical unfolding. The Formula of Concord[4] too is still aware of this, for it teaches that "good works do not precede faith, nor is sanctification prior to justification. First the Holy Spirit kindles faith in us in conversion through the hearing of the Gospel. Faith apprehends the grace of God in Christ whereby the person is justified. After the person is justified, the Holy Spirit next renews and sanctifies him, and from this renewal and sanctification the fruits of good works will follow." For the rejection of the opinion is immediately added that "true faith could coexist and survive for a while side by side with a wicked intention." Rather, faith "is at no time ever alone," without works (S.D. III, 41). Accordingly, succession is bracketed by contemporaneity.

This bracketing of the temporal concepts also explains the great unconcern with which the Apology and the Smalcald Articles make their statements about justification as regeneration, when, e.g., in the well-known definition of Ap. IV, 72, justification is defined in the first place as a making righteous and in the second place as a pronouncing righteous.[5] Similarly Luther defines justification by

[4] To be sure, history-of-dogma investigation would establish that in the Formula of Concord there are already the germs of the later doctrine of the *ordo salutis,* in which the temporal aspect of the various steps becomes increasingly more significant. It must not be overlooked, however, that these suggestions of a temporal serial development in the Formula of Concord are always transcended at the decisive point, and that thus the Formula of Concord does remain an exposition of the Augsburg Confession in this matter.

[5] The much controverted *"quia"* at this place (*Bek.,* p. 174, l. 37) also loses its force with regard to its causal significance, since the statements concerning justification evince no interest in a temporal succession. Therefore, this sentence does not permit us to deduce that regeneration is the basis for justification, that is to say, that justification is an analytical judgment. Rather, *"quia"* designates here only two meanings of the one justifying act of God as belonging inseparably together. This is true already in the retention of the punctuation as found in the Latin text. The possibility of such a misunderstanding is entirely excluded by the German text and the thought-provoking suggestions of Loofs, O. Ritschl, and Kunze, to read lines 37 to 44 of the Latin text as one sentence, with lines 41 ff. as apodosis. In this case the clause *"significat et . . . scriptura"* would be parenthetical. Cf. *Bek.,* p. 174, n. 2.

saying "that by faith . . . we get a new and clean heart and that God will and does account us altogether righteous and holy for the sake of Christ, our mediator" (S.A. III, xiii, 1). But all this does not mean that the renewal is the presupposition for God's pronouncing us righteous. This would destroy the doctrine of justification. The Confessions can speak as they do because they are not interested in the temporal succession and because they do not understand the "and" (S.A.) temporally. They are, furthermore, not interested in a distinction between the "beginning" and the "state" of justification,[6] but every man should and may repent at any time, i.e., he may regret his sins and be comforted by forgiveness; and this again means receiving justification and the Spirit of renewal and of new obedience. It is *one* act of grace, whereby God forgives and renews, justifies and sanctifies. But human language can extol this one act of God in no other way than in a succession of concepts. If in this succession faith is usually mentioned first and then renewal and then good works, but not vice versa, this signifies that our love has its source in God's love, but not that God's love has its source in our love. The love of God is the reality of the sending and the suffering of his Son. This deed precedes faith as well as the works of faith in which the Christian always lives simultaneously.

5. In presenting the wealth of the effects of divine grace in regeneration and new obedience, the status of man is again called into question.

If we hold fast to what was said in the preceding chapter about justification and faith, the doctrine of regeneration and of the new obedience can actually become a trial for faith. This may be demonstrated by following once more the trend of thought presented in theses 1 through 3.

[6] Thus in the doctrine of justification in the Apology we cannot consistently refer "justum effici" to the modus conversionis and "justum reputari" to the entire earthly life (Loofs, Die Bedeutung der Rechtfertigungslehre der Apologie, pp. 629 ff.), and distinguish them as the initial becoming righteous and the permanent state of being righteous, as actus and as status (J. Kunze, Die Rechtfertigungslehre in der Apologie, pp. 375 ff.), as initium justificationis and as the state of being pleasing to God on the part of the regenerate. O. Ritschl, Der doppelte Rechtfertigungsbegriff in der Apologie, pp. 331 ff. It is also impossible to deduce a temporal serial development and succession of steps in the Spirit's work from S. C. II, 6: ". . . just as he calls, gathers, enlightens, and sanctifies the whole Christian church on earth and keeps it with Jesus . . ." We do not have here an ordo salutis in the sense of the later Lutheran dogmatics. Cf. J. Meyer, Hist. Kommentar, pp. 361 ff.

The first thesis now raises the questions: If faith is both life and power in the heart, both joy and bold confidence, is any further salvation available for one who is despondent and downcast, for one who lies prostrate in impotence? If faith cannot coexist with sin, with sinful desires, or with the intention to sin, whose faith is then still faith? Who can discover in himself such a hostility to sin that he can claim to have faith? If justification is also the transformation of the sinner, who can still be sure of his justification? Who does not see himself ever again as the old man who still has not at all become pious and holy? If justification cannot remain without love toward God and man, what will become of me with my lovelessness which is active and assertive even after I have been justified? Does not this "must"—this insistence on the necessity of the act of faith—nullify justifying faith? Is anybody at all a believer, if he must also prove himself obedient?

We proceed to thesis 2. If in regeneration the enslaved will becomes a liberated will, this means that the liberated will is "able" not only to accept grace, but also to reject grace. "All who stubbornly and perseveringly resist the Holy Spirit's activities and impulses, which take place through the Word, do not receive the Holy Spirit but grieve and lose him" (S.D. II, 83). Is not the result of this my condemnation, if the continued presence of the Holy Spirit—and therewith my remaining in salvation, my blessedness—depends on my decision, which is "able" to grieve and expel the Holy Spirit, though it should not do this? Is not the Holy Spirit always and constantly the unconditional glorious victor over the one who must necessarily decide against him?

Finally, the statements of thesis 3 suggest looking on good works as an "indication of salvation" (S.D. IV, 38) and seeing in them "testimonies" of the presence of the Holy Spirit (Ep. IV, 15). To be sure, this thought is expressed in the Formula of Concord only in passing and is not further developed systematically; rather, any significance of works for salvation and the knowledge of salvation is expressly rejected in ever-new statements. Yet is it not rather obvious and is it not, after all, the thought expressed here that the state of sanctification which becomes manifest is a sign of justification? After all, the Apology does draw this inference from the statement that "good works must necessarily follow" justification: "Baptism and the Lord's Supper, for example, are signs that constantly admonish, cheer, and confirm terrified minds to believe more firmly. Those who fail to do good do not arouse themselves to

117

believe but despise these promises. But the faithful embrace them and are glad to have signs and testimonies of this great promise. Hence they exercise themselves in these signs and testimonies" (Ap. IV, 276). Here the attack on our faith has reached its climax. How is that sinner to be saved who can find in himself only the absence of such "signs and testimonies"? Does not this doctrine of regeneration and of the new obedience rise up against and devour the word of justification by faith? Is not the Gospel refuted by this doctrine?

All of these questions, which are to be put particularly to the believers and the regenerate and by no means to heathen only, may be summarized thus: ". . . who loves or fears God enough? Who endures patiently enough the afflictions that God sends? Who does not often wonder whether history is governed by God's counsels or by chance? Who does not often doubt whether God hears him? Who does not often complain because the wicked have better luck than the devout . . . ?" 'Again, who lives up to the requirements of his calling? Who is not angry with God in trials, when God hides himself? Who loves his neighbor as himself? Who is free from all sorts of evil lusts?' (Ap. IV, 167). There is only one answer to all of these questions—no one!

This long list of questions which we have drawn from the doctrine of regeneration and the new obedience is introduced in the Apology in this way: "The *law* always accuses us." However, these questions are put to man not only by God's law, but also by the doctrine of regeneration and the new obedience, which, of course, also includes God's law. The doctrine of the gifts of grace in regeneration and new obedience thus not only offers a promise, but also confronts man with questions. The more something is taught as being a gift, the more also God's law is established, if the gift is to become *manifest* in our lives. The message of that gift of sanctification which is to become apparent in our human lives, namely, in our hearts, in our thoughts, in our new emotions, in a new manner of life—this message is at the same time a preaching of the law. For regeneration means renewal of the will for a free assent to God's *law,* and the new obedience consists of deeds in agreement with the Ten Commandments. Even if the *"debet"* and *"oportet"* is taught in the sense that surely obedience *will* grow out of faith, the "thou must" and "thou shalt" of the Ten Commandments is nevertheless thereby also prescribed for all who lack this obedience. The law is taught again, and not primarily by means of the explicit third use of the law, but already by means of the doctrine of the gracious gifts of regeneration and of the new obedience which transforms man.

6. Since the regenerated man and his new obedience in this age remain imperfect, the regenerated man is not only in the law, but also under the law. There, however, he sees all of his works as sin.

When the righteousness of faith is thus called into question the Confessions first reply by stating this fact: The regenerated man is still imperfect and his obedience is still impure.

Positively, regeneration means that in the regenerate 'the new, yes, the *eternal life* has begun'; but this implies, negatively, that the new life has *only begun.* 'There still remains a remnant of sin and evil lust, and the law still finds many things of which to accuse us' (Ap. IV, 161). Nothing more can be said than that "holiness has begun and is growing daily," that we are "only halfway pure and holy." This is true until the day when "our flesh will be put to death, will be buried with all its uncleanness, and will come forth gloriously and arise to complete and perfect holiness in a new eternal life" (L.C. II, 57 f.). Accordingly, the Formula of Concord too expressly denies a complete renewal of corrupt man before the resurrection and understands Rom. 7:14 ff. and Gal. 5:17 as statements of Scripture concerning the regenerated man (S.D. VI, 8; cf. Ep. IV, 13; S.D. II, 17). The Formula of Concord knows not only of a beginning and a growth in the new life, but also about the ups and downs of fluctuations. "But since in this life we have received only the first fruits of the Spirit, and regeneration is not as yet perfect but has only been begun in us, the conflict and warfare of the flesh against the Spirit continues also in the elect and truly reborn. Again, there is not only a great difference between Christians, one being weak and the other strong in the Spirit, but even the individual Christian in his own life discovers that at one moment he is joyful in the Spirit and at another moment fearful and terrified, at one time ardent in love, strong in faith and in hope, and at another time cold and weak" (S.D. II, 68).

Accordingly, in the statements about regeneration various quantitative terms are used: begin and grow, imperfect and perfect, weak and strong, half and half, more and less. Not only the regenerated person, but even regeneration itself can be described as "not complete." Yes, in this connection quantitative statements are made even about faith: as a living, joyful, confident thing it can "grow and be strengthened" (Ap. IV, 142, 350), "grow and increase" (Ap. IV, 189), but it can also decrease and disintegrate. And these qualifications and negations are as a rule found immediately after statements in which the new life, the liberation of the enslaved will, and all the transforming effects of regeneration are extolled.

Similarly, the new obedience of the regenerated man is impure. After all, only individual good works are ever done, whereas God's law demands complete obedience. Even 'our best works, even after the grace of the Gospel has been received . . . , are still weak and not at all pure. For sin and Adam's fall are not such a trifling matter as reason thinks or imagines; it exceeds all human reason and thought what a horrible wrath of God has been handed on to us by that disobedience' (Ap. IV, 163 f.). Hence, it is quite generally true that "in this life we cannot satisfy the law (not even "Christians and saints"), because our unspiritual nature continually brings forth evil desires, though the Spirit in us resists them" (Ap. IV, 146). Thus the new obedience is described in the same quantitative terms as regeneration. The new obedience too begins and grows, is manifested *magis magisque,* "more and more" (Ap. IV, 124, 136), but also more or less.

Because the renewal of the old man remains imperfect till the resurrection, and the activity of the renewed man remains impure, the regenerate man lives not only *in* God's law, but also *under* God's law. To the extent that sinners are reborn, they live in the law. To the extent that the regenerate are still sinners, however, they remain together with all other sinners under the law which accuses and judges them, which terrifies them and reveals God's wrath to them.[7]

For the regenerate, living *in the law of the Spirit,* God's law represents no threat and no coercion, no occasion for fear, no word of wrath, but it is the basis for joy and gratitude. For him the law is a "certain rule and norm for achieving a godly life and behavior in accord with God's eternal and immutable will" (S.D. VI, 3), and "a mirror in which the will of God and what is pleasing to him are correctly portrayed" (S.D. VI, 4). This mirror, this rule and standard for the regenerate, is a help, a light on his way. God's kindness shows the regenerate through the law the way of the Spirit

---

[7] For the following, cf. especially Art. V of the Formula of Concord, in which the antinomistic controversy was settled by rejecting the doctrine of Agricola. See the literature in *Bek.,* p. 951, n. 1.

and admonishes them "to serve God not according to their own notions" (S.D. VI, 3). Thus God's law is a means of preserving the regenerate from falling into religious fanaticism. In this sense we should probably understand Luther's statement that "no prophet, whether Elijah or Elisha, received the Spirit without the Ten Commandments" (S.A. III, viii, 11).

At the same time the regenerate continue to be *under God's law and judgment.* "For the old Adam, like an unmanageable and recalcitrant donkey, is still a part of them and must be coerced into the obedience of Christ, not only with the instruction, admonition, urging and threatening of the law, but frequently also with the club of punishments and miseries" (S.D. VI, 24). But if the law forces, beats, punishes, and troubles the regenerate like the old sinner who is "lazy, negligent, and recalcitrant" because of the flesh (S.D. VI, 12), then the law is over him as the revelation of the divine wrath and divine enmity against all sin. The office of the law remains the office of wrath over the Christian as sinner and brings him no help but rather death. Not *before* the Christian's life, but *over* his life Luther's word about the law is valid: "This, then, is the thunderbolt by means of which God with one blow destroys both open sinners and false saints. He allows no one to justify himself. He drives all together into terror and despair. This is the hammer of which Jeremiah speaks, 'Is not my word like a hammer which breaks the rock in pieces?' (Jer. 23:29). This is not *activa contritio* (artificial remorse), but *passiva contritio* (true sorrow of the heart, suffering, and pain of death)" (S.A. III, iii, 2). In his repentance the regenerate man realizes anew every day that he is under God's law, i.e., under God's terrible judgment and tangible wrath.

So, in the first place, the law produces "external discipline and decency against dissolute and disobedient people" (S.D. VI, 1). Secondly, the law as "a schoolmaster unto Christ" drives people to a knowledge of sin and to despair. But for those who by faith have been justified and regenerated, the law is a help and a comfort in so far as they walk in the Spirit, but a schoolmaster and a club in so far as they are still sinners. In this sense the Formula of Concord distinguishes a threefold use of the law (Ep. VI, 1).[8]

[8] The Confessions prior to the Formula of Concord do not contain a precise distinction of the three *usus* of the law. Actually there was no primary dogmatic interest in distinguishing them. Only *what* must be preached as law, and that it is to be preached to *every* man is decisive. The three *usus* will find their application as a matter of course in the event of the correct preaching of the law. This follows also from an analysis of the Catechisms. The ar-

A review of all statements about the law in Chapters 3 and 4 makes clear that no man, but God alone is Lord over the three-fold use of the law. Neither the person who hears the preaching of the law nor the preacher of the law himself can control in what use and to what benefit the law operates in him and through him. The church has the sole commission to preach God's holy law to everybody. But the church is not to ask what happens as a result and cannot predetermine the result of this preaching. The church is not permitted to demand an isolated, external, civil righteous-ness which ignores or openly denies the triune God. Furthermore, the church is not permitted to drive men to despair by a preaching that isolates the law. The church must always preach the law as the one unchangeable will of the triune God, but together with the Gospel. It is God who uses the law in a threefold manner, either leaving and confirming a man in the delusion of civil righteousness, or leading others to fear and despair, or, in the case of the believers, terrifying and gladdening them, bludgeoning or gently leading them. But the latter is accomplished through the operation of the Gospel, through the Holy Spirit.

Because of the imperfection of the regenerated man and of his new obedience *all* of his works are indeed to be acknowledged as sin. No partial obedience can stand before the law of God. Partial obedience is total disobedience. Transgression of individual com-mandments of God is transgression of the whole law of God. Thus Christians in daily repentance realize "that we are all utterly lost, that from head to foot there is no good in us. . . . Repentance . . . lumps everything together and says, 'We are wholly and altogether sinful.' . . . nothing is left that we might imagine to be good enough to pay for our sin. One thing is sure: We cannot pin our hope on anything that we are, think, say, or do" (S.A. III, iii, 35 f.). "In the case of a Christian such repentance continues until death" (S.A.

rangement of the first two chief parts, which in Luther's Catechisms are different from most catechisms before his time (J. Meyer, *Hist. Kommentar,* pp. 82 ff.), must indeed be evaluated as a conscious dogmatic decision: The law (I) is to be a schoolmaster to drive men to Christ (II). But the exposition in the Large Catechism makes clear that the Ten Commandments in the first chief part are not only schoolmasters but also a comfort and an occasion for doxology, as well as a demand for external civil discipline. Since in the Catechisms the chief parts stand side by side as independent units, without explicit dogmatic integration, in spite of the dogmatic significance of the arrangement—law first and faith second—the task remains to interpret the law for the *believer* and thus also to interpret the law *after* the Credo. From the first word on, the Catechism is intended for the instruction of the baptized. Moreover, even the Catechism itself speaks of the law not only before, but also after the Credo. S. C. V, 20.

III, iii, 40),[9] for God's law remains God's immutable, holy will in view of which our sin is revealed daily anew and more exclusively. Contrition does not grow smaller, but greater. In daily contrition the Christian recognizes himself more and more as a total sinner who stands under God's wrath and is in need of forgiveness. Referring to Augustine, the Apology therefore teaches that 'even the good works which the Holy Spirit creates in us please God in no other way than in that we believe that for Christ's sake we are acceptable to God, and that the works are not in themselves God-pleasing' (Ap. IV, 172). Forgiveness which must be appropriated anew every day determines the quality of the works of the regenerate and of the unregenerate man.

Thus our investigation has returned to the point from which it started in Chapter 3 in the doctrine of the law.

At the end of Chapter 3 it might have appeared that the relationship between law and Gospel had been clarified by a logical, linear trend of thought leading from the law and God's wrath by way of Christ's deed to the Gospel. Now, however, much seems again confused and even inextricable that before had seemed already clarified. Thus, for example, the repeal of the law by the Gospel, and the establishment of the law by the Gospel are placed in antithesis. In antithesis are the doctrine of the necessary connection between faith and the new obedience, and the attack which this doctrine launches against the harassed believer and presses on him anew each day. Nevertheless, no study of the Lutheran Confessions, after going the way that leads from the law to the Gospel, may omit following the additional path which begins with the unfolding of the Gospel and, by way of regeneration and the new obedience, again leads back to the law and the revelation of God's wrath. Whoever restricts himself to the first way, as so often happens, falsifies Lutheran doctrine no less than the person who grants validity to only the second way and would like to understand justification on the basis of man's renewal. Only when both ways—the way from the law to the Gospel (Chap. 3, 1-10) and the way from the Gospel to the law (Chap. 4, 1-6)—have been traversed to the end do the questions with which all theology is confronted by the Word of God become clear. Only then can we truly see the problem that must be called the theme of the entire

[9] For the doctrine of repentance see below, pp. 141 ff.

Lutheran theology—the distinction between law and Gospel. This distinction is the guarantee of the *gloria Christi*.

It is to this theme that we now address ourselves when we undertake to specify the dialectical relationship—a dialectic men can never dissolve—which exists between justifying faith and regeneration on the one hand (thesis 7) and between justifying faith and the new obedience on the other (thesis 8). We shall endeavor to clarify the matter by following a parallel line of thought in the treatment of both theses.

7. Justification does not occur because of regeneration.

a) Justification and regeneration must not be torn apart. Justification is forgiveness and regeneration, a declaring righteous and a making righteous. Faith is trusting reception and renewal in the heart; it is joy, peace, etc. (cf. theses 1 and 2).

b) Justification and regeneration must be distinguished as clearly as possible. The clarification of this distinction is the contribution of Article III of the Formula of Concord ("The Righteousness of Faith Before God"), which treats the problem of Osiander and expressly urges care so that "the renewal which follows justification by faith will not be confused with justification and so that in their strict senses the two will be differentiated from one another" (S.D. III, 18). The distinction follows on the one hand from a clarification of the term "regeneration." It is used, "in the first place, to include both the forgiveness of sins solely for Christ's sake and the subsequent renewal which the Holy Spirit works in those who are justified by faith. But this word is also used in the limited sense of the forgiveness of sins and our adoption as God's children" (S.D. III, 19). Now, however, regeneration is to be understood specifically as the renewal and transformation of the sinner.[10] On the other hand, however, the distinction also follows from the definition of the concept "justification." In the Apology justification means forgiveness of sins and regeneration. Now this term is defined as follows: "The word 'justify' here means to declare righteous and free from sins and from the eternal punishment of these sins" (S.D. III, 17). By faith in the righteousness of Christ

---

[10] This very limited and special definition alone is the presupposition for the following peculiar antithesis of justification and regeneration. It must be remembered that here the Formula of Concord did not incorporate the full content of the Lutheran idea of regeneration. Cf. pp. 94 f., 108 ff.; also the doctrine of Baptism, pp. 148 ff., 181 ff.

the sinner is altogether righteous. All of his sins are covered because of Christ's obedience. Regarding renewal, however, it must be said that when "we teach that through the Holy Spirit's work we are reborn and justified, we do not mean that after regeneration no unrighteousness in essence and life adheres to those who have been justified and regenerated" (S.D. III, 22). As true as it is that the believing sinner by God's verdict of justification "is absolved and declared utterly free from all his sins" (S.D. III, 9), it is equally true of the same wholly righteous man that "the inchoate renewal remains imperfect in this life and . . . sin still dwells in the flesh even in the case of the regenerated" (S.D. III, 23). In his renewal man is still imperfect; in his justification he is perfect. Regeneration as the renewal and transformation of the old man means that the battle between flesh and spirit is still being waged. Justification, however, declares that this battle is already over, for the righteousness of the risen Lord is ours. "Similarly, although renewal and sanctification are a blessing of Christ, the mediator, and a work of the Holy Spirit, it does not belong in the article or matter of justification before God" (S.D. III, 28).

c) Justification does not occur because of regeneration. The state of regeneration—the change in the sinner which becomes manifest —does not enter into consideration at all in justification and it has no influence on God's acquitting word of forgiveness. Like the Apology, the Formula of Concord condemns the statement that "faith saves because by faith there is begun in us the renewal which consists in love toward God and our fellowman" (Ep. III, 19). Going beyond this, the following sentence is also condemned: "That faith indeed has the most prominent role in justification, but that also renewal and love belong to our righteousness before God, not indeed as if it were the primary cause of our righteousness, but that nevertheless our righteousness before God is incomplete and imperfect without such love and renewal" (Ep. III, 20). This is the most penetrating distinction between justifying faith and regeneration. The transforming effects of regeneration dare neither be the comfort and basis of justifying faith—Christ's deed alone is that comfort—nor need the deficiencies and imperfections in the regenerated persons indicate the end of justifying faith. On the contrary, every confusion of justification and renewal snatches away the comfort of forgiveness and denies that the Christian, who daily sees nothing but sin in himself, is loved and accepted by God.

d) In spite of these distinctions both justification and renewal must be taught. The fact that renewal is not the ground of justification can never mean permission to be silent about renewal as a gift and a demand of God. Even though the doctrine of renewal and a look at its fruits have no place in justifying faith, nevertheless regeneration, like justification, must be taught with all emphasis as the work of God and must be taken seriously. Thus, now as before, justification and regeneration are acknowledged as the one deed of divine grace. But we human beings cannot bear witness to this one deed in any other way than by distinguishing two "articles." The distinction dare not be understood "as though justification and sanctification are separated from each other in such a way as though on occasion a genuine faith could coexist and survive for a while side by side with a wicked intention" (S.D. III, 41). While the Formula of Concord distinguishes both, it does not tear them apart, but teaches at the same time that justifying faith "is never alone, but is always accompanied by love and hope" (Ep. III, 11; cf. 17). To those who are justified for Christ's sake, "there is given the Holy Spirit, who renews and sanctifies them and creates within them love toward God and their fellowman" (S.D. III, 23; cf. 26, 36, 41).[11]

8. Justification does not occur because of the new obedience.

a) Justification and new obedience must not be torn apart. Good works follow faith "surely" and "necessarily"; they "shall" and "must" follow faith (cf. theses 1 and 3). Good works must "certainly and indubitably follow genuine faith," "like fruits of a good tree" (Ep. IV, 6).

b) Justification and new obedience are to be distinguished as clearly as possible. The clarification of this distinction was the particular task of Article IV of the Formula of Concord ("Good Works"); it is undertaken in debating the antithetical propositions of the controversy between Major, Menius, and Amsdorf: "Good works are necessary for salvation"; "good works are detrimental to

[11] This diastasis and synthesis of justification and regeneration is apparent already in the Apology. Thus Frank ("Rechtfertigung und Wiedergeburt," *Neue kirchl. Zeitschr.* [1892], p. 871) correctly explains the statement *"justificatio est regeneratio"* in this way: "Justification is the acquittal from our sins for Christ's sake, indeed through faith and not without faith; but not on account of faith, as though faith were a human work and merit; not without immediate renewal, but not because of it, and never in the sense that there could be justification without simultaneous renewal." It is, nevertheless, true that the unity of justification and regeneration appears more strongly in Ap. IV than the Formula of Concord is willing to recognize.

salvation." In trying to arrive at a distinction, the Formula of Concord starts by sharpening the term "necessary." On the one hand, good works are necessary because "it is God's will, ordinance, and command that believers walk in good works" (S.D. IV, 7). "Likewise, Holy Scripture itself uses words like 'necessity,' 'necessary,' 'needful,' 'should,' and 'must' to indicate what we are bound to do because of God's ordinance, commandment, and will" (S.D. IV, 14), because of "the order of God's immutable will" (S.D. IV, 16), hence because of the commandments of the divine law. "Necessary" does not mean, however, that God takes pleasure in works of coercion, which remain "specious works" of external obedience. "Necessary" is the free, voluntary obedience of the children of God. On the other hand, good works are not necessary for salvation. For the work of Jesus Christ alone is the basis of justification. Accordingly, justification and new obedience must be distinguished as clearly as possible. ". . . the reckoned righteousness of faith" and "the inchoate righteousness of the new obedience" must "not be confused with one another or introduced simultaneously into the article of justification by faith before God" (S.D. III, 32). Although the believers "possess the beginning of renewal, sanctification, love, virtues, and good works, these should and must not be drawn to or mingled into the article of justification before God, in order to preserve the glory due to Christ, the redeemer" (S.D. III, 35). This is true because the new obedience of the believers is imperfect, while Christ's obedience is perfect. With regard to his good works the regenerate person remains a sinner; with regard to his faith, however, he is completely righteous because the obedience of Christ is his.

c) Justification does not occur because of new obedience. It occurs neither because of the works of the law done by natural man, nor because of the good works of the regenerate man. Nor are the fruits of the Holy Spirit the basis of justification. For with Christ's work everything is finished for us. As soon as works are "drawn into and mingled with the article of justification and salvation," as soon as men direct the eyes of the believers to the fruits of the Spirit instead of the work of Christ alone as the ground of faith, they "deprive tempted and troubled consciences of the consolation of the Gospel, give occasion for doubt, are dangerous in many ways, confirm presumptuous trust in one's own righteousness and confidence in one's own good works" (S.D. IV, 22 f.). If even in the least the gift of new obedience is drawn into the doctrine of justification, this doctrine again becomes law, and the threefold result of the law becomes evident—an Epicurean life, work-righteousness, and despair. The Confessions, therefore, emphatically condemn the statements that "good works are necessary to salvation; likewise, that no one has ever been saved without good works; likewise, that it is impossible to be saved without good works" (Ep. IV, 16). Justification remains a reality even for the one who believes again and again, and who again and again fails to see any fruits of the Spirit in himself. Whoever denies this will by his denial make his good works injurious to salvation. "If anyone draws good works into the article of justification and rests his righteousness or his assurance of salvation on good works in order to merit the grace of God and to be saved thereby, it is not we, but Paul himself who declares no less than three times in Phil. 3:7 ff. that good works not only are useless and an impediment to such a person but are actually harmful" (S.D. IV, 37).

d) Nevertheless the good works of the new obedience are demanded by God. The fact that justification is based exclusively on the work of Christ by no means implies the permission to remain silent about the necessity of good works. Rather, the delusion is expressly condemned "which some dream up that it is impossible to lose faith and the gift of righteousness and salvation once it has been received, through any sin, even a wanton and deliberate one" (S.D. IV, 31), "as if there could simultaneously be in a single heart both a right faith and a wicked intention . . ." (S.D. IV, 15). Thus justification and sanctification are not torn apart, but they are distinguished. The one justifying and sanctifying act of God cannot be witnessed in this world of sin and death except in the distinction of two articles of doctrine. Although reference to good works has no place in the context of justifying faith, good works are very definitely to be inculcated as God's deed and demand. But why still do good works, if we are saved without them? (Because God demands them!)[12]

[12] This line of thought employed by the Formula of Concord says nothing new in the decisive aspect over against the Augsburg Confession: "It is also taught among us that such faith should produce good fruits and good works and that we must do all such good works as God has commanded, but we should do them for God's sake and not place our trust in them as if thereby to merit favor before God. For we receive forgiveness of sin and righteousness through faith in Christ, as Christ himself says, 'So you also, when you have done all that is commanded you, say, We are unworthy servants.'" A. C. VI, 1 f.; cf. Ap. IV, 111 f.

9. Although in the law Gospel too is revealed—and in the Gospel, law—law and Gospel must nevertheless be distinguished.

Accordingly, man is addressed simultaneously by two different proclamations of God, the law and the Gospel, the commandment of obedience and the gracious word of justification. By the one God demands everything; by the other he gives everything. By the one God demands works and wants us to offer ourselves to him; by the other he requires faith, that is, he bestows benefits which we need merely allow to come to us, yes, he gives himself. The Gospel proclaims that Christ has accomplished everything, his good work is definitive. The law demands, "You must do good works!" The Gospel says, "Good works are not necessary before God, since Christ's work has rendered satisfaction!" The law says, "Good works are necessary, for God demands them!" "Now you see that the Creed is a very different teaching from the Ten Commandments. The latter teach us what we ought to do; the Creed tells what God does for us and gives to us. The Ten Commandments, moreover, are inscribed in the hearts of all men. No human wisdom can comprehend the Creed; it must be taught by the Holy Spirit alone. Therefore the Ten Commandments do not by themselves make us Christians, for God's wrath and displeasure still remain on us because we cannot fulfill his demands. But the Creed brings pure grace and makes us upright and pleasing to God" (L.C. II, 67 f.; cf. in the Apology the frequent contrasting of *"fides,"* or *"promissio,"* and *"lex,"* e.g., Ap. IV, 44, 49, 79, 106). Hence, law and Gospel in God's Word are to be distinguished as a twofold proclamation of God to the sinner. This distinction is elementary in the real sense of the term: "Since the beginning of the world these two proclamations . . . have continually been set forth side by side in the church of God with the proper distinction" (S.D. V, 23).

If, while we live in this world of sin and death, we attempt to resolve this distinctiveness and to proclaim only *one* word instead of these two, we hear and say neither of the two. If we say only, "God demands everything of us; we must do good works," we slander the work of Christ. But this slander of the work of Christ is at the same time a slander of the divine law, for his work is obedience to the demands of the law. If, on the contrary, we say only, "God gives everything; we need only believe," we slander God's eternal holy will and thereby we also slander Christ's glory and work. For his glory is his suffering and death for us, and this death is obedience to the same will of God which the law reveals. A logical resolution of the distinction between law and Gospel separates man from the revealed God and plunges him either into libertinism or into work-righteousness or into despair, but in every case exclusively under the law which condemns us. Neither dare the law be subsumed under the Gospel, nor dare the Gospel be traced back to the law, but the church must always proclaim law and Gospel together in their distinctiveness.

Again, the distinction between law and Gospel is taught incorrectly if their unity is ignored. This unity consists in the fact that the same triune God utters both words, the word of the law and the word of grace. The unity of law and Gospel accordingly becomes a reality in Jesus Christ, whose obedient suffering preaches forgiveness and calls to obedience at the same time. Likewise, the unity of law and Gospel is the reality of the Holy Spirit, who creates faith and new obedience. But even though "we are in the Christian church, where there is full forgiveness of sin"—both that "God forgives us, *and* we forgive, bear with, and aid one another" (L.C. II, 55)—the Christian church is nevertheless, neither in its knowing nor in its acting, lord over the unity of divine forgiveness and human forgiveness, of divine mercy and human obedience. And though there is a unity of law and Gospel in God's Word, we do not thereby receive a concept which would enable us to resolve the distinction of the two doctrines. But as we submit ourselves to the Word of God we stand under the reality of the triune God himself, in whom the unity is contained.

The church, then, can bear witness to the unity of law and Gospel only by distinguishing between them. The task of theology is by no means only to make a distinction between the Word of God and the word of man, but above all to make a distinction within the Word of God: 'One must . . . rightly cut and divide the Word of God, the law in one place and the promise of God in another.' We must 'separate as far as the heavens are from earth, the promise of God and the grace that is offered, on the one hand, and the law, on the other hand. Only then shall we rightly understand the benefits of Christ and the great treasure of the Gospel (Ap. IV, 188, 185). Only then do we properly distinguish between God's Word and man's word, between the revelation of God and human religion.[13]

---

[13] Thus even the real problem of the doctrine of the law is not the relation between the natural law written in the hearts and the law revealed in the Word and written in the Bible, but the relation of law and Gospel.

Thus the Confessions make the "distinction between law and Gospel" the most important task of theology, whereby the "Word of God" is "divided rightly" (Ep. V, 2). This distinction must be maintained and carried through "with all diligence," "in order that both doctrines, law and Gospel, may not be mingled together and confused so that what belongs to one doctrine is ascribed to the other. . . . Such a confusion would easily darken the merits and benefits of Christ, once more make the Gospel a teaching of law, as happened in the papacy, and thus rob Christians of the true comfort which they have in the Gospel against the terrors of the law" (S.D. V, 27). Only through this distinction will the Holy Scriptures, "the writings of the holy prophets and apostles . . . be explained and understood correctly" (S.D. V, 1).

How are the law and the Gospel correctly distinguished?

One might first contrast the Old and the New Testament as law and Gospel, or more specifically, Moses and Christ. But this distinction is an over-simplification. It alone would be too easy and would at times most surely obscure the Gospel. The distinction between law and Gospel runs through the Old Testament as well as the New, through Moses as well as through Christ's word and work. Yes, however paradoxical it may sound, the distinction between law and Gospel runs through both law and Gospel. This means that whoever would correctly distinguish them must know both about the Gospel in the law and about the law in the Gospel.

a) The Gospel in the law—If we call the whole Old Testament law, we must realize immediately that in the Old Testament the word of the gracious forgiveness of sins, and hence the Gospel, is most consolingly proclaimed. 'And such faith and trust in God's mercy are extolled as the highest form of worship, especially in the prophets and the psalms. For although the law does not primarily proclaim grace and the forgiveness of sins as does the Gospel, yet the promises of the coming Christ were transmitted from one patriarch to another, and they knew and believed that through the blessed Seed, Christ, God wished to grant blessing, grace, salvation, and comfort. . . . Therefore they received the forgiveness of sins, grace and salvation without any merit and were saved by faith in the divine promise, the Gospel of Christ, just as we and the saints of the New Testament' (Ap. IV, 57). Even though this quotation contrasts the law as Old Testament, since it does "not primarily" preach the forgiveness of sins, with the Gospel, that is, the New Testament, the Gospel *in* the Old Testament is clearly acknowledged. For

131

already in the Old Covenant man was saved only by faith in the Gospel. Therefore it follows quite logically that 'even the holy patriarchs were accounted pious and holy before God not by the law, but by God's promise and faith' (Ap. IV, 60). Within the Old Testament itself we must distinguish between law and Gospel. "These are the two chief works of God in men, to terrify and to justify and quicken the terrified. One or the other of these works is spoken of *throughout* Scripture. One part is the law, which reveals, denounces, and condemns sin. The other part is the Gospel, that is, the promise of grace granted in Christ. This promise is repeated continually *throughout* Scripture; first it was given to Adam, later to the patriarchs, then illumined by the prophets, and finally proclaimed and revealed by Christ among the Jews, and spread by the apostles throughout the world" (Ap. XII, 53 f.; cf. IV, 5).

If we speak about law in a narrower sense as the *Mosaic law,* this likewise will be done correctly only when we are conscious of the fact that this law too bears witness to the Gospel. 'For the slaughter of oxen and sheep in the law signified the death of Christ and the office of preaching the Gospel' (Ap. XXIV, 34). On the basis of the Mosaic laws concerning sin offerings the people in the Old Covenant were to know that they would be redeemed and justified not because of their own merits, but because of the merits and blood of someone else, namely, because of the sacrifice of Christ. Isolating the Decalogue from the ceremonial and political provisions of the Mosaic law, as we did at the beginning of Chapter 3, indicates that within the law of Moses law and Gospel must be distinguished.

But even when the *Ten Commandments,* apart from ceremonies and political matters, are proclaimed as law, it must not be forgotten that the Lord who gives the Ten Commandments reveals himself and his commandments by saying: "I am the Lord *your* God." This little word "your" is already a word of grace. And though these words have been omitted in the text of the first chief part in the Small and Large Catechisms, they are not eliminated as far as their contents are concerned. They are omitted because the Catechism adds the Three Articles to the Ten Commandments and the two chief parts are now most closely related. The Credo now takes the place of "I am the Lord your God." In the Creed "your" is expounded; in it the triune God is confessed as the Lord of the Ten Commandments. But when the triune God has become known through the Gospel, then even the Decalogue can be extolled as the gift of God.

b) The law in the Gospel—If, corresponding to the line of thought just presented, the *New Testament* as a whole is called Gospel, we must remember that all Scripture has these "parts"— law and Gospel. The New Testament too has been "distributed" into these two works of God, "to terrify, and to justify and quicken the terrified." Even though "the New Testament immediately adds the consoling promise of grace in the Gospel" which "is to be believed" to the mortifying office of the law, yet "this function of the law is retained and taught by the New Testament" (S.A. III, iii, 4, 1; cf. S.D. V, 14). This assertion by no means follows merely as a logical deduction from a general premise; it is documented in detail.

If *Jesus Christ* as the Gospel is contrasted with Moses as the law, it must be borne in mind that in the Sermon on the Mount Christ himself "takes the law into his own hands and explains it spiritually" (Ep. V, 8). This "spiritually" does not involve the abrogation of the law, but, as Luther's explanation of the Ten Commandments— based on Matt. 5—in the Large Catechism shows, it tremendously intensifies and unveils the law. "Then 'God's wrath is revealed from heaven' over all sinners." On the basis of the Sermon on the Mount men "learn from it for the first time the real nature of their sin, an acknowledgement which Moses could never have wrung from them" (*ibid.*). This explanation of the law which condemns man is called "spiritual," because "the Spirit of Christ must not only comfort but, through the office of the law, must also convince the world of sin" (S.D. V, 11, quoting John 16:8).

If we wish to see especially the Gospel in that word by which Christ before his ascension commands his disciples that penitence and forgiveness of sins should be preached (Luke 24:47), we must add: 'The Gospel convicts all men that they are born in sin and are all subject to eternal wrath and death, and it offers them for Christ's sake the forgiveness of sins and righteousness' (Ap. IV, 62). If "the sum of the proclamation of the Gospel" is this, namely, "to denounce sin, to offer the forgiveness of sins and righteousness for Christ's sake" (Ap. XII, 29), then in fact the same thing must be said of the Gospel and its results as of the law: 'The teaching of repentance, or this voice of the Gospel, Amend your lives, repent! terrifies the conscience when it truly penetrates the heart, and is no jest but a great terror in which the conscience feels its misery and sin and the wrath of God' (Ap. IV, 62). But if the Gospel is defined as the preaching of repentance and of the forgiveness of sins, then evidently one must also distinguish between law and Gospel within this Gospel. Thus the Formula of Concord, in agreement with the distinction between law and Gospel which the Apology itself makes in other places, calls this definition of Gospel a *"generalis definitio,"* which represents a description of the word "in its broad sense and apart from the strict distinction of law and Gospel" (S.D. V, 5). The same is true when the first four books of the New Testament are called Gospels and when formulations such as these are used: '. . . the Gospel does not bring new laws concerning worldly government but it commands and expects that we obey the laws and the government' (*"evangelium . . . praecipit . . . et jubet,"* Ap. XVI, 3).

But we must go one step farther. If the Gospel is defined as the message of Christ's work—hence, his obedience, his life and death— the question must be asked: "In fact, where is there a more earnest and terrible revelation and preaching of God's wrath over sin than the passion and death of Christ, his own Son?" (S.D. V, 12). Even "the proclamation of the suffering and death of Christ, the Son of God, is an earnest and terrifying preaching and advertisement of God's wrath which really directs people into the law" (Ep. V, 9). Yes, the preaching of Christ's passion can even be "Moses and the law pronounced upon the unconverted" (S.D. V, 12). Thus even the message of the cross is law and Gospel. "Nevertheless, as long as all this—namely, the passion and death of Christ—proclaims God's wrath and terrifies people, it is not, strictly speaking, the preaching of the Gospel" (Ep. V, 10). On the contrary, the message of the cross as Gospel preaches the Christ who died for us, for whose sake God is merciful to us and forgives sin. Likewise the message of the obedience of Christ is not only Gospel but also law. It is Gospel inasmuch as he obeyed the law in our stead; but it is law inasmuch as his obedience confirmed the law, explained it, and by his call to follow him established it. The Gospel is Jesus' death for us; the law is Jesus' death because of us. The Gospel is Jesus' obedience in our stead; the law is his obedience as a model— "Be obedient like me."

c) The distinction between law and Gospel—But how are law and Gospel to be distinguished if God reveals the Gospel also in the law, and the law also in the Gospel? How are we to carry out this distinction if even the word of the cross is both law and Gospel?

Article V of the Formula of Concord, which aims at composing the controversies caused by Agricola, answers the question once more by appealing to Paul and then also to the Apology and to Luther in the following antithetical statements: The law "is an office which kills through the letter and is a 'dispensation of condemnation,' but the Gospel is 'the power of God for salvation to everyone who has faith,' a 'dispensation of righteousness' and 'of the Spirit' " (S.D. V, 22). " 'Everything that preaches about our sin and the wrath of God, no matter how or when it happens, is the proclamation of the law. On the other hand, the Gospel is a proclamation that shows and gives nothing but grace and forgiveness in Christ' " (S.D. V, 12).

This suggests a further question: Is the distinction of law and Gospel merely a distinction of the divine operation or is it also a distinction of the words spoken by God and witnessed by Holy Scripture? For example, does the preaching of the Ten Commandments accomplish condemnation as well as forgiveness, howsoever it pleases God? For the Confessions the distinction of law and Gospel is not only a distinction of the divine operation, but also of the divine Word. The Ten Commandments are not the word of forgiveness; the sinner is not justified by them, nor does he through them receive the Holy Spirit who renews him. Although the Ten Commandments no longer condemn the regenerated man and no longer show him God's wrath, they do not give him the spirit of life. And although the Ten Commandments become a benevolent and fatherly directive of God for the regenerated man, they do not bestow life; at the most they preserve him in the life given to him by showing him how to walk in the new life. They preserve the dead unto death and the living, whom nothing can separate from the love of God, unto life. The Ten Commandments do not renew, nor do they give the renewed man the Spirit of renewal, of whom he stands in daily need. This is the weakness of the law. Although "the Gospel illustrates and explains the law and its doctrine; nevertheless the true function of the law remains, to rebuke sin and to give instruction about good works" (S.D. V, 18). Forgiveness and life, renewal and salvation are the gift of the Gospel alone.

The same question could also be worded thus: Is the distinction of law and Gospel merely the distinction between unbelief and belief over against God's Word? Does the same Word of God become law for one who does not believe, and is it Gospel for the believer? Certainly the distinction of law and Gospel can be made only through faith. Already at the beginning of Chapter 3 we began with the proposition that the law of God cannot be known except through faith in the Gospel. But faith distinguishes on the basis of the fact that law and Gospel have already been distinguished in the Word of God. Faith does not create the distinction. It is not faith that produces the Gospel; the Gospel produces faith. The antithesis of law and Gospel is already the presupposition of faith itself; for faith, the Holy Spirit, and eternal life are not the gift of the Ten Commandments but of the word of the cross. The difference between law and Gospel is neither solely a difference between the illuminating and the nonilluminating operation of the Spirit of God, nor is it solely the difference between man's acceptance and rejection, but it is the difference between the two "parts" of Scripture.

Nevertheless, this doctrine very obviously indicates that the church cannot have and possess the distinction between law and Gospel, but can only receive it again and again. Though even the word of the cross is the revelation of God's wrath and law for one who does not believe, this distinction of the two parts of Scripture does not imply that man is Lord over God's act of punishing and saving, over God's wrath and God's mercy. Since the distinction of law and Gospel is a gift of the Spirit and is possible only in faith, it cannot be caged, even by the most precise dogmatic formulation, in such a manner as to make this formula a recipe to be handed down and used once for all. Even the knowledge of the doctrine of justification does not guarantee the correct distinction of law and Gospel. The *notitia* of the doctrine of justification is not yet the reception of justification. Just as the merit of Christ is not yet known in the intellectual apperception of his cross, but rather only in the use of his cross, so also the proper distinction of law and Gospel takes place not in formal theology but by experience alone, that is, through a believing appropriation. The distinction between law and Gospel is possible only in the act of accepting by faith the gifts which the Gospel promises.

At this place theological thinking passes over into the act of the confession of sins and into the eager approach to absolution and the sacraments. Thinking becomes praying and pleading, a "return" to the Baptism which has taken place, and an approach to the Lord's Table which is prepared for the sinner. The distinction between law and Gospel is ever again God's own gracious deed.

10. The Word of God is, strictly speaking, the Gospel.

All previous statements about law and Gospel and about Gospel and law would be simply unintelligible if their distinction were regarded as a dialectic in which law and Gospel are with equal stress united as *God's* Word and again separated as two *different* words of God in equally stressed antithesis. The Confessions are not interested in an antithetical dialectic as such. If we separate law and Gospel 'as far apart as heaven and earth,' if we 'rightly cut and divide the Word of God, the law at one place and the promise of God at another place,' then we shall 'see, what the Scripture says of the promise and what it says of the law. For Scripture commands and commends good works in such a way that it, nevertheless, ranks God's promise and the true treasure, Christ, *many* thousand times higher' (Ap. IV, 186 ff.). The comparative elevates the Gospel far above the law. It is 'plainly evident in all syllables of the Bible that faith is commended and extolled as the *highest,* noblest, greatest, most pleasing, best worship of God' (Ap. IV, 60). The superlative is not used in connection with works and with the law, but it places faith and Gospel far above the law. Only by means of such comparatives and superlatives does the distinction between law and Gospel, as it is put into practice in all Lutheran Confessions, find its comprehensive expression. The Confessions do not distinguish law and Gospel for the sake of a dialectic, but to extol the Gospel and exalt it far above the law. The Gospel, however, as the liberation from the curse of the law, can be extolled only because it is a word completely different from the law.

What is the basis of these effusive comparatives and superlatives? The total previous discussion served to answer this question. Here we shall merely call attention to the following:

Elevating the Gospel above the law is not the work of man. One might be tempted to offer an anthropological reason: Under the law man feels God's wrath; through the Gospel he receives divine mercy. The law hurls man into despair; the Gospel makes him new, free, and happy. The law and the works of the law do not help the sinner; the Gospel and faith cure him once for all. One might indeed think that a gift with so great a benefit would be sufficient reason for man to place the Gospel "many thousand times" higher than the law. But without a doubt this is not the reason.

The church has to exalt the Gospel far above the law, because God by giving up his Son has revealed himself as the Father whose love is a thousandfold greater than his wrath. To be sure, God terrifies and condemns through the law, but this terrifying is his "alien work" (*opus alienum*). "God's own proper work (*opus proprium*) is to quicken and console." He terrifies only in order to

137

demolish man's security and to quicken him. He does his alien work only for the sake of his own proper work (Ap. XII, 51).

Again and again the Gospel is extolled in this distinction between "alien" and "proper": Although Christ's work not only proclaims forgiveness but also God's wrath, his suffering and death—"as long as all this . . . proclaims God's wrath and terrifies people"—is "an 'alien work' of Christ by which he comes to his proper office— namely, to preach grace, to comfort, to make alive" (Ep. V, 10). Although the Spirit has not only the office of Comforter but also "through the office of the law" rebukes the sinful world, this is not really his proper office: "he must perform . . . 'a strange deed' (that is, to rebuke) until he comes to his own work (that is, to comfort and to preach about grace). To this end Christ has obtained and sent us the Spirit, and for this reason the latter is called the Paraclete" (S.D. V, 11). Although the Gospel calls us to repent and believe in the forgiveness of sins, "we believe, teach, and confess that the Gospel is not a proclamation of contrition and reproof, but is, strictly speaking, precisely a comforting and joyful message which does not reprove or terrify but comforts consciences that are frightened by the law, directs them solely to the merit of Christ . . ." (Ep. V, 7). In an improper sense, therefore, Christ's word is, "You *shall* be perfect." In reality he says, "My perfection *is* yours." In an improper sense God's Word demands, "You *shall* sanctify yourself." In reality the Word gives a gift and says, "The Son's holiness *is* yours." Greater than the word which establishes the law is the message, "You are forever free from the law!"

Thus also the power of the keys which Christ has given to his church is indeed a twofold power—to forgive sin and to retain sin. But the real power of the keys, strictly speaking, is absolution. This is emphasized so strongly that the office of the keys and the office of preaching the Gospel are identified. Absolution is "the very voice of the Gospel" (Ap. XI, 2). The same powerful accent recurs in the statements about confession. Confession, indeed, consists of "two parts" (S.C. V, 16; L.C. Conf., 15)—confession of sins and absolution. But the emphasis rests on absolution; it is "the surpassingly grand and noble thing that makes confession so wonderful and comforting" (L.C. Conf., 15); it is "the very necessary second part" (L.C. Conf., 16). "We should therefore take care to keep the two parts clearly separate. We should set little value on our work but exalt and magnify God's Word" (L.C. Conf., 18). Therefore Confession is actually synonymous with absolution (S.A. III, viii, 1), and private absolution is urged so strongly because there a "precious treasure," "advice, comfort, and strength" are to be obtained (L.C. Conf., 20, 13). "We urge you, however, to confess and express your needs, not for the purpose of performing a work but to hear what God wishes to say to you. The Word or absolution, I say, is what you should concentrate on, magnifying and cherishing it as a great and wonderful treasure to be accepted with all praise and gratitude" (L.C. Conf., 22). Not determining sins, but comforting the sinner is the real art and function of the confessor (cf. S.C. V, 29). For the Gospel is so incomparably more glorious than the law that by comparison the law is without glory.

This effusive comparative, as we shall see later,[14] is the determining factor in all doctrinal sections of the Confessions, not only in the doctrine of the sacraments, but also of the church and the world, of the spiritual and the temporal office. It is the determining factor in the whole proclamation of the church.

All this means to say that God's Word is, strictly speaking, the Gospel. God's Word and Gospel are interchangeable terms (cf., e.g., A.C. V, 4: *"Wort des Evangelii"* corresponds to *"verbum"*; cf. also the Latin and German texts at other places). Either law and Gospel or the Gospel alone are mentioned as the content of Scripture. But God's Word and the law are never equated, and the law alone is never called the summary of Scripture. Over against the Gospel of God the law is the Word in an improper sense. In the antithesis of law and Gospel the glory belongs to the Gospel, not to the law.

Thus in this time of sin and death *the distinction between law and Gospel* is the acknowledgment of God's final judgment in which *all* men will be judged according to their works. Jesus Christ will then pronounce the sentence of condemnation upon some without pardoning them, and he will receive the others without condemning them on account of their sins. Then for some he will make the word and threat of the law a reality without the word of grace, and to the others, without using the word that condemns, he will grant the reality which they have believed on the basis of the Gospel. Law and Gospel are to be distinguished in such a manner that in the church's teaching a place is allowed for the twofold final judgment of Christ on the Last Day: He will pardon apart from the law and he will judge without further recourse to any forgiveness.

[14] Cf., e.g., pp. 152, 176 f., 187, 198 f., 222 f., 251 ff., 267 f., 275 ff., 286 f.

The doxology of the Gospel far above the law is the expectation of the believers' resurrection and it signifies the daily straining of the believers toward the new creation. Even now in manifold trials they may be sure that Jesus Christ will not condemn them in his judgment but will receive them. But only in the resurrection in Jesus Christ will the distinction between law and Gospel come to an end, and the antithesis of law and Gospel reach its definitive conclusion.[15]

[15] Cf. pp. **287 f.**

BAPTISM AND THE LORD'S SUPPER

1. Daily repentance through contrition under the law and through faith in the Gospel is a daily "return" to Baptism and a daily approach to the Lord's Supper.

As the one Word of God confronts the sinner with a twofold address, namely, as law and as Gospel, so the sinner's response to the Word of God must always be twofold—contrition and faith. In this duality it is *one* response, repentance. The "two parts" (*"partes,"* Ap. XII, 1, 47, 91, etc.) of this response—which alone is pleasing to God—are contrition and faith. "Properly speaking, true repentance is nothing else than to have contrition and sorrow, or terror, on account of sin, and yet at the same time to believe the Gospel and absolution (namely, that sin has been forgiven and grace has been obtained through Christ)" (A.C. XII, 3-5). Accordingly, "Confession consists of two parts. One is that we confess our sins. The other is that we receive absolution or forgiveness from the confessor as from God himself, by no means doubting but firmly believing that our sins are thereby forgiven before God in heaven" (S.C. V, 16). The confession of sins which is made in confession is "contrition itself" (Ap. XII, 107).

Contrition and faith are united in the act of repentance, yet they appear in completely different contexts and may not be intermingled in theological thought. They must be distinguished as "two parts" just like *mortificatio* and *vivificatio:* 'That we are dead to sin takes place by contrition and its terrors, and that we should rise again with Christ takes place when by faith we again obtain consolation and life' (Ap. XII, 46, referring to Rom. 6).

Contrition has its place under the law. "Reflect on your condition in the light of the Ten Commandments." In this way the Small Catechism directs people to acknowledge their sin in confession (S.C. V, 20). Hence contrition is not something abstract, but concrete; it is the acknowledgment of concrete transgressions against God's concrete commandments, e.g., "I have cursed. I have set a bad example by my immodest language and actions. I have injured my neighbor . . ." (S.C. V, 23; cf. 22). It is true, man does not know all the sins he has committed. Therefore, in confessing it is "not necessary to enumerate all trespasses and sins, for this is impossible. Ps. 19:12, 'Who can discern his errors?' " (A.C. XI, 2). Demanding a full enumeration of sins would "ensnare their consciences" and would force them into "a great torture" (Ap. XI, 6), since in that case no one could know "when he had made a sufficiently complete or a sufficiently pure confession" (S.A. III, iii, 19). Nevertheless, contrition is the sorrow of the heart over concrete sins that have been committed, and the advice is given: 'It is of advantage to accustom coarse, inexperienced men (those who are not conscious of any sin or know about sin only as something abstract)' to enumerate some sins when they go to confession. (Ap. XI, 6; cf. S.C. V, 24). This concreteness of contrition does not mean that it is restricted to concrete thoughts, words, and deeds. Rather, in such concrete action it becomes manifest that we not only *committed* individual sins but that we *are* sinners, that "from head to foot there is no good in us" (S.A. III, iii, 35). Once we have truly come to acknowledge at least one sin, the debate stops about "what is sin and what is not sin." Genuine contrition "lumps *everything* together and says, 'We are wholly and altogether sinful' " (S.A. III, iii, 36). It is conscious of no single sinless thought, for it knows that not only the deed but also the doer belongs under God's demand and judgment (S.A. III, iii, 37). The terror of the divine enmity against every sin, even if there were only "one or two" (S.C. V, 24), turns all casuistry in the matter of contrition into moralistic child's play. This contrition of the sinner concerning all of his activity is precisely not abstract but in deadly earnest: 'We call that genuine contrition when the conscience is terrified and begins to feel its sin and God's great wrath over sin, and when it grieves that it has sinned' (Ap. XII, 29) and confesses that God is "justified in condemning and punishing" (Ap. XII, 108). This is not only attrition, that is, thought, intention, or even beginning of contrition, but this is contrition itself (S.A. III, iii, 16 ff.), and again this is "not *activa contritio* (artificial remorse), but *passiva contritio* (true sorrow of the heart, suffering, and pain of death)" (S.A. III, iii, 2).

Unlike contrition, faith clings entirely to the Gospel; it is the "yes" in response to the question of the confessor, "Do you believe that the forgiveness I declare is the forgiveness of God?" (S.C. V, 27). The sinner receives this forgiveness neither because of *attritio* nor because of *contritio,* neither because of an enumeration of sins nor because of despair over the countless number of sins, neither because of contrition over the sins committed nor because of attempts to atone for what has been done (Ap. XII, 18 ff.; cf. IV, 83). Nor do we obtain forgiveness of sins "because of our contrition or love" (Ap. XII, 75), or because of contrition accompanied by serious purposes of amendment. All this would imply trying to merit grace by our own works (Ap. XII, 17). Whoever teaches this would offer *"nothing but* the teaching of the law" after "the elimination of the Gospel and the abolition of the promise of Christ" (Ap. XII, 75). The sinner receives forgiveness only because of the merit of Christ, "not because of our contrition but because of the word of Christ, 'Whatever you bind on earth, etc.' " (Ap. IV, 397, quoting Matt. 16:19). Because Christ is the sole basis of forgiveness the absolution may in principle be given also to such a sinner as is not able in confession to mention a specific sin (S.C. V, 25), because faith alone receives the forgiveness.

In repentance, then, contrition and faith must be carefully differentiated. Their unity is as little subject to logical comprehension as is the distinction between law and Gospel. They indeed have their unity in the activity of the one Holy Spirit in one and the same human being. But the "how" of this unity is beyond analysis. The look at the law and the look at the Gospel, the despair of contrition and the confidence of faith, the antitheses of terror and peace are joined in the act of repentance, not indeed as a result of contrition and faith but as simultaneous experiences. The "how" of this unity eludes any attempt at psychological analysis.

"In the case of a Christian such repentance continues until death" (S.A. III, iii, 40). His whole life is repentance in obedience to the law and the Gospel, in contrition and faith, in the death of the old man and the resurrection of the new man. This must now be said also in this way: The total life is a "return" to Holy Baptism and an approach to the Lord's Supper.

Repentance "is really nothing else than Baptism. What is repentance but an earnest attack on the old man and an entering upon a new life? If you live in repentance, therefore, you are walking in Baptism, which not only announces this new life but also produces, begins, and promotes it." "Repentance, therefore, is nothing else than a return and approach to Baptism, to resume and practice what had earlier been begun but abandoned" (L.C. IV, 74, f., 79 f.; cf. S.C. IV, 12). Repentance means that the baptized sinner should always "head for" his once-for-all Baptism as to the saving ship "and cling to it until he can climb aboard and sail on in it . . ." (L.C. IV, 82).

Just so, every reception of Holy Communion is repentance. From the beginning the Confessions teach that the reception of the Lord's Supper must not be separated from confession. "The custom has been retained by us of not administering the sacrament to those who have not previously been examined and absolved" (A.C. XXV, 1; cf. XXIV, 6). Thus "the two parts of repentance" recur in the invitation to receive the Lord's Supper: "If you are heavy-laden and feel your weakness, go joyfully to the sacrament and receive refreshment, comfort, and strength" (L.C. V, 72).

The whole life of the Christian is a *daily* repentance. This calls for the further assertion: The mortification of the old Adam followed by the resurrection of the new man both take place in us as long as we live so that "a Christian life is nothing else than a *daily* Baptism, once begun and ever continued. For we must keep at it incessantly, always purging out whatever pertains to the old Adam, so that whatever belongs to the new man may come forth" (L.C. IV, 65).[1] If the life of the Christian as daily repentance is "daily Baptism," the Lord's Supper also "is given as a *daily* food and sustenance so that our faith may refresh and strengthen itself and not weaken in the struggle but grow continually stronger" (L.C. V, 24). The Lord's Supper is to be used as "a great . . . treasure which is daily administered and distributed among Christians" (L.C. V, 39). The Confessions never tire of admonishing, inciting, and summoning the baptized to receive the Lord's Supper frequently. (To this purpose Luther devotes the longest section in his treatment of the Lord's Supper in the Large Catechism.) Such remarks about daily sacraments have no intention of permitting a repetition of Baptism. In the life of each Christian Baptism remains final, once-for-all. Rebaptism is rejected in the strongest terms. Whereas, on

[1] In the interpretation of all these passages it must be remembered that repentance is primarily faith in the Gospel, that is, reception of the benefit of Baptism, and that the "old Adam" is primarily *unbelief*. To the question (C. Dieterici, *Institutiones Catecheticae*, IV, 28), "how is that old Adam in us drowned?" we may not answer, as Dietrich does, "By daily mortification and repentance, that is, by resisting and suppressing the evil desires and keeping them in check." Such resistance grows out of repentance only as a fruit of faith. The daily mortification of the old man dare not be confused with the human work of moral perfectionism, because in repentance man finds in himself only sins; in Christ alone does he find righteousness.

the contrary, the Lord's Supper is to be received frequently, here too no demand is made that every Christian should actually commune daily. Rather, we are given to understand that daily repentance is a constant event between both sacraments, that as a matter of principle it can never be separated from them, but becomes a reality every day only in looking forward to the next approach to the Lord's Table and in looking backward to the Baptism that was received once for all.

2. Baptism is not only natural water, but water comprehended in God's Word, that is, in Christ's baptismal command and baptismal promise.

The question "What is Baptism?" is answered in the Small Catechism as follows: "Baptism is not merely water, but it is water comprehended [*gefasset*] in God's command and connected with God's Word." Or to put it another way, Baptism is "the water comprehended in God's ordinance" (L.C. IV, 31). Conversely, it is also asserted that God's Word is in the baptismal water, that God "has implanted his Word in this external ordinance and offered it to us so that we may grasp the treasure it contains" (L.C. IV, 29). "For the nucleus in the water is God's Word or commandment and God's name" (L.C. IV, 16). Inverting the statements regarding the essence of Baptism which make *water* the subject,[2] we may also define: "Baptism is nothing else than the *Word of God* in water" (S.A. III, v, 1).

Now, whether Baptism is defined as water in God's Word or as God's Word in the water, the admonition must at all events be heeded "that these two, the water and the Word, must by no means be separated from each other. For where the Word is separated from the water, the water is no different from that which the maid cooks with . . ." (L.C. IV, 22). This also means that apart from the baptismal act, that is, apart from the Word proclaimed at Baptism, the water is and remains "simply common water."

The Word of God in Baptism consists of two words of the risen

[2] The definition of Baptism which begins with the water must not be weakened by saying, "*Definitio haec non est accurata, sed popularis,*" as was done by J. Benedict Carpzov (*Isagoge* [3rd ed.], p. 1085) and even more recently in current explanations. Rather, beginning with water in defining the essence of Baptism must be regarded as a highly pregnant theological antithesis against the Enthusiasts. Nor is the reversing of terms in the definition of Baptism an accidental way of speaking, but it presents a kind of analogy to the relation of the human and divine natures in Christ.

Christ, above all, the baptismal command (Matt. 28:19) "Go therefore and make disciples of all nations, baptizing them in the name of the Father and of the Son and of the Holy Spirit." Furthermore, as "the words upon which Baptism is founded" (L.C. IV, 3) the Catechisms mention Mark 16:16, "He who believes and is baptized will be saved; but he who does not believe will be condemned."

In several respects this Word of God in Baptism is decisive:

a) First, as "God's Word and *command,* which have instituted, established, and confirmed Baptism" (L.C. IV, 8). Because God has commanded Baptism, no one may doubt "that Baptism is of divine origin, not something devised or invented by men," "no human plaything" (L.C. IV, 6), not "useless. It is a most precious thing, even though to all appearances it may not be worth a straw" (L.C. IV, 8). This command is universally valid; "men, women, children, and infants" are to be baptized; yes, "it is necessary to baptize children, so that the promise of salvation might be applied to them according to Christ's command (Matt. 28:19), 'Baptize all nations' " (Ap. IX, 2).

b) Moreover, God's Word in Baptism is the *name* of God. "To be baptized in God's name is to be baptized not by men but by God himself. Although it is performed by men's hands, it is nevertheless truly God's own act" (L.C. IV, 10).

c) Finally, Christ's word, Mark 16:16, embraces the water as "Word and *promise* of God" (S.C. IV, 6). The promise is intended for faith and awards salvation to it. According to the baptismal command of Christ this promise is intended for all nations and hence also for the children. ". . . they are included in the promise of redemption" (S.A. III, v, 4).

If we ask further, which is the active agent in the sacramental act, the water or the Word, we receive the answer, "It is not water that produces these effects, but the Word of God . . ." (S.C. IV, 10). This sentence is all-inclusive. For the very inclusion of water in the sacrament of Baptism is in no way to be ascribed to anything the water is or does, but exclusively to the act of the Word of God. All statements about the symbolic qualities or possibilities of water are lacking, as is any discussion of a symbolic-indicative significance which the natural process of immersion as such could already have of itself. Rather, in the strongest terms the inherent nullity of the water and of the washing with water is stressed: It is "to all appearances" not "worth a straw" (L.C. IV, 8; cf. 22). The water as such is not yet an indication of God's gracious will, but rather conceals the Word of grace like a gross, external mask, "as we see the shell of a nut" (L.C. IV, 19). At this point too a natural theology is excluded. In themselves, the elements and events of the fallen world provide here no arguments or even hints which could be taken up by the teaching of the church. Water is rather lifted out of the multiplicity of elements and out of their symbolic nothingness by God's Word alone, "as if God were to pick up a straw" (L.C. IV, 12). Only by this means does the water become theologically significant, "because here something nobler is added; God himself stakes his honor, his power, and his might on it" (L.C. IV, 17). Because the *Word* embraces the water, the water embraces the Word. Because the *Word* is in the water, the water is in the Word. Only after this has been established can we speak "finally" also of the "observance" and the significance of the act of being dipped into the water and of being drawn out again. This signifies "slaying the old Adam and the resurrection of the new man" (L.C. IV, 64; cf. S.C. IV, 11 f.).[3] This significance is a reality because the risen Christ by his Word has given the water this significance; he has put the water into this symbolic relationship. The Word is monergistically the agent in creating the sacrament. In this sense Augustine is quoted: " 'When the Word is joined to the element it becomes a sacrament' " (L.C. IV, 18; cf. S.A. III, v, 1 *et al.*).

On the basis of the Word, however, it is true also of Baptism that "it is not simply common water" but "a divine water" (L.C. IV, 14), "a divine, blessed, fruitful, and gracious water" (L.C. IV, 27), "the salutary, divine water" (L.C. IV, 33). "Baptism is a very different thing from all other water, not by virtue of the natural substance but because here something nobler is added. . . . Therefore it is not simply a natural water, but a divine, heavenly, holy, and blessed water . . . all by virtue of the Word (L.C. IV, 17). It is "a gracious water of life and a washing of regeneration in the Holy Spirit" (S.C. IV, 10, referring to Titus 3).

[3] Of course, on the basis of the Word the reference made to the natural process is not omitted, for "the effect of the water consists not only in washing and cleansing, nor only in surrounding and covering on all sides, but the water may also have a killing effect: the 'old man' drowns in the water." At the same time it must be noted that Luther's doctrine of Baptism did not maintain any of these points of comparison with any striking consistency. C. Stange has shown in detail how Luther's expressions have varied the sense of the symbolism in Baptism, shifted its emphasis, yes, even "turned it into the direct opposite." *Studien zur Theologie Luthers*, I, 358 ff. To give a symbolic interpretation of Baptism on the basis of the graphic process of immersion can establish only an accumulation of contradictions within the doctrine of Baptism.

These formulations are not to be understood in a magical sense as though the baptismal water were fruitful and salutary independently of the faith or unbelief of the person baptized. Nor, however, are they merely a manner of speech which in plerophoric inexactness transfers effects and qualities of the Word to the water. Luther rejects the doctrine of Scotus that the washing away of sins takes place "only through God's will and not at all through the Word or the water" (S.A. III, v, 3), and this "or" is to be taken seriously. The water in Baptism is gracious and salutary like the Word in Baptism. For in the sacrament the Word and the water can no longer be separated. Hence Baptism can be defined as "the Word of God in water" and " 'the washing of water with the Word' " (S.A. III, v, 1). In the definition of the sacrament either the Word *or* the water can be the predicate noun. Faith can cling both to the Word and to the water. Whoever does not receive the water of Baptism does not receive the promise of the Word of Baptism. God effects salvation not only through the Word but through Word and water, through the Word in the water and the water in the Word. Water and Word are now in one another. The Word is visible in the water of Baptism. Therefore one may and should believe that he may "receive in the water the promised salvation" (L.C. IV, 36).

3. Baptism is the washing of regeneration which effects forgiveness of sins, deliverance from death and the devil, and grants eternal life.

"What gifts or benefits does Baptism bestow? Answer: It effects forgiveness of sins, delivers from death and the devil, and grants eternal salvation . . ." (S.C. IV, 5 f.). In Baptism God pours out on us "the superabundant and boundless riches of his grace" by calling it a " 'new birth,' whereby we are made free from all tyranny of the devil, from sin, death, and hell, become children of life and heirs of all the blessings of God, and God's very children and Christ's brethren" (*Tauf.*, 8).

Baptism is the forgiveness of sins. Even though evil lust remains in the baptized until the resurrection, Baptism "overcomes and takes away sin" (L.C. IV, 83). Even though "original sin remains after Baptism," it is still true "that Baptism removes the guilt of original sin" (Ap. II, 35).

Baptism is redemption from the power of the devil. The devil is, indeed, the lord of this world who like a wild beast stalks the baptized. As long as they live in this world they are assailed by him daily. And yet they are taken out of his dominion, since Baptism "snatches us from the jaws of the devil" (L.C. IV, 83). The command: "I adjure thee, thou impure spirit, . . . that thou depart . . . and make room for the Holy Spirit" is effective in Baptism (*Tauf.,* 11, 15; *Bek.,* pp. 538-39).[4]

Baptism is liberation from death. Even though the baptized in their earthly life are still moving toward death, they are delivered from death. "Now, here in Baptism there is brought free to every man's door just such a priceless medicine which swallows up death and saves the lives of all men" (L.C. IV, 43). The baptized have already died and they are living with Christ in eternal life. This eternal life, however, is granted not only to the soul but also to the body. Because Baptism is Word and water, and the water affects the body while the Word strikes the soul, therefore "body and soul shall be saved and live forever: the soul through the Word in which it believes, the body because it is united with the soul and apprehends Baptism in the only way it can. No greater jewel, therefore, can adorn our body and soul than Baptism, for through it we obtain perfect holiness and salvation, which no other kind of life and no work on earth can acquire" (L.C. IV, 46).[5] Just as Christ lives forever as the Risen One, so he gives his disciples eternal life in bodily resurrection from the dead, in "the resurrection of the body" (Apost.).

All of these fruits of Baptism are comprehended for Luther in the phrase, the "purpose of Baptism is to save . . . To be saved, we know, is nothing else than to be delivered from sin, death, and the devil and to enter into the kingdom of Christ and live with him forever" (L.C. IV, 24).[6] For Baptism gives "God's grace, the entire Christ, and the Holy Spirit with his gifts" (L.C. IV, 41).

---

[4] For the controversy regarding the inclusion of the *Taufbuechlein* (Pamphlet on Baptism) in the Book of Concord, see *Bek.,* p. XLIII.

[5] Cf. pp. 164 f.

[6] It must not be overlooked that this sentence, like the answer to the question in the Small Catechism concerning the benefit of Baptism ("it effects forgiveness of sins, delivers from the death and the devil . . ."), agrees with the explanation there of the Second Article ("redeemed . . . from all sins, from death, and from the power of the devil . . . , that I may live under him in his kingdom . . ."). This agreement must be understood as linking Baptism with the "holy, precious blood" and the "innocent sufferings and death" of Jesus Christ. Cf. L. C. IV, 37. Even though this linking of the act of Baptism with Christ's death and resurrection, thus making both contemporaneous, is not expressed in the Catechisms with the same clarity as in the New Testament, it is impossible to say that in the Catechisms "virtually a second work

Accordingly, Baptism is "the washing of regeneration in the Holy Spirit" (Titus 3), for this is the power of Baptism—the "slaying of the old Adam and the resurrection of the new man" (L.C. IV, 65). This is the work of the Holy Spirit whom God bestows through Baptism. In Baptism the Holy Spirit changes slaves of sin and the devil into children of God; he changes enemies of Christ into brethren of Christ. For to be born again means to put on Christ. Thus in Baptism the Holy Spirit breaks through the enslavement of the human will and grants the baptized a liberated will (S.D. II, 67); he renews the hearts to love God and to take pleasure in his commandments.

This doctrine concerning the benefit of Baptism must be delimited in two directions:

a) Baptism is the offer of divine grace, but not merely an offer. Thus the Augsburg Confession teaches that through Baptism "grace is offered" (*"offeratur gratia Dei"*) and that children through Baptism are 'being offered to God' and 'are *received* into his grace' *recipiantur in gratiam Dei* (A.C. IX, 2). The Apology presents the same ambivalence of expression: 'In and with Baptism . . . the universal grace and the treasure of the Gospel are *offered*.' At the same time little children are to be baptized 'so that they may become *partakers* of the Gospel, the promise of salvation and grace' (Ap. IX, 2). Baptism is not only the offer of grace but also the gift of grace; it is *"efficax ad salutem"* [efficacious for salvation] (Ap. IX, 1); it makes "God our own" (L.C. IV, 83).

b) Baptism is the promise of salvation, yet not only the promise. On the one hand, on the basis of the promise the baptized are "'*heirs* in *hope* of eternal life'" (S.C. IV, 10). The event of Baptism "signifies that the old Adam in us . . . *should* be drowned by daily sorrow and repentance and be put to death . . ." (S.C. IV, 12). After Baptism the death of the old man and the resurrection of the new man shall, must, and will last "our whole life long" (L.C. IV, 65), until we rise again at the Last Day. This prayer is

of redemption, namely Baptism, is placed beside God's work of redemption in Christ's death and resurrection. First Christ redeemed us from sin, death, and devil, and now Baptism redeems us from them." P. Wernle, *Der evangelische Glaube, I Luther*, p. 258. Incidentally, J. Meyer detects a cryptic christological reference in the baptismal doctrine of the Small Catechism in a perhaps not insignificant change within the quotations from Rom. 6, so that it reads "in death" instead of "unto death" (S. C. IV, 14). This change "becomes meaningful only if this death is not referred to the death of our old man which Baptism serves to accomplish (this would have demanded "unto death"), but rather to the death of Jesus in which we experience this burial of our sins." *Hist. Kommentar*, p. 457.

therefore offered to God at Baptism: May this child serve Thee throughout his life "fervent in spirit, joyful in hope, *in order that* with all believers he may become worthy of Thy promise to inherit eternal life" (*Tauf.*, 14). On the other hand, it is stated most emphatically that "Baptism effects salvation . . ." (S.C. IV, 6). Baptism not only promises forgiveness but bestows forgiveness; it not only promises eternal life but translates into eternal life. In the act of Baptism regeneration is effected, that is, in Baptism the old man dies and the new man arises. Even though the baptized is still moving toward his temporal death, he moves as one who has already died, as one who has been liberated from death. Even though he hastens onward in hope to the eternal life of the resurrected, he hastens on toward it as one who already possesses this eternal life. Baptism, therefore, is already the eschatological event of the resurrection from the dead which it promises. For this reason alone the invitation to a daily return to Baptism makes sense. Baptism as *promissio salutis* is not only a promise but also the bestowal of what is promised, just as the Gospel as *promissio* is both promise and assurance.

4. The benefit of Baptism is received only through faith, which is at the same time both produced and strengthened by Baptism.

Baptism "grants eternal salvation to all who believe, as the Word and promise of God declare . . . , 'He who believes and is baptized will be saved; but he who does not believe will be condemned'" (S.C. IV, 6 ff.). This Scripture passage (Mark 16:16) teaches that "faith alone makes the person worthy to receive the salutary, divine water profitably" (L.C. IV, 33). Whoever receives Baptism without faith does not receive the benefit of Baptism—eternal salvation (L.C. IV, 33-37). Not for one moment must the benefit of Baptism be separated from faith, either in the act of Baptism or in the later life of the baptized.

What does faith mean in this connection? As resolutely as in the doctrine of justification faith is separated from works in the doctrine of Baptism. "So this single expression, 'He who believes,' is so potent that it excludes and rejects all works that we may do with the intention of meriting salvation through them" (L.C. IV, 34). In no way is faith added in a synergistic sense to the action of God in Baptism; rather, here too it is pure reception. ". . . faith does not constitute Baptism but receives it" (L.C. IV, 53). Faith receives—that means the believer is embraced by God's grace. Faith apprehends—that means the believer is apprehended by God's grace. Faith brings nothing that it could bestow upon God; rather it is simply that trust which is bestowed by God. In passivity the believer knows himself exposed to the activity of God's grace. "Thus faith clings to the water and believes it to be Baptism in which there is sheer salvation and life, not through the water, as we have sufficiently stated, but through its incorporation with God's Word and ordinance and the joining of his name to it. When I believe this, what else is it but believing in God as the one who has implanted his Word in this external ordinance and offered it to us so that we may grasp the treasure it contains?" (L.C. IV, 29).[7] Such faith, such "clinging" and "grasping," is so completely a reception of grace that every psychological description of this process must be eliminated. Nor can the act of reception be bound to psychological presuppositions. It is only logical for Luther not to exclude the possibility of faith in children but to presuppose it expressly, although their ability to think and to express their thought is still undeveloped (L.C. IV, 55, 57; *Tauf.*, 23 ff.). It is nevertheless surprising that in this connection contrition is hardly mentioned alongside faith, even though the "return" to Baptism is called repentance and is, therefore, contrition and faith. By repeatedly specifying faith as that which receives the benefit the effusive comparative is again stressed whereby the Gospel is exalted far above the law, so that the summary of Scripture is not the law but the Gospel. Even though the return to Baptism is repentance, that is, contrition and faith, the worthiness of the person baptized consists only of faith in the promise of the Gospel which is imparted to him in the water of Baptism.

Baptism, then, must be received by faith. This faith is also to be expected as a result of Baptism. The sacraments have been instituted by God "for the purpose of awakening and strengthening our faith. For this reason they require faith, and they are rightly used when they are received in faith and for the purpose of strengthening faith" (A.C. XIII). Hence faith is not only the presupposition of the salutary reception of the sacrament but also its effect, and accordingly faith itself is the benefit of the sacrament. Not only is faith required for the reception of the sacrament but it is also produced

[7] Cf. also the rejection of the Enthusiasts' misconception of Baptism as man's work. L. C. IV, 35 ff. Over against the objection of the Enthusiasts the opposite is true: Whoever does not receive Baptism as God's work must necessarily confuse his own faith with man's work. In that case faith would be resting on itself.

and strengthened. As a matter of fact, faith is required because it is also produced and strengthened by the sacrament. It is true not only of the Lord's Supper but also of Baptism that "through the Word and the rite God simultaneously moves the heart to believe and take hold of faith, as Paul says (Rom. 10:17), 'Faith comes from what is heard' " (Ap. XIII, 5).[8]

Baptism is to be received by faith. This faith is also to be expected as the divine answer to the congregation's intercession: "We ask Thee of Thy boundless mercy, look graciously upon this N. (i.e., the person to be baptized) and bless him with true faith through the Spirit" (*Tauf.*, 14; *Bek.*, p. 539). This intercession for the child is stressed in the strongest terms, and the sponsors are most urgently requested to join sincerely in the prayer. Yes, Luther thinks that "people have turned out so badly after Baptism because they were treated so coldly and negligently and were prayed for in Baptism without any real earnestness." Believing that such a prayer is heard, the sponsors vicariously answer "yes" to the questions addressed to the child: "Do you believe in God the Father almighty . . . ? Do you believe in Jesus Christ, his only Son . . . ? Do you believe in the Holy Spirit . . . ?" (*Tauf.*, 4; 23 ff.; *Bek.*, pp. 536, 540). Such believing intercession on the part of pastor and sponsors demonstrates in a special way what it means to be "received into the Christian community" (L.C. IV, 2). The Holy Spirit, "placing us upon the bosom of the church, . . . brings us to Christ" (L.C. II, 37). The faith of the church always precedes the faith of the individual.

"We do the same in infant Baptism. We bring the child with the purpose and hope that he may believe, and we pray God to grant him faith. But we do not baptize him on that account, but solely on the command of God" (L.C. IV, 57). More than our "purpose" and "hope" that the person to be baptized may believe is in no case possible, not even in the case of an adult candidate for Baptism. Only God's command is sure (cf. Ap. IX, 2). This command is, above all, the baptismal command which makes no exceptions. To this is added the Gospel selection used in Baptism, Mark 10:13-16: "Let the children come to me, do not hinder them" (*Tauf.*, 16; *Bek.*, p. 539). How then could we withhold Baptism from the children

---

[8] Thus it is true in a comprehensive sense that in Baptism "the 'dead' are addressed by the living and effectual Word of God." "Baptism is to accomplish that which can only be compared with God's act on the first day of creation or with Christ's resurrection and the resurrection of the dead." H. Asmussen, *Seelsorge* (4th ed.; Munich, 1937) p. 94.

who are assured of the kingdom of heaven by Christ's invitation and Word? Is there something greater than the kingdom of heaven?[9]

It is clear, therefore, that the benefit of Baptism and faith are inseparably conjoined. Now, it is possible to receive, not indeed the benefit, but the washing of Baptism without faith. From this follows both the possibility that the fruit of Baptism is received later than Baptism, as well as the opposite possibility that the benefit received in Baptism can be lost, if the baptized later casts his faith away and no longer uses his Baptism in a daily "return." Nevertheless, it is true that the sacrament of Baptism "in itself . . . is infinite, divine treasure" and remains such (L.C. IV, 34). ". . . when the Word accompanies the water, Baptism is valid, even though faith be lacking" (L.C. IV, 53; cf. 54 ff.). "Gold remains no less gold if a harlot wears it in sin and shame" (L.C. IV, 59). Thus Baptism "always remains valid and retains its integrity" (L.C. IV, 60).

What, then, does this statement mean: ". . . where faith is lacking, it remains a mere unfruitful sign" (L.C. IV, 73)? The treasure has been offered to you but you did not make use of it. Baptism is a treasure "in itself," but it has not become a treasure for you. ". . . it is not the treasure that is lacking; rather, what is lacking is that it should be grasped and held firmly" (L.C. IV, 40).

This distinction of Baptism and benefit can be profoundly terrifying and can drive one into desperate questioning as to whether he really received Baptism in faith and whether he is using it in faith today. In the Confessions, however, this distinction is presented primarily as the joyful assurance that no abuse of man can nullify the divine deed in Baptism, and as the comforting invitation: "But if anybody falls away from his Baptism let him return to it. As Christ, the mercy-seat, does not recede from us or forbid us to return to him even though we sin, so all his treasure and gifts remain" (L.C. IV, 86). And so also Baptism abides daily as long as we live. Thus in a superabundant measure the doctrine of Baptism is a doxology of grace, even in its statements about faith. For faith is not so much required as permitted, enticed, aroused, and strengthened. For the rest, these statements obligate the congregation to offer up the most sincere intercession for every baptized child and to provide faithful instruction for those baptized, that they may in faith make use of their Baptism. To this extent the composition of the Cate-

[9] In the Large Catechism there is not so much the assertion of infant faith as the rejection of its impossibility and a discussion of its possibility—to be taken seriously—and the *hope* of its reality.

chisms results from this doctrine of Baptism (cf. S.C. Pref., 11). This much is sure, the Confessions are not interested in an isolated treatment of the essence of Baptism apart from the reception of its benefit. Rather, all statements about the essence of Baptism remaining intact even when salvation is not received, have the purpose of guaranteeing the benefit of Baptism *for the believer*. That the Confessions are concerned with the unseparated essence and benefit of Baptism is made clear by the statements which without differentiation call either the Word in Baptism (L.C. IV, 16), or the benefit of Baptism (L.C. IV, 26), or finally even the Baptism received without benefit (L.C. IV, 43) a "treasure."

5. The Lord's Supper is not only natural bread and wine, but bread and wine comprehended in God's Word, that is, in Christ's words of institution.

"As we said of Baptism that it is not mere water, so we say here that the sacrament is bread and wine, but not mere bread or wine such as is served at the table. It is bread and wine comprehended in God's Word and connected with it" (L.C. V, 9). What is true of Baptism applies also here: ". . . if you take the Word away from the elements or view them apart from the Word, you have nothing but ordinary bread and wine" (L.C. V, 14). Accordingly, bread and wine are not the sacrament apart from the event in which God's Word is spoken to the person eating and drinking. Since here too "the Word" means the words of the institution of Jesus Christ, the Formula of Concord expressly obligates "that in the celebration of the Holy Supper the words of Christ's institution should under no circumstances be omitted, but should be spoken publicly, as it is written, 'the cup of blessing which we bless' (I Cor. 10:16; 11:23-25). This blessing occurs through the recitation of the words of Christ" (Ep. VII, 9).

In the union of the Word and the element, the element is entirely passive in the Lord's Supper just as in Baptism. As in the doctrine of Baptism so also here the Confessions are not at all interested in exhibiting any symbolical significance which bread and wine might have in themselves and by which bread and wine as such might be set apart from other elements of this world. In themselves bread and wine are "mere bread or wine such as is served at the table" (L.C. V, 9), and they share the same nothingness as do water and straw, among other elements, and do not of themselves point to Christ's death and God's grace. We find no symbolic interpretation of the bread's derivation from kernels of grain and of the wine's derivation from grapes offered up for the sake of our nourishment. We find no symbolic interpretation of the natural process of eating and drinking; nor is the community of the meal as such a topic of theological significance. In no way does the doctrine of the Lord's Supper start with the empirical impressions produced by physical processes and their symbolic possibilities. Not bread and wine but only God's Word creates the sacrament of the Lord's Supper. "The Word must make the element a sacrament; otherwise it remains a mere element" (L.C. V, 10). Again the word of Augustine is quoted: " 'When the Word is joined to the element it becomes a sacrament' " (*ibid.*). God's Word takes bread and wine out of the nothingness of the things of this world and apprehends and embraces them by the free decision of the divine institution. Bread and wine became the elements in the Lord Supper only because Christ took them and added his Word to them. Only through this act did they receive theological significance, namely, as signs of divine grace. Here too the Confessions are free from all natural theology. Here too there is no teaching of nature's receptivity for grace; rather, the enslavement of this world of sin and death is acknowledged. As God sent his Son into the world in mercy which is incomprehensible and without any basis whatever in man, so God takes hold of the element by his Word in a condescension which is utterly without basis in the element.

Not only before God's Word takes hold of bread and wine, however, but even afterward bread and wine, as well as eating and drinking, are conceded no independent significance and symbolism which go beyond the statements of the Word. On the contrary, in the doctrine of the Lord's Supper and in its administration the Confessions forego any exhibition of even such symbolical features as might be suggested by the New Testament reports of the institution of the sacrament. They show no interest in supporting the proclamation of the Lord's death by the demonstrative symbolism of breaking the bread, or to enliven the memory of Jesus' last meal in a representative repetition of this meal, or in the symbolic emphasis on the fellowship of the communicants. From beginning to end attention is focused in both Lord's Supper and Baptism on the Word and thereby on the gift of God. Accordingly, both sacraments in their real essence are not "signs by which people might be identified outwardly as Christians"—this they are also—but "they are signs and testimonies of God's will toward us" (A.C. XIII, 1; cf. Ep. VII, 27; S.D. VII, 115).

God's Word in the sacrament of the Lord's Supper comprises the words of institution which Jesus spoke in the night in which he was betrayed, as reported in the New Testament accounts. They are quoted in the Catechisms in a harmonized version of the reports in the Synoptic Gospels and of I Cor., with I Cor. 11 as the basis. Both in the Small and the Large Catechisms the eschatological words are missing. In the case of I Cor. 11:26 this might be explained by the fact that here the apostle is speaking. All the more striking is the omission of Luke 22:16 and 18.

The words of institution of Jesus Christ are important in several respects. The Large Catechism unfolds this importance in four directions:

a) God's Word is, in the first place, God's "ordinance or command. . . . For the Lord's Supper was not invented or devised by any man. It was instituted by Christ without man's counsel or deliberation" (L.C. V, 4). God's ordinance or command is Christ's institution as a whole; especially, however, within these words of institution the command: "Do this in remembrance of me." "These are words of precept and command, enjoining all who would be Christians to partake of this sacrament" (L.C. V, 45). These words command the reception and the distribution of this sacrament. This command to repeat—"Do this"—is the constitutive factor in the doctrine of the Lord's Supper to such an extent that a celebration without this command would be null and void. Accordingly, the Formula of Concord gives the express direction to speak or chant this command in every service in which the Lord's Supper is celebrated (S.D. VII, 79 ff.).

b) God's Word is the power that makes of bread and wine a sacrament, so that it is not "mere bread and wine," but is "rightly called Christ's body and blood" (L.C. V, 10). By means of the Word, Christ's body and blood come to the bread and wine; hence "you here have Christ's body and blood by virtue of these words which are coupled with the bread and wine" (L.C. V, 18). As words which bring the sacrament into being these words especially are mentioned: "Take, eat; this is my body"; "Drink of it, all of you, this is the new covenant in my blood" (cf. L.C. V, 13). The importance of these words is underestimated if we call them merely *"Deuteworte"* [words which represent or signify].

c) God's Word "brings" forgiveness through the sacrament. For "the whole Gospel" is "embodied in this sacrament and offered to us through the Word" (L.C. V, 32)—especially the words, "given for you," "shed for you." The Word in the Lord's Supper not only speaks of forgiveness but gives it (L.C. V, 33) and offers it (L.C. V, 35). And whoever believes the Word not only hears about forgiveness, but "has" it (*ibid.*).

d) Finally, God's Word in the Lord's Supper has a didactic significance. Through Christ's words of institution the Christian knows what he receives in the sacrament (L.C. V, 2) and against which errors he must take a stand (L.C. V, 19). Yet this didactic function never becomes autonomous. As is the case with the doctrine of justification, the instruction is completely enclosed in the comforting assurance of the Word, and the informed understanding is enclosed in the believing reception.

As in Baptism, so also in the Lord's Supper God's Word is both command and promise (L.C. V, 64; cf. Ap. XIII, 3, *et al.*), and this is true of the entire Word by which Jesus Christ instituted the Lord's Supper, even though within the compass of this Word some words are especially stressed as command and some as promise. Still it becomes evident that the same distinction of command and promise in the two sacraments includes statements that differ widely. For in Baptism we have no analogy for the words, "This is my body"; "this cup is the new covenant in my blood."

This difference is of the greatest importance for the whole structure of the doctrine of the Lord's Supper. For if the words of institution in the two sacraments agreed also in form, we should have to continue: The Lord's Supper is not merely natural bread and natural wine, but divine, blessed, gracious bread, and divine, heavenly, salutary wine. The Word, however, not only makes bread and wine gracious food, as it makes water the washing of regeneration, but the Word causes the sacrament of the Lord's Supper to be "rightly called Christ's body and blood" (L.C. V, 10). It is the "true sacrament (that is, Christ's body and blood," L.C. V, 16). Unlike the answer to the question, "What is Baptism?" the Small Catechism, in answering the question, "What is the Sacrament of the Altar?" does not start out with the element, but the answer states at once, "It is the true body and blood of our Lord Jesus Christ, under the bread and wine." The Small Catechism does not make use of this opening statement which would be altogether possible and analogous to Baptism: The Sacrament of the Altar is not only ordinary bread and wine but it is bread and wine used according to God's command and connected with God's Word. This silence at once emphasizes the uniqueness of the words, "This is my body." Because of these words the Large Catechism at once answers the question thus: "It is the true body and blood of the Lord Christ" (L.C. V, 8). The definition of the Lord's Supper as "bread and wine comprehended in God's Word and connected with it," with which we started, *follows* after the opening statement about Christ's body and blood. Corresponding to this order, the Large Catechism speaks of the Lord's Supper as of that bread and wine which are Christ's body and blood *and* with which the words are coupled (L.C. V, 28).

6. *The Lord's Supper is Christ's body and blood given and shed for the forgiveness of sins.*

The body and blood which are offered and received in the Lord's Supper are not the body and blood of man in general but the body and blood of the incarnate Son of God. Again, the Lord's Supper is not the body and blood of Christ in material independence, but the body and blood of Jesus Christ which are not for a moment to be separated from the person of the incarnate Son of God. On the one hand, the Confessions from the beginning reject the idea that only the spirit of Christ, but not his body is present in the Lord's Supper (Ap. X, 1). On the other hand, also from the beginning, it is taken for granted that the presence of the body and blood of Christ is "the presence of the living Christ" (Ap. X, 4). The firmness with which a mere presence of the divine person of Christ without his human nature is rejected is matched in the way the Formula of Concord asserts that the presence of the true body and blood of Jesus Christ at the same time means "that the Lord Jesus Christ is present in his Supper truly, essentially, and alive" (S.D. VII, 6). The divine nature of Christ is not without the human nature and the human nature is not without the divine nature. The doctrine of the Lord's Supper in all its assertions derives from the presupposition of the incarnation of the Son of God.

The body and blood of Christ can no more be separated from the fact of his death on the cross than they can be separated from the divine person. The objection that the body and blood of Christ are not given and shed for us in the Lord's Supper is answered by Luther with the self-evident statement that "the work was accomplished and forgiveness of sins was acquired on the cross" (L.C.

159

V, 31). This linking of all statements about Christ's body and
blood in the Lord's Supper with the event of Christ's death on the
cross dare not be lost sight of for one moment, even though it
appears to receive little explicit mention. This connection is assured
and kept in steady awareness by means of the constantly repeated
quotation of the words of institution, "given for you," "shed for
you." These words speak of the giving of the body and the shedding
of the blood on the cross.[10] Thus the Lord's Supper is the body
and blood of Christ "through which forgiveness is obtained" (L.C.
V, 28). We cannot pit one against the other—obtaining forgiveness
through Jesus' suffering and death *or* through the giving of Jesus'
body and blood. The sacrifice of the human body is at the same
time the dying of the incarnate Son of God.

The words "given and shed for you" are referred, however, not
only to Christ's death on the cross, but also to the act of giving
the body and blood of Christ in the Lord's Supper. Christ says,
" 'Given *for you*' and poured out *for you,*' as if he said, 'This is
why I give it and bid you eat and drink, that you may take it as
your own and enjoy it' " (L.C. V, 34). This surely does not mean
that the "giving" and "shedding" occurs in the Lord's Supper instead
of on the cross. But in the act of distributing the Lord's Supper
the event of the cross is a contemporaneous reality. The same
Christ who once gave his body on Calvary now gives his body
in the Lord's Supper and this makes us contemporaneous with his
death on the cross. The fact that this twofold meaning of the words
"given for you," "shed for you," is as a rule inseparably fused in
the Confessions is an acknowledgment of this contemporaneity.[11]
This also means that in the Lord's Supper not only the crucified
but also the exalted Christ is acting, who today offers his congregation the body once given on the cross. "In this sacrament he
offers us all the treasure he brought from heaven for us" (L.C. V,
66). Christ's body and blood in the Lord's Supper are the body
and the blood which Christ, after his condescension from heaven

[10] Cf. J. Meyer, *Hist. Kommentar,* p. 469. A physical understanding of the
Small Catechism's definition apart from the crucifixion and death of Jesus is
possible only if this definition is torn away from the immediately following
words of institution. This misunderstanding is made impossible by the fact
that the Large Catechism inverts the order and brings the confessional statements as inferences from the preceding words of institution.

[11] Hence Christ's death on the cross is still happening for me, namely, in
the distribution. It is inaccurate for A. Hardeland to say that Luther is not
thinking of the crucifixion but of the distribution; for in the distribution
Luther lets the crucifixion become the timeless present for us, and therefore
does not exclude it." *Ibid.*

into the flesh, once gave and shed on Calvary and which he now as the exalted Christ gives to us. Not only the dying Christ but also the exalted risen Christ acts in this giving. Not only he who is on the way to the cross but also he who sits at the right hand of the Father is present in the Lord's Supper.

The identity of the giving of the body, once on the cross and now in the Lord's Supper, has its basis in the words of institution of Jesus Christ and in the identity of the crucified and risen Lord: The exalted Lord acknowledges as his own, and acts according to, the words which he spoke in his humiliation when he instituted his Supper. In the Lord's Supper the body of the crucified and the body of the exalted can no more be torn apart than the crucified and exalted Christ himself. 'We are talking about the presence of the living body (so Jonas translates *praesentia vivi Christi*); for we know, as St. Paul says, that death no longer has dominion over him' (Ap. X, 4). We dare not ignore the resurrection of the body given on the cross when today we receive Christ's body and blood. If the living Christ is present bodily in the Lord's Supper, then we must also believe that the glorified, resurrected body of the exalted Lord is given and received. If this were denied, all statements about the presence of Christ's body, that is, the bodily presence of the living Christ who did not remain in the grave, would be untenable. On the other hand, the exalted body is never for a moment to be separated from the body given on the cross, the marks of which it bears. The question whether in the Lord's Supper the crucified or the glorified body is received is in every way improperly put. For the glorified body is the same body which had been suspended on the cross. In the doctrine of the Lord's Supper this truth must be stressed: The exalted Christ is present bodily *as* the crucified Christ, and the body and blood of the exalted Christ are present *as* the body given on the cross and blood shed on the cross.[12]

When the Sacrament of the Altar is defined as "the true body and blood of our Lord Jesus Christ, under the bread and wine" (S.C. VI, 2), and when we teach "that the true body and blood

---

[12] This emphasis is admittedly clearer in the Large Catechism than in the Formula of Concord, which places its expressions concerning the body and blood of the exalted Christ into a definite polemical framework to a degree that the connection with the event of the cross recedes noticeably into the background. But even in the Formula of Concord it is made perfectly clear that according to the words of institution we may speak of the body of the exalted Christ as present in the Lord's Supper in no other way than "of his true, essential blood, which was shed for us on the tree of the cross for the forgiveness of sins." S.D. VII, 49.

of Christ are really present in the Supper of our Lord under the form of bread and wine" (A.C. X), the true body in all such statements is to be understood as qualified above. In all texts of this kind it is impossible to separate the body and blood from the person of Jesus Christ and from the event of the giving of his body on the cross, and to ignore the fact of the exaltation of the crucified and of his present action. A separation of Christ's person from his body given on the cross is equally impossible.[13] This intimate unity remains a fact even if one understands that in the total complex of Melanchthon's theology there is an immediate interest in the person of Christ—in the presence of which person Christ's body and blood are also present—whereas it is precisely in the presence of body and blood that Luther's doctrine of the Lord's Supper confesses the present Christ. But even in the confessional writings authored by Melanchthon it becomes perfectly clear that the statement *"vere et substantialiter adesse"* [are truly and substantially present] affirms not only the true substantial presence of Christ but also the true and substantial presence of Christ's true body and blood (Ap. X, 1 ff.). For this reason a quotation from Cyril is used to reject the idea that we are joined to Christ only spiritually by faith and love but not by his flesh, and that we are one body in Christ only because of the spiritual blessings but not through the communication of Christ's flesh (Ap. X, 3). Thus the presence of Christ's body in the Lord's Supper restrains us in the doctrine concerning the Lord's Supper from speaking prematurely about the church as the body of Christ. In view of the propositions of Zwingli and other opponents it is understandable why in this doctrine the Catechisms refrain entirely from speaking of the church as Christ's body. For it is not that the Lord's Supper is the true body of Christ because the church is the body of Christ; rather, the church

---

[13] Cf. pp. 178 f. H. Gollwitzer judges differently: "Forgiveness of sins has been won for us not by the fact that the eternal Logos took the human destiny of death on himself, but by the fact that he sacrificed for us this his body which has become immeasurably valuable through its union with him. In other words, we were redeemed not really by the act of dying, but by the material price, the body." "Luther regards the body of Christ as independently active (i.e., "apart from a free, personal activity of Christ himself"); he brings deliverance not on the basis of a decision but on the basis of his natural being. . . . The operation of Christ's body is not identical with Christ's free operation through his Word and Spirit, but it is the automatic operation of a matter treated well or badly by the recipient to his own benefit or harm." *Coena Domini*, p. 63. But this separation of the human nature from the divine person and from the work of Jesus Christ contradicts Luther's Christology. Cf. E. Sommerlath, *Der Sinn des Abendmahls*, pp. 28 ff., 42 f., 47 ff. Incidentally, is "believing" synonymous with "treating"?

is the body of Christ because Christians receive Christ's body in the Lord's Supper and are nourished by it and thus incorporated into Christ. Like the Gospel, the Lord's Supper is "the means whereby we are united with Christ and are incorporated into the body of Christ, which is the church" (S.D. VII, 59). But this is true precisely because in the eucharistic words even the word "body" is "not speaking of a symbol of his body, or of a representation of his body in a figurative sense, or of the virtue of his body and the benefits which he has won for us by the sacrifice of his body. He was speaking of his true, essential body, which he gave into death for us . . ." (S.D. VII, 49). In this sense every metaphor and metonymy in the interpretation of the words of institution is rejected.

The benefit of the distribution of Christ's body and blood is the forgiveness of sins. "We are told [this] in the words 'for you' and 'for the forgiveness of sins.' By these words the forgiveness of sins, life, and salvation are given to us in the sacrament" (S.C. VI, 6). Thus the words of institution, which make a sacrament out of bread and wine so that they are Christ's body and blood, also "give" the forgiveness secured for us by Christ's body and blood on the cross. This gift of forgiveness is so great a treasure that it is not mentioned without being expounded at once: "For where there is forgiveness of sins, there are also life and salvation" (*ibid.*). This exposition is presented in many and varied statements running through almost all Confessions, statements which extol the greatness of the reality of forgiveness in words of an effusive gratitude. In its benefit it becomes evident that the Lord's Supper is nothing less than the antidote against all poisons which could harm the baptized. "For here in the sacrament you receive from Christ's lips the forgiveness of sins, which contains and conveys God's grace and Spirit with all his gifts, protection, defense, and power against death and the devil and all evils" (L.C. V, 70; cf. also 22). In an all-inclusive sense the Lord's Supper is a "remedy" (L.C. V, 78).

In an attempt to systematize the abundance of statements in which the gift of forgiveness is expounded and extolled, we first call attention to the fact that just as in the doctrine of justification "declaring righteous" and "making righteous" are united in one act of God, so also in the Lord's Supper forgiveness is not merely the nonimputation of sins but also the strengthening and encouragement of the sinner in the battle against sin. The Lord's Supper is comfort, refreshment, and invigoration for faith and the new obedience. Conversely, he who withdraws from the Lord's Supper will day by day "become more and more callous and cold" (L.C. V, 53). But through the reception of the sacrament the heart will be quickened, "warmed and kindled" (L.C. V, 54).

Thus the Lord's Supper is given as a "comfort" so that man in the battle with the devil may here obtain "new strength and refreshment" (L.C. V, 27). Forgiveness is both power and protection against the devil. The Lord's Supper does not redeem from the dominion of the devil in the sense that it places the prisoner of Satan under the dominion of Jesus Christ. This was done in Baptism. But the Lord's Supper provides protection against the ever-recurring concrete attacks and temptations with which Satan constantly stalks and attacks the Christian.

The forgiveness of sins is affirmed and extolled particularly as life, and the Lord's Supper is described as life-giving food and as protection, guard, and gift against death. Even though Christians must die at the end of their earthly pilgrimage, the Lord's Supper is the completely adequate protection against death. After all, Christians have already died in Baptism and there remains only one death to be feared—apostasy from eternal life in Christ. The Lord's Supper preserves the Christian in the eternal life into which he has been translated through Baptism. Therefore with Hilary, Luther urges the Christian not to stay away from the sacrament "lest he deprive himself of life" (L.C. V, 59). The power of forgiveness and the new life granted with it would, of course, remain unrecognized if this life were understood only ethically as new obedience. When the Lord's Supper is called a "food of the soul since it nourishes and strengthens the new man" (L.C. V, 23), it is clear that the eschatological reality of the new man is recognized; and, indeed, all the Confessions know that the new man is the sinner rising from the dead. The resurrection from the dead is, however, not only forgiveness and new obedience but also the gift of a new body. Since this new body has been most definitely promised through Baptism, the baptized even now, in the midst of this world of sin and death, are such as have been born again and renewed to eternal life. Against this background we are to understand the teaching of the Large Catechism about the Lord's Supper that it is "a pure, wholesome, soothing medicine which aids and quickens in both *soul and body*. For where the soul is healed, the body has benefited also" (L.C. V, 68). These assertions say not only that the Christian receives Christ's body and blood in a bodily manner, with his mouth, but in addition that through Christ's body he receives eternal life for the body.[14] Even though the believer is still walking in his terrestrial body he receives eternal life "in both body and soul." After all, he is the same person who is now walking in his perishable body and who in the resurrection will one day be clothed with the imperishable eternal body. This relationship between our receiving terrestrial body and the eternal life of the new body follows from the fact that the crucified Christ as the exalted Lord in the sacrament gives us his glorified body which was offered on the cross.

This, then, is the benefit of the Lord's Supper—that 'through this food we are united with Christ' (Ap. XXII, 10). Jesus Christ is giver, gift, and benefit at the same time. The Lord's Supper is "a true bond and union of Christians with Christ their head and with one another" (S.D. VII, 44; cf. 59). This union with Christ is a union with the incarnate Son of God, the crucified and risen one who has ascended into heaven and will return. Uniting us

---

[14] Luther's remarks about the benefit of the Lord's Supper for the body of the communicant must not be ignored or weakened. Nor are they unexpected excrescences of massive polemics in the context of Lutheran theology, or exaggerated conclusions drawn from the fact of the physical reception of Christ's body. They are bound to appear surprising to one who in the sense of Greek anthropology opposes soul to body, or, in the modern idiom, personality to physical nature. In Lutheran anthropology, however, person and nature are not separated in this way, but they are interchangeable terms. Cf. p. 43, n. 6. Just as the whole man—person and nature—is God's creature, so also the whole man is the recipient of grace. Luther's remarks would also be strange if a man's body had succumbed to the corruption of sin more than the soul, and if the body had remained God's creature less than the soul. But the whole man—body and soul—is at the same time creature and corrupted by sin, and the promise of the new creation applies to the whole fallen creature. The decisive antithesis is not soul and body, person and nature, but flesh and spirit. Soul *and* body, person *and* nature are flesh, and *both* are renewed by the Spirit of God. It is therefore decisive for the proper understanding of the expressions concerning the bodily benefit of Baptism and the Lord's Supper to see them in view of the resurrection of the body, in expectation of the Last Day. Just as now through a believing reception of the sacraments we obtain pardon and eternal life, so also through this reception we are already entering the eschatological separation of creatureliness and corruption. Cf. p. 271 f. "Now, because this poor bag of worms, our body, also has the hope of the resurrection from the dead and of eternal life, this body must also become spiritual and digest and consume all that is carnal in it. And that is what this spiritual food accomplishes: if a man eats it bodily, it will digest his flesh and transform him, so that he too *becomes* spiritual, that is, eternally alive and blessed, as Paul says (I Cor. 15), 'It is raised a spiritual body.' To use a crude illustration, the effect of this food is as if a wolf had devoured a sheep which proved to be so powerful a meal that it transformed the wolf into a sheep. Similarly, when we eat the flesh of Christ in a bodily and spiritual manner, this food is so powerful that it transforms us into it and turns carnal, sinful, natural men into spiritual, holy, living men. This we are already, but still concealed in faith and hope. *WA* 23, p. 205. For further study of the whole question see the important explanations and documentation in E. Sommerlath, *Der Sinn des Abendmahls*, pp. 81-90.

with himself, he makes his death and his life, his righteousness and his holiness, his first and second Advent our property and we are "incorporated into the body of Christ, which is the church" (S.D. VII, 59).

Hence the Lord's Supper is not only an offer, but the gift of forgiveness in all its fullness. The power and fruit of the Lord's Supper are not merely proffered but we may "seek and obtain" them; we receive them; we "obtain" them when we receive the sacrament (L.C. V, 20-22). In this respect the words "for you" embrace us with consoling power, since they proclaim to us positively that the treasure, the power, and the benefit of the Lord's Supper have actually become yours and mine.

So then the power of the Lord's Supper is not merely the promise of forgiveness but the imparted presence of forgiveness, life, and salvation. At the same time it must not be overlooked that all of these gifts are eschatological realities, i.e., that forgiveness, in its determining essence, is the acquittal in the Last Judgment, and that life is the eternal life of those who have risen from the dead. The doctrine of the benefit of the Lord's Supper is eschatologically determined for the very reason that in the context of the Confessions all statements about the attacks of Satan on the church and about the protection and help of the church militant must be understood as statements referring to the last times preceding the Last Day. To be sure, in the doctrine of the Lord's Supper our attention is not directed to the time which separates us from the returning Christ, but in the reception of the sacrament the advent of Jesus Christ and his gifts is the most certain presence. While we receive the body and blood of Jesus Christ faith leaps over the interval of the still-imminent battle and wins the victory over sin, death, and the devil.

The statements about the Lord's Supper as the body and blood of Christ and about the benefit of the Lord's Supper are, as we know, made by the Small Catechism in successive answers to two different questions. The statements are separated to the extent that the first answer does not speak of the benefit at all, even though the first question is quite comprehensive: "What is the Sacrament of the Altar?" This fact raises the questions: Are these two answers separated merely in the interest of a serial development of theological explication, the first question being answered not only by the first answer but also by the elaboration of the additional questions; or is there a basic theological concern involved in this separating of the body and blood of Christ in the Lord's Supper from forgiveness? In other words, does the benefit, forgiveness, belong to the essence of the Lord's Supper or does it not?

Even though the separation of essence and benefit in the Small Catechism and the Large Catechism may not be only a matter of explanation, we must, in the first place, say quite definitely that the primary concern of all statements both about Christ's body and blood and about forgiveness is to show the close interrelation and unity of essence and benefit. The whole sacrament is *both* "essence" and "effect and benefit" (L.C. V, 33), that is, Christ's body, *"through and in which"* we obtain the forgiveness of sins" (L.C. V, 22). Christ's body and blood, received in the Lord's Supper, are not only a sign of the benefit of the Lord's Supper, but they themselves are "a source of blessing to me" and this not only as a "sure pledge and sign" of forgiveness but also as "the very gift he has provided for me against my sins, death, and all evils" (L.C. V, 22). We are to "seek and obtain" the "benefit" of the sacrament *in* its "essence," not beside it (L.C. V, 20). "Christ's body can never be an unfruitful, vain thing, impotent and useless" (L.C. V, 30). For when the body of Christ in the Lord's Supper becomes "yours" and "mine" (L.C. V, 29 and 22), the death of Christ as accomplished for you and me is applied to you and me. Because Christ's body in the Lord's Supper is in essence the body given on the cross *for us,* it is indeed quite natural to define the Lord's Supper at times simply as the body and blood of Christ without explicitly mentioning the benefit of forgiveness. In a different way the statements about essence and benefit come close to being tautological when the benefit of receiving the sacrament is presented as union with Christ. At all events, forgiveness is to be sought in Christ's body and blood, and, accordingly, the benefit of the Lord's Supper is to be sought in the essence. This does not contradict the statement made at another place that the forgiveness of sins "cannot come to us in any other way than through the Word" (L.C. V, 31). For this intimate relationship between essence and benefit has its basis in Christ's words of institution by the power of which we have both Christ's body and blood and the forgiveness of sins. The statement that we receive forgiveness in the Lord's Supper through the Word therefore does not contradict the assertion that we receive forgiveness in the Lord's Supper through Christ's body and blood. Nor is there any contradiction in the Small Catechism which first defines the sacrament as Christ's body and blood (S.C. VI, 2) and

167

then declares Christ's Word to be "the chief thing in the sacrament" (S.C. VI, 8). For, "comprehended in the Word," Christ's body and blood are "offered to us" (L.C. V, 30).

The same primary interest in the close connection between essence and benefit in the Lord's Supper is manifested in the references of the Large Catechism to the treasure in the Lord's Supper. Both Christ's body and blood (L.C. V, 22, 29 f.) and the Gospel (L.C. V, 32) are the treasure. The Gospel is the treasure in the Lord's Supper because it brings us the forgiveness purchased by Christ's death; likewise, Christ's body given for us is the treasure because forgiveness was purchased by it and it "can never be an unfruitful, vain thing, impotent and useless" (L.C. V, 30). Because of the body and blood given for us the word of forgiveness is called the treasure, and because of forgiveness the gift of the body and blood in the Lord's Supper is called the treasure. In every case "this treasure is fully offered in the words" (L.C. V, 36). Only because essence and benefit are thus viewed together in determining the concept "treasure," does it become possible to say: "But he who does not believe has *nothing*. . . . The treasure is opened and placed at everyone's door, yes, upon everyone's table, but it is also your responsibility to take it and confidently believe that it is just as the words tell you" (L.C. V, 35; cf. 36 ff.). This statement by no means denies that the unbeliever also receives Christ's body and blood in the Lord's Supper. If he still "has nothing," this "nothing" is Christ's body and blood without the benefit of forgiveness. On the other hand, Christ's body and blood given and shed *for me* are everything in the Lord's Supper. The fact that the treasure in the Lord's Supper is extolled with such surprising unconcern for a nice distinction of essence and benefit shows clearly that there is no primary and independent interest in this distinction and, accordingly, in the problem of the unbelieving reception of the sacrament. Even though the unworthy guests receive the sacrament of the Lord's Supper, that is, the true body and blood of Jesus Christ, and receive it to judgment, the focus of these statements is immediately directed to the sacrament as Gospel, as the reality of forgiveness in Christ's body and blood. This is the primary concern— that we all receive Christ's body and blood for the forgiveness of sins. Only as faith views this close relation of essence and benefit do the overwhelming doxology of the Lord's Supper and the thoroughly enticing and joyous invitation to all to come to the Lord's

Supper become possible, as we find them especially in the Large Catechism.[15]

7. *In the Lord's Supper bread and wine are Christ's body and blood; in, with, and under the bread and wine Christ's body and blood are offered and orally received.*

The two answers to the question about the essence of the Lord's Supper: "It is the true body and blood of our Lord Jesus Christ" (S.C. VI, 2) and it is "bread and wine, comprehended in God's Word and connected with it" (L.C. V, 9) do not stand side by side independently but are most intimately connected by God's Word itself through the word "is." Not only is the sacrament Christ's body and blood but in the sacrament the bread is Christ's body and the wine is Christ's blood. The forgiveness of sins is not given through bread and wine, "since in itself bread is bread—but [we are making this claim] of that bread and wine which are Christ's body and blood and with which the words are coupled" (L.C. V, 28; cf. S.A. III, vi, 1). Hence the Lord's Supper is "the true body and blood of our Lord Jesus Christ, under the bread and wine . . ." (S.C. VI, 2); "the true body and blood of the Lord Christ in and under the bread and wine which we Christians are commanded . . . to eat and drink" (L.C. V, 8). And the sacrament is not only *called* Christ's body and blood by the church, but it "is," and "*is rightly called* Christ's body and blood" (L.C. V, 10). Only because the "is" is true is the "is called" also true. It is not because we "call" them this that bread and wine are Christ's body and blood; rather, the "is" is true because God's Word—that is, Christ's words of institution—calls them this. "Bread

[15] The fact that the Large Catechism alternately calls Christ's body and blood and the benefit the treasure, and ascribes forgiveness of sins both to the Word and to Christ's body and blood, constitutes an "inconsistency" and a "difficulty" in Luther's doctrine of the Lord's Supper (Gollwitzer, *Coena Domini*, pp. 60, 64; cf. pp. 188 f.) only if these texts are separated from the act of a believing reception of the sacrament. What the Catechisms say about the Lord's Supper must be understood as the confession of those who *by faith* receive Christ's body and blood, that is to say, receive Christ's body and blood for the forgiveness of sins. An "inconsistency" develops only when the remarks about the Lord's Supper are made from a point beyond the believing and unbelieving reception—in other words, when the question concerning the *manducatio indignorum* is made an *independent* theological concern. This happened soon in the interconfessional controversies of early Lutheran Orthodoxy. It will not do, however, to read back the problems raised by this emerging spectator attitude into Luther's doctrine of the Lord's Supper, the entire pathos of which concerns the immeasurable treasure the embattled *believer* receives in the Lord's Supper.

and wine comprehended in God's Word" (L.C. V, 9) *is* Christ's body and blood "in and under the bread and wine" (L.C. V, 8). But as decisive as are these definitions of the relationship of bread and body and of wine and blood in the Large Catechism, so startling is their brevity compared with the extensive discussions about Christ's body and blood and about the benefit of the Lord's Supper, as well as about worthy reception.

In the Latin text of the Augsburg Confession the elements are not mentioned, and therefore no statement is made about the relationship of bread and body and wine and blood. It is taught only that 'in the Supper of the Lord' 'the body and blood of Christ are truly present and are distributed to those who eat' (A.C. X). One may here see a shift of emphasis from the elements to the sacramental act, as it is present in the whole of Melanchthon's teaching on the Lord's Supper. But the fact must not be ignored that Christ's body and blood are distributed to those who eat bread and wine, and that the German text expressly teaches the presence of Christ's body and blood "under the form of bread and wine" "in the Supper of our Lord." The latter wording must not be interpreted as being directed only against the denial of the cup in the Roman church and as favoring the distribution under both kinds.[16] These words have rather been understood by the church of the Augsburg Confession in the sense of Luther's "under the bread and wine," and this interpretation is indirectly confirmed by Melanchthon's dilution of the text of Article X of the Augsburg Confession in 1540, where he omitted the words *"vere adsint"* and added *"cum pane et vino."*[17] This formulation, however, leaves the question open whether the two different processes of receiving the bread and wine, on the one hand, and of receiving the body and blood, on the other, are simultaneous or not. It is true the Apology too does not say "under the form of bread and wine," but *"cum . . ."*—"with the visible elements, bread and wine" (Ap. X, 1). But this "with" is safeguarded against a separation of bread and body and

---

[16] So H. Heppe, *Die confessionelle Entwicklung der altprotestantischen Kirche Deutschlands* . . . (Marburg, 1854), p. 65, and A. Ebrard, *Das Dogma vom hlg. Abendmahl,* II, 357. Contrariwise, it is true in any case "that the phrase 'under the form' points to a relation of bread and body, wine and blood." H. Schmid, *Der Kampf der lutherischen Kirche* . . . , pp. 69 f.—a relation which excludes a side-by-side distribution of body and bread, blood and wine, as well as a side-by-side oral and spiritual reception.

[17] The article was weakened further by dropping the words *"et improbant secus docentes"* and *"exhibeantur,"* a word whose meaning wavers between "presenting" and "exhibiting," "distributing" and "profferring." The text of Variata X is given in *Bek.,* p. 65, ll. 45 f., n. a.

wine and blood by the quotations from the fathers which follow, in which a downright transforming of the elements is expressed. These quotations must not be interpreted as though transubstantiation is taught in the Augsburg Confession and the Apology. The *"cum"* makes this interpretation impossible. Rather, the point of comparison in these quotations is the "bodily presence of Christ," which the Augsburg Confession wishes to maintain in agreement with the Greek and the Roman church. Thus these quotations make impossible a rejection of the Lutheran "in and under" in the light of the preceding *"cum."* Nevertheless, it is no accident that the interpretation of the *"cum"* in the Apology, as well as of the corresponding expressions in the Augsburg Confession, again and again became the subject of controversy. The definition of the relationship between bread and body and wine and blood was not a paramount question in the doctrine of the Lord's Supper as it was developed there so as to require a comprehensive clarification of this point. After all, even the wording "under the form of bread and wine" (A.C. X), if isolated from other statements, does not exclude the transforming of the *materia* of the elements while the *forma* remains.

In the Formula of Concord the "in" and "under" of the Catechisms and the "with" of the Apology are combined in the formula that the body of Christ is present "under the bread, with the bread, in the bread" (S.D. VII, 35, 37 ff.). It is in this sense that the bread is Christ's body and the wine is Christ's blood. In each case one preposition is to guard against a misunderstanding of the other and, again, the whole formula protects against definite false doctrines which must be rejected; they do so, however, without trying to explain "the sacramental union" of bread and body and of wine and blood. "All attempts at more precise definition of the manner of the union of the elements with Christ's body and blood and of the manner of receiving the former with the latter have a purely limiting character" (W. Elert, *Morphologie*, I, 267). Thus transubstantiation is rejected, for in the Lord's Supper we are concerned about "the sacramental union between the untransformed substance of the bread and the body of Christ" (S.D. VII, 35; cf. 107 f.). On the other hand, the doctrine is rejected "that the bread and wine are only figures, images, and types of the far-distant body and blood of Christ" (Ep. VII, 28; cf. 29-32, 36; S.D. VII, 115 ff.). The bread in the Lord's Supper is Christ's body without ceasing to be bread, and wine is Christ's blood without ceasing to be wine. But especially when we now follow in detail these modifying statements about the "how" of the presence of Christ's body and blood in, with, and under the bread and wine, statements clothed in negations and condemnations, we find that "the formula 'sacramental union' which is to summarize all that can be said (S.D. VII, 37) also means merely a waiving of any attempt to describe the manner more precisely" (Elert, *op. cit.,* p. 268). When we make this statement there can be no doubt *that* Christ's body and blood are present and are offered in, with, and under the bread and wine. But *how* they are present and offered in, with, and under the bread and wine exceeds our ability to describe. For Christ's words, "This is my body," are an absolutely unique expression (S.D. VII, 38). "This expression is called *inusitata* [uncommon] by us because in *usitatis linguis* [ordinary language] no example can be found which can be completely compared with it" (Apologia F. C. 154a; cf. *Bek.,* p. 984, n. 4). These statements which define the relationship of bread and body and of blood and wine merely wish to ward off ideas which contradict the words of institution, but not to reveal the mystery of the sacramental union. The *fact* that Christ's body and blood are given for forgiveness surely is not hidden; it stands in the very center. What is said about the relationship of bread and body *serves* the certain expectation and the doxological acknowledgment of this fact. Only in polemics do they receive an apparently independent and monographic significance.

Basically the same situation arises when we ask what kind of eating of Christ's body and drinking of Christ's blood occurs in the Lord's Supper.

In the first answer of the Small Catechism the statement "under the bread and wine" is placed between the two statements "the true body and blood of Jesus Christ" and "given to us Christians to eat and to drink." The question is debatable as to whether the words "under the bread and wine" belong to the first or to the second statement. The Latin translation of the Large Catechism (L.C. V, 8) favors the first. The punctuation of the German text (S.C. VI, 2; L.C. V, 8) favors the second, although punctuation is, of course, not decisive. Of greater importance is consulting parallel passages in Luther's writings.[18] But no matter how the question is answered, under no circumstances may the following connection be overlooked: If Christ's true body and blood are present in and under

---

[18] *WA* 30, I, 260, ll. 2 f.; 315, ll. 19 f.

the bread and wine, then the body and blood are also eaten and drunk in and under the bread and wine, and vice versa. The "bodily eating and drinking" (S.C. VI, 7) therefore receives not only bread and wine but Christ's body and blood under the bread and wine. This suggests the deduction that in and under the bread and wine Christ's body and blood are received in the Lord's Supper with the mouth. To be sure, neither the Small Catechism nor the Large Catechism expressly draws this conclusion. But even though the kind of sacramental eating and drinking is not determined more precisely, and though the primary concern is to make clear that the sacramental treasure of forgiveness is not seized with the fist but by faith (L.C. V, 35-38), yet in all statements it is evident that Christ's body and blood—and therewith the benefit of the Lord's Supper—are received not beside, but in the bodily taking, eating, and drinking.

The Augsburg Confession and its Apology do not give a more precise answer to this question, but in the Formula of Concord we find a somewhat definitive formula in the decision that while the reception of Christ's body and blood occurs "with the mouth, the mode is spiritual" (S.D. VII, 105). Yet even this definition evidently is not an explanation and description of the sacramental eating and drinking, but merely a delimitation of this process over against false expressions without explaining the process itself. On the one hand, the thought is warded off that in the Lord's Supper there occurs a separate reception of Christ's body and blood by the spirit, and of the bread and wine by the mouth. No, *in* the act of eating the bread I eat Christ's body and *in* the act of drinking the wine I drink Christ's blood. With the mouth Christ's body and blood are received in the Lord's Supper (S.D. VII, 48, *et al.*). Just as emphatically, on the other hand, the claim is rejected that in the Lord's Supper there occurs "Capernaitic eating of the body of Christ as though one rent Christ's flesh with one's teeth and digested it like other food" (Ep. VII, 42); that would be a gross, carnal understanding of the sacramental eating. No, in the Lord's Supper Christ's body and blood are with the mouth "received, eaten, and drunk spiritually." The word "spiritually" is here understood as "the spiritual, supernatural, heavenly mode according to which Christ is present in the Holy Supper, not only to work comfort and life in believers but also to wreak judgment on unbelievers" (S.D. VII, 105; cf. also 61-66). It is obvious that neither delimitation is meant to explain the process of sacramental participation, but in

173

their open dialectic they wish simply to paraphrase the mystery of the oral reception of Christ's body and blood in its incomprehensibility. The Formula of Concord feels obligated by the words of institution to make these delimitations. But beyond that it consigns to the judgment of God "all presumptuous, sarcastic, and blasphemous questions" which attempt to define precisely the act of sacramental participation (Ep. VII, 41). For the human mind and reason cannot comprehend the process of this "true, though supernatural" eating and drinking; rather, our reason is to be brought into captivity to the obedience of Christ (Ep. VII, 42).

However, the question would be put incorrectly if it were asked whether the Lutheran doctrine of the Lord's Supper is chiefly concerned about the presence *or* the giving of the body and blood of Christ in, with, and under bread and wine; about the substance of the body and blood *or* about the event of receiving the body and blood. In spite of possible shifts in emphasis it must be maintained that in the definition of the Lord's Supper the presence, the giving, and the taking, the *"adesse et exhiberi"* (Ap. X, 1) are inseparably conjoined. The Lord's Supper is "the true body and blood of our Lord Jesus Christ, under the bread and wine, given to us Christians to eat and to drink" (S.C. VI, 2; cf. L.C. V, 8; S.A. III, vi, 1). Thus the presence of Christ's body and blood in, with, and under the bread and wine is an actual event in various respects; as the event of the offering of Christ's body and blood on the cross, it is actual in the event of the proclamation of the words of institution, and the distribution and oral reception of bread and wine.

8. The benefit of the Lord's Supper is received only by faith which is both produced and strengthened by the Lord's Supper. The unbeliever receives Christ's body and blood to his judgment.

The power of the Lord's Supper is the forgiveness in Christ's body and blood. Who, then, is the person who "receives this power and benefit"? "It is he who believes what the words say and what they bring" (L.C. V, 33). "Who, then, receives this sacrament worthily? . . . He is truly worthy and well prepared who believes these words: 'for you' and 'for the forgiveness of sins'" (S.C. VI, 10). True worthiness consists of faith in Jesus' words of institution and especially the words "given for you." ". . . he who believes these words has what they say and declare: the forgiveness of sins" (S.C. VI,

8). But "he who does not believe these words, or doubts them, is unworthy and unprepared, for the words 'for you' require truly believing hearts" (S.C. VI, 10). Faith relies on this word. For in the words "for you," (cf. L.C. V, 34), which cannot be stressed too strongly, the forgiveness through Christ's body and blood is pronounced to *me,* and in these words, so to speak, the treasure of the sacrament is concentrated. But "the promise is useless unless faith accepts it" (Ap. XIII, 20; cf. A.C. XIII, 2). Yes, in the reception of the sacrament faith is so vital that Justus Jonas [in his German text], citing Augustine approvingly, even adds: 'it is faith in the use of the sacrament which justifies before God, and not the sacrament' (Ap. XIII, 23).

The worthiness of the communicants does not consist in "fasting and bodily preparation" (S.C. VI, 10). Even though this is a "good external discipline" (*ibid.*), it is not once admitted that "outward preparation" *too* is a part of worthiness (Ep. VII, 38). Nor does worthiness consist in previous moral improvement. Who would then dare to approach the Lord's Table? "If you choose to fix your eye on how good and pure you are, to work toward the time when nothing will prick your conscience, you will never go" (L.C. V, 57; cf. 73). For no one is "perfectly pure." To every person in the presence of the sacrament, inquiring about his own purity, "it appears like a dark lantern in contrast to the bright sun, or as dung in contrast to jewels" (L.C. V, 56). In the question concerning worthiness there is no place for good works. And these are not the works of pagans but of people who have been reborn in Baptism and have often been strengthened in their faith by Word and sacrament. Thus, in the question concerning worthiness, not even the statement that faith may not remain without the new obedience stands over against the approach to the Lord's Supper as condition and prohibition. Worthiness consists exclusively of faith, and that not as a living, strong, active faith; rather, here—as in the doctrine of justification—faith is pure reception. To be sure, it is stated that "those who are shameless and *unruly* must be told to stay away, for they are not fit to receive the forgiveness of sins, since they do not desire it and do not want to be good" (L.C. V, 58). But who are these shameless and unruly people? They are not characterized as people guilty of scandalous or criminal behavior, but they are people who do not yearn for grace, people who do not want to receive forgiveness and life. Shameless and unruly are those too who, because of their good works, or even because of their new obedience, imagine that they do not need forgiveness.

"If you are heavy-laden and feel your weakness, go joyfully to the sacrament and receive refreshment, comfort, and strength" (L.C. V, 72). "Therefore they alone are unworthy who neither feel their infirmities nor admit to being sinners" (L.C. V, 74). From such statements one might possibly draw the conclusion that in addition to faith also the agony of yearning, the suffering of thirst, and the sensation of weakness and sinfulness are the prerequisites for a salutary reception of the sacrament. But such an understanding is nullified and all words concerning the thirst of the worthy guests are radically outdistanced by the answer to the question, "What shall I do if I cannot feel this need or experience hunger and thirst for the sacrament?" The answer states conclusively, ". . . the less you feel your sins and infirmities, the more reason you have to go to the sacrament and seek a remedy" (L.C. V, 75, 78). In the final analysis, calling attention to the thirst and the suffering because of sins committed does not constitute a condition or raise a barrier but is the invitation addressed to those who labor and are heavy-laden. Next to faith there is no condition for the reception of the Lord's Supper; the feeling of our weakness is no more such a condition than are good works. Here too faith escapes psychological determination. Faith is neither thirst nor lack of thirst, neither sensation of weakness nor lack of sensation, but it is the reception of divine grace. From this viewpoint we understand why in the Small Catechism worthiness is defined not as contrition and faith, but simply as faith. Though we must not approach the Lord's Table without confession—and hence not without repentance, that is, not without contrition and faith—worthiness in the reception of the sacrament itself, as in the doctrine of Baptism, is defined in ever-new ways as faith alone. These passages too demonstrate the superabundant glory by which the Gospel surpasses the law. Though the Formula of Concord defines worthiness as true contrition, true faith, and sincere intention of amendment, yet here also faith alone is the decisive factor (cf. Ep. VII, 18 f.). Here too whatever goes beyond these statements is intended above all as an urgent invitation. "True and worthy communicants . . . are those timid, perturbed Christians, weak in faith, who are heartily terrified because of their many and great sins, who consider themselves unworthy of this noble treasure and the benefits of Christ because of their great impurity, and who perceive their weakness in faith, deplore it, and heartily wish that they might serve God with a stronger and more cheerful faith and a purer obedience. This most venerable sacrament was instituted and ordained primarily for communicants like this" (S.D. VII, 69 f.; cf. 68).

If faith as trusting reception constitutes worthiness, then worthiness does not consist in the act of receiving but in the treasure received, not in faith as a human act but in faith as in him who is believed. Therefore it is stated conclusively: "We believe, teach, and confess that the entire worthiness of the guests at this heavenly feast is and consists solely and alone in the most holy obedience and complete merit of Christ alone, which we make our own through genuine faith" (Ep. VII, 20). "And worthiness does not consist in the weakness or certainty of faith, be it greater or smaller, but solely in the merits of Christ" (S.D. VII, 71). Our worthiness is faith as it receives the worth of Christ.

Here the statements indicating the casual relationship of faith and sacramental benefit execute a turn of 180°. Not only does faith receive Christ's body and blood for a benefit, but faith is also the benefit of Christ's body and blood. The Lord's Supper "is given as a daily food and sustenance so that our faith may refresh and strengthen itself and not weaken in the struggle but grow continually stronger" (L.C. V, 24). The Lord's Supper was instituted so it "might strengthen our faith and we might publicly confess our faith and announce the blessings of Christ" (Ap. IV, 210). Faith, then, is both the presupposition and the fruit of the Lord's Supper: The sacrament was instituted to 'strengthen the faith' of the terrified consciences 'when they believe' (Ap. XXII, 10). It was instituted 'to awaken our faith and comfort our consciences when we perceive that through the sacrament grace and forgiveness of sin are promised us by Christ. Accordingly this sacrament requires faith . . .' (A.C. XXIV, 30). This last quotation might almost justify the inference that since faith is stimulated and strengthened by the Lord's Supper, the Lord's Supper requires faith. At all events, nothing is required of man in the sacrament that God does not himself give to man in the sacrament. That is to say, here God only gives and he requires nothing. Since the Lord's Supper requires faith and gives faith, it is altogether a gift. We need add nothing to God's grace. We need merely accept and receive his gift. It is literally placed into our mouth.

At this point in the doctrine of the Lord's Supper there is disclosed the proper understanding of the command of Jesus Christ to remember him. What is the meaning of "in remembrance of me"? To 'remember Christ is to remember his benefits and realize that they are truly offered to us; and it is not enough to remember the history, for the Jews and the ungodly can also remember this' (A.C. XXIV, 31 f.). The remembrance of Christ is that faith which receives the gift that these words in the Lord's Supper convey.

The fact that faith is simply reception but adds nothing to the sacrament is definitely assured through the propositions regarding the reception of the Lord's Supper on the part of the unworthy: "Even though a knave should receive or administer it, it is the true sacrament (that is, Christ's true body and blood) just as truly as when one uses it most worthily" (L.C. V, 16; cf. S.A. III, vi, 1). Neither the unbelief of the celebrant nor the unbelief of the communicant can invalidate the fact that Christ's true body and blood are present, are distributed and received in, with, and under the bread and wine, if only the Lord's Supper is administered according to the words of institution. Of all who receive the sacrament in the contempt of unbelief it is true that they receive it "to their harm and damnation. For such people nothing can be good or wholesome, as when a sick person wilfully eats and drinks what is forbidden him by the physician" (L.C. V, 69). It is the unanimous doctrine of all Lutheran Confessions that such unbelieving despisers, even though they abuse the sacrament, still receive Christ's body and blood. To be sure, this doctrine is not expressly stated in the Small Catechism, the Augsburg Confession, and the Apology. But it is inescapably implied whenever the terms "under," "under the form of," "in," and "with" are defined in the sense in which this is done in the Confessions from the beginning. The silence of the Augsburg Confession and the Apology on the question of the reception of Christ's body and blood by the unbelievers cannot be interpreted to mean that this question should be answered negatively. This is impossible already in view of the frank use of quotations from the canon of the mass, from Theophylact and Cyril.

In the Lord's Supper Christ's body and blood are received by the believers to the forgiveness of sins and by unbelievers to their judgment, but this does not imply that man now becomes lord over the efficacy of the sacrament and that he may manipulate the benefit of the sacrament. After all, faith is not man's work but the work of the Holy Spirit operating in man through Gospel and sacrament. Just as little may this thesis be used to assert that in the case of unbelievers the material substance of the body and blood of Christ as such causes harm. As in the whole doctrine of the Lord's Supper, so here also Christ's body is the person of the living Christ himself in his corporeal presence. He himself confronts the unbelievers in the Lord's Supper, now however not as Saviour but as "a strict judge" who "is just as much present to exercise and manifest his judgment on unrepentant guests as he is to work life and consolation in the hearts of believing and worthy guests" (Ep. VII, 17). Here too the contemporaneity with the event of the crucifixion of Jesus Christ is at stake; the unworthy guest at the Lord's Table becomes guilty of profaning the body and blood of the Lord Jesus Christ and he "dishonors, abuses, and desecrates him who is there present as certainly as did the Jews when they actually and in deed laid violent hands upon the body of Christ and murdered him" (S.D. VII, 60). Whether the Lord's Supper is received for forgiveness or for judgment, in every case Christ is the Lord in action; he is the divine Saviour and judge.

Here indeed essence and benefit of the Lord's Supper are separated, and not only as a distinction to explain matters for our mode of thinking. For in the reception by the unbelievers Christ's body and blood, the gift of the Lord's Supper, are separated from the benefit. But we have already seen that even in its fixing of terms the Large Catechism is primarily interested in the close interrelation of essence and benefit. This concern probably explains the silence of the Small Catechism, the Augsburg Confession, and the Apology concerning the *manducatio indignorum* which, however, is not denied by them. For in all Confessions the statements about receiving Christ's body and blood to one's judgment are embraced and far surpassed by the permission for one to approach the Lord's Table in faith and expect to receive the strengthening of his faith from the Lord's Supper. The expressions concerning the reception of the sacrament to one's judgment are embraced and far surpassed by the unqualified invitation which addresses itself ever again to all the baptized and asks for no precondition except hunger—in fact, not even hunger, but only the approach in the knowledge that a lack of hunger is displeasing to God.

The statements about the *manducatio indignorum* stand *between the demand and the promise of faith*. In the last analysis these statements are far less terrifying than comforting and reassuring. For they immediately direct our attention away from the question, "Am I worthy or unworthy, believing or unbelieving?" to the reality which in every case is present and given in the Lord's Supper, namely,

Christ's body and blood. Christ's body and blood, however, are given with the promise, and are never impotent but always full of power and effect. "For Christ's body can never be an unfruitful, vain thing, impotent and useless" (L.C. V, 30). The sacrament makes the wavering trustful, the secure sinners terrified, the unworthy guests worthy. Therefore the passionate desire of the doctrine of the Lord's Supper is not to warn, examine, reprove—all this is concluded in Confession before the Lord's Supper—but to invite, that is, "draw and impel." For Christ himself "most graciously invites us" (L.C. V, 66). His promises "most powerfully draw and impel us" (L.C. V, 64). Obedience toward this loving and gracious coaxing on the part of the bidding Christ is not obedience to the law, and it is not produced "from compulsion and fear of man's commandments" (L.C. V, 51), "not from compulsion, coerced by men, but to obey and please the Lord Christ" (L.C. V, 45). It is an obedience which, incited by the Gospel and thereby released from strains and tensions, no longer resists the grace of God. For the "command" to approach the Lord's Table is permission: "Go joyfully to the sacrament and receive refreshment, comfort, and strength" (L.C. V, 72). This is the meaning when the Large Catechism speaks with infinitely greater fullness about the invitation to the Lord's Supper than about the *manducatio indignorum,* and devotes more space to this enticing and inviting than to the first two sections about the essence and benefit of the Lord's Supper.

All statements, then, testify that not death but life, not judgment but forgiveness is the proper effect of the Lord's Supper. Also, in the doctrine of the Lord's Supper we find the most powerful testimony that Christ's proper office is not condemning but saving.

9. The sacraments are the individual application of the promise of the Gospel under visible signs, indeed, the realization and the gift of what is promised.

In thesis 1 we started with the thought that a Christian's life until death is daily repentance and as such a daily "return" to Baptism and an eager approach to the Lord's Table. The Christian's whole life, then, is spent between the two sacraments, in constant hastening to both sacraments. Hastening to Baptism is a going back, while approaching the Lord's Supper is a hastening forward. Thus both sacraments embrace the believer at every moment.

What does it mean to live between the sacraments? What does

repentance mean as a daily return to Baptism and as a daily going forward to the Lord's Supper?

Baptism is the washing of regeneration through the Holy Spirit. In Baptism the old man dies and a new man is created. Every Christian should "regard his Baptism as the daily garment which he is to wear all the time, . . . suppressing the old man and growing up in the new" (L.C. IV, 84). "Thus a Christian life is nothing else than a daily Baptism, once begun and ever continued" (L.C. IV, 65). Because we have died in Baptism, let us live daily! Because in Baptism we have been reborn to a new life, let us walk in a new life! Because the old Adam has been drowned in Baptism, we should drown the old Adam in us by daily contrition and repentance, and the lusts and works of the old Adam should daily decrease! (S.C. IV, 12; L.C. IV, 67, 71). Because in Baptism the new man has arisen, "the new man should come forth daily and rise up, cleansed and righteous, to live forever in God's presence" (S.C. IV, 12),[19] and shall grow and increase! Here too we speak of growing and increasing in the fruits of regeneration. But if Baptism were only the beginning of this increase, only the beginning in a quantitative sense, then the daily "return" to Baptism would be retrogression, and the daily entrance into Baptism would be a daily flight from the eschatological consummation. But this is precisely not the case.[20] Rather, the return to Baptism is also a hastening forward to the Last Day. For in Baptism the believer has already reached the goal, even though the life of the regenerated man is spent in the midst of the ebb and flow of fluctuations, of increase and decrease in the fruits of regeneration, that is, of the works of the new obedience. Baptism is not a partial, but a total beginning for the new man.

The daily approach to the Lord's Supper—even though the Christian does not receive it daily, his life is oriented to the next ap-

[19] The *exercitium fidei* "*actualizes* the one-time *act of Baptism* as a remembrance of Baptism that is continually and believingly exercised, which as a remembrance of the divine *promise* is likewise also an expectation of Baptism. The baptized Christian lives between remembrance and expectation of Baptism as 'once baptized by the sacrament, but always as through faith to be baptized.' " *WA* 6, 535, l. 10; H. Diem, "Zum Verstaendnis der Taufe bei Luther," *Ev. Theol.* (1935), pp. 413 f.

[20] There is no reference here to a threefold or triple regeneration, e.g., (1) a baptismal regeneration; (2) a regeneration in conversion; (3) a rebirth (restoration) of all things. Cf. W. Laible, "Sind die Aussagen des kleinen Katechismus Luthers ueber die Sakramente noch haltbar?" in *Das Erbe Martin Luthers, Festschrift fuer L. Ihmels* (Leipzig, 1928), p. 375. Rather, the regeneration in Baptism, the daily *vivificatio* in repentance, and the resurrection at the Last Day are in an overwhelming manner "ultimately" identical for the believing reception.

proach to the Lord's Table—is the advance to the crucified body of our Lord through whom forgiveness and with it life eternal are granted us. Returning to the cross on Calvary the way of the Christian is also a hastening forward to the returning Lord who in the Last Judgment will acquit us of all sins and will for all eternity free us from death and the devil. This acquittal is imparted to us through Christ's body and blood in the Lord's Supper. Receiving the Lord's Supper we are united with Christ who in one person is the crucified and risen, the exalted and returning Lord.

What bearing has this on the relationship of the two sacraments to each other? Here we must first establish the fact that the doctrine of the sacraments is developed in the Confessions in two separate articles and that the interest in a general sacramental concept recedes rather strikingly into the background. To be sure, there are also some important pronouncements about the sacrament in general (A.C. XIII; Ap. XII, 42; XIII, 3 ff.; XXIV, 49, 69, etc.). But neither the doctrine of Baptism nor the doctrine of the Lord's Supper is derived from a general sacramental concept. It surely is not an accident that in the structure of the Augsburg Confession the general definition of a sacrament (A.C. XIII) does not precede but follows the article on Baptism (A.C. IX) and the Lord's Supper (A.C. X). To start with the general concept of a sacrament is impossible because the institution of the Lord's Supper in the decisive words, "This is my body," is without analogy in the institution of Baptism. The important difference involved in the absence of this analogy is taken into account in the method of presenting the Lutheran doctrine of the sacraments in that the Lutheran teaching develops the doctrine of Baptism independently from the words that institute Baptism, and develops the doctrine of the Lord's Supper just as independently from the words that institute the Lord's Supper.

Nevertheless, as deductions from the specific doctrines of Baptism and the Lord's Supper we find definitions and recapitulations such as the following: The Lord's Supper "is appropriately called the food of the soul since it nourishes and strengthens the new man. While it is true that through Baptism we are first born anew, our human flesh and blood have not lost their old skin. There are so many hindrances and temptations of the devil and the world that we often grow weary and faint, at times even stumble. The Lord's Supper is given as a daily food and sustenance so that our faith may refresh and strengthen itself, and not weaken in the struggle but grow continually stronger. For the new life should be one that develops and progresses" (L.C. V, 23 f.). Thus Baptism is the new birth, and the Lord's Supper is the protection and strengthening of the reborn man. Baptism is the beginning of the new life, and the Lord's Supper is the food of life which has this effect: that the life which has begun does not cease but increases constantly. Baptism is deliverance from the devil, and the Lord's Supper is protection against the devil, who steadily encircles the redeemed. But though we acknowledge this distinction, we maintain that the benefit of Baptism and of the Lord's Supper is one and the same, namely, forgiveness, life, and salvation. The fruit of both sacraments is the new man who, delivered from the devil and death, lives the eternal life of the resurrected in the midst of the rebellion of sin, death, and the devil.

What does it mean, therefore, to live between the sacraments? It means to return daily to the once-for-all Baptism and to go forward daily to the Lord's Table, which is prepared for us again and again. Thus the Christian's life at every moment is completely surrounded and embraced by the event of Christ's death on the cross. At every moment the Christian comes from Christ's death and hastens on to Christ's death. He is therefore not only surrounded by Christ's death but also given into Christ's death. But in that case he also partakes daily of the life of the risen Lord. For the crucified and the risen Lord cannot be torn apart. In Baptism we receive Christ's eternal life, and in the Lord's Supper we receive Christ's vicarious death, his given body and his shed blood. Again, in Baptism we receive the death of our old man, and in the Lord's Supper we receive Christ's body and blood as the bread of life. In the believing reception of both sacraments the Christian's life on earth—his present life and even the remainder of his life on earth—proves to be so completely encircled and encompassed by Christ's first and second Advent that the present and still prospective interval loses the power to lead him astray. In the reception of the two sacraments the believer is translated out of the problem area of his visible existence into the eternal life which will become visible at Christ's return.

It must, however, not be overlooked that God grants forgiveness, life, and salvation not only through the sacraments but also through preaching. Indeed it is one and the same forgiveness which is received through absolution and through the sacraments. It is one and the same life which the believer receives when he hears the Gospel or when he receives the sacraments. For it is the same Christ who "regenerates through Word and sacrament" (Ap. IX, 2). It is likewise the same Holy Spirit who works through Word and sacrament and gives us faith and life. In other words, the one Gospel comes to the sinner both through preaching and through Baptism and the Lord's Supper; the Gospel "offers counsel and help against sin in more than one way, for God is surpassingly rich in his grace: First, through the spoken word, by which the forgiveness of sin (the peculiar office of the Gospel) is preached to the whole world; second, through Baptism; third, through the holy Sacrament of the Altar; fourth, through the power of keys; and finally, through the mutual conversation and consolation of brethren" (S.A. III, iv). The whole Gospel is "embodied" and "offered" in the words in the Sacrament of the Altar, and these are "the very words which we hear everywhere in the Gospel" (L.C. V, 32). The same is true of Baptism. The Gospel in the sermon and in the sacrament is so completely identical that to deny the benefit of the Gospel in the sacrament is equivalent to asserting "that the whole Gospel or Word of God apart from the sacraments is of no value" (*ibid.*). The same truth is indicated when the Augsburg Confession and the Apology summarize preaching and the sacraments as *"promissio."* Just as the one Jesus Christ—not Moses—by his Word has instituted the Gospel ministry and Baptism and the Lord's Supper, so, through the preaching of the Gospel, Baptism, and the Lord's Supper Jesus Christ performs his proper work; not punishing and killing, but forgiving, quickening, and saving. For through the preaching of the Gospel, Baptism, and the Lord's Supper he gives us the merit of his suffering and death so we may receive his blessings and be saved. Thus in the preaching of the Gospel, in Baptism, and the Lord's Supper he speaks his proper word: "Your sins are forgiven you!" and is active in his proper office: as Saviour and life giver.

Why, then, are sacraments needed in addition to preaching, and why preaching in addition to sacraments? Are Christ and his gift received only partially through the sacraments? No, indeed. Already Baptism brings "the entire Christ, and the Holy Spirit with his gifts" (L.C. IV, 41), and the same is true of the Lord's Supper. Or are the merits of Jesus Christ and forgiveness received only partially and incompletely in absolution? By no means! Why then preaching *and* sacraments? The only answer is, "Because God commands both and because Christ has instituted both—the preaching of the Gospel and the sacraments." [21] We are forbidden to eliminate or even to

---

[21] This disposes of the question whether the Lutheran doctrine accords priority and greater significance to the Word *or* to the sacraments.

overlook this divine institution. This prohibition is confirmed by the statements which say the sacraments are necessary for salvation: 'Our churches teach that Baptism is necessary for salvation' (A.C. IX, 1; cf. Ap. IX, 1; Ep. XII, 6-8, 23). This is true also of the Lord's Supper: ". . . let it be understood that people who abstain and absent themselves from the sacrament over a long period of time (namely 'a year, or two, three, or more years') are not to be considered Christians" (L.C. V, 42, 40). "If you want such liberty, you may just as well take the further liberty not to be a Christian; then you need not believe or pray" (L.C. V, 49).

What, then, distinguishes the sacraments from preaching?

In the Lord's Supper "you have both truths, that it is Christ's body and blood and that these are *yours* as your treasure and gift" (L.C. V, 29). "Christ bids me eat and drink in order that the sacrament may be *mine* and may be a source of blessing to *me* as a sure pledge and sign" (L.C. V, 22). In the administration of the sacraments the Gospel is applied personally to every individual—to you and to me. Here no doubt need remain as to whether the grace that is proclaimed is for me, or whether perhaps it is intended for my neighbor in the pew, yes, perhaps for all others who hear the sermon with me except for me. The "for you" can indeed not be written too large; it excludes the fear that *we* in human caprice and greed have applied the Gospel to ourselves. In the inescapable directness of distribution and reception it means, "Given for you and for me." [22] The same is true of Baptism. From this viewpoint we understand why the Gospel pronounced personally by the absolution in Confession is also occasionally called a third sacrament (Ap. XII, 41; XIII, 4).

Moreover, in distinction from preaching the sacraments are not only an audible word but a "visible word" (*verbum visibile*), "a sort of picture of the Word" (*pictura verbi*), 'a painting whereby the same is signified as is proclaimed through the Word' (Ap. XIII, 5), 'a seal and confirmation of the Word and promise' (Ap. XXIV, 70). Hence the sacraments are not only the Word, but there are "two parts to a sacrament, the sign and the Word. In the New

[22] We must beware of using these peculiarities of the sacraments to deduce a *theory* about the necessity or feasibility of the sacraments alongside the Word. Cf. B. P. Tschackert: "This already answers the question *why* there are sacraments beside the Word at all. For since the Word of God proclaims the promise of grace in general, the sacrament effects the individual appropriation of salvation." Tschackert, *Entstehung*, p. 349. The juxtaposition of Word and sacrament is recognized by the Confessions purely as God's gracious ordinance and is not made evident by further proofs.

Testament, the Word is the added promise of grace" (Ap. XXIV, 69). We call sacraments 'the external signs and rites which have God's command and an added divine promise of grace' (Ap. XIII, 3). Already at this point it becomes clear why the absolution in Confession is really no sacrament because to the promise of grace no visible sign has been added by *God's* institution (the sign of the cross and the laying on of hands are mere human customs). Thus the sacraments act not only on the ears but also on man's other senses and strike his perception in a more comprehensive manner: "Through the Word and the rite God simultaneously moves the heart. . . . As the Word enters through the ears to strike the heart, so the rite itself enters through the eyes to move the heart. The Word and the rite have the same effect" (Ap. XIII, 5). Thus the sacraments are "signs and testimonies of God's will toward us" (*"signa et testimonia voluntatis Dei erga nos,"* A.C. XIII, 1); ' "signs of the New Testament," testimonies of grace and of the forgiveness of sins' (Ap. XIII, 14); 'a seal and sure sign' (Ap. XXIV, 49).

What does "sign" mean in these definitions? In the doctrine of the Lord's Supper one might think first of bread and wine, but the terms *"ritus"* and *"ceremonia"* point beyond these elements to the act of offering and receiving the bread and wine. The Apology ultimately uses the term "sign" to designate also the sacrament as a whole. In a different way the Large Catechism calls Christ's body and blood "a sure pledge and sign" (L.C. V, 22). It is clear that the Confessions do not use this word uniformly.[23]

Whom or what does the "sign" designate? In the Apology, does it designate Christ's body and blood or the gracious will of God, i.e., the forgiveness of sins? In both the Large Catechism and the Apology it is the latter. However, this is not a strict either/or. For Christ's body and blood are not only "a sure pledge and sign," but "the very gift he has provided for me against my sins, death, and all evils" (L.C. V, 22). Christ's body and blood and the forgiveness of sins are interwoven. Also, in the doctrine of the sacraments in the Apology—despite divergences from the Catechisms—signs, promises, and the promised gift cannot be separated. Through the sacraments as "signs of the promises" the "promised gifts" (*res promissae*) are themselves offered and received (Ap. XIII, 20; cf. XXIV, 18).

[23] For the differences in the concept "sign" within Lutheran doctrine, and for the meaning of *"signum"* in the writings of Melanchthon especially, see Gollwitzer, *Coena Domini,* pp. 64, 65 ff., 101 ff., 163, 167 ff., *et al.*

Therefore faith should cling not only to the Word but also to the visible sign. 'As God gives the promise to create such faith, so also the external sign has been added and placed before the eyes in order to move the heart to believe and to strengthen faith. For through these two, the Word and the external signs, the Holy Spirit is active' (Ap. XXIV, 70). "Thus faith clings to the water" (L.C. IV, 29), and the same is true of bread and wine. For we dare not "separate faith from the object to which faith is attached and bound. Yes, it must be external so that it can be perceived and grasped by the senses and thus brought into the heart, just as the entire Gospel is an external, oral preaching" (L.C. V, 30). Faith must "have something to believe—something to which it may cling and upon which it may stand" (L.C. V, 29). In the reception of the sacraments faith rests not only on the Word but also on the sign, and it is called forth not only by hearing but also by seeing, feeling, and tasting. The sacraments accordingly strengthen faith in that they make clear by signs that the promise of the Gospel is meant for the *whole* man.

The sacraments, therefore, are the rock to which the Christian on trial clings; yes, on which he may leap and stand erect in the midst of the distress into which God's law brings him, the sinner, by means of ever-new attacks. In the midst of the storm caused by distinguishing between law and Gospel, contrition and faith, being righteous and being sinner, being reborn and yet only partially renewed, the sacraments stand firm. Here God lets you, you yourself personally, not only hear but also taste and feel that in Christ all this distinguishing has already been ended. In the believing reception of the sacraments the final superiority of the Gospel over the law is visibly demonstrated in all its comforting and convincing attraction.

10. Even as the one who is exalted at the right hand of God, Jesus Christ is still present on earth according to his divine and human natures.

This statement follows already from Article X of the Augsburg Confession. For in his congregation's celebration of the Lord's Supper Jesus Christ is truly present, not only as visualized by the congregation in faith, but in the reality of his person, and again, not only according to his divine nature but also according to his human nature. For he is present bodily. Hence he is present not only at one place but simultaneously at many places on earth, wherever in his church the Lord's Supper is distributed and received, even when this happens at the same time at places far apart from each other.

This fact is attested in the Confessions' doctrine of the Lord's Supper from the very beginning, but before the Formula of Concord it is nowhere the topic of independent christological reflections. Its meaning for Christology is systematically unfolded for the first time in the Formula of Concord (VIII), where it is incorporated into the teaching on the two natures of Christ. Thus the teaching about ubiquity proves to be something secondary, in the temporal and conceptual structure of the Book of Concord, both in terms of chronology and of content. That which is primary, which the teaching on ubiquity exists to serve, is the doctrine of the Lord's Supper. The comforting assurance of receiving Christ's body and blood, and therewith the comfort of the incarnation of the Son of God, is to be strengthened, fortified, and protected by the doctrine of the ubiquity. The important thing here is "that according to and with the same assumed human nature, Christ can be and is present wherever he wills, and in particular that he is present with his church and community on earth as mediator, head, king, and high priest. Not part or only one half of the person of Christ, but the entire person to which both natures, the divine and the human, belong is present. He is present not only according to his deity, but also according to and with his assumed human nature, according to which he is our brother and we flesh of his flesh and bone of his bone (Eph. 5:30). To make certainty and assurance doubly sure on this point, he instituted his Holy Supper that he might be present with us, dwell in us, work and be mighty in us according to that nature too, according to which he has flesh and blood" (S.D. VIII, 78 f.).

The christological content of the doctrine of the Lord's Supper is systematically delineated in three main ways:

a) Article VIII of the Formula of Concord not only teaches the fact that the exalted Lord is present bodily in the Lord's Supper, but beyond this makes certain pronouncements concerning the possibilities of his exalted body being spatially present in general.

Thus it is taught that Christ at the right hand of the majesty and power of God has received majesty also according to his human nature and that therefore "also according to and with this same assumed human nature of his, Christ can be and is present wherever he wills, and in particular . . . with his church and community on earth . . ." (S.D. VIII, 78). At the same time the Confessions reject a spatial understanding of Christ's session at the right hand of God. The point at issue here is that "the right hand of God . . . is not a specific place in heaven." It is "precisely the almighty power of God which fills heaven and earth, in which Christ has been installed according to his humanity in deed and truth [*realiter*]" (S.D. VIII, 28). The rejection of spatial conceptions is made even more pointed by the rejection of the words "that the human nature of Christ is locally extended to every place in heaven and earth" (Ep. VIII, 29). On the contrary, the exalted Christ in his divine superiority is Lord of space, being confined neither by a specific place in space, nor restricted in his power by the co-ordinate system of spatiality. He is the Lord not only as true God but also as true man, also in his human corporeality. Expressly rejected is the notion "that Christ is present with us on earth in the Word, in the sacraments, and in all our necessities only according to his deity, and that this presence does not at all concern his human nature" (Ep. VIII, 32; cf. 30). Luther's *Great Confession Concerning the Holy Supper*[24] is quoted with approval: " 'No, comrade, wherever you put God down for me, you must also put the humanity down for me. They simply will not let themselves be separated and divided from each other. He has become one person and never separates the assumed humanity from himself' " (S.D. VIII, 84). It is true, there still remains in this systematic development the lack of clarity which is indicated by the difference between Brenz and Chemnitz, between the Wuerttemberg and the Lower Saxony Christology; that is, the difference between the absolute omnipresence and a multivolipresence.[25] Chemnitz's 'wherever he wills' [*ubicunque velit*] which plainly appears in several passages as a qualifier (S.D. VIII, 29, 78, 92) has not been thought through as to its christological implications; it has been systematically harmonized neither with the occasional unqualified statements of the Formula of Concord about the omnipresence of Christ's human nature (e.g., *Bek.*, p. 808, ll. 11, 18), nor with similar quotations from Luther's writings (cf. esp. S.D. VIII, 81 ff.).

[24] *Vom Abendmahl Christi, Bekenntnis* (1528); *WA* 26, 332-33.
[25] It is not correct to say, "The whole Christology of the Formula of Concord essentially reproduces the teaching of Chemnitz." C. E. Hay (trans.), R. Seeberg's *Textbook of the History of Doctrines* (Baker, 1954), Vol. II, Book III, part II, 1, pp. 387 f. We are here faced with a compromise in which neither Chemnitz nor Brenz had his way.

b) The Formula of Concord teaches not only the omnipresence but also the omnipotence and omniscience of the exalted Christ's human nature:

". . . inscrutable, ineffable, heavenly prerogatives and privileges in majesty, glory, power, and might above every name that is named, not only in this age but also in that which is to come" (S.D. VIII, 51) belong to it. Not only as true God but also as true man Christ knows all things (Ep. VIII, 16, 30-38; S.D. VIII, 73 ff.) and has the power to quicken, to judge, and to forgive (S.D. VIII, 55). This is not meant to be a mere christological manner of speaking which out of deference to the divine person of Jesus Christ says unwarranted things about his human nature (Ep. VIII, 24-26; S.D. VIII, 36 ff., 56 f.). No, omnipresence, omnipotence, omniscience are actually given to the human nature of Jesus Christ. But, on the other hand, this must not be made to say that thereby the human nature of Christ has become unlike our human nature "in such a way that the human nature in Christ had completely laid aside its natural and essential properties and is now either transformed into the Godhead or by means of these communicated properties has become intrinsically equal with the Godhead" (S.D. VIII, 62; cf. 72). Quite the contrary! Even at the right hand of God Jesus Christ is and remains true man, one of us. Between the two rejected misinterpretations the doctrine of the *communicatio idiomatum* is developed. Appealing to the christological formulas of Chalcedon, both the commingling as well as the severing of Christ's human and divine natures are rejected, and a nonreversible penetration of the human nature by attributes of the divine nature is taught. While the Confessions decline the picture of two boards glued together, they do approve the ancient simile of glowing iron to elucidate the personal union of the two natures in Christ: "Thus there is and remains in Christ only a single divine omnipotence, power, majesty, and glory, which is the property of the divine nature alone. But it shines forth and manifests itself fully, though always spontaneously, *in, with, and through* the assumed exalted human nature of Christ. Just as in glowing iron there are not two powers of illumination and combustion—the power of illumination and combustion is the property of fire—but since the fire is united with the iron, it demonstrates and manifests its power of illumination and combustion in and through the iron in such a way that on that account and through this union the glowing iron has the power of illumination and combustion . . ." (S.D. VIII, 66; cf. 18 f.).

c) Furthermore, Article VIII teaches not only the omnipotence, omniscience, and omnipresence of the human nature of the ascended Lord, but that all these divine attributes and potentialities belong to the human nature of Christ itself: "But Christ did not receive this majesty, to which he was exalted according to his humanity, only after his resurrection from the dead and his ascension, but when he was conceived in his mother's womb and became man and when the divine and human nature were personally united" (S.D. VIII, 13). Not only through the ascension but already in the incarnation the human nature of Jesus Christ "has been elevated to the right hand of majesty, power, and might over every name that is named not only in this age but also in that which is to come" (S.D. VIII, 12). This majesty of his human nature Jesus Christ "kept . . . hidden during the state of his humiliation and did not use it at all times, but only when he wanted to" (S.D. VIII, 26). He indeed revealed it through his miracles in word and deed (S.D. VIII, 25), and yet "concealed and restrained" it (S.D. VIII, 65). Only with the exaltation through resurrection and ascension can it be said that "since the form of a slave has been laid aside, it takes place fully, mightily, and publicly before all the saints in heaven and on earth" (S.D. VIII, 65), now he is "established in the full use, revelation, and manifestation of his divine majesty" (Ep. VIII, 16). This, however, does not make the human nature master of the divine nature, either in the humiliation or in the exaltation of Jesus Christ; rather, the divine fullness shines with its majesty in the human nature always "spontaneously and when and where he wills" (S.D. VIII, 64). Even though in this way the humiliation is understood as concealing the complete possession of the divine glory of the human nature (cf. also Ep. VIII, 39), there still remains the difficulty of reconciling these statements with other statements of the Formula of Concord, according to which the human nature of Jesus Christ was not placed in complete *possession* of the divine majesty until after the resurrection and ascension (S.D. VIII, 26, 51), after his humiliation when he could "increase in age, wisdom and favor with God and men" (Ep. VIII, 16). Here too dissonances between the Christology of Brenz and of Chemnitz and future doctrinal controversies are suggested.[26]

One will not do justice to the Christology of the Formula of

---

[26] Especially the controversy between the Lutheran theologians of Tuebingen and Giessen at the beginning of the seventeenth century. Cf. O. Ritschl, *Dogmengeschichte des Protestantismus*, IV, 180 ff.

Concord if one does not recognize its real concern, which finds most emphatic expression at the close of the positive presentation in the Solid Declaration. Its real concern is the "highest comfort" of Christians, namely, the "promises of the presence and indwelling of their head, king, and high priest, who has promised that not only his unveiled deity, which to us poor sinners is like a consuming fire on dry stubble, will be with them, but that he, he, the man who has spoken with them, who has tasted every tribulation in his assumed human nature, and who can therefore sympathize with us as with men and his brethren, he wills to be with us in all our troubles also according to that nature by which he is our brother and we are flesh of his flesh" (S.D. VIII, 87).

In spite of this, it is doubtful whether the Christology of the Formula of Concord follows with theological cogency from the earlier Lutheran Confessions and can really be termed "restatement and explanation" of an article of the Augsburg Confession (cf. F.C. title page). In the Apology knowledge of Christ was identical with receiving the benefits of Christ, but in the Formula of Concord the relationship of the two natures increasingly becomes an independent theological concern, separate from the redemptive act.[27] All statements of the former Confessions witnessed to the gracious mercy of God, but the Formula of Concord directs its attention to the omnipotence, omniscience, omnipresence of God and to the problem of the participation in these divine attributes on the part of the human nature of Jesus Christ. "These, taken by themselves, fit the *Deus absconditus* just as well" (W. Elert, *Morphologie,* I, 203). Moreover, we must ask whether this Christology is to be considered an interpretation or an abrogation of the christological formulations of Chalcedon to which the church of the Augsburg Confession always felt obligated.[28] The former assumption was soon denied, and not only by Reformed critics. Besides, we must also bear in mind that the church of the Augsburg Confession itself did not with a clear conscience dare to deny territorial churches which declined to accept the Christology of the Formula of Concord the right to be churches of the Augsburg Confession.

[27] "Thus within Reformation territory itself it has been established how destructive is the *contueri Christi naturas et modos incarnationis,* which the Reformation had once forbidden." F. Loofs, *Leitfaden,* p. 921.

[28] Thus Vilmar regards the creed of Chalcedon as an obligatory presupposition of the Augsburg Confession alongside and among the three Ecumenical Symbols with which the Book of Concord begins. *Dogmatik,* I, 129. Cf. the Catalog of Testimonies, *Bek.,* p. 1105.

But no matter how one may judge the Christology of the Formula of Concord, at all events we must conclude from the doctrine of the Lord's Supper in the Confessions that by his ascension Jesus Christ has not been removed from his church but dwells in its midst as true God and man. Thus Jesus Christ will not only return in the future but he is even now present in the midst of his congregation according to his divine and human natures. As the Lord sitting at the right hand of God he dwells among his own as they suffer and strive here on earth, and he purifies, refreshes, and guides them.

VI

THE CHURCH

After having treated the doctrine of the Gospel and the sacraments in the foregoing chapters it would seem obvious to start immediately with the definition of the church as given in Article VII of the Augsburg Confession. It comes to us naturally as a result of the previous line of thought. Nevertheless, we shall look first at the antithesis between the devil's kingdom and Christ's kingdom, for only against the background of this bitter conflict does the doctrine of the church and of the ministry, as well as of the office of the civil government, really become clear.

1. The devil's kingdom is the tyrannical power with which the devil stupefies fallen man through false teaching, incites him to vices, and keeps him a prisoner in the sphere of sin and death.

Through Adam's disobedience "all men were made sinners and became subject to death and the devil" (S.A. III, i, 1). The devil lords it over them all. They are all "members of the devil's kingdom" (Ap. VII, 16), for "human nature is enslaved and held prisoner by the devil" (Ap. II, 47). The unlimited rule of the devil over all sinners corresponds to the universal reality of original sin. By bringing the child to Baptism the church confesses before God that it is "possessed by the devil" (*Tauf.*, 2). The church knows about the personal reality of the angelic powers who revolted against their Creator and whose impious dominion God permits to exist until the Last Day. They are not an invention of men, nor are they merely personified symbols of psychological processes. Man's enslaved will is not merely an anthropological fact. Rather, the will of man after the fall is not free to do good since, being subject to the devil's slavery, it is held fast by him in the sphere of sin. This satanic imprisonment is complete. Human nature is "far too weak to be able by its own strength to resist the devil"

194

(Ap. IV, 138). This subjection of all men under the dominion of the devil is a punishment like death (Ap. II, 46).

The devil rules over his subjects by seducing them to false teaching and thereby stupefying them. The whole history of the world shows the tremendous power of the devil's kingdom: 'It is apparent that the world, from the highest to the lowest, is full of blasphemies against God and full of great errors and wicked doctrine against God and his Word. In these strong fetters and chains the devil keeps many wise men, many hypocrites who appear as saints before the world, in wretched captivity' (Ap. II, 49). Thus the devil lures men to devise their own gods and cults and he fans into blasphemy and idolatry the small spark of their knowledge that there is a God. Thus the devil entices man to devise laws of his own and to trust in his works, and thus he falsifies the Decalogue even with respect to the second table which is inscribed in the human heart. The devil does not fail to use the terms "good" and "bad," not even the name of God, but he misuses them for their devilish opposite and permits no unoccupied, neutral space between idolatry and service to the true God. Thus the world is "full of sects and false teachers, all of whom wear the holy name as a cloak and warrant for their devilish doctrine" (L.C. III, 47); so that his name is used "to cloak lies and make them acceptable" (L.C. III, 41).

The devil thus incites to "all kinds of sins" (Ap. II, 47), not only to blasphemies but also to vices (Ap. II, 49). He misleads man not only to a corruption of the Decalogue in his thoughts but also to transgressions in the act of murder, adultery, greed, etc. Both sins—blasphemies and vices—are inseparably connected; ungodly deeds are produced by ungodly opinions. The devil seduces men by stupefying them. They imagine that they are wise, whereas they go astray as fools, and they think they are good even while they do evil.

This, then, is the dominion of the devil, that he ensnares in ever-new sin men to whom paradise has been closed, and at the same time prevents them from recognizing their sin. In this way the devil completely holds in the sphere of death those who are abandoned to death. This rule of his which consists in enslaving slaves all the more securely and in binding the fettered more firmly is properly called tyranny. The devil's dominion is tyranny because it treacherously and forcibly suppresses faith and obedience toward God. Not every kind of rule is tyranny. But there is no tyrannical rule apart from the devil. Since he rules the world and fills it with blasphemies and vices, the devil's kingdom may also be called the kingdom of the world. In so far as the world is viewed as being preserved by God in spite of sin and death, the kingdom of the world must be distinguished from the devil's kingdom, just as the divine institution of civil government is differentiated from the devil's activity. But in so far as the world is corrupted by sin and is subject to death, it is also entirely subject to the tyranny of the devil.

2. Christ's kingdom is the rule through which Jesus Christ redeems fallen man from sin, death, and the devil, and gives man righteousness and eternal life.

Whereas the devil binds the sinner in sin, Jesus Christ gives the sinner righteousness. Whereas the devil keeps the dead in the realm of death, Jesus raises and liberates the dead to eternal life. Whereas the devil deceives and stupefies through lies, Jesus Christ is the truth opening the eyes of the blinded. Thus he is the Lord "who has redeemed me, a lost and condemned creature, delivered me and freed me from all sins, from death, and from the power of the devil" (S.C. II, 4).

However, these two kingdoms are distinct not only as regards their rulers: one kingdom is ruled by a creature, the other by the Son of God and, hence, by God himself; therefore the kingdom of Christ and the kingdom of God are interchangeable terms (cf. L.C. III, 51). One kingdom is governed in enmity against God, the other in communion and essential unity with God. Nor are the two kingdoms differentiated only by their completely opposite purposes and effects. Rather, the very terms "Lord," "property," "service" in each case mean something radically different. Jesus Christ is my Lord as my redeemer (L.C. II, 27), who has redeemed me "not with silver and gold but with his holy and precious blood and with his innocent sufferings and death" (S.C. II, 4). Christ is Lord as the one who has humbled himself to be the servant of those whom he governs. He does not, after the manner of other lords, demand their lives that they might die for him, but he gives his life that they might live. He is the Lord in a paradoxical sense, so different from all human lords and also from the devil, that the redeemed man actually realizes: "Before this I had *no* Lord and King but was captive under the power of the devil" (L.C. II, 27).

To "be his" (S.C. II, 4) in the kingdom of Christ means something altogether different than it does in the devil's kingdom. To be Christ's own does not mean to be a servant and slave; rather, I am his own as his brother, and I belong to God as his child. I belong to him not as a prisoner but as a freed man. So also service in his kingdom is not the service of a slave but the cheerful, free service of the newborn children of God; it is not coercion but a gracious permission. Yes, this service is not service in the usual sense at all; it is not so much service as fellowship. For Christ has redeemed me that "I may . . . live under him in his kingdom, and serve him in everlasting righteousness, innocence, and blessedness, *even as* he is risen from the dead and lives and reigns to all eternity" (S.C. II, 4). To live *under* Christ in Christ's kingdom means to live *with* Christ; to serve him means to rule with him.

In agreement with this the Apology teaches that "the kingdom of Christ is the righteousness of the heart and the gift of the Holy Spirit" (Ap. VII, 13). The kingdom of Christ consists in this that he "quickens by his Spirit" (Ap. VII, 18), that he 'inwardly rules, strengthens, and comforts hearts, and imparts the Holy Spirit and manifold spiritual gifts' (Ap. VII, 13). Christ's kingdom is, therefore, Christ's act of giving; he gives us his righteousness and through the Holy Spirit renews us to his image. He exercises this rule through the preaching of the Gospel and the administration of the sacraments. The same holds true of God's kingdom: It is "righteousness and life in the heart"; it consists in this that 'inwardly the Holy Spirit enlightens, purifies, and strengthens our hearts, and that he produces a new light and life in the hearts' (Ap. XXVII, 27). Christ's kingdom is God's kingdom, since Christ is exalted by God to be Lord over all creation. Even though he now exercises his rule in seeming weakness through Word and sacrament, yet Christ's victory over the devil's kingdom is assured.

Until Christ's return both of these kingdoms must never be thought of as static but as in constant opposition, conquering and reconquering, advancing and repelling, holding fast, freeing and, under certain circumstances, recapturing. Through Word and sacrament Christ snatches the slaves of the devil from their enslavement. The devil, on the other hand, tempts the freed men and tries to make them his slaves again. There is no peace and no neutral ground between the two kingdoms. Man is either a member of the devil's kingdom or a member of Christ's kingdom. This battle is fought with every man as a prize and it is waged on this earth. As the Word and sacraments through which Christ rules are an external Word and earthly elements in the external Word, so the

THEOLOGY OF THE LUTHERAN CONFESSIONS

battle of the devil against Jesus Christ, the exalted Lord, becomes manifest on earth as a conflict centering around Word and sacrament, that is, as centering around the church.[1]

3. The church is "the assembly of all believers among whom the Gospel is preached in its purity and the holy sacraments are administered according to the Gospel" (A.C. VII, 1).

The church is defined as the assembly of all believers and the assembly, in turn, is defined by what is done in its midst.

First, we must note that the Word of God is not named here in general, nor is the law, but only the Gospel, and that in connection with "preaching." The Gospel in its essence is the oral proclamation of forgiveness. In the German and Latin texts "preaching" and

[1] In almost all cases the decision as to whether the Lutheran doctrine of the church is correctly presented is not made with the explanation of the statements about the church, but with the doctrine concerning Word and sacrament, yes, in essence with the correct understanding of the incarnation of the Son of God. One who does not recognize that the living Word of God comes to us only as external Word in the word of men and concealed under water, bread, and wine, or one who fails to see that this external Word is not man's possession but God's *viva vox*, must necessarily miss the point in the doctrine of the church. Between these two errors lie the manifold misinterpretations of recent times. When, for example, E. Troeltsch understands the Lutheran concept of the church as a saving institution in the sense of a reformed but not transcended Roman, institutional concept of the church, this caricature rests on the misconception of the Lutheran doctrine of the Word, namely, the distinction between law and Gospel and, again, the relationship between Gospel, preaching, and Scripture. From this point it is impossible to say, "The Bible is the heart of the church, the inspired authority, and the saving power which is operative through its inherent converting power." "Die Soziallehren der christlichen Kirchen und Gruppen," *Ges. Schriften* (Tuebingen, 1919), I, 462. "The Word" is "an objective treasure chest set up for all individuals, a treasure owned by the institution, to be dispensed in an orderly way by officials designated for that purpose." *Ibid.*, p. 449. But God's Word is God himself, who speaks and acts in the law and the Gospel, over whose killing and quickening we have no control whatever as we might have over a book or a treasure. In an entirely different way R. Sohm caricatures the Lutheran doctrine of the church when, in pointed polemics against all "institutional" aspects, he divorces the church as a fellowship of the Spirit from the church as an external fellowship and equates the latter with the world. In the last analysis this misinterpretation too rests on a false view of the Word: "The external visible Word and sacrament, belonging to the external visible 'bodily' Christendom, is as such *not* identical with the true Word and sacrament," it is the "dead Word"; the living Word, on the contrary, is "invisible." Such statements are impossible in the context of Lutheran doctrine. The very pathos of the Lutheran doctrine is the witness to the incarnation of the Word, the condescension of God, who is present in the words of men and in, with, and under the external elements, quite independent of whether his Word is heard by believers or unbelievers, and whether the sacrament is received by worthy or unworthy communicants. Sohm's statements go far beyond the Reformed distinction of *verbum efficax* and *verbum inefficax* and are spiritualistic-enthusiastic. Cf. the discussion with Troeltsch in *Kirchenrecht* (Muenchen-Leipzig, 1923), II, 132 f.

'teaching' (that is, *doctrina evangelii,* A.C. VII, 2) correspond. Not the silent possession of doctrine is meant here but the act of oral teaching and, again, not a teaching that ignores assurance and comfort but a teaching that is preaching.[2]

Likewise the stress is not placed on knowing about the sacraments but on their actual administration. They are to be administered "according to the Gospel" (A.C. VII, 1), "in accordance with the divine Word" (A.C. VII, 2). This involves, first, that each sacrament is to be administered according to its words of institution. A celebration of the Lord's Supper without the words of institution would be no celebration (cf. p. 155). However, this qualification must not be restricted to the liturgical rubrics of the administration of the sacraments. "According to the Gospel" includes also the proclamation related to the sacraments. Again, the church is characterized in her essence not by the silent possession of a doctrine of the sacraments in agreement with the Gospel, but by the "administration" of the sacraments, that is, through the actual giving and receiving. This attention to the event is also "according to the Gospel."

If, then, the Gospel and the sacraments belong to the concept "church," the essence of the church includes the only "means" through which "God gives the Holy Spirit" (A.C. V, 2), and through which the Holy Spirit is active.

In the definition from A.C. VII, given above as the topic sentence, "the assembly of all believers" and the preaching of the Gospel and the administration of the sacraments are connected by means of the controversial words "among whom," *"in qua."* In a similar connection the Small Catechism has a corresponding "in": ". . . the Holy Spirit has called me through the Gospel, enlightened me with his gifts . . . just as he calls, gathers, enlightens, and sanctifies the whole Christian church on earth. . . . *In this Christian church* [*Christenheit*] he daily and abundantly forgives all my sins, and the sins of all believers" (S.C. II, 6; cf. L.C. II, 54 f.). The Holy Spirit calls the Christian church through the Gospel and preaches the Gospel in the Christian church. These very statements indicate that in the total context of the Confessions the words *"in"* and *"bei"* of the Augsburg Confession (VII) are to be explained by taking various factors into consideration:

[2] Just as *"doctrina"* must be interpreted in terms of "preaching," so "preaching" must be interpreted in terms of *"doctrina."* That is to say, the content of the sermon is a report concerning a definite event, a report that may be comprehended in sober doctrine.

a) The Gospel and the sacraments are "in" the assembly of all believers as instruments through which the Holy Spirit produces faith and creates the assembly of believers.

b) The Gospel and the sacraments are "in" the assembly of believers as the service which is entrusted to the assembly of believers and which is performed by it.

This twofold significance[3] may be designated with Luther as follows:

a) ". . . where Christ is not preached, there is no Holy Spirit to create, call, and gather the Christian church" (L.C. II, 45). Through Word and sacrament the Holy Spirit awakens the believers and gathers the assembly of the faithful.

b) The Holy Spirit "has appointed a community on earth through which he speaks and does all his work" (L.C. II, 61). It "is the mother that begets and bears every Christian through the Word of God. The Holy Spirit reveals and preaches that Word, and by it he illumines and kindles hearts so that they grasp and accept it, cling to it, and persevere in it" (L.C. II, 42; cf. 41). The community of believers exists prior to my faith. The Holy Spirit "first leads us into his holy community, placing us upon the bosom of the church, whereby he preaches to us and brings us to Christ" (L.C. II, 37). The community of believers creates faith through Word and sacrament.

Hence it follows that in the Augsburg Confession's definition (VII) the words "assembly of all believers" and the statement of the relative clause are inseparable. The relative clause does not add anything new to the definition "assembly of all believers," but explains it. Thus it is possible to define the church, without mentioning Gospel and sacrament, as "the assembly of all believers and saints" (A.C. VIII), which says nothing else than A.C. VII. For the assembly of believers can never exist without Gospel and sacrament. Without preaching and the sacraments the church would dissolve into nothing and would never have come into existence.[4]

---

[3] Both imply something quite different from what is currently suggested by neo-Protestants who say that Word and sacrament spring from the fellowship of faith, or that faith creates an avenue of expression for itself in Word and sacrament.

[4] "Unity of faith and unity in Word and sacrament" must never be separated. This does not lead to a "double concept of church" in the sense of an either/or, as is claimed. W. Kahl says that the church "is *either* a 'spiritual inner Christendom,' united by the unity of faith and the communion of the Spirit; *or* a 'bodily, outward Christendom,' united through the cultus . . ." However, the distinction must be made ". . . depending on whether the fellowship of the members rests purely on the unity of faith and the Spirit, *or*, in case this

Because of this essential connection between the church and the means of grace it is necessarily true of the church that without it "no one can come to the Lord Christ" (L.C. II, 45). ". . . outside this Christian church (that is, where the Gospel is not) there is no forgiveness" (L.C. II, 56).

We must note at this place that the church in the Augsburg Confession is not defined as the assembly of believers in which good works are done![5] These are surely not excluded, but they are fruits of faith. The Holy Spirit who creates faith is not received

unity were lacking, at least on the fact of the common possession of the cultus or some other external sign." *Der Rechtsinhalt des Konkordienbuchs, Sonderabdruck a.d. Festgabe fuer O. Gierke* (Breslau, 1910), pp. 21 f. Rather, the fellowship of the members of the "spiritual inner Christendom" rests also on the fellowship of the "cultus," because the external marks, Word and sacrament, are not only to be "brought forth" by the church, but they above all bring forth the church, that is, the "spiritual, inner Christendom." J. Stahl separated the two concepts of the Augsburg Confession (A.C. VII), "assembly of believers" and "pure doctrine," even more drastically. He says: "They are not identical, nor inseparable. A living and believing congregation can exist with serious doctrinal errors, yea more, a congregation with pure doctrine can be without a living faith." *Die Kirchenverfassung nach Lehre und Recht der Protestanten* (2nd ed.; Erlangen, 1862), p. 42. But has not this transformed into a quantitative possession of doctrinal formulations the pure doctrine of the Gospel, that is, the event of bestowing pardon by grace alone, without which there can be no faith? Over against this view A. Ritschl is justified in saying: "Since the Reformers do not at all present the congregation of saints without these tangible means of the gracious operation of God (that is, not without Word and sacrament), the relative clause, '*in qua evangelium recte docetur*, etc.,' is not a synthetic, but an analytical judgment with respect to the *congregatio sanctorum.*" "Die Begruendung des Kirchnrechtes im evangelischen Begriff von der Kirche," *Ges. Aufsaetze* (Freiburg-Leipzig, 1893), p. 105. Reversing the concepts, in an analytic judgment concerning the "*congregatio . . .* , in qua EVANGELIUM *pure docetur,*" the *congregatio* is qualified as "*congregatio* SANCTORUM," or "assembly of all *believers.*"

[5] A. Ritschl moved in this direction when he viewed the definition of A.C. VII as a dogmatic formula about the church and suggested that it be supplemented with an ethical one. He proceeded from the fact that the church under identical operation of the Holy Spirit manifests degrees of gifts, effects, and callings. He also pointed to the experience of the variety of activities and orders in which the ethical self-activity of the sanctified and of their self-conscious volition manifests itself. Thus the church is "an ethical, autonomous reality, inasmuch as her members exercise their common priestly privileges by confessing God and Christ in prayer and in the observance of the Lord's Supper, and also inasmuch as through their gifts of charity they enable their needy fellow members to join in their joint worship." *Ibid.*, pp. 107, 114, 136. However, the Confessions will not admit such a distinction between dogmatic and ethical. Does not the definition in A.C. VII already contain the ethical statements that should be made on the basis of a proper distinction between law and Gospel in this connection, namely, as the Word of God is properly the Gospel which pardons and sanctifies, and not the law which reveals and retains sins, so also the permission to believe—"Here is the church"—is full of abundant grace. This is true because the definition of the church skips over the confession, sacrifice, and prayer that should be present in the congregation, yet is always very imperfectly present, and mentions directly God's work in the congregation, which creates faith and the new obedience.

through works. It is even more striking that the Confessions are not mentioned in the relative clause,[6] even though the question about the meaning of the terms *"pure," "recte," "according to the Gospel,"* at once suggests Confessions or Creeds—and even the Augsburg Confession attaches great importance to agreement with the creeds of the ancient church. However, the Confessions are the response to the preaching of the Gospel and they are the fruit of the Holy Spirit, but they are not his instruments as Word and sacrament are. Finally, it is noteworthy that in this definition no mention is made of the office of the ministry.[7] This is done in Articles V, XIV, and XXVIII; therefore in Article VII we must not think of a preaching and an administration of the sacraments separated from the ministerial office. Since here the ministry is implied but not mentioned, our attention is fixed on God's act through the Gospel, and it becomes clear that the ministry is not an independently existing institution but only a service to the Gospel.

This definition, moreover, does not stay with a locally circumscribed assembly, but has its eye immediately on "the assembly of *all* believers." Though the Gospel is always proclaimed in a local fellowship of believers, A.C. VII looks beyond the size, large or small, of local assemblies to the whole Christian church on earth.

[6] Note the differing formulation in Article XII of the Schwabach Articles, the primary source for the Augsburg Confession: "Such a church is nothing else than the believers in Christ who maintain, believe, and teach the above-mentioned articles and doctrines and suffer persecution and pain because of them. . . ." Here the definition of the church includes not only the preaching of the Gospel and the use of the sacraments but also creedal articles concerning the Trinity, the deity of Christ, the work of the Incarnate, death, original sin, etc. The fact that the wording of A.C. VII does not repeat Schwabach XII must not be overemphasized, but neither must it be overlooked.

[7] At this point Stahl begins his attempt at supplementing the Augsburg Confession. In A.C. VII "the organic side of the church has been ignored, namely, office and government. Only the spiritual forces and their free activity have been included in the definition, but not the institutional structure that must bear them. Only the divine aspect is emphasized, namely, the operation of the Holy Spirit in men's hearts, and the Word and sacrament, but not the medium of the human aspect, the external order and alignment under men through whom the Word is to be purely preserved and proclaimed." *Kirchenverfassung,* pp. 43 f. However, A.C. VII cannot be taken out of the context of V and XIV. But then it becomes clear that on the basis of the right distinction between law and Gospel there necessarily follows the emphasis on the "divine aspect" and the omission of the "human aspect," certainly in the sense of a constitutionally normative and fixed church activity such as Stahl envisions. For this activity and the result contained in the constitution cannot be named alongside Word and sacrament in the concept of the church. As a purely human activity it must constantly yield to the Word. What "has become historically legal on the basis of divine establishment" cannot be valid as a divine "institution," as "something established and arranged by God," nor can it confront the congregation as something "higher" in this sense.

The Augsburg Confession speaks not only of *the* church but also of the *churches* ("*ecclesiae apud nos docent*," A.C. I, 1; II, 1; III, 1; etc.). Like the Christian church on earth the Christian congregation at a specific place, being an assembly of believers, is the church of Jesus Christ in the most real sense. The definition of A.C. VII does not deny this but from the beginning precludes an independentistic concept of the church which wrongly isolates the individual congregation.

4. As the assembly of believers the church is the communion of saints.

In the German text of A.C. VII the church is called "the assembly of all believers," while the Latin has "the congregation of saints." Both terms designate the same assembly of the same people. The believers are the saints; the saints are the believers. The "association of faith and of the Holy Spirit in men's hearts" (Ap. VII, 5) is "the assembly of saints who share the association of the same Gospel or teaching and of the same Holy Spirit, who renews, consecrates, and governs their hearts" (Ap. VII, 8). Faith is not without renewal, and justification is not without sanctification.[8]

"I believe that there is on earth a little holy flock or community of pure saints under one head, Christ. It is called together by the Holy Spirit in one faith, mind, and understanding. It possesses a variety of gifts, yet is united in love without sect or schism" (L.C. II, 51). In it the Holy Spirit "creates and increases sanctification, causing it daily to grow and become strong in the faith and in the fruits of the Spirit" (L.C. II, 53). Here Luther speaks not only of faith but also of love, not only of receptive faith but also of active faith, a faith producing fruits. Sanctification is justification and renewal. The Holy Spirit through Word and sacrament gives faith and new obedience in love. Both are a reality in the church. Neither can be separated from the other. Therefore "*communio sanctorum*" is not only the assembly of the saints but also "the sharing of the members with one another, each becoming a partner with all others,

---

[8] Regarding W. Elert's emphasis that, according to A.C. VII, "sinners belong in the church and only sinners" ("Die Botschaft des VII. Artikels der Augsb. Konf.," *Allg. Ev.-luth. Kirchenzeitung* [1927], p. 1059), already K. Thieme pointed out (*Die Augsburgische Konfession*, p. 224, n. 1) that, in view of the lament in A.C. VIII over the sinners mixed with the church, this statement would need to be formulated far more carefully. The church is the assembly of believing sinners who, justified, are at the same time renewed to obedience toward God's commandments.

each active for the other"; "the brothers are in a fellowship of grace and of burden—and their fellowship is a sharing in each other's grace and burden" (P. Althaus, *Communio sanctorum,* I, 40). This mutual giving of oneself to the other and working for the other in love has its basis in the common hearing of the Gospel through which the Holy Spirit gives love together with faith, and this love unites the believers into one body. Accordingly, the believers are the "holy believers and sheep who hear the voice of their Shepherd." Their "holiness . . . consists of the Word of God and true faith" (S.A. III, xii, 2 f.).

As the assembly of "holy believers" the church is a "spiritual people," "God's true people, reborn by the Holy Spirit" (Ap. VII, 14; cf. 16). But all action of the Holy Spirit is at the same time the action of Jesus Christ who "renews, consecrates, and governs by his Spirit" (Ap. VII, 5). The church as the work of the Holy Spirit is Christ's work and property. Thus the assembly of believers is "the living body of Christ" (Ap. VII, 12; cf. 5). He is the head; the believers are the members. Thus the church is also called 'Christ's bride' (Ap. VII, 9).

5. The Holy Spirit gathers the church under Christ, the head, as the "one, holy, catholic, and apostolic church" (Nic.).

The church is *holy* as the community of those whom the Holy Spirit has sanctified.

The church is *apostolic* as the assembly of believers among whom the same Gospel is preached which Jesus Christ once commissioned the apostles to proclaim. "If it has and holds fast to the word of the apostles, it is living and truly apostolic. If it has departed from the apostolic word, it is dead," "un-apostolic," "even if it had been founded by apostles and lived on the very graves of apostles" (W. Loehe, *Drei Buecher von der Kirche* [Guetersloh, 1883], p. 18).

The church is the *one* and, at the same time, the *catholic* church which embraces all believers of all times and in all places. Both characteristics, unity and catholicity, are indeed always in contrast when viewed from the standpoint of church history, since, wherever the church gives expression to her unity in the fellowship of the same order and even the same creeds, not all believers are united. For the observation of church history, the universality of the church calls its unity into question, and the unity of the church calls the catholicity into question. But the unity and the catholicity of the church are identical not in our observation but in faith. The one, holy, catholic, and apostolic church is to be believed and is confessed in the same faith which confesses the triune God (Apost., Nic., Art. 3). "I believe that there is on earth a little holy flock or community of pure saints under one head, Christ. It is called together by the Holy Spirit in one faith, mind, and understanding. It possesses a variety of gifts, yet is united in love without sect or schism" (L.C. II, 51).

It is "not necessary for the true unity of the Christian church that ceremonies (*"traditiones humanas seu ritus aut ceremonias"*), instituted by men, should be observed uniformly in all places" (A.C. VII, 3). ". . . as the different length of day and night does not harm the unity of the church, so we believe that the true unity of the church is not harmed by differences in rites instituted by men" (Ap. VII, 33). We must be careful not to construe the terms "rites," "traditions," "ceremonies" too narrowly in this context. They include not only definite festivals and seasons but, as a matter of principle, everything pertaining to order in the church that has been instituted or taken over by the believers themselves in the liberty of faith, be it the order of service or the government of the church. The unity of the church does not require the unity of one man governing it (S.A. II, iv, 7 ff.), nor even the identity of the church constitution in the various territories of the church. Yes, the unity of the church could be realized even without a church government placed over the local congregations. The yardstick to determine what is necessary for the unity of the church is the question whether it is "necessary for righteousness before God" (Ap. VII, 34); that is, are the forgiveness of sins and the gift of the Holy Spirit imparted thereby? ". . . it is sufficient for the true unity of the Christian church that the Gospel be preached in conformity with a pure understanding of it and that the sacraments be administered in accordance with the divine Word" (A.C. VII, 2). The true unity of the church is a "spiritual unity, without which there can be no faith in the heart nor righteousness in the heart before God" (Ap. VII, 31). The unity of the church is the unity of faith. The features of territorial churches, free churches, and the like,[9]

[9] This by no means excludes the necessity of coming to grips by faith with questions concerning the church's structure. Though the unity of the church does not consist in the unity of outward forms, the church never exists without external form, which, however manifold and mutable, is never left to the whim of the world. It is entrusted to the liberty of the believers with

are not a part of the concept of church in the Lutheran Confessions. Hence differences in human ordinances are expressly rejected as a warrant for renouncing church fellowship (Ap. VII, 32).

Even though uniformity in the ritual and legal order of the church and her office are not necessary for the unity of the church, they are by no means forbidden by this fact. Rather, such uniformity is used and sought with pleasure and gratitude, since it is conducive to a well-ordered and tranquil training of the people (Ap. VII, 33). Adjustments in external ordinances result again and again from the unity of faith as works of love and fruits of spiritual unity. Nevertheless, changes in church ordinances instituted by men are, in the final analysis, as unimportant as the diversity of styles of clothing (Ap. VII, 34). Yes, uniformity in church ordinances would be of the devil the moment they were designated as being necessary for salvation.

Even though in the statements of the Augsburg Confession about the unity of the church no direct mention is made of the unity of creed, this unity is incomparably more urgent than uniformity in external ordinances. For the Confession is nothing but the formulation of the *"consentire de doctrina evangelii et de administratione sacramentorum"* (A.C. VII, 2), which, though considered sufficient, is yet demanded as necessary for the true unity of the church. The Confession is nothing but the unanimous fixing of the *"pure"* and *"recte"* of the preaching of the Gospel and the administration of the sacraments in accordance with the Scriptures. Since the Confession grows out of the unanimity of the preaching of the Gospel and of faith and serves the preservation of the preaching of the Gospel and of faith, the unity of the church is essentially also the unity of Confession. At this place it need not be shown again that the Confessions themselves attach great importance to showing their agreement with the ancient creeds and hence with the *doctrina evangelii* of the church of all times.[10] In this connection we refer again to the constant quoting of the church fathers.[11] The unity of the church does not exist without the unity of creed. However, in accordance with the Lutheran conception of Scripture and Confession which always centers about the *preached* Gospel, the whole weight of this statement rests on the *contents* of the Confession,

the command to preach the Gospel. Hence the church must constantly reexamine her concrete form in the light of the question whether it serves this command.

[10] Cf. pp. 12 f., 19 f., 60 ff.
[11] Cf. pp. 17 f.

on the Gospel itself. Unity of the churches can, therefore, exist even where—as before 325 or before 1530—this unity has not yet, or only partially, been expressed in creedal statements. If only the one Gospel is preached with common consent! The unity of the church can exist also where churches do not at all, or only partially, have the same Confessions; compare, for example, the evaluation of the Greek Orthodox church by the Reformers. If only these creeds agree in the teaching of the Gospel![12] However reticently the Confessions speak about the relationship of church unity and the acknowledgment of the same Confessions,[13] they still lead unequivocally to the conclusion that there is no true unity of the church where the pure Gospel is not taught and the sacraments are not administered according to the Gospel. This applies also where Confessions are in force which teach falsely about the Gospel and the sacraments. It is inadmissable to see church unity in areas where the Confessions of one church condemn those of another in the doctrine of the Gospel or of the sacraments.[14] For this reason it becomes necessary

[12] It follows that strong impulses toward ecumenical activity must go out from the church of the Augsburg Confession, for its Confession permits and orders the Lutheran church to seek and find assemblies of believers also in those areas where no one is pledged to the Augsburg Confession. At the same time, however, this ecumenical activity must remain inexorable in a decisive respect, namely, that it may recognize the unity of churches only where the one Gospel is preached and believed. This unity does not yet result and manifest itself in the practical co-operation of churches, but only in the event of the *consensus de doctrina*. Thus the unity in love will be expected not from a joint activity, but solely from the unity of faith.

[13] This applies at all events to the Confessions before the Formula of Concord. The latter indeed opens with the provision that "the primary requirement for basic and permanent concord within the church is a summary formula and pattern unanimously approved, in which the summarized doctrine commonly confessed in the churches of the pure Christian religion is drawn together out of the Word of God" (S.D. Sum. Form., 1), in other words, that the unity of the church requires the same creedal statements. One could ask whether this "requirement" is to be understood in the sense of a constitutional or a dogmatic necessity. If taken in the latter sense, this claim does not seem to follow from the expressions of the Augsburg Confession but is of a piece with the shift of dogmatic concern from the norm of the preached Gospel to the formal norm of Holy Scripture, as it comes to view in the doctrine of the Formula of Concord concerning the Scriptures.

[14] From this standpoint the unions which were consummated in the nineteenth century between Lutheran and Reformed churches in Prussia, Baden, the Palatinate, and Hesse must necessarily be placed in question whenever the Lutheran doctrine of the church is taken seriously. Defining the relationship between Scripture, Gospel, church, and Confession permits and even requires the church of the Augsburg Confession to acknowledge church unity with every other church that has expressly revoked errors formerly held in the doctrine of the Gospel and sacraments. Furthermore, this definition of relationships in principle does not exclude the possibility of compelling the church of the Augsburg Confession to correct a hitherto-maintained position in her own Confession by means of Scripture in the consensus of her teachers and congregations. But in every case it is forbidden to grant equal rights in

for the church in all ecumenical endeavors first of all to ask definite questions about doctrine and to make clear that the consensus in doctrine must be the prerequisite for all talk about the *una sancta,* and for all proper action in her name.

If A.C. VII denies the necessity of identical church constitutions and does not even mention specific Confessions as constituting the unity of the church, this fact, like the rejection of human merit in the doctrine of justification, has a christological basis, the acknowledgment of the glory of Christ's sole merit, the reverently watchful faith in Jesus Christ as the only Lord of the church. His activity in the church through Word and sacrament is the only reality of its unity; that is to say, the unity of the church is the sole reality of the Spirit of God within it. For it is true that " 'there is one body and one Spirit, just as you were called to the one hope that belongs to your call, one Lord, one faith, one Baptism' " (Eph. 4:4, 5, quoted in A.C. VII, 4).

This conception of the unity of the church necessarily includes its catholicity. The Creed "says 'the church catholic,' lest we take it to mean an outward government of certain nations. It is, rather, made up of men scattered throughout the world who agree on the Gospel and have the same Christ, the same Holy Spirit, and the same sacraments" (Ap. VII, 10). The one church embraces all believers, whether gathered locally in large congregations, or scattered in lonely places, 'in all the world, in various kingdoms, islands, lands, and cities, from the rising of the sun to its setting' (Ap. VII, 20). For the one Christ is the Lord to whom all power is given and who rules all saints. Since the catholicity of the one church has its reality in the rule of the one Christ, *"catholica"* is rendered in the Lutheran Confessions simply "Christian" (Apost., Nic.). This christological title of honor, "catholic," is therefore not surrendered to the Roman church but is expressly ascribed to the assembly of believers among whom the one Gospel is preached. The catholicity of the church is the catholicity of its commission with which the Lord sends his people to all nations, and the catholicity of its Lord, who is present and active wherever the Gospel is preached according to his commission and the sacraments are administered.

the one church of Jesus Christ to several creedal statements which anathematize each other in the doctrine of the Gospel or even in only one sacrament. This would mean the repeal of any confessional obligation, and, beyond that, the introduction of an even greater dissensus between Lutheran and Reformed doctrine, namely, the modernistic dissolution of the consensus even in those doctrines that were not in controversy.

The unity and catholicity of the church are identical in the *unity* of the Son of God to whom *all* men are subject, and therewith also the *unity* of the Holy Spirit who creates *every faith* in Jesus Christ and without whom there is no saint on earth.

6. The conflict between the devil's kingdom and Christ's kingdom is waged not only between church and nonchurch, but always also within the external fellowship of the church.

The line of thought developed in theses 3 through 5 follows: ". . . the true people" "according to the Gospel," ". . . the church is the kingdom of Christ, the opposite of the kingdom of the devil" (Ap. VII, 16; cf. 17). The believers as members of the church are members of Christ's kingdom. The members of the devil's kingdom do not belong to Christ's kingdom, nor are they living members of the church.

But the devil still lords it over this world. Daily the baptized are exposed to him. Even when as saints they are no longer members of his kingdom, on earth they "are daily under the dominion of the devil who neither day nor night relaxes his effort to steal upon you unawares and to kindle in your heart unbelief and wicked thoughts against all these commandments" (L.C. I, 100; cf. 71). "Therefore you must continually keep God's Word in your heart, on your lips, and in your ears." Since God's Word is active and living, "the devil is cast out and put to flight" (L.C. I, 102).

But "where the heart stands idle and the Word is not heard, the devil breaks in and does his damage before we realize it" (L.C. I, 100). Within the circle of the baptized, then, there are "evil men and hypocrites." They are in "the outward fellowship of the church" and are "members of the church according to the outward associations of the church's marks—that is, Word, confession, and sacraments" (Ap. VII, 3). Outwardly they share in the church, since they hear the Gospel, receive the Lord's Supper, and even represent the true confession. But they do this without the obedience of faith. Inasmuch as they do not believe, it applies to them that they "in whom Christ is not active are not members of Christ." They are only "dead members of the Church," while the believers alone are the living members (Ap. VII, 5). The "wicked are part of the church only in name and not in fact, while the godly are part of the church in fact as well as in name" (Ap. VII, 10). For "the church is made up of those persons in whom there is true knowledge and the confession of faith and truth" (Ap. VII, 22).

The baptized who do not believe—these are the wicked—are merely "mingled" with the church (Ap. VII, 3). They can take part in the outward signs of the church in a twofold manner: By hearing the Gospel *and* by preaching the Gospel, by receiving *and* by administering the sacraments. In the outward fellowship we must reckon with wicked men not only in the pew but also with "ungodly teachers" in the pulpit (Ap. VII, 22; cf. 47). Hypocrites and wicked men also "hold offices in the church" (Ap. VII, 28). This does not imply necessarily that they preach false doctrine and no longer administer the sacraments according to the Gospel. Often the wicked man will hypocritically submit to the church's Confession and in his words accommodate himself to the requirement of the Gospel. In this case "the sacraments are efficacious even if the priests who administer them are wicked men" (A.C. VIII, 1; cf. Ap. VII, 3, 19, 28). However, this does not in the least excuse the wicked men in the office of the church, it only manifests the glorious superiority of Christ's person who acts redemptively also through unworthy men (namely, through his Gospel even though unworthy men preach it). But even though the wicked men in the church's office *need* not be false teachers, yet unbelief and vice will impel them toward false doctrine. Again, false doctrine as a rule does not remain uncontaminated by vice, it leads to tyranny.

These "dead members of the church" are "members of the kingdom of the devil." Even though the wicked take part in Word and sacrament "they are not the true kingdom of Christ and members of Christ" (Ap. VII, 19). Even while they are members of the church, they are members of the devil, not members of Christ. Even though they are "within the church" itself (Ap. VII, 9), it must be said of them that since they "belong to the kingdom of the devil, they are not the church" (Ap. VII, 17).

Thus the boundary line between Christ's kingdom and the devil's kingdom does not run between the outward fellowship of the church and the masses of the unbaptized, but it cuts through the number of the baptized. It is not a fixed boundary but a battle front in constant flux. The devil invades the church with ever-new attacks in order to destroy Christ's kingdom. It is he who produces one heresy after another in order to seduce and beguile the members of the church. He bewitches them with work-righteousness (L.C. I, 120) and with religious fanaticism (S.A. III, viii, 5, 10); he demands masses, pilgrimages, etc., and rides the pope (S.A. II, ii, 16 ff.). As he makes use of the natural knowledge of God and of the categories of good and evil for the purpose of benumbing the heathen, so he uses the name of Christ to blind the Christians, but at the same time he removes Christ's benefits through work-righteousness and religious fanaticism. Thus he permits the Lord's Supper to be celebrated, but he cuts through the words of institution and removes Christ's blood and hides Christ's body in the doctrine of the *opus operatum*. He also speaks of love, but substitutes the love of men for God's love to us. The Confessions say little about the dangers threatening the church from without on the part of the heathen, in spite of the acute danger from the Turks; the most dangerous assault of the devil's kingdom occurs within the church through the members enslaved by the devil.

The Confessions indulge in no illusions about the extent to which the devil's kingdom has entered and daily enters the church. They know that "in this life *many* false Christians, hypocrites, and even open sinners remain among the godly" (A.C. VIII, 1). "There is an *infinite* number of ungodly within the church who oppress it" (Ap. VII, 9). They threaten to destroy the communion of saints.

7. The church must exclude from its fellowship those who persist in false doctrine, manifest vices, and contempt of the sacraments.[15]

The "battles by which Christ restrained the devil and drove him away from the believers" (Ap. IV, 190) are fought in the dangers, labors, and sermons of the believers. Christ "pits the witness of the saints against the rule of the devil" (Ap. IV, 189), and through the holy works of the believers—through their confession, their trials, works of love, mortifications of the flesh—he triumphs over the devil "who is determined that nothing happen to the praise of God" (Ap. IV, 192). This indicates that the church receives the equipment for its warfare against the devil's kingdom exclusively through the Word and the sacraments. The Word is the church's weapon as the Gospel through which the Holy Spirit strengthens the tempted and converts the fallen. The church fights by glorifying the grace

[15] The statements of the Lutheran Confessions concerning church discipline have their most important exposition in the Lutheran church constitutions. Here the brief, essentially only basic, hints of the Confessions are unfolded in concrete directives regarding the premises and method of disciplinary procedure. The fact that there is so much disparity in detail demonstrates that these regulations were established by the church in the liberty of faith without confusing the identity of the church with the identity of a specific constitution.

of God and by proclaiming God's forgiveness through Word and sacrament. Only in this way is the sinner delivered from the dominion of the devil and strengthened for holy works.

However, in accordance with the Lord's commission the church must fight against the devil's kingdom not only by means of the word of the forgiveness of sins but also through the denial of forgiveness; not only by giving the Lord's Supper but also by excluding from the sacrament. For Christ has entrusted a twofold word to his disciples: to forgive sin and to retain sin (John 20:23; cf. Matt. 16:19; 18:18). The power of the keys in the church is therefore always twofold (S.A. III, vii, 1). On the basis of this power of the keys entrusted to the whole church—not "to the person of one particular individual" (Tr. 24, 28)—pastors and bishops have the power to exclude sinners from the Christian congregation by means of excommunication, and "all this is to be done not by human power but by God's Word alone" (A.C. XXVIII, 21), i.e., not by the greater excommunication which is coupled with the imperial ban, but by the so-called lesser excommunication.[16] The "lesser (that is, the truly Christian) excommunication excludes those who are manifest and impenitent sinners from the sacrament and other fellowship of the church until they mend their ways and avoid sin. Preachers should not mingle civil punishments with this spiritual penalty or excommunication" (S.A. III, ix). This statement seems to be contradicted by Luther's demand in the Preface to the Small Catechism regarding excommunicated persons "that parents and employers should refuse to furnish them with food and drink" and "that the prince is disposed to banish such rude people from his land" (S.C. Pref., 12). But this measure is not to be understood as a measure of the spiritual office but of the civil, even though here Luther, the incumbent of the spiritual office, suggests and approves this measure. The separation of the two offices finds its limits here as in the statements of the Confessions about the duties of Christians in a civil office.

Who is to be excluded from the church? First, the false teacher. The bishops should not only "condemn *doctrine* that is contrary to the Gospel" (A.C. XXVIII, 21) but also exclude the false *teachers*: "We should forsake wicked teachers because they no longer function in the place of Christ, but are antichrists" (Ap. VII, 48). Not every teacher who has sinned is at once to be called a *"doctor*

---

[16] This must not be confused with a differentiation between the greater and the lesser excommunication *within* the discipline of the church. See, for example, Vilmar, *Die christliche Kirchenzucht*, pp. 57 ff.

impius," but one who advocates and spreads false doctrines. And here we must distinguish between "unprofitable opinions," by which "many weak people" build stubble, but do not 'overthrow the foundation, Christ, and therefore are still Christians,' and "wicked error," whereby the doctrine of justification is rejected and the foundation is removed (Ap. VII, 20 f.). In the proper sense, only the champion of such lethal doctrines is a false teacher, not every brooder with his peculiar notions. Similarly the Formula of Concord distinguishes between "those persons who err ingenuously and who do not blaspheme the truth of the divine Word" and "false and seductive doctrines and their stiff-necked proponents and blasphemers." Only the latter should "not by any means" be tolerated "in our lands, churches, and schools" (B. of C. Pref., p. 11). Not every teacher departing from doctrine but only the teacher abrogating the Gospel is to be excluded from the church by excommunication, and again, not every teacher abrogating the Gospel but only the teacher who in spite of all admonition obstinately persists in his error. Thus, as a matter of principle, it is possible to condemn *theologoumena* without condemning their author. In individual cases it is not always easy to draw the line between unprofitable opinions and lethal error. The line cannot be fixed once for all by formulating definite fundamental articles, but *in concreto* the line must be drawn ever anew, since the devil invades the church with ever-new infatuations of error. In this case exclusion from the congregation is commanded both when the false doctrine is spread by a *"doctor impius"* in the real sense, by a pastor who has been called *"rite,"* and when false doctrines are spread obstinately and seductively by laymen. But despising the Gospel through indifference and ignorance can also be a reason for exclusion from the Lord's Supper: "For we do not intend to admit to the sacrament and administer it to those who do not know what they seek or why they come" (L.C. V, 2). Those who are unwilling to learn the Catechism should not "be admitted to the sacrament, be accepted as sponsors in Baptism" (S.C. Pref., 11).

Excommunication is also to be pronounced against the "openly wicked" ('those who live in manifest vices, fornication, adultery, etc.' Ap. XI, 4; cf. XXVIII, 13). Excommunication should not result from 'trifles,' dealing with nonobservance of fasts or festivals (Tr. 75), nor from serious transgressions if the sinner has turned from them in sincere repentance. Rather, by excommunication sins are to be retained against "manifest and *impenitent* sinners" (S.A. III, ix), 'those who are *guilty* of [*liegen in*] notorious crimes' (Tr.

60; cf. 74) and persist in them. Even though fornication is here especially mentioned, persistent transgression against other commandments may also result in excommunication. Stressing the obstinacy of such transgressions shows that excommunication is based not on the act as such, but on the denial of the Gospel. For the sinner has had the Gospel pronounced to him often in absolution, yet has either not lived a new life in the strength received in absolution, or has even disdained contritely to hear absolution. Whoever does not desire forgiveness, or desires it only as a cloak for persisting in vice, is to be excluded from the church.

From this we can understand why "the despisers of the sacrament" are mentioned in the same breath with the "openly wicked" (Ap. XI, 4). Their excommunication follows from the expressions about the necessity of the sacraments and, by the way, from the very fact that the despisers of the sacrament have excluded themselves from the Lord's Supper. Since the same Gospel is received in the sacrament and in Confession, despising the latter also becomes a cause for excommunication. If you "despise it and proudly stay away from confession, then we must come to the conclusion that you are no Christian and that you ought not receive the sacrament. For you despise what no Christian ought to despise and you show thereby that you can have no forgiveness of sin" (L.C. Conf., 29).

The Confessions give no specific directions about the procedure of excommunication, since this is the function of the actual constitutions. The Confessions neither prescribe a specific formula of excommunication nor clarify the relationship of congregation, pastor, and bishop in bringing about excommunication. Since, however, only "impenitent" sinners are to be excommunicated, it is presupposed that they have been admonished repeatedly. Furthermore, the stress on "open" sinners implies not only an evaluation of their especially pernicious and seductive power, if they are openly tolerated in the congregation, but also the restriction of excommunication to transgressions which have really been proved. Since "this is a very serious charge, nobody should be condemned without due process of law" (Tr. 75). Moreover, excommunication can be pronounced against several persons for the same reason, e.g., for a specific false teaching, if they advocate it and persist in it. The greater the number of these teachers and of their adherents in the congregations, the more can excommunication assume the significance of an ecclesiastical division, that is, it can lead to the elimination of a heretical pseudo-church from the church of Jesus Christ.

Like absolution, so also excommunication is the voice of God himself speaking through the mouth of his authorized human servant. As absolution pronounced here on earth in the name of God testifies that the sins are forgiven in heaven, that is, in the verdict of the Last Judgment, so the excommunication of the church is the retaining of sins by God and by his Son returning for the Last Judgment. Nobody can rid himself of this excommunication, except again the church to whom the twofold power of the keys has been entrusted. The excommunicated sinner must repent; not his contrition, however, but only absolution will release him. The ministry of the church has the authority not only to excommunicate but also "again to absolve them if they are converted and ask for absolution" (Ap. XXVIII, 13). Excommunication can actually be understood as the last radical attempt to save the lost, as the last summons of the judgment which, we hope, may terrify them and move them to return. But this dare not weaken the significance of excommunication as God's act of judgment. Accordingly, excommunication, whereby *God* retains the sinner's sin, is by no means merely the exclusion of the sinner from the outward fellowship of the church, but it is exclusion from the true church, the communion of saints. The sinner who has separated himself from the saints by his action is excluded from the communion of saints. He is no longer a member of the body of Christ.

8. For the rest, the church must tolerate members of Satan's kingdom in its external fellowship.

Excommunication is not to be applied against "unprofitable opinions," even when they are wrong, nor against errors even when they depart from the Gospel, nor against hypocrites who quietly betray the Gospel or secretly draw others away from the Gospel, nor against sinners whose vices are not manifest or whose sins seem to be "trifles" (cf. Ap. VII, 20 f.). Furthermore, the church may not ban those who have indeed lapsed into manifest heresies or vices, who for the present, however, are not to be excluded as obstinate, but are to be admonished in love. All of this signifies that excommunication cannot purge the church of all members of the devil's kingdom, nor even rid the offices of the church of them. Even if the church excommunicates according to its obligation, the fact remains that "in this life many false Christians, hypocrites, and even open sinners remain among the godly" (A.C. VIII).

Moreover, it must not only be "conceded" that evil persons are mingled with the church, but this condition is to be endured: "We concede that in this life hypocrites and evil men are mingled with the church and are members of the church according to the outward associations of the church's marks . . ." (Ap. VII, 3). The Confessions expressly forbid the church to separate itself from all evil people. Why should these people be tolerated in the communion of saints? The reason is not primarily that in practice it is impossible for the church to excommunicate all sinners, since it does not know the secret sins. But the church is forbidden to execute that separation of the good and the evil, of the members of Christ and the members of the devil's kingdom, a separation which only the returning Christ will perform. The parables of Jesus concerning the tares among the wheat and concerning the dragnet are here taken seriously. Human beings not only *cannot* put an end to the mingling of saints and sinners in the church, but they *should* not attempt this. By renouncing the attempt to recognize and to eliminate the evil persons by any particular method beyond the special cases mentioned above, the church honors Jesus Christ as its Lord before whom as the returning judge *all* men shall appear, also the so-called good men.[17]

From this point results the distinction between "the church properly so called" (*ecclesia proprie dicta*) and "the church in the larger sense" (*ecclesia large dicta*). For although such evil persons are to be tolerated in the church, they are not on that account members of Christ. The real church is "the body of Christ" (Ap. VII, 29), "the assembly of saints who truly believe the Gospel of Christ and who have the Holy Spirit" (Ap. VII, 28; cf. 22). It is "the true church" (Ap. VII, 19), "the pillar of truth" (Ap. VII, 20). It and it alone is the kingdom of Christ upon earth. "The church in the larger sense includes both the godly and the wicked" (Ap. VII, 10); it includes all who hear the preaching and receive the sacraments, whether they receive the benefit or not. This distinction between the real church and the outward fellowship of the church is a conceptual distinction of faith and hope but not an empirical distinction to be realized concretely. The latter would be the human

---

[17] The question involuntarily suggests itself: "Why practice church discipline at all, if the sinners may not be excluded from the church before Christ's return?" The Confessions provide no further basis for church discipline. Since it cannot be the church's purpose to purge itself, the concern remains in force to protect the church by means of discipline against offense and seduction. However, the decisive reason is that Christ has commanded his church to forgive *and* to retain sin. The church has no right to cut this command in half.

anticipation of Christ's return. The church must not separate the saints from all sinners but sanctify the sinners through the Gospel.

The true church, then, is hidden in the outward fellowship of the church; "the church is hidden under a crowd of wicked men" (Ap. VII, 19). ". . . because the kingdom of Christ has not yet been revealed, they are mingled with the church" (Ap. VII, 17). Christ's kingdom is the true church, the communion of saints. It is hidden under the superior force of the members of the devil's kingdom. They are the cross by which Christ's kingdom is covered (Ap. VII, 18). The cross is the wickedness and ungodliness which not only attacks the church from the outside, but also arises within the church and here assails, suppresses, and conceals the true church through hypocrisy, vices, and false doctrines.

9. Although the true church is hidden under the external fellowship of the members of Christ and the members of the devil's kingdom, the true church is, nevertheless, a reality on this earth and can be recognized by the preaching of the Gospel and the administration of the sacraments according to the Gospel.

Though the members of the devil's kingdom are mingled with the church and because of their great number suppress Christ's members and conceal Christ's kingdom, yet the assembly of the believers, the kingdom of Christ, does exist on this earth. Christ's kingdom on earth is not only an object of hope but a present reality, even though it has "not yet been revealed" (Ap. VII, 17 f.). The one, holy, apostolic, catholic church is not an idea of which the churches on earth are merely imperfect copies, but it exists really and truly on earth. The church is not an ideal toward which Christians are striving without ever reaching it in this time, but the church is present on earth prior to the individual Christians; only out of its reality does the Christian come into being. "We are not dreaming about some Platonic republic ('about an imaginary church which is to be found nowhere'), . . . but we teach that this church actually exists ('is truly on earth'), made up of true believers and righteous men scattered throughout the world" (Ap. VII, 20).

Moreover, the true church which is Christ's kingdom does not merely *exist* on earth but it is also to be *found* on earth. Since there would be no believers without the Gospel and since the Gospel does not come to the believers without the oral, external Word and without the visible elements, the community of believers is not without distinguishing marks. "The church is not merely an association of outward ties and rites like other civic governments, however, but it is mainly an association of faith and of the Holy Spirit in men's hearts. To make it recognizable, this association has outward marks, the pure teaching of the Gospel and the administration of the sacraments in harmony with the Gospel of Christ" (Ap. VII, 5). "To make it recognizable" does not mean to add the outward marks as something that really does not belong to the church as the community of the Holy Spirit, but it emphasizes the paradox of the "inward" and "outward" in the concept of the church, which in principle is none other than the paradox of the revelation of the Son of God in the flesh and that of the communication of the Holy Spirit through human words and earthly signs. The church is never without the outward signs. Gospel and sacrament are the essential cause of the communion of believers—Christ is present in them and makes them what they are by giving himself in them—and as essential cause they are at the same time the ground of recognition for the believers. The church is recognized by the Word and the sacraments; for it is produced by the Gospel and has the commission to preach the Gospel to all the world. To be sure, the church can be recognized and found only by faith, since faith alone knows the Gospel and is able to distinguish it from the false teachings of a human world view.[18] Whoever tears the doctrine of the church out of the articles of the Christian Creed (Apost., Nic.) will not find the church on earth, since in its essence it can be recognized only by its message and, hence, only by faith in this message. But even though faith alone recognizes the true church by its marks, these marks by no means cease to be external. Through them Christ not only edifies the believers in their hearts but by means of them Christ daily advances his battle lines into the world.

The works of the saints performed out of love to God and man

[18] From this R. Sohm concludes that "the church of Christ is invisible." For "the church in the religious sense, the church as the people of God on earth, is an object of *faith*, and 'what is believed is not seen,' it cannot be seen with the eyes of natural man." *Kirchenrecht*, II, 130. However, the doctrine of the church in the Confessions wishes to be regarded in its totality precisely as a confession of faith and not a confession of natural man. Both the statements concerning the hiddenness of the true church as well as the statements concerning the external visible marks of its reality on earth are expressions of faith, as are the statements concerning the divine *and* the human natures of Jesus Christ. Hence, from the fact "that the living Word as Word of *God* is visible only for believers," it by no means follows that it is "invisible." *Ibid.*, p. 137. Likewise, from the fact that only faith recognizes the external marks of the church as marks of the true church, it by no means follows that the church is invisible.

are not marks of the church. These works are not thereby denied. They are done in the church 'as prayers of thanksgiving to God' (Ap. IV, 189), to "glorify" God (A.C. XX, 27; cf. Ap. XIII, 17), and they are the weapons of Jesus Christ against the devil (Ap. IV, 189 ff.). The church is to "be diligently joined together in unity of doctrine, faith, sacraments, prayer, works of love, etc." (S.A. II, iv, 9), and will never be without love, as faith is never without works. But the hypocrites too can produce works, and it is precisely for the believer himself that one's good works are hidden.

Furthermore, a definite form of organization is not a mark of the church. Organization is not thereby made an insignificant matter. The Confessions contain numerous weighty statements indicating the bounds within which the church in the liberty of faith may establish proper ordinances (cf. Chap. 7). But the church can still be recognized even when the hitherto existing forms of its ordination and church government are demolished.

Finally, church discipline is not a mark of the church, even though the Lord himself has commanded the church to practice it and the church is bound to administer it. Expressly rejected and condemned is the view "that it is no true Christian congregation in which public expulsion and the orderly process of excommunication do not take place" (Ep. XII, 26; cf. S.D. XII, 34). The mark of the church is the preaching of the Gospel—not the Word that condemns but the Word that liberates; not the Word that expels from the church but the Word that calls into the church.

With Loehe one may point out that neither age nor extent, neither external succession nor external miracles are called marks of the church. Only the external means by which Christ acts in a saving way and by which the Holy Spirit is given are properly marks. Accordingly, not the believers as such are marks, but the Gospel in Word and sacrament, the Gospel which is never weak but produces believers wherever it is proclaimed.[19]

[19] In opposition to this Stahl has said: "It cannot be asserted that pure doctrine as such is *the* mark of the communion of saints. And in so far as it is *a* mark, it is not the only one. Among the marks one may also mention the proof of faith in life, charity, church discipline, abstinence, and contempt of death. In reality true doctrine is not the *external mark* of the church but rather the mark of the *external* church. The true external church is recognized by true doctrine. This is not the case with the internal church, the communion of saints." *Kirchenverfassung* (2nd ed.), pp. 42 f. Here too the question must be asked in all seriousness whether such additions to the Lutheran doctrine of the church do not already imply its repeal; furthermore, whether these attempts do not deny the distinction of law and Gospel, of faith and works, inasmuch as the wrath of God against the sinner is ignored. In addition, there is here a docetic kind of separation of external and internal

Hence the Confessions consistently speak of only two marks of the church—Word and sacrament. Occasionally the Apology also mentions the confession (Ap. VII, 3). Along the same line Nicholas of Lyra is quoted in support of the view that "therefore the church is made up of those persons in whom there is true knowledge and the confession of faith and truth" (Ap. VII, 22). Since confession always and essentially is an external, public statement, calling it a mark of the church alongside Word and sacrament readily suggests itself. After all, so far as content is concerned, the confession is most intimately associated with Word and sacrament, since it must make statements about what constitutes pure preaching of the Word and proper administration of the sacraments. It might seem obvious to call the Confessions, if not a third mark of the church, at least a mark in a derived sense, since they teach and confess the two true marks of the church, the Gospel and the sacraments. Nevertheless we must speak guardedly in this matter on the basis of the Confessions themselves. As the norm of the church is the *proclaimed* biblical Gospel, and as the church is defined by the *preaching* of the Gospel and the *administration* of the sacraments, so the Confessions are not *per se*, as *written documents,* a mark of the church, but in *preaching and administration of the sacraments,* as performed according to the Confessions, i.e., in conformity with the Gospel. The church is not to be recognized where the correct Confessions have constitutional validity but are not observed in practice. Conversely, the church may be found where no particular creeds are recognized but where, nevertheless, the Gospel is properly preached and the sacraments rightly administered.[20] However important Creeds are for the church's proclamation and however irresponsibly a church body acts which refuses to have any creeds, yet, if A.C. VII is taken seriously, the Confessions are a mark of the church only when they are put into practice by the church's preaching in conformity with them. This does not mean that the Confessions as such may be dissolved into ever-new acts of personal confession, but it does have this implication for the question of the marks of the church: The Confession is a mark of the church exclusively *in*

church. The preaching of the Gospel in the "external church" is, rather, the external mark of the "internal church."

[20] In no case does this mean that "the church of Christ is not a confessional church" (Sohm, II, 138), but rather the opposite. The church of Christ is always a confessional church, even though no specific creeds should receive official recognition. The unity of the church consists in the consensus of preaching and, hence, of doctrine, no matter whether this consensus of confession is fixed in a creedal statement or not.

the two marks of Gospel proclamation and administration of the sacraments. Since the Confessions by their very nature are to serve the preservation of Gospel preaching and the proper administration of the sacraments, they are a mark of the church *in* this their service. The Confessions are, furthermore, no mark of the church inasmuch as this mark coincides with the other two marks and can be recognized as a mark of the church only *in* them. Correspondingly, the Confessions themselves consistently mention only Word and sacrament as marks, and the cited passages of the Apology do not mention any specific Confessions.[21]

All of these considerations lead to the conclusion that "the church, properly speaking," is to be found only in "the church in the larger sense." The communion of believing saints is to be found only in the fellowship of the outward marks. For the church can be recognized only by the outward marks in which the lip-Christians too participate. In other words, Christ's kingdom on earth is to be found only within the outward church fellowship of the believers and the ungodly. Here it must be noted that in the Confessions "the true church" and "the church in the larger sense" are not contrasted as the invisible and the visible church. Even though the statements about Christ's kingdom, being still a hidden and not yet manifest kingdom, approach very closely in content the correctly understood concept of the invisible church, the severing of the visible and the invisible church[22] and the sequestering of the invisible church into

---

[21] Both of these points have frequently been overlooked in the more recent Lutheran ecclesiology, including the confessional revival theology of the last century. Thus, e.g., Loehe in theses 3 through 5 of Book Two of his beautiful *Drei Buecher von der Kirche* says: "The Confessions are the marks of a particular church," "the scripturalness of the Confession is the mark of the purest church, the church par excellence," "the Lutheran Church has the distinguishing mark of a scripturally correct Confession." Such statements give the Confessions an emphasis that not even the ecclesiology of the Confessions contains. Also, unless we are prepared to draw the most incisive conclusions regarding churches of a different confessional obligation, the necessity follows of going too far in the other direction, that is, of weakening the significance of the Confession through the concept of denominationalism. In this way the divergent denominations and, with them, doctrine and heresy, would be placed side by side in a unique manner. See, for example, also Delitzsch: "It is in the nature of a tree to spread out in branches, but the production of diverse fruits on the branches results from the unequal character of the tree. So the Confession is a fruit, and since the character of the congregations which are the branches of the whole church is not the same, there are diverse Confessions, as there are many branches with dissimilar fruits on one tree having one and the same root." *Vier Buecher von der Kirche,* pp. 126 f.

[22] This was done in manifold variations and with varying implications for the churchly life and action of the men involved, as, e.g., by J. Mueller and J. W. F. Hoefling. Even G. Chr. A. Harless is not entirely free. He says, "The divinely ordained reciprocity between the 'spiritual inner Christendom'

a sphere of ideal other-worldliness,[23] as is done commonly in neo-Protestantism, is made completely impossible. No, the kingdom of Christ, which is hidden among the wicked in the outward church fellowship, is at the same time manifested in the outward church fellowship. Only because it is *manifest* here, only because here Christ acts through the outward Word and sacrament, do we know that it is *hidden* among the enemies, that it is *not yet revealed* in glory. The true church becomes visible in the outward church fellowship as surely as the sacrament is *verbum visibile*. If we do want to use the terms "visible" and "invisible," we must make clear that in the visible church the invisible church is real and visible for the believer.

The Confessions, however, speak not only of the church hidden among the ungodly, but in accordance with Scripture they also apply the term "church" to the wider visible circle of the believing and unbelieving baptized who are gathered about Word and sacrament. When the distinction is made of *ecclesia proprie* and *late dicta,* we dare not overlook the fact that in both cases the term "church" is used. It is immeasurable grace that this structure of believers and ungodly, of saints and wicked men may be called *"church."* The reverse would seem to have just as much in its favor, namely, that God, *in spite* of saints and because of the wicked, *in spite* of the believers and because of the ungodly, would deny the name "church" to this assemblage. But he does call this assemblage "church" *in*

and the 'bodily outward Christendom' (*externa societas signorum ecclesiae*) is not the same as the inseparable unity of soul and body in natural man in that the Lord must be where the body is." "The mere claim of the external possession of the visible means of grace does not constitute a tangible proof for the existence of a truly believing, Christian, holy people." *Kirche und Amt nach lutherischer Lehre* (Stuttgart, 1853), pp. 7 f. In opposition to this view, Loehe, Delitzsch, and Vilmar, each in his own way, have said: "Contrary to the teaching of nearly all dogmaticians of the evangelical church we maintain that the evangelical creeds do *not* teach an abstract doctrine of an invisible church as the only true church in this age." Vilmar, *Dogmatik,* II, 203.

[23] This is finally done by R. Sohm: "The church of Christ is invisible. Hence there is no visible fellowship which, per se, would be the church. Even to the extent that it possesses and administers Word and sacrament, the visible 'bodily' Christendom is *not* the church of Christ. It has Word and sacrament only in an external, apparent manner. Especially as far as it is the true Word of God that is used in visible Christendom, it does not belong to the visible, but rather to the hidden, invisible Christendom. Visible Christendom does not have the Spirit of God, is not the people of God, does *not* have the Word of God. Visible Christendom is no longer a double reality, as it once was in the Middle Ages. Today it is only the Christian *world,* not also the Christian church. Even to the extent that it produces fellowship in Word and sacrament it is only *world,* not church. There is *no visible* church." *Kirchenrecht,* II, 135. And if Sohm does say occasionally that "the church is *visible* for the believer," we would answer that the doctrine of the Confessions *is* the doctrine of faith.

spite of the ungodly and for the sake of the believing saints, i.e., for the sake of the Gospel. Here too it becomes evident that the Gospel is more glorious than the law, and the grace of God greater than the judgment of God. If law and Gospel were of equal importance placed in dialectical antithesis, no assemblage on earth could be called "church"; for nobody knows of his neighbor whether he believes, and every believer acknowledges himself to be a sinner before God. Because the Gospel is victorious as the power of God we are permitted to believe that we and others who hear the Gospel with us are *saints,* even though we do not see it.

Where, then, is the one, holy, apostolic, catholic church to be sought and found on this earth *in concreto*? There is no doubt that the Confessions answer first: The church is to be found in our churches where the Gospel is preached and the sacraments are administered according to the Gospel. The epithet 'Lutheran' (German version of Ap. XV, 44; *Bek.,* p. 305, l. 52), applied by their opponents, is not taken over by themselves as their own name for these churches, but the entire pathos and their entire confidence is the assurance that the one, holy, apostolic, *catholic* church is a reality in these confessing churches. It must be added at once that the churches of the Augsburg Confession are the one, holy, apostolic, Christian church in communion with all believers on earth, in communion both with the fathers of the ancient church and with the contemporary brethren in other churches. We must expect to find such brethren also in heretical churches from which the church of pure Gospel preaching had to separate, as from the Roman church. Even though in the Roman church bishops, teachers, and monks taught righteousness through works and thus obscured the office of Christ, nevertheless "the knowledge of Christ has remained with some faithful souls" (Ap. IV, 392). Even though in the erring Roman church of the late Middle Ages before the Reformation the marks of the church were mutilated in preaching and in the Mass, yet also during this time, as always, there existed a communion of saints on earth. And though in a heretical church the Gospel is witnessed only in its liturgical prayers (Ap. IV, 385), and even if the marks of the church are present only in a valid Baptism, yet because of the superabundant grace of God we must expect to find believers also here in the Diaspora. But it follows from this that the Roman church is not called "church" without some dialectic. It is indeed often called "church" together with the churches of the Augsburg Confession, and yet Luther's insight is valid: "We do not concede to the papists that they are the church, for they are not. . . . For, thank God, a seven-year-old child knows what the church is, namely holy believers and sheep who hear the voice of their Shepherd" (S.A. III, xii, 1 f.). To the degree that an erring church's marks are not the pure preaching of the Gospel—this is the voice of the good Shepherd—and the administration of both sacraments in conformity with the Gospel, that church is not truly church.[24]

10. "It is also taught among us that one holy Christian church will be and remain forever" (A.C. VII).

"We see the infinite dangers that threaten the church with ruin. There is an infinite number of ungodly within the church who oppress it." And yet we know that the "church will abide nevertheless" (Ap. VII, 9).

The devil impels ever-new hordes of the godless to attack Christ's kingdom, men who 'despise, bitterly hate, and most violently persecute the Word, as, e.g., the Turks, Mohammedans, other tyrants, heretics, etc. Besides, the true doctrine and church are often so utterly suppressed and lost, as happened under the papacy, as if there were no church, and it often seems that the church has completely

[24] From this viewpoint the doubts concerning the concept "denomination" arise. In the more recent confessional literature this concept is almost common property, which is not the case in the Confessions. It represents a derailment from theological to phenomenological thinking to the extent that the reason for calling a denomination a "church" is less and less the pure preaching of the Gospel and correct administration of the sacraments, and more and more the self-styling and even the sociological structure of the so-called religious organizations. Thus the church of the Augsburg Confession is aligned with all other so-called churches as one among others and the sum total of all is said to be the church of Jesus Christ. The dialectical evaluation of heretical churches as church or nonchurch becomes a quantitative way of speaking: The several denominations do not all possess the full truth, only more or less truth; they do not all mediate full certainty, only more or less, etc. This makes possible the most diverse speculative theories by means of which theological thinking, preferably in parables drawn from the realm of organic growth, seeks to bridge the chasms of ecclesiastical schism and master the *una sancta*. But who will determine the boundary line where the error of a denomination becomes greater than its truth and its quantum of scripturalness less than its unscripturalness? Taking all their statements together, we find that the Confessions refer to the Roman church both as church and as nonchurch, and do this in a manner that leaves things unadjusted and unsatisfactory for systematic thinking. The question is left open whether the church is still there and where it is to be found there. This shows the humble and reverent attitude of the Confessions in that in final eschatological expectation they leave the answer to this question up to God himself. Such a dialectical way of speaking makes it more difficult to be calm about the denominational cleavages and to regard them as a historical development "by God's providence."

perished' (Ap. VII, 9). Whenever heresies are unmasked the devil counters with a swarm of new heresies; he responds to every excommunication from the communion of saints with new revolts of the godless in the congregation. These attacks of the devil's kingdom against the church do not decrease but increase beyond comprehension. The overwhelming majority of the godless will in these last days cover and conceal the church to such an extent that it seems to be exterminated.

Yet it remains true "that one holy Christian church will be and remain forever" (A.C. VII). This "will" is not a demand of the law but the future tense of the gracious promise (". . . *quod una sancta ecclesia perpetuo mansura sit*"). The church has the promise "that it will always have the Holy Spirit" (Ap. VII, 22). And the church, having the Holy Spirit, has God's eternal Spirit who never ceases to be because he is God himself. Who could frustrate his eternal activity whereby he gives sinners eternal life? As the work of the Holy Spirit the church will continue "forever." It does not, like Israel, have the promise that it will continue in a specific country and at a specific place, but it will never cease to exist, even though it might be in flight or in hiding. The church does not have the promise to exist and continue at all places but only at all times, until Christ's return. However it will always exist on this earth and not just in heaven. The preaching of the Gospel may be suppressed on earth, but it can never be exterminated.

After all previous statements about the church as Christ's kingdom these statements should not cause surprise. The church will continue throughout the oppressions of the last times, 'just as there will always be and remain a Christ who in time was crucified and who now rules and governs in everlasting glory in heaven' (Ap. VII, 18). Even when the church seems to have been killed it remains. Even when it is soiled by malice and godlessness it will be revealed in glory. It remains on earth as the communion of saints who live eternally because Christ, who was crucified and who rose, is the church's Lord and head and bridegroom. It remains as the body and the kingdom of the eternal, only-begotten Son of God.

VII

CIVIL AND ECCLESIASTICAL GOVERNMENT

1. Civil government is the power of the sword providing for external righteousness and peace.

In the article on "Civil Government" the Augsburg Confession teaches "that Christians may without sin occupy civil offices or serve as princes and judges, render decisions and pass sentence according to imperial and other existing laws, punish evil-doers with the sword, engage in just wars, serve as soldiers, buy and sell, take required oaths . . ." (A.C. XVI, 2; cf. Ap. XVI, 1). Thus this article defines the function of civil government by referring to the Christian in and under this government, not by referring to this government as such. From the outset, as is the case with the Confessions' doctrine in general, the doctrine of government is presented as a doctrine that is preached and is to be preached, a doctrine that is directed to the congregation of Jesus Christ and calls it to the obedience of faith. The church does not call civil government as such to the obedience of faith, but the people in and under this government. For civil government as such, as a "good order," is not to be called in question. The Gospel is addressed not to the office of government but to the person in the office. Therefore, as a matter of course, we must not expect the Confessions to offer a comprehensive treatise on political science, much less prescriptions for a concrete political system; they teach only so much as the believer must know in order to obey God in and under civil government. *All* statements of the Confessions are to be understood as presenting what is to be preached to the Christian *congregation,* even though they are worded as statements about this office as such.[1]

The power of civil government is the sword. Even when government rules by means of words—laws, commands, and judicial

[1] This hortatory concern is largely overlooked not only by the presentations in the area of liberal arts and jurisprudence, but also in the area of theological commentary on this doctrine of the Confessions.

226

decrees—the power of all those words is the sword standing behind them. As the Fifth Commandment does not apply to God, so also it does not apply to the civil office to which God has given the power over life and death. "Therefore what is here forbidden applies to private individuals, not to governments" (L.C. I, 181). The same truth applies here as to the commands of the Lord not to judge and be angry with the neighbor (Matt. 5); "it forbids anger except, as we have said, to persons who occupy the place of God, that is, parents and rulers. Anger, reproof, and punishment are the prerogatives of God and his representatives, and they are to be exercised upon those who transgress this and the other commandments" (L.C. I, 182).

The sword is given to civil government to punish evildoers. Examination and proof of the offense must precede punishment, and "decisions" and "sentence" are to be administered according to prevailing laws, that is, "imperial and other existing laws" (A.C. XVI, 2). On the other hand, the distinction between "imperial and other existing laws" indicates that the judicial activity of government is by no means merely an administration of justice through a conservative interpretation of existing laws, but it is at the same time the determination of justice through laws issued by the emperor and other authorities. In this respect the power "of a king," as a matter of principle, always means acting "above the law" (*supra legem*) in word and deed (Ap. XXVIII, 14). But this power is not equivalent to the right to judge and render a verdict "without a definite law" (*sine certa lege*). Rather, by putting into effect new laws beyond those already given, the government binds its judgment and verdict to these laws and foregoes an arbitrary use of its power.

The sword is given to civil government not only to punish evildoers within the circle of its subjects but also to be used as a weapon against such as turn against the government and its subjects from without. Thus government is to "engage in just wars, serve as soldiers" (*jure bellare, militare,* A.C. XVI, 2), 'to use the sword, horses, and armor' (Ap. XVI, 8). But even the conduct of war is not left to the caprice of civil government, but is to be done *jure*. War as "redress and punishment of evil" is also imposed on government as a duty. The "various kinds of public redress are court decisions, punishments, wars, military service" (Ap. XVI, 7). By a just war vengeance 'is done as God's work' (Ap. XVI, 8); God's vengeance itself is at work and he punishes the evildoers through the government. Therefore the Christian in public office and by authority of the public office is to use the sword in all its sharpness with a good, unsullied conscience.

Thus civil government serves the establishment and maintenance of justice and peace. War is to be waged not for the sake of war but for the 'common peace' (Ap. XVI, 7). All measures of the government as, e.g., the collection of taxes and the concrete form and constitution of the government, are to serve the preservation of justice and peace. "It would therefore be fitting if the coat-of-arms of every upright prince were emblazoned with a loaf of bread instead of a lion or a wreath of rue, or if a loaf of bread were stamped on the coins, to remind both princes and subjects that through the office of the princes we enjoy protection and peace and that without them we could not have the steady blessing of daily bread. Rulers are worthy of all honor, and we should render them the duties we owe and do all we can for them, as to those through whom we enjoy our possessions in peace and quietness, since otherwise we could not keep a penny. Moreover, we should pray for them, that through them God may bestow on us still more blessings and good things" (L.C. III, 75). "Through civil rulers, as through our own parents, God gives us food, house and home, protection and security" (L.C. I, 150).

What is striking in all of these statements is that the functions of civil government are defined within the area of the second table of the Decalogue. Government is not supposed to proclaim the triune God or to pronounce forgiveness of sins. Therefore the righteousness which it produces is in its essence merely external righteousness, not the righteousness that avails before God. 'For God the Lord desires the gross sins to be restrained by external discipline and to maintain this he has given laws, established governments, provided learned and wise men who are qualified for government' (Ap. IV, 22 f.). This becomes especially clear in the right of government to demand oaths. For an oath presupposes the untrustworthiness of all other human protestations and promises, although God's law demands of man truthfulness in all his words. Government is able to protect 'from manifest harm,' "from the power of others" (A.C. XXVIII, 11), but immeasurably much injustice and brutality, by its very nature, escapes the intervention of even the best government. Neither by punishment nor by pardon can it remove the evil nature of the human heart. Yes, in the very civil righteousness sin attains its apex, namely, in work-righteousness, though civil unrighteousness is punished by the government according to God's will. Civil government does not make righteous but merely maintains order in the midst of unrighteousness. This limitation is not to be criticized but is fixed by God himself. In the same manner the peace which this government serves is not the "peace of God, which passes all understanding," but the peace of the discord of this world, the external restraint of the revolt of all against all. In this sense the statements must be understood that "temporal power does not protect the soul, but . . . body and goods" (A.C. XXVIII, 11). Civil government does not liberate from the power of sin and eternal death, but by means of this government God in spite of sin and death preserves man in the realm of sin and death.

2. Spiritual government is the office of preaching the Gospel and administering the sacraments.

The power of spiritual government is God's Word alone, not a word backed by the sword of civil power but the Word which is the "sword of the Spirit" (Eph. 6:17). Since Christ comes among his people through the Word committed to the church and since the Holy Spirit is given to men through his Word, this Word is God's power and spiritual energy. Therefore the power of the church and its government does not require some other, some civil power for its establishment or its maintenance. It "is used and exercised only through the office of preaching" (A.C. XXVIII, 10), without external force.[2] The Gospel which the church is committed to preach, the sacraments which the church is committed to administer are the power of the spiritual rule—this rule of civil impotence.

Thus spiritual power is the office of the Word, the office of the Gospel, more exactly, 'the ministry of teaching the Gospel and administering the sacraments' (A.C. V, 1). The ministry of the spiritual realm is completely circumscribed by the commission to preach the Gospel and administer the sacraments. All additional statements of the Confessions do not add anything new to this de-limitation but merely unfold it. To preach the Gospel always in-

---

[2] Stahl in his commentary on these words is right in rejecting the common misunderstanding that the church is authorized "merely to proclaim the Word of God but not to insist on its application." This would mean that the church may inform heretics and servants of vice that they are unworthy of the sacrament and fellowship, but then it must not actually exclude them. On the contrary, these words mean that "the instruments of compulsion available to the church are those only that are contained in the Word of God, i.e., suspension from the sacraments and excommunication." *Kirchenverfassung*, pp. 146 f.

volves preaching the law and the Gospel. To forgive sins always involves administering the office of both keys, loosing and binding. Gospel without law would not be Gospel. Authority to forgive sins without authority to retain sins would not be authority to forgive sins. For Christ has given his church the twofold power, to loose and to bind. To preach the pure Gospel involves recognition and exposure of, and separation from, false doctrines as such. To serve the Gospel, furthermore, involves providing for the preservation of the preaching of the Gospel and for the calling and sending of ministers of the Gospel. In this sense A.C. V is unfolded as follows: The power of the bishops "according to the Gospel . . . is a power and command of God to preach the Gospel, to forgive and retain sins, and to administer the sacraments" (A.C. XXVIII, 5). "According to divine right, therefore, it is the office of the bishop to preach the Gospel, forgive sins, judge doctrine, and condemn doctrine that is contrary to the Gospel, and exclude from the Christian community the ungodly whose wicked conduct is manifest. All this is to be done not by human power but by God's Word alone" (A.C. XXVIII, 21). These remarks apply not only to the bishops in their capacity as overseers of the congregations but, as a matter of principle, to every pastor as the bishop of his congregation. 'Bishops *or* pastors' are, in principle, distinguished neither in A.C. XXVIII, nor elsewhere in the Confessions. For there is only *one* office of preaching the Gospel and administering the sacraments.

Through the spiritual power, i.e., through Word and sacrament, "are imparted not bodily but eternal things and gifts, namely, eternal righteousness, the Holy Spirit, and eternal life" (A.C. XXVIII, 8; cf. A.C. V). In distinction from civil government which preserves the sinner in the realm of sin, the spiritual rule frees him from his sins through forgiveness. Here righteousness is not only demanded but also bestowed. The righteousness which the ministry proffers is not merely an external righteousness before men but righteousness before God; not only the righteousness of works but of the heart and hence of the entire man. Yes, in this respect it is even against civil righteousness, inasmuch as work-righteousness has always been the greatest enemy of faith and, on the other hand, men who were rejected by civil righteousness—publicans, malefactors —received the righteousness of faith. In distinction from civil government which produces external peace among men, the peace of God comes through the spiritual rule. Here not only the body and bodily things are defended but man himself, the "soul," is touched and brought to peace with God. In distinction from civil government which preserves the life of death-bound sinners until their death, the spiritual power provides final deliverance from death, namely, regeneration to eternal life. Through the spiritual office man is protected not only in the area of sin and death against the grossest injustice and a premature death, but he is snatched from the jaws of sin, death, and the devil. Through Word and sacrament he is not only preserved but created anew.

The doctrine of the spiritual government must never be separated from the doctrine of the church. Where the church is, there is also the ministry, and where there is preaching of the Gospel and administration of the sacraments, there the church always is also. But as in the concept of church the Christian church on earth and the congregation of believers in the different places on earth, in other words, the geographically circumscribed congregation of *some* believers and "the assembly of *all* saints and believers" (A.C. VII, 1) dare never be severed, so the spiritual power in the local congregation must, in principle, not be separated or even differentiated from the spiritual power which governs and serves a large number of congregations and their pastors.[3] As the local congregation is altogether the church of Jesus Christ—it lacks no mark of the Christian church on earth—so the ministry in this congregation is the office of bishop in its full dimension. Thus, in the very nature of the case every pastor has the right to excommunicate and to ordain. As the church of Jesus Christ in its essence is catholic, so also the ministry in the individual congregation participates in the commission of proclaiming the Gospel which is given to the other congregations and acknowledges this community in the form of a superior church government which examines the teaching in the congregations, excludes false teachers, and ordains true pastors. As the one church is a reality both in every individual congregation and in the whole Christian church on earth, so the one ministry is a reality in the office of the pastors and of the bishops.

---

[3] This approach in the doctrine of the church is of the greatest significance for the whole doctrine of the ministerial office. Whoever views the local congregation as the sum of individual believers and the church as the sum of local congregations must necessarily fail in the correct understanding of the ministry. Such a one is not only in danger of asserting the independent existence of the individual congregation, or is at least in the dilemma of having to establish the supervisory office of the church government by the analogy of political, especially democratic, constitutional forms, or even to turn the church's administration over to the political authority, but he will also see in the local pastor only the executor of the believers' orders.

3. Civil and spiritual authority are divine ordinances and derive their dignity from the Word of God.

"Thus our teachers distinguish the two authorities and the functions of the two powers, directing that both be held in honor as the highest gifts of God on earth" (A.C. XXVIII, 18). ". . . because of God's command both authorities and powers are to be honored and esteemed *with all reverence* (*"religiose venerari"*) as the two highest gifts of God on earth" (A.C. XXVIII, 4). If anyone were to honor only the spiritual office he would not truly honor it, because he does not honor God who was pleased to institute two kinds of authority. If anyone were to honor only the civil authority he would not truly, i.e., "with reverence," honor it, because he does not know that *God* who has instituted the civil power and who manifests himself only through the preaching ministry as the triune giver of the gift of civil government. The praise of the knowledge of God which is received through the spiritual authority does not involve any disparagement of civil government but rather leads to praise and thanksgiving for the divine gift of this civil power.

Both powers are ordinances of the triune God.[4] Even though, in speaking of the two, the word "ordinance" [*ordinatio*] is used in a different sense the fact remains that neither has been instituted by man but by the triune God. The triune God has ordained civil government and confirmed it by the command and the obedience of his Son, but confirmed it also by creating obedience to this government in the hearts of believers through the Holy Spirit. The triune God has instituted the spiritual authority through the Word of Jesus Christ and through this power, i.e., through Gospel and sacrament "as through means" (A.C. V, 2), gives the Holy Spirit.

In both realms God himself is at work even though it is always men who act in them, and God wants men to act in both offices. Like the parents the government has "received the command to do us all kinds of good. So we receive our blessings not from them,

---

[4] It must not be overlooked that the Confessions designate as divine ordinances not only the civil and spiritual powers but also marriage and family and the orders of nature, as, e.g., the change of seasons. Restricting ourselves in this chapter to the two first mentioned is proper because the Confessions had not yet developed the later doctrine of the *triplex ordo,* nor fixed systematically the threefold number of divine ordinances. On the concept *ordo* and *ordinatio Dei* in the B. of C., cf. H. Sasse, *Das Volk nach der Lehre der evangelischen Kirche* (München, 1934), pp. 17 ff. By developing the doctrine of the civil and spiritual powers in a strictly systematic parallelism, the specific characteristics of each are bound to emerge the more clearly as the parallelism is dissolved.

but from God through them. Creatures are only the hands, channels, and means through which God bestows all blessings. For example, he gives to the mother breasts and milk for her infant . . ." (L.C. I, 26). The same triune God who acts through the civil government also acts through the church's ministry. We are permitted to know that 'God wills to preach and be active through men and those who have been chosen by men' (Ap. XIII, 12). "On the basis of another's Word rather than on the basis of their own" (Ap. XXVIII, 18)—because God speaks through the ministers, not because they themselves speak—should we give them credence. Their absolution in the decisive point is "not the voice or word of the man who speaks it, but it is the Word of God, who forgives sin, . . . as much as if we heard God's voice from heaven" (A.C. XXV, 3 f.). We are permitted to believe that the promise of Christ, "He who hears you hears me," applies to the word of the spiritual authority (Luke 10:16; cf. the numerous quotations of this passage in the Index of Biblical References, B. of C., p. 642). Through the church's ministry Christ himself speaks to the world whose sins he bore. Similarly the office of the Word, and the Word preached in this office, is that "means through which God the Holy Spirit teaches people" (Ep. XII, 22).

If the triune God acts through both authorities, through civil government as creator and preserver and through the spiritual government as redeemer, sanctifier, and new-creator, both actions have in common that they are done through men, which also implies that they are done in spite of men. In both authorities God condescends to men by taking into his service and veiling his action in their action, his Word in their word. In this condescension God exercises his sovereign rule. This becomes most evident in the fact that in both offices he acts also through such men as are not members of the kingdom of God but of the kingdom of the devil, men who did not receive the benefits of Christ but who revile the cross of Christ through unbelief and persistent vices. Thus God acts even through a heathen in the office of civil government. Even though the heathen has not yet been delivered from the power of the devil's kingdom—this is done through Baptism—God commands us through the Gospel "to obey the existing laws, whether they were formulated by heathen or by others." The laws enacted by heathen can be God's commands too to such an extent that they cannot be annulled by the preaching of the Gospel and the law by the church: "The Gospel does not introduce any new laws about the civil estate"

(Ap. XVI, 3). This cannot imply that heathen in civil office and their laws always and everywhere provide for justice and peace according to God's will. This does not even apply generally where Christians act in the civil office. Yes, heathen government, at least the Roman designation of rulers as "fathers of the country," can be held up to Christians as a model which puts them to shame (L.C. I, 142).[5] Moreover, it is true both of a heathen and of a "Christian" in civil government that "God sometimes permits much good to come to a people through a tyrant or scoundrel" (S.A. II, iv, 3).

God acts with the same condescension and sovereignty through the ministry. "Word and sacraments are efficacious even when wicked men administer them" (Ap. VII, 19), "for they do not represent their own persons but the person of Christ, because of the church's call, as Christ testifies, 'He who hears you hears me.' When they offer the Word of Christ or the sacraments, they do so in Christ's place and stead" (Ap. VII, 28; cf. 47). This applies even to Judas, the betrayer. This doctrine of the spiritual office most effectively challenges the incumbent. Even when God blesses the congregation through the pastor's service, the pastor's person can be lost. But at the same time this doctrine of the divine glory of the spiritual authority is the highest comfort for pastor and congregation: Even though I, a sinner, preach to the congregation, God himself speaks to the congregation through my word; and even though a sinner pronounces the forgiveness of my sins to me, it is God who forgives them.

Now, of course, the statement that God acts through the action of evil men in the civil and spiritual realms by no means applies to any activity whatever. If Luther praises the government of the Turks and Tartars over against the rule of the pope, he does this because, "great as is their enmity against Christians, . . . those who desire to do so they allow to believe in Christ, and they receive bodily tribute and obedience from Christians" (S.A. II, iv, 11).

[5] This makes doubtful, to say the least, whether the idea of a *corpus Christianum* as a higher unity embracing both church and state is the presupposition of the Lutheran doctrine of both realms. It will not do to say in general: "Christendom is the basic concept. God has established two swords (two realms) within *Christendom,* namely, the spiritual and the civil. Both have the duty to govern Christendom . . ." Sohm, *Kirchenrecht,* I, 548 f. In the Confessions Christendom means "the church." The civil government, however, is God's ordinance among all people, Christian and pagan. That the incumbent of the civil government is a Christian is to be viewed as a special case within the Lutheran doctrine of the civil office, but not as its premise.

Even though they are enemies of the kingdom of God and his Son, in their governmental activity they remain in the sphere of the commission given to civil government by God, to provide for justice in the area of the second table. They do not interfere with their subjects in the area of worship. Basically, in like manner, we can think of an efficacy of Word and sacrament only where they are proclaimed and administered according to the commission given to the spiritual office, that is, where sinners—even though hypocritically—preach the Gospel and administer the sacraments in accordance with the Gospel.

All of these statements show clearly that the concept of office in the Confessions is a decidedly functional one.[6] The office is not determined from the standpoint of the person but of the divine institution. The words and deeds performed in the office do not receive their quality from the person—for example, from the fact that this person is a member of Christ's kingdom—but only from the action of God who in his offices too acts even through his enemies. The boundary for the divine action through the civil and the spiritual office is not man as such but in every case it is the commission given by God with the office. This functional character of the office becomes evident most paradoxically in the fact that God wars against the devil's kingdom even through such members of the devil's kingdom as function in the civil or spiritual realm.

[6] This is true already with respect to the secular office. But especially is the functional character of the ministry emphasized again and again, and this with an express devaluation of the incumbent persons. Hence it is improper to deduce from the Augsburg Confession that "God not only ordained that the *functions* be *carried out* in preaching, baptizing, absolving, and excommunicating, but that God has also ordained to assign these functions to *special persons* as their *life's calling,* to be carried out regularly by them alone." Stahl, *Kirchenverfassung,* p. 109. According to this, "not only the *office* of preaching but also the *class* of preachers,"—"class in the specific ecclesiastical sense of a special profession which determines also the *entire orientation* of life"—are of divine institution. "This is evidenced by the fact that the servants of the Word are to find their living too in the church and are not to engage in other gainful employment." *Ibid.,* p. 110. The Confessions omit such ideas. These signify, on the one hand, a secularizing transformation of the call as a profession, and, on the other hand, the elevation of the persons in church office—not the office itself—above the other believers by means of a special divine consecration. This doctrine has many serious implications. It is most intimately connected with the distinction between church and congregation, as Stahl expresses it: "Congregation designates the *people united* in faith, while church designates the *divine establishment over the people.* The congregation comes into being through the will and deed of men, their inner decision to believe, their external membership; the church is a work, institution, kingdom established and continually preserved by God." *Ibid.,* p. 67. However, neither church and ministry nor church as fellowship and as institution may be thus placed in opposition. Otherwise man would obtain, contrary to the Confessions, a value in himself.

Even though God acts in the civil and spiritual dominion also through members of the devil's kingdom, he has established both dominions in opposition to the devil's kingdom and protects them daily against the devil's power. The devil is "not satisfied to obstruct and overthrow spiritual order, so that he may deceive men with his lies and bring them under his power, but he also prevents and hinders the establishment of any kind of government or honorable and peaceful relations on earth. This is why he causes so much confusion, murder, sedition, and war; why he sends tempest and hail to destroy crops and cattle; why he poisons the air, etc. In short, it pains him that anyone receives a morsel of bread from God and eats it in peace" (L.C. III, 80). To be sure, through civil government nobody is liberated from the power of sin, death, and the devil; all men in and under civil government, in spite of all their righteousness, remain members of the devil's kingdom until they believe the preaching of the Gospel. And yet, "here lurks a sneaky, seditious devil who would like to snatch the crown from the rulers and trample it under foot and would, in addition, pervert and nullify all God's work and ordinances" (L.C. IV, 62). Why does the devil fight not only against the spiritual office through which God takes the sinner away from him, but also against the civil office through which God preserves the sinner in the power of sin, death, and the devil? Because the devil is not only a liar but also a murderer from the beginning. But lawful governments "are truly ordinances of God and are preserved and defended by God against the devil" (Ap. VII, 50). For God wishes to preserve his creatures through this office, so that they may be saved through the Gospel.

The dignity of both realms consists in God's Word. After what has been said, this applies immediately to the spiritual office. For it is the office of the Word. This office cannot exist for a moment without God's Word, for the Word is its power. God's Word, however, also constitutes the dignity of the civil government. "If we regard these persons (civil authority) with reference to their noses, eyes, skin and hair, flesh and bones, they look no different from Turks and heathen. . . . But because the commandment is added, 'You shall honor father and mother,' I see another man, adorned and clothed with the majesty and glory of God. The commandment, I say, is the golden chain about his neck, yes, the crown on his head, which shows me how and why I should honor this particular flesh and blood" (L.C. IV, 20). Even though in civil government things can be done correctly without knowing God's

Word, yet God's Word remains the dignity of this realm too. It is related to the person in this office like the kernel in the nut to the shell, yes, like the Word to the element in the sacrament. Though the person in civil office shares in the dignity of this office without knowing about God's Word, he knows nothing about the divine dignity of his office apart from God's Word. The dignity of this office is to be recognized empirically as little as the dignity of all other ordinances of God. The divine majesty and glory of civil government is hidden in its empirical reality for both lord and subjects and is visible in the Word alone.[7] Both realms must be honored and esteemed "because of God's command" (A.C. XXVIII, 4).

Though both realms have their dignity in God's Word, this truth at once reveals the differences of both. The dignity of civil government is an objective reality even without a subjective knowledge of the Word of God. Even when civil government does not know God's Word, its rightful laws are God's commandments. In the spiritual office, however, not a single word can be spoken as God's Word without the acknowledgment of God's Word, even if only in a hypocritical way, and without express reference to the testimony of the Word of God in Scripture. The dignity of the spiritual office is solely the witnessed Word of God. Apart from this witness the spiritual office has no dignity. Accordingly, heathen government may occasionally be presented to the Christian as a model for his thinking about civil government; but in no case may the heathen cultus be a model for Christian worship. It is evident from these differences that the two authorities are distinct, and not only as to the functions assigned to them by God; the very concept of *"ordinatio"* has a completely different content in both cases.

4. Civil government is God's good creature and ordinance.

"All government in the world and all established rule and laws" are "instituted and ordained by God for the sake of good order" (*"bona opera Dei,"* A.C. XVI, 1). They are 'God's good creatures and divine ordinances' (Ap. XVI, 1). What does the expression "creatures and divine ordinances" mean? "It is legitimate for Christians to use civil ordinances, just as it is legitimate for them to use the air, light, food, and drink. For as this universe and the fixed movements of the stars are truly ordinances of God, and are

[7] Cf. pp. 53 f.

preserved by God, so lawful governments are ordinances of God and are preserved and defended by God against the devil" (Ap. VII, 50). The Gospel "subjects us to them, just as we are necessarily subjected to the laws of the seasons and to the change of winter and summer as ordinances of God" (Ap. XVI, 6); we may use lawful civil governments "just as" God "lets us make use of medicine or architecture, food, or drink, or air" (Ap. XVI, 2). Civil government, accordingly, is an ordinance of God the Creator and as such it is God's creation. God preserves the ordinance of civil government as he preserves his creation, and he preserves man through the ordinance of civil government as he preserves him through the gifts of nature.

These statements involve no pondering of the question whether the ordinance of civil government existed already in paradise or was added after the fall. As the Confessions do not use the term "orders of creation," so they also lack a distinction of orders of creation and of preservation. In this connection we again note the refusal to distinguish between God's creation and his preservation, a refusal which keeps the constantly active Creator in view.[8] God not only created in the beginning before man sinned, but as Creator he is also at work on the sinner. But even though the Apology does not expressly state that civil government as an ordinance of God follows sin, we must still note that the assertions of the Apology about the function of civil government, i.e., to provide for outward justice and peace, presuppose the unrighteousness of the sinner. God the Creator preserves the sinners by protecting them through civil government from mutual annihilation. Perhaps sin is also presupposed in the comparison of the change of seasons (Ap. XVI, 6) and the heavenly bodies (Ap. XVI, 50), if we assume that Melanchthon was thinking of the covenant with Noah in which God guaranteed the preservation of the sinful human race and the change of summer and winter, of day and night.

In the Large Catechism the derivation of civil government from the parental office corresponds to these statements. "Out of the authority of parents all other authority is derived and developed. Where a father is unable by himself to bring up his child, he calls upon a schoolmaster to teach him; if he is too weak, he enlists the help of his friends and neighbors; if he passes away, he confers and delegates his authority and responsibility to others appointed for the purpose. . . . Thus all who are called masters stand in the

[8] Cf. pp. 38 ff.

place of parents and derive from them their power and authority to govern. In the Scriptures they are all called fathers because in their responsibility they act in the capacity of fathers and ought to have fatherly hearts toward their people" (L.C. I, 141). Since God established matrimony "as the first of all institutions, and he created man and woman differently . . . to be true to each other, be fruitful, beget children, and support and bring them up to the glory of God" (L.C. I, 207), from this too the designation of parental and civil government as God's creation and ordinance follows. At the same time, the fact that Luther bases civil government on the parental office shows clearly that it was not the parental office as such, but only the interference with and the inability of this office which necessitated a superordinate civil government. For this reason, in the authority of the parental office, civil government steps out of the father's estate and stands over against it. Nevertheless, this government is God's creation, even if it did not at the outset arise from the parental union of man and wife.

Just as marriage does not begin only when man and wife hear God's Word but already exists as the work of God the Creator in the union of man and wife even before God the Creator reveals himself to them in the Word of grace, so government exists among all nations, among Christians and pagans. The office of civil government is God's good creature, even though the person in this office does not honor the Creator but, instead, derives the dignity of his office from the sword in his hand, or from the will of the people, or from some other source. This does not mean, however, that the existing empirical ordinances of the civil government are simply to be equated with the divine institution of this government. Man's investiture in the divine ordinance of civil government indeed does not first take place through God's proclaimed Word; yet not every use of civil power can be equated with the activity of God through his establishment of civil government. All statements about government as God's ordinance rather presuppose that the government is lawful ("legitimae," A.C. XVI, 1). God permits us to "make outward use of legitimate political ordinances" (Ap. XVI, 2). God does not act as avenger through every penal sentence and through every war conducted by the civil power, but civil government has the duty to "prescribe legal punishments, engage in just wars" (Ap. XVI, 1). And this applies to both Christians and pagans in this realm. Thus the divine ordinance of government is not as such identical with the activity of the civil power; it is rather at once concealed in this activity, that is hidden under unlawful activity.

But what does "legitimate" mean here? If it means "according to the valid laws," we must immediately ask: "What is the norm of the law that is valid in the statutes and measures of legitimate, even though pagan, government?"

The Confessions are remarkably uninterested in an explicit answer to this important question. When we approach Luther's statements in the Large Catechism with this question, we are in the main again and again directed only to God's activity, who through the government gives us food, protection, and safety (L.C. I, 150; III, 74, 77 f., 80). This fact is its glory. God acts through it when it provides "us our daily bread and all the comforts of this life" (L.C. III, 74). An answer going beyond this may be derived from the Apology where the "civil righteousness" (*justitia civilis*) and the "righteousness of reason" (*justitia rationis*) are equated. Natural human reason "to some extent" understands the Decalogue and in this unclear and constantly distorting comprehension of the divine law it understands "the external works that reason can somehow perform" (Ap. IV, 7).[9] Thus the second table of the law, even in the distortion of the natural knowledge of the law, is the norm in the laws of the lawful pagan government. Significant in this connection as is the natural knowledge of the law, in spite of its separation of the two tables, significant namely as a means through which—through an indistinct knowledge about good and evil, about the crimes of murder, adultery, theft, perjury, etc.—God preserves the sinner, it still follows from the norm of the natural knowledge of the law that civil righteousness in its very essence is restricted to the punishment of *coarse, external* wrong.

While the treatment of civil government in the Confessions does not answer more than this to the question about the norm of the laws and of the activity of legitimate government, we dare not forget that they do not give political advice to pagans, but profess the content of the *church's* proclamation about civil government. This implies that this preaching is never done, either to subjects or to rulers, on the basis of the natural knowledge of the law but always and only on the basis of the norm of the divine Word, hence never separated from the Gospel and the preaching of the unseparated *two* tables of the Decalogue. To be sure, the Decalogue with its few prohibitions cannot serve as a legal code for the civil govern-

[9] Cf. pp. 49 ff.

ment. Just as little, however, is the Christian permitted—be it in civil government when laws are enacted, be it under civil government in obeying its laws—to disregard the commandments of the second table as the commandments of God who has revealed his will in both tables.

5. *The spiritual office was instituted by God in the calling of the apostles through Jesus Christ.*

In the statements about the spiritual office we speak about *"ordinatio"* and *"ordo"* in a very different sense from that used in the doctrine of civil government. God has "instituted the office of the ministry" (A.C. V), not "created and instituted" (A.C. XVI, 1)[10] but instituted by command and promise. *"Ordinatio"* here does not mean "creature and ordinance" (Ap. XVI, 1) but a "calling through the Word of God." The same word, *"ordinatio Dei,"* here receives a special meaning. The spiritual office does not already exist where God the Creator is active in preservation, without revealing himself in the Word. But apart from the revelation of the Word of God and its preaching there is no ministry at all. God's Word is the dignity of this office only as the Word that is heard and proclaimed. The spiritual office as distinct from the civil government does not exist everywhere and at all times but it is instituted in a specific historical event of the divine address, i.e., in the commissioning of the apostles by Jesus Christ.

Jesus Christ empowered the apostles through the command, "As the Father has sent me, even so I send you" (John 20:21). Furthermore, for the Confessions the authority of the spiritual office is specifically defined by the word of Jesus, "He who hears you hears me" (Luke 10:16). To these are added the other words by which the Lord commissioned and sent the apostles to gather and edify congregations. Consistently these commands and promises given to the apostles are referred to the public ministry through which at all times the Gospel is to be preached in the midst of the congregation and before all the world. This approach to the doctrine of the ministry is of decisive significance. The public ministry of all times was instituted with the calling of the apostles, without disparagement of the unique church-founding position of the apostles. The "glorious promises" which the ministry "has" are also acknowledged by means

---

[10] The B. of C. rendering of *"geschaffen und eingesetzt"* as "instituted and ordained" is not literal enough to serve as the basis for Schlink's argument which follows.—Trans.

241

of the apostolic and prophetic word, Rom. 1:16, "The Gospel is the power of God for salvation to every one who has faith." Likewise, Isa. 55:11, "My word that goes forth from my mouth shall not return to me empty, but it shall accomplish that which I purpose" (Ap. XIII, 11).

The Word by which Jesus authorizes the apostles is also the authorization for the entire church. The words "You are Peter, and on this rock I will build my church" (Matt. 16:18 f.) are interpreted to mean that Jesus builds his church not on the authority of a man but on the office of the confession which Peter had made, "not on the man but on the faith of Peter," that is, on the foundation of the faith and confession, "You are the Christ, the Son of the living God" (cf. Tr. 25 ff.). Jesus Christ himself is therefore the rock and foundation of his church. Referring to John 20:23, the statement is added that Peter is not addressed as an individual but as the representative of the apostles. Again, the power of the keys according to Matt. 18:18 is entrusted not only to the apostles but to the whole church. The "keys do not belong to the person of one particular individual but to the whole church," and that "immediately" (Tr. 24; cf. S.A. III, vii, 1).

Thus the apostles were commissioned by Jesus Christ not only as the servants of the first church but as servants and representatives of the church at all times. Therefore, "wherever the church exists, the right to administer the Gospel also exists" (Tr. 67). The fact that according to the testimony of the ancient church a layman may in an emergency absolve and become the minister and pastor of another (Tr 67), and the fact that the Gospel is to be applied "through the mutual conversation and consolation of brethren" (S.A. III, iv), show plainly that the loosing power of the keys is entrusted not only to particular persons but to all members of the church. Peter's word is indeed true, "You are a royal priesthood" (Tr. 69). 'The person adds nothing to this Word and office ordained by Christ. No matter who it is who preaches and teaches the Word, if there are hearts that hear and adhere to it, something will happen to them according as they hear and believe because Christ commanded such preaching and demanded that his promises be believed' (Tr. 26). The authority to preach the Gospel includes the authority to send out other messengers with the authority to preach the Gospel. Together with the power of the keys the whole church has been given also the right to ordain; together with the Gospel, also the responsibility for the spread and preservation of the Gospel. "Where the true church is, therefore, the right of electing and ordaining ministers must of necessity also be." "Wherefore it is necessary for the church to retain the right of calling, electing, and ordaining ministers" (Tr. 67).

Under these presuppositions, what does it mean that, according to A.C. XIV, "nobody should publicly teach or preach or administer the sacraments in the church without a regular call" *("nisi rite vocatus")*? This article does not deny the royal priesthood of all believers but presupposes it. Because the spiritual office has been entrusted to all believers, its administration is not left to the whim of every individual believer. The public administration depends, rather, on the authorization of the assembly of believers. Because the ministry is entrusted to the church, the church calls the particular believer into the office of public preaching and administration of the sacraments. But the believer does not become a priest through this call. The relationship between the power of the keys given to all believers and the power of the public ministry can be characterized, with Harless, in this manner that we, on the one hand, "clearly distinguish between the priestly and ministerial call and, on the other hand, seek the essence of the ministry of the Word in nothing else than in what belongs also to every believing Christian by virtue of his priestly calling" *(Kirche und Amt,* p. 16). "Ministerial," then, means that in the congregation the preacher of the Gospel serves the priestly commission which God has given the whole congregation. Under no circumstances therefore may the right of every believer to forgive the brother's sins be treated as nonexistent, or as provided only for a case of emergency, or only as done in trust for the public ministry. The call into the public ministry and the activity in this office at all times presupposes the royal priesthood of all believers and does not abolish it.[11]

Having been entrusted with the Gospel, the church has also been commissioned to spread the Gospel, and, having been given the ministry, the church is also authorized to call men into the ministry. It is, therefore, only consistent that the call into the public ministry, like public preaching, cannot be done arbitrarily. Like public preaching, the calling into the ministry by the church should as a rule be done through the men properly called into the public ministry.

[11] In view of these presuppositions, may we say that ordination "bestows the Holy Spirit in all his reality and gives the ability to forgive sins . . ."? Vilmar, *Dogmatik,* II, 277. In view of the royal priesthood of all believers, may the Christian in the public ministry be distinguished from other Christians by such an "ability"?

Ordination, which in the Confessions is not clearly distinguished from the call and election, is the function of pastors and bishops. But this does not abolish the right of all believers to ordain. This right does not, as a result of the above rule, become a "superfluously" or "fictitiously" provided emergency right (cf. A.F.C. Vilmar, *Die Lehre vom geistlichen Amte,* pp. 73 f.). Nor can it be an "inviolable rule" that "the judgment whether a person is competent to fill the office of pastor, and that the installation of a person found competent (fit, worthy) in the office of pastor can proceed *only* from a pastor."[12] Even one layman, who in case of necessity was called by another layman, deals with that very layman as pastor in the full sense of the term (Tr. 67). In this connection the Treatise also points out that formerly the episcopal ordination was merely the ratification by another bishop of the bishop called by the congregation (Tr. 70).

At this point it might seem natural to infer that the public ministry grows out of the royal priesthood of all believers and that it comes into being through the enabling commission of the congregation; that its authority is the authority of the congregation transferred to one of its members. The public ministry would then be an "emanation," a "concentration," or an "organization" of the universal priesthood of all believers, a "community office" based on the "collective right" of the whole congregation, and the pastor would preach the Gospel and administer the sacraments in the name and at the direction of the congregation—"for the community and on behalf of the community."[13] In this case, he would "represent" the congregation

---

[12] Vilmar *(op. cit.,* pp. 70 f.) maintained this very firmly in his polemics against the dissolution of the concept of the ministerial office by Hoefling and others. He also understood the contrary statements of the Treatise as superfluous remarks about the emergency rights of the congregation in the practically inconceivable emergency of the absence of all pastors called by pastors. In view of this it will be difficult to find a theologial basis for this emergency right of the congregation. The "emergency right" does not rest on the emergency but on the fact that the office of the ministry has been entrusted to the entire congregation. This does not only become real in an emergency but is the universally valid premise for every act of calling into the pastoral office by pastors, and is already present in each of these acts.

[13] Hoefling, *Grundsaetze der evangelisch-lutherischen Kirchenverfassung,* p. 56. Correspondingly, it would have to be said also of the supervisory church administration that it could *not* act in the name of God but only in the name of the fellowship. "That which acts on behalf of the community is the organ of the universal priesthood of believers, imbued with the omnipresence and omnipotence of Christ." *Ibid.,* pp. 234 f. It is the abiding church-historical achievement of Loehe, Kliefoth, Vilmar, Dieckhof, and, in spite of everything, also of Stahl to have opposed this still widely held theory of transference (initiated by Justus Henning Boehmer, d. 1749).

in the divine service (A. Ritschl). But these conclusions are false.[14] The public ministry is not a creation of the congregation demanded by the moral principle of order but it is an immediate institution of God through the command and promise of Jesus Christ. The Confessions do not permit us to place the universal priesthood as a divine institution over against the public ministry as a human institution. The idea of a transfer of the rights of the universal priesthood to the person of the pastor is foreign to the Confessions. The church does not *transfer* its office of preaching the Gospel and administering the sacraments to individuals in its membership, but it *fills* this office entrusted to it by God, it *calls* into this office instituted by God. In this office the pastor therefore acts in the name and at the direction of *God* and in the stead of *Jesus Christ*. He acts with authority not on the basis of an arrangement made by believers but on the basis of the divine institution. This becomes especially evident in the occasional designation of this *"ordo"* as a sacrament (Ap. XIII, 11 ff.). This term is questionable inasmuch as the *mandatum* by which God instituted the ministry does not comprise an external sign; the laying on of hands at ordination, for example, was not commanded by Christ like water, bread, and wine. But not even for a moment could the Confessions here speak of the ministry and the laying on of hands as a sacrament if God himself did not call into the ministry through the calling word of men, that is, the church, "for we know that God approves this ministry and is present in it" (Ap. XIII, 12). Like all promises of God, so also the application of the promises connected with the laying on of hands at the filling of the ministerial office is *God's* deed. He himself calls into the ministry through the mouth of men.[15] The pastor does not merely occupy his office as a member

[14] Such conclusions reach their ultimate result in the views of R. Sohm: "From the church in the religious sense arises only that office which is 'common property of all Christians,' namely, the 'ministerial office' that is inherent in the *universal* priesthood of every believer. This common office, untrammeled by any constitutional provisions, exists *'jure divino,'* that is, by virtue of the essence of Christianity." The *public* office, however, equipped with specific rights, rests on *human* liberty which for the sake of order transfers to an individual what *jure divino* belongs to all. This office is part of "the external order of *visible* Christendom" and hence is not part of the church but of the world. It is a *"worldly"* office, and it is "expendable." "From a *religious* point of view not only the 'how' of the constitutional provisions for the office of the ministry and for the congregation but also the 'that,' the *existence* of the public office in a properly constituted congregation, is a matter of indifference." *Kirchenrecht,* II, 140 f.

[15] If, however, the pastoral office is only the orderly commissioning of a member by the congregation, the ordination can be nothing more than an "act of ecclesiastical benediction" which "can claim neither a specific *man-*

commissioned by the congregation; rather, he stands over against the congregation as God's representative in God's commission. The word proclaimed by the ministry is not only the voice of a man but it is God's own voice coming down from heaven. The call into the ministry through the church is proper only in the acknowledgment of the divinely posited polarity between God's Word and church, i.e., when we acknowledge the divine institution of the public ministry. The Confessions place this polarity of office and congregation so much in the foreground that they regard the spiritual office, ministry, and *public* ministry as identical concepts, though they acknowledge the royal-priestly authority given to all believers.

The question could be raised whether the ministry antedates the congregation or vice versa; whether the ministry is above the congregation or vice versa. Such an either/or is out of order,[16] just

datum divinum, nor a specific *promissio divina.*" "It is not God who is acting here, as in the sacraments, to bestow a specific grace and mental competence, rather it is men who act in the presence of God, who through prayer consecrate, hallow, strengthen, and confirm their God-pleasing, God-ordained relation to each other." Hoefling, *op. cit.,* p. 80. Even though the ritual of ordination within the frame of Lutheran doctrine may legitimately be understood as an act of benediction and as public ratification of the call and the election, it is nevertheless true of the *entire process* of the call, election, and ordination—not clearly distinguished in the Confessions—that through this action of the church, or the church government, performed on a member of the church, *God* is calling into the pastoral office. For the church calls by God's command. Thus the act of benediction rests on a specific *mandatum divinum,* and the prayers have a specific *promissio divina.*

[16] In the last century A. Harless and Th. Harnack came closest to avoiding the twin dangers of denying either the universal priesthood or the divine institution of the public ministry, the dangers of viewing the office either as a rank or as being under the control of the congregation. As a matter of fact, we must refrain from setting up an immediate, logically acceptable relationship between office and congregation. *Both* things must be said: "Precisely because all have the calling to proclaim Christ and the praises of him who has called us out of darkness, no individual has the right to do this arbitrarily and publicly before the congregation but must await a special election or call to do so, because the believing congregation regards it as its duty to make provisions for election and call in an orderly way." "From the fact that the congregation in an orderly election or call summons someone into the ministry of reconciliation it by no means follows that such ministry is purely a congregational service or arrangement or authorization. On the contrary, it is precisely because the believing congregation acknowledges this ministry to be an institution, ordinance, and authorization of Christ—founding, building, and preserving his Christendom through his Word and the ministry of his Word—that the congregation issues a call for this office." Harless, *Kirche und Amt,* pp. 18 f. In opposition to the misrepresentations of the Lutheran doctrine of the pastoral office, Th. Harnack rightly maintained this thesis: "The church possesses an office not because it has believing or spiritually endowed persons, but because it has the means of grace and the mandate of its Lord. Both hierarchism and the common fraternalism, each in its own way, fail to understand this. Though proceeding from opposite premises, both arrive at a point where the office disappears behind the persons; for both shift the focus to the *personal,* the one hierarchically, the other charismatically." *Die Kirche, ihr Amt, ihr Regiment,* p. 52.

as in another way the question about the priority of the visible or the invisible church is falsely put. The relationship between office and congregation cannot be presented clearly in a direct statement of their relationship at all, but only in the relationship of both to their Lord Jesus Christ who through the ministry governs his kingdom, the communion of believers, the freedmen, those who live and reign with him. Because the Confessions look to this *Lord* who governs the congregation through the external Word, they are not at all interested in a logically satisfying clarification of the relationship between the universal priesthood and the public ministry. This much is established, namely, that Lutheran doctrine places "the office over the persons and the church over the servants" (Th. Harnack), and that the relationship between office and congregation is never that of a one-sided authentication and influence, be it on the part of the office or of the congregation. The relationship is rather a reciprocal one, like that which exists between the church and the preaching of the Gospel according to the *"in qua"* of A.C. VII: The church comes into being where the Gospel is preached and the church exists by preaching the Gospel. The church preaches the Gospel by calling the believer into the ministry of preaching the Gospel, and the church is built when the called believer preaches the Gospel. This dual relationship must never be forgotten. But just as the Gospel creates the church, and not inversely the church the Gospel—the church can only bear witness to the Gospel—so in the doctrine of the ministerial office attention is directed above all to the speaking of God through this office, and not to the human word which calls into this office and is heard in this office. Thus, neither the congregation nor the person of the pastor is the final authority, but the Lord of both in royal sovereignty governs both pastor and congregation through the Gospel and the sacraments.[17]

6. The function but not the concrete form of both authorities is revealed in God's Word. Only according to human law is the office of church government distinguished from the pastoral office.

The articles concerning the spiritual and civil authorities have in common that they either make no statements about the concrete

---

[17] The controversy about the priority of the office or the congregation in a certain way reminds one of the question whether the hen or the egg was there first. Vilmar, *Lehre vom geistlichen Amt*, p. 98. Here too we shall have to say that God the Creator was there first of all.

form of both offices or at least do not in these statements make a specific form or constitution of these offices confessionally binding. Even though the doctrine of the spiritual and civil powers sets definite limits of action for both, it is not possible to extract a code of constitutional law or a code of church government from the Confessions.

Here must be noted, on the one side, the peculiar lack of concern according to which civil government is designated by a variety of terms without any attempt at closer definition: *politia, oeconomia, respublica, societas civilis, imperium, regnum, magistratus, status civilis*, etc. (cf., e.g., Ap. XVI, 5-8). This variety of terms not merely designates the identical form of government from different points of view but leaves room for the variety of forms of civil power, monarchy, estates, democracy, and others. Nor do the Confessions contain any doctrinal statements about the way in which one may legitimately enter civil office. The corresponding lack of concern for the form of civil government recurs in the designation of the laws according to which the government acts. They are 'the imperial laws and others in present force,' 'common law and customs having the force of law,' whether they have been framed by heathen or by others (Ap. XVI, 1, 3, 12, 13). This lack of interest in the form of civil government is also shown by a comparison of the Latin and German texts of the same passage. The diversity of these forms has the concept of the "legitimate" as a unifying factor. But this term is so wide that, even when its content is determined in the sense of the second table of the Decalogue, no concrete form of a political constitution nor an even approximately adequate concretion of a criminal code results.[18]

The same applies also to the concrete form of the ministerial office. To be sure, the Confessions make basic statements about the relationship of church and Gospel, church and ministry, and also about the identity of the pastorate and the episcopate in accord with the fact that the one catholic church becomes a reality in the local congregation and in the Christian church on earth. But the Confessions lack binding assertions of a specific nature delimiting the functions of pastorate and episcopate, even though a delimitation must take place. What would happen to churches if every pastor were arbitrarily to exercise administrative functions affecting

---

[18] "The legal provisions of the Confessions are not legal pronouncements, but legal principles." W. Kahl, *Der Rechtsinhalt*, p. 1. This sentence applies not only to canon law but, in basically the same manner, also to the Lutheran doctrine of the state.

the whole church, if, e.g., he wanted to ordain arbitrarily? Furthermore, there are no specific directives for the relationship of the ministry and the congregation. To be sure, the universal priesthood of all is definitely presupposed, and even in a church with an episcopal government this finds expression at least in the provision that the congregation is to examine the doctrine of the bishops and in special cases refuse to obey them (A.C. XXVIII, 23 ff.). The congregation may confer ordination "with the assistance of their pastors," [19] yes, in case of necessity, even without them (Tr. 72; 66 f.). But there is no concrete specification of the organs through whom the congregation acts in this case. Furthermore, there are no concrete instructions about the relationship of ordination, pastoral election, installation, and the conditions that must be satisfied in calling a member of the church into the ministry. What, specifically, is meant when it is said that they shall be 'suitable persons' (Tr. 65), not 'crude asses' (Ap. XXVIII, 3)? There are no binding prescriptions about who should perform the ordination—the pastor or the bishop. From this it follows that the Confessions do not obligate the church to a specific constitution. They contain no more than guiding principles for the determination of various constitutions.

The questions suggested by this presentation may be discussed in greater detail by referring to the confessional assertions concerning the office of the church administration to which a number of local congregations and their pastors are subordinated.[20] As far as the divine commission is concerned this church administration

---

[19] *"Adhibitis suis pastoribus"* is not translated in the B. of C. rendering of the passage.—Trans.

[20] None of the following statements has escaped attack within the Lutheran church during the past hundred years. By invoking the Confessions it was argued whether a superior church administration was divinely ordained or established by human right only; whether such an arrangement was necessary, possible, or even impermissible; whether this pertained to the ministerial or the civil office, to civil government as such or only to Christians in government; whether the church administration was identical with the pastoral ministry or constituted an entirely different ecclesiastical office; whether in the highest instance it would have to be synodical or episcopal; whether the administration would have to adopt the same confessional basis as the congregation or whether it would have to be acknowledged by congregations of a divergent doctrinal position; whether and to what extent the church government could demand compliance, etc. The scope of this book will not permit further discussion of these diverse theses. It is clear, however, that some of these necessarily result from the various distortions of the Lutheran concept of church and ministry. Since these distortions rest ultimately on a misunderstanding of God's revelation in the external Word, it would be ill advised to seek the cause of this confusion in the Confessions themselves. They are quite clear on this matter when viewed from the center, but only then, namely, in the proper distinction between law and Gospel. Getting involved without the necessary clarity in present-day arguments about the pastoral office and church

is identical with the pastorate. According to A.C. XIV, every properly ordered public ministry is "ecclesiastical order." The Confessions know of no superior church administration having a divine commission different from the pastorate. The one church power is active in different forms or, in other words, "Bishop and pastor are two functions of the same office" (W. Trillhaas, *Die lutherische Lehre 'De potestate ecclesiastica,'* p. 507). The church administration has the same duty for its diocese as the pastor has for his congregation. Even though the church administration does not personally preach in all congregations and distribute the sacraments to all the people in the diocese, it has the responsibility to see to it that the Gospel is really preached in all congregations of the diocese and that the sacraments are administered according to the Gospel.

The differences of authority by which the church administration is distinguished from the pastorate are a human arrangement. Therefore it is possible "for the sake of love and unity" (S.A. III, x, 1) to grant ordination to the bishops alone, even though every pastor has the right to ordain (Tr. 65 ff.). In this case the pastor does not lose his right, but for the sake of order in the church he makes no use of his right as long as ordinations are performed properly by the bishop. Likewise, it is possible that certain functions of the power of the keys, namely, excommunication, are delegated in a special manner to the bishop, even though the pastor is empowered by God to do this. Here too we have a human arrangement which does not give the bishop a divine right nor take it away from the pastor. But for the sake of love and unity now the pastor, now the bishop refrains from insisting on his rights. To this may be added certain powers pertaining to church administration which are delegated to the bishops and in which the pastor obeys, such as the fixing of festivals, orders of service, and matters of administration.

Frequently the episcopate is presupposed as the form of church administration. But this does not necessarily mean that according to the Lutheran Confessions the episcopate is the divinely ordained form of superior church order. Administrative decisions in this sense are expected also of synods. These provide for the church "the power

---

administration is all the more culpable for the Lutheran churches, because all the questions of the present time were actually posed with great precision in the debates of the last century. And this was done not only in a theoretical way but even more through the decisions made in practice. So, for example, the much-neglected individual doctrinal reasons for the "separation" of the Lutherans in Prussia from the Union, and the considerable splits within this "separated" church, are most painfully relevant today.

of making judgments and decisions according to the Word of God."
"The decisions of synods are decisions of the church" (Tr. 56; cf.
40, 49 f.). To be sure, the councils are here viewed as levels of
church government superior to the bishops and they are placed in
opposition to the pope. Yet in principle it is permissible to say
that the "alternative, 'bishop or synod,' is a question of expediency
and is out of order where not the 'how' but the 'that' of genuine
church government is concerned." [21] For in individual passages it
is difficult to determine to what extent the confessional expressions
regarding the episcopate are conditioned by the actual presence of
Roman bishops with whom they had to deal, or to what extent they
demand this office as a matter of principle. The Confessions do
definitely reject the claim that "the pope is . . . the head of all
Christendom by divine right or according to God's Word" (S.A.
II, iv, 1). As an extreme concession Melanchthon is ready to say
in subscribing to the Smalcald Articles that, if the pope would
allow the Gospel, "we, too, may concede to him that superiority
over the bishops which he possesses by human right . . ., for the
sake of peace and general unity . . ." (B. of C, pp. 316-317).

At all events, it is established that only the church itself has the
power to direct the affairs of the church and that this is to be done
through the ministry.[22] Since the church is determined by the Gospel,
the church cannot be directed without the recognition and preaching of the Gospel. Since, however, the Gospel should not be
preached publicly without a regular call, the guidance of the church
is essentially the function of the spiritual authority. The Confessions nowhere speak of another authority for the church; yes, it is
in principle excluded by their doctrine of church and ministry. But
the form of this control, including the limiting of its functions apart
from those of the pastorate, is a matter of "human right."

[21] Trillhaas, *Die lutherische Lehre 'De potestate ecclesiastica,'* p. 505. The
question regarding the mutual relationship of bishops and synods in the sense
of a superior or inferior position is not determined by the Confessions any
more than the either/or of bishop or synod.

[22] It is today almost universally recognized that this statement is a necessary
inference from the Confessions. For the individual points, cf. the arguments
which Stahl and Vilmar have introduced against the theses of O. Mejer (that
Lutheran doctrine assigns the government of the church as a matter of principle to the Christian ruler, *Die Grundlagen des Lutherischen Kirchenregiments*
[Rostock, 1864]) and of Hoefling (that "only in an emergency and under
certain circumstances" the ministerial office could take charge of the government of the church, *Grundsaetze . . . ,* p. 128). While R. Sohm (*Kirchenrecht*,
I, 506 ff.) first refutes these theses in an excellent way, he then proceeds even
to top them: "The government of the visible church can only be a *secular*
one, a government *by the state.*" *Ibid.,* 139.

What do "divine right" and "human right" mean in this connection?[23] The "divine right" of ecclesiastical power is the commission by which God has instituted it, that is to say, the authority given to it, the power of the keys. The "human right," conversely, is not the right of the world but the right of the church, not a right of men as such but the right of believers to put church ordinances into effect in the liberty of faith. The distinction between divine and human right concerns a distinction between God and man in the recognition of the Gospel which binds man to the work that Jesus Christ did for us and which frees man from the law and the works of the law. This, then, is a distinction of the church itself which alone is able to distinguish to what extent the Gospel binds and frees, to what extent man is bound by the commission to preach the Gospel and by this very obligation is authorized in the liberty of faith to put ordinances into effect which serve the preaching of the Gospel. As the Gospel is the source of this liberty, so it is also the norm and the goal. Ecclesiastical order must always be constituted anew in such a way as to "offer the office of the ministry a maximum of possibilities to accomplish its service of preaching the pure Gospel and of properly administering the sacraments in the name and by the command of the Lord of the church" (H. Sasse, *Kirchenregiment und weltliche Obrigkeit nach lutherischer Lehre,* p. 60). Liberated by the Gospel for service to the Gospel, "man" establishes ordinances in the church for examinations, ordinations, and installations, for the relationship of congregation, pastor, and church administrations for the unfolding of the functions of the *one* spiritual office in various offices arranged by the church, for the cooperation of the voice of the universal priesthood of believers in the activity of church administration, etc. The fact that the Confessions do not prescribe canonical rules for all these matters— though the church must have order in these matters if confusion is not to result—is felt as a lack and a weakness the moment the church has forgotten about the freedom of faith. Then the silence of the Confessions becomes a pretext for constant yielding, for

---

[23] Though the term *"jus divinum"* comes from the language of canon law, it is directed by means of incisive polemics against that law to the degree that *jus divinum* and *jus humanum* are now distinguished within the *jus divinum* of canon law. *Jus divinum* does not originate with the church or the pope, but it is the Word of God, especially the command and promise of divine institution. "It is to be understood everywhere in the general sense of *ordinatio*, or as *mandatum Dei*, not in the technical sense of a legal statute." Cf. Kahl, *Rechtsinhalt des Konkordienbuches*, p. 44. In this sense *jus divinum* is the norm of all enactments of human law and is unalterable.

indolence and betrayal. But the church which lives by faith in the Gospel as the fellowship of liberated saints receives from this doctrine of the Confessions an unheard-of possibility and impetus for its devotion to the preaching of the Gospel and is permitted the most extensive missionary activity. Since even the New Testament statements concerning ecclesiastical order and its offices are not imposed as a law but are received in the liberty of faith, the church is commanded to shout the Gospel into the world in ever-new advances, in ever-new forms and arrangements of the one spiritual office. If the bishops no longer ordain according to the Gospel, the pastors must do it. If the pastors no longer do it, the laymen must do it in this hour of need, so that the Gospel may never be silenced. If the church is attacked in those ordinances having only *jure humano* validity, then, in the very freedom in which the church fashions its ordinances, it will become invincible for the world and the world's will to extirpate the church. The ministry cannot cease as long as two believers are gathered together.[24]

[24] This is not contradicted when we designate as a lawful provision the current church order, and as canon law the essence of the directives by which the church regulates its service in obedience to its commission. This designation corresponds to the frequent use of the terms *"jus divinum"* and *"jus humanum"* in the Confessions in connection with church order. Besides, this designation is in principle suggested by the far-reaching thought parallelism employed in the material concerning the civil and the ministerial "office," both of which are called "authority," "power," "order," etc. However, just as the civil and the ecclesiastical office are distinguished, so also civil and canon law must be distinguished. The problem of the existence of canon law arises only when canon law and civil law are not carefully differentiated. This distinction concerns both the basis and the structure of both orders. In distinction from civil law the entire ecclesiastical administration must be determined by the command to preach the Gospel and administer the sacraments. Church government is derived from the divine institution of the ministry in the midst of the congregation for service to all the world. All administrative directives must promote this service. Contrary to civil government, the power of the church is the power of the keys, and obedience within the sphere of church government means the proclamation and acceptance of the Gospel and the giving and receiving of the sacraments. The obedience to church authority as such is the expression of the liberation bestowed by the Gospel. The difference between civil and ecclesiastical authority is most strongly expressed in that, according to the Lutheran distinctions of both authorities, church authority does not depend on its being recognized by the civil power. As a divine institution the office of the ministry is *jure divino*, and in its structure established *jure humano* it is independent of both the recognition and the opposition of the civil government. Yet, in spite of all differences, not only the secular but also the ecclesiastical order is an external, visible arrangement in this world, because the Gospel is the *oral* Word, the sacraments are *external* signs, the congregation is a *local* assembly of the baptized, and the ministry is the *public* service of *specific* men who were called *rite*. "The church of God is . . . independent of every law," *Kirchenrecht*, I, 5337; "The power of the ministerial or teaching office to govern the church is not a legal power," *ibid.*, p. 239; "an episcopal government of the church with legal power is contrary to Christianity," *ibid.*, p. 539; church order "is never a matter of 'church' law, but is always only

Hence it is true of both ecclesiastical and civil authority that they have been instituted by God. But only their institution, commission, and authority, and not their concrete form, is asserted by the Confessions. In neither case does this imply that the form of the two offices is left to human arbitrariness. Rather, the form of both ecclesiastical and civil office must be determined by the commission given them by God. In both cases the form of the office must serve the divine commission.

7. God demands of every man obedience to both authorities.

The obedience to the civil power which the Confessions demand is, by the very nature of the Confession, not the obedience of pagans but of Christians. It is, therefore, obedience to the triune God who has instituted civil power and has revealed himself in the redemptive work of Jesus Christ; it is the obedience arising from faith in the Gospel. "For without faith and without Christ human nature and human strength are much too weak to do good works, . . . diligently [to] engage in callings which are commanded, render obedience, avoid evil lusts, etc. Such great and genuine works cannot be done without the help of Christ, as he himself says in John 15:5, 'Apart from me you can do nothing'" (A.C. XX, 37 ff.). Hence proper obedience to the government is not the external obedience of works, but the free obedience of the renewed heart. For

civil and *secular* law," *ibid.,* II, 143: these theses of Sohm, on the one hand, follow quite logically from his explicitly secular "legal concept of law" (singularly unresolved in Vol. I, but clearly stated in II, 48 ff.). This concept generally dominates his expositions concerning civil and church law. His definitions concerning the "autonomous fellowship" as source of law, and concerning the significance of duress in the legal order of the fellowship do, in fact, make the application of this concept of law—but of *this one* only—to the church order impossible. However, even within the doctrine of civil government it is improper to speak of the autonomous association as a source of law. Furthermore, Sohm's theses are the inevitable result of his tearing "visible" and "invisible Word," and visible and invisible church apart. If the Spirit of God is no longer imparted only through the external Word, and if the invisible church is no longer recognizable as being present only in the visible church, then all legal order of the church is necessarily only the legal order of the civil government. In consequence of misreading the distinction of law and Gospel in the external Word there is also a peculiar legalism in the polemics against legalism, namely the peculiarly legalistic pathos of insisting on the wholly unregulated free operation of the Spirit. "Catholicism teaches that Christ gave His church a legal equipment, established and unalterable in its main features. Sohm teaches that from the beginning Christ gave His church an alterable organization of such a nature that it, in principle and for all time, excluded every connection with the law. The one is as wrong as the other. Protestantism teaches that Christ has neither granted, nor withdrawn, legal orders." W. Kahl, *Lehrsystem des Kirchenrechts und der Kirchenpolitik* (Freiburg-Leipzig, 1894), I, 74.

"the *Gospel* commands" us to obey the government, and this "not only from fear of punishment" but also "for the sake of conscience" (Ap. XVI, 5; cf. 3), "for God's sake" (L.C. I, 327). Like all obedience to God's law, so also obedience to the government is an act of love; the Gospel "commands us . . . in this obedience to practice love" (Ap. XVI, 3; cf. A.C. XVI, 5). Like every obedience to God, so also obedience to the government is prayerful obedience. For government is not honored as a divine ordinance without intercession to God, the Creator of this government, "to endow the emperor, kings, and all estates of men, and especially our princes, counselors, magistrates, and officials, with wisdom, strength, and prosperity to govern well and to be victorious over the Turks and all our enemies; to grant their subjects and the people at large to live together in obedience, peace, and concord. On the other hand, to protect us from all kinds of harm to our body and our livelihood, from tempest, hail, fire, and flood; from poison, pestilence, and cattle-plague; from war and bloodshed, famine, savage beasts, wicked men, etc." (L.C. III, 77 f.). Prayer for civil government is included in the command to pray for daily bread, and in this petition "the greatest need of all is to pray for our civil authorities and the government, for chiefly through them does God provide us our daily bread and all the comforts of this life" (L.C. III, 74).

By the prayerful obedience of faith in the Gospel "Christians are obliged to be subject to civil authority and obey its commands and laws in *all* that can be done without sin" (A.C. XVI, 6 f.). This is to be done whether Christians or heathen, believers, or hypocrites are in charge of the civil offices, no matter in what form the civil government rules over its subjects. This obedience is to be the concrete obedience to concrete requirements of the government. For the Gospel "commands us to obey the existing laws" (Ap. XVI, 3). Nor is this obedience restricted to specific directives and laws of the government; rather, in the expressly acknowledged swearing of oaths and paying of homage to the hereditary sovereign there is included also obedient loyalty to the bearer of the civil authority (S.D. XII, 20).

Obedience to the divine ordinance of civil governments is required not only of subjects but also of rulers. For what is said about activity in the civil government is not restricted to granting the Christian *permission* to participate—'Christians are permitted to hold civil office' (A.C. XVI, 2)—and to condemning the claim "that no Christian *can* hold an office in the government with an inviolate conscience" (S.D. XII, 18). Rather, a Christian in governmental activity is *obligated* to act legitimately, 'to decide matters by the imperial and other existing laws, to award just punishments, to engage in just wars' (A.C. XVI, 2). The ruler is no more lord over the divine ordinance and over the legitimacy of civil power than the subject. Man in civil government must rather obey the divine ordinance by commanding, judging, and killing within the sphere of this ordinance. Every ruler, therefore, owes obedience to the triune God and to that end is to be reminded by the church: ". . . do not imagine that the parental office (in this case, the civil office) is a matter of your pleasure and whim. It is a strict commandment and injunction of God, who holds you accountable for it" (L.C. I, 169).

Obedience to the ecclesiastical authority is above all faith in the Gospel. Though the spiritual office preaches law and Gospel and thereby demands obedience also to the law, this obedience is realized only as a fruit of faith which cannot, of course, remain dead. The obedience of faith is commanded, no matter whether believers or hypocrites preach the Gospel and administer the sacraments. This obedience is commanded, no matter in what form the church authority confronts man, whether through admonition by the brethren, the pastors, or the bishops. The latter is expressly stated: ". . . parish ministers and churches are bound to be obedient to the bishops, according to the saying of Christ in Luke 10:16, 'He who hears you hears me' " (A.C. XXVIII, 22). Yes, they are 'bound by divine law (*necessario et jure divino*) to be obedient.' Disobedience to the bishop is disobedience to God. Over against this it cannot be urged that the institution of a superior church government and the delimitation of its authority is by human right, that is, the outgrowth of the free arrangement of the church. For obedience to the church administration is taken out of the area of the free interests of individuals or those of the congregations, because the preaching by the bishop and the ordinations and excommunications which he performs are done not by human but by divine right in the office of the Word. Moreover, we should not only obey the preaching but also the regulations which the church has adopted in the unity of faith and love for the preservation of preaching. No Christian exists by himself, but he is a member of the congregation. "It is proper for the Christian assembly to keep such ordinances for the sake of love and peace, to be obedient to the bishops and parish ministers in such matters and to observe the regulations in such a way that one does not give offense to another and so that there may be no disorder or unbecoming conduct in the church. However, consciences should not be burdened by contending that such things are necessary for salvation . . ." (A.C. XXVIII, 55 f.; cf. XV, 1). Also disobedience to an ordinance of the church instituted by human right is disobedience to God since it violates the law of love.

Obedience to the ordinance of the ecclesiastical power is required not only of the hearers of the Word but of the preachers themselves, and again, not only of pastors but also of bishops. Bishops are forbidden "to exercise lordship as if they had power to coerce the churches" (A.C. XXVIII, 76). "A bishop does not have the power of a tyrant . . ., nor that of a king. . . . But he has a definite command, a definite Word of God, which he ought to teach and according to which he ought to exercise his jurisdiction. Therefore it does not follow that since they have a certain jurisdiction bishops may institute new acts of worship." 'For the Gospel does not authorize them to exercise authority apart from the Gospel' (Ap. XXVIII, 14).

A special obligation toward the church's authority results for the Christian in civil government. The emperor has the special obligation before God "to maintain and propagate sound doctrine and to defend those who teach it. God demands this when he honors kings with his own name and calls them gods (Ps. 82:6): 'I say, "You are gods." ' They should take care to maintain and propagate divine things on earth, that is, the Gospel of Christ, and as vicars of God they should defend the life and safety of the innocent" (Ap. XXI, 44). As "chief members of the church, the kings and the princes," should "have regard for the interests of the church and to see to it that errors are removed and consciences are healed" (Tr. 54). They should also help the church against the pope and see to it "that the church is not deprived of the power of making judgments and decisions according to the Word of God" (namely, in the decisions of their synod, Tr. 56). These demands do not apply to civil government as such but to the Christian in civil government. These demands addressed to the Christian in civil government presuppose the church's authority as a special authority and do not imply that the civil government assumes control over the church.[25] It is rather

---

[25] It is impossible to deduce from these statements that according to the teaching of the Confessions the territorial prince may assume control of the church. On the contrary, these and similar expressions must be seen from the following three viewpoints:

a) Every civil government as such must be concerned with preventing in its domain disturbance and rebellion due to religious controversies. It is the duty of the chief members of the church (*praecipua membra ecclesiae*) to provide for the preservation and protection of the spiritual authority. They must not interfere with the pure doctrine of the church but acknowledge it, provide free course for it, and remove hindrances.[26] They must not proclaim the Gospel themselves, but by faith in the Gospel they must do all they can so that the ministry may reach all subjects with the glad tidings. For no Christian, including a Christian in public office, may in any action overlook the fact that as a member of the kingdom of Christ he owes his neighbor, be he subject or lord, the witness to this royal rule of Christ.

To sum up: Every Christian must obey the government, and through the ministry every subject is called to the obedience of faith. The Christian in the spiritual office too is obligated to obey the civil power. Conversely, the lords—emperors, kings, magistrates, judges, etc.—are obliged to render the obedience of faith to the spiritual power, i.e., the Gospel, lest they be lost. For the person

obligated to provide for peace and external justice. In times of danger to the civil order from religious differences the principle of *"cujus regio ejus religio"* and the exile of dissenters may result. In this sense the *custodia utriusque tabulae* [the protection of both tables of the law] belongs to the duty of the civil government itself, regardless of whether a Christian or non-Christian is active in this government.

b) In times of ecclesiastical *emergency* the Christian in government is obligated to lend his arm to the church for the restoration of its order. Such an emergency exists when the church government collapses. In that case the congregation itself must fill the pastoral office through call and ordination. Within the sphere of this duty the Christians in civil government with their "outstanding" facilities for creating order must support, and even substitute for, the other Christians in restoring order in the church in case of emergency. Especially must they make provision in an "outstanding" manner for filling the church's supervisory offices. Thus in time of distress the Christian in civil government stands at the head of the congregation to perform a task for which the whole congregation is responsible. In this sense the emergency aid of the territorial prince aims at restoring an ordered ecclesiastical control, not at consolidating the prince's rule over the church.

c) Although such an emergency was the historical presupposition of the Confessions, their remarks concerning the duties of a Christian ruler are not limited to extraordinary times of crisis but are, in part, of general import. The Christian in civil government is obligated *at all times* to make and to preserve a place for the Gospel in his domain and, hence, also for a separate ecclesiastical office.

[26] This remains the framework also for the subscriptions of the princes and counselors to the Augsburg Confession (A.C. I, 1; Con. 6). By means of their signatures they accept as their own the doctrine of the church (*"ecclesiae magno consensu apud nos docent . . ."*) as also the doctrine of the ministry (*"confessio . . . eorum, qui apud nos docent"*); and they represent this doctrine as their own Creed before the superior government of the emperor (*"confessio nostra"*). The signatures as such do not imply that in the Augsburg Confession the princes are acting as territorial and municipal rulers over the church, or that they are giving account of their administration of the church.

who in legitimate civil government provides for external peace and external righteousness is not for this reason righteous before God. The model *pater patriae* of the heathen is a sinner before God, as are the criminals whom by divine authority he punishes with the sword. Neither the non-Christian nor the Christian, neither the lord nor the subject is righteous before God because of the goodness of his political acts, but he is righteous only for Christ's sake by grace through faith. Conversely, however, the faith of a man who does not obey civil government is doubtful. For how can faith continue without obedience to God's commandments?

Thus the problem of the concrete co-ordination of the two powers arises. Both extend over *all* men. The spiritual office is to preach repentance and grace to *all* men, and civil government is to protect *all* people within its borders against external injustice. God does not permit individuals to be excused from the requirement of obedience to either of the two authorities—neither the lords from the claim of the ministry, nor Christians from the claim of the government. There is, then, no person in office, no area in this world in which the claims of both realms do not overlap. This overlapping cannot be removed by granting power over life and property to civil government and the right over souls to the spiritual office. This is not what the Confessions have in mind when they distinguish between body and soul in their doctrine of the two offices. For the ecclesiastical office through the preaching of the Ten Commandments requires also the obedience of the body, and the Christian's obedience to the government is not only the obedience of the body but rather obedience in love and for conscience's sake. This overlapping must be kept plainly in view. Even the apparent exception of the pagan state is in the shadow of the Lord's command, "Go into *all* the world and preach the Gospel to *all* nations" (Mark 16).

8. The ecclesiastical and civil offices must not be intermingled, but differentiated.[27]

Because of God's ordinance church and civil power are to be revered as the two chief blessings of God on earth. However, they

---

[27] If in the following the subject is not the relationship of church and "state," but of church and civil government, or the ministerial and the secular office, the purpose is to uphold the difference between the Lutheran concept of government and the more recent concepts of the "state." The Lutheran Confessions are dealing with government as the divinely ordained office of civil authority, which is also the meaning of *"politia,"* whereas the modern concept of the "state" embraces the entire ordered community of government and subjects,

are honored as such only in the recognition of their difference (A.C. XXVIII, 4 and 18). ". . . the Gospel does not teach an outward and temporal but an inward and eternal mode of existence and righteousness of the heart. The Gospel does not overthrow civil authority . . ." (A.C. XVI, 4); "temporal authority is concerned with matters altogether different from the Gospel. Temporal power does not protect the soul, but with the sword and physical penalties it protects body and goods from the power of others. Therefore, the two authorities, the spiritual and the temporal, are not to be mingled or confused" (A.C. XXVIII, 11 f.).

God commands every man to make this distinction and to make it ever anon. The prohibition against mingling the two offices applies not only to the *doctrine* of civil government and public ministry but also to the *activity* in and under both offices. The concern is that neither "invade the function of the other" (A.C. XXVIII, 13), either in ruling over it or in rendering it obedience.

This distinction, however, also implies a bracketing of the two offices, that is, a distinction in obedience to the one commanding God. Spiritual power does not "interfere with" and does not "subvert" civil power, but commands subjection and proclaims the divine dignity of civil power in God's Word. Civil power, on the other hand, grants the church the freedom of proclamation; indeed, the Christian in civil government protects the spiritual power and even makes provision for the maintenance of preaching. This bracketing of both offices in their distinction involves neither theocracy nor a state church, as little as the distinction of the offices bracketed in God releases from obedience to both offices. The unity of God, the giver of both powers, is dissolved as little by this distinction as by the distinction of the three articles of the Creed.

Both offices are actually mingled when the spiritual power pre-

---

as a rule in the bracketing of state and nation. This point of view is almost totally absent in the Confessions and they do not contain the modern idea that "the state is the Nation [*Volksstaat*] and, as such, more than the constituted government. The state is not only the instrument of God to suppress the evil but it is also in the service of God's creative will, who uses the state to make of a people what it can and ought to be." P. Althaus, *Kirche und Staat nach lutherischer Lehre*, p. 747. Within the scope of this book we cannot answer, but can only keep alive the question whether such and similar views may stand as a legitimate supplement to the Lutheran doctrine concerning the civil authority. An examination of this question is bound to miss the mark if the Lutheran concept of civil government is restricted to ecclesiastical recognition of contemporary governmental forms. We must rather take terms like "office," "authority," "estate," "order" as theological terms in the strict sense, terms which are valid independently of the concrete form of the civil authority.

sumes to exercise functions of the civil power, either negatively or positively, either destructively or constructively. It "should not set up and depose kings, should not annul temporal laws or undermine obedience to government, should not make or prescribe to the temporal power laws concerning worldly matters. Christ himself said, 'My kingship is not of this world,' and again, 'Who made me a judge or divider over you?'" (A.C. XXVIII, 13 f.; cf. Tr. 32). The fact must be maintained that the sword of the spiritual power is the Word and its power is God's Spirit (cf. A.C. XXVIII, 15-17; Tr. 31).

Both offices are also mingled when civil power presumes to exercise spiritual power. To be sure, the demand for a distinction of both offices is illustrated primarily in the encroachment of spiritual power upon the domain of civil power—the encroachment of the pope and the bishops—hardly in the encroachment of civil power upon the spiritual domain. In view of this historically conditioned distinction we must be very careful not to confuse principle and illustration. The principle of not mingling the two offices is expressed in general terms and applies with equal obligation to each of the two offices over against the other. Only the elucidation of this principle emphasizes the acute form of the confusion that prevailed at the time. The prohibition not to interfere with the office of the other applies also to the civil government, and it was "a serious neglect of the Lutheran theology of the past that it did not always and everywhere teach distinctly what consequences result from the principles of A.C. XXVIII, e.g., that according to the sense civil government must be admonished: Let it not abrogate the laws of the church; let it not abolish lawful obedience . . . let it not prescribe laws to the bishops concerning the form of the church" (H. Sasse, *Kirchenregiment und weltliche Obrigkeit*, p. 14). Civil government has no right to exercise spiritual power, to preach and to administer the sacraments, to forgive and retain sins, to examine or even reject doctrine, to ordain and install into the ministry, to fix church ordinances either by establishing or by abolishing them. Civil power can only punish sins but not remove them. Therefore it invades another's office when it installs or deposes church authorities—be it in the form of the pastorate or of the superior church administration—when it exercises spiritual power or determines its exercise. Even the concrete regulation of the spiritual office, which has only *jure humano* validity, is not left to civil government as such, since the regulation of the spiritual office is to serve the Gospel and its implementation presupposes faith in the Gospel and a legitimate call by the church.

Every time the two offices are mingled, no matter which office takes the first step, both offices are distorted and are placed more or less in contradiction to their divine institution. Such mingling and distorting produces tyranny. God "does not want to have knaves or tyrants in this office and responsibility" (L.C. I, 168 f.), and this is true even though God in the transcendent freedom of his preservation "sometimes permits much good to come to a people through a tyrant or scoundrel" (S.A. II, iv, 3). The very essence of tyranny is the mingling of the two powers. This important concept of the Lutheran Confessions is determined in detail by the following factors: Removal of obligation to definite laws in favor of arbitrary action (*"sine certa lege,"* Ap. XXVIII, 14) and the use of civil force for the suppression of the Gospel and the spread of heresies. Mingling the two powers must necessarily lead to heresy and lawlessness, since according to God's ordinance the spiritual office justifies by faith even the evildoer whom the civil government punishes, and addresses as a sinner the "righteous man" whom the civil power praises and rewards. If the civil office were to forgive the evildoer and the ministry were to declare the "righteous man" of the civil order a saint, arbitrariness and heresy would be inevitable. As a rule it would result that tyrants would strive "to receive homage" (L.C. I, 168). Whenever the Gospel is abrogated the Lord God is denied.

Here the question arises whether in practice the mingling of the two offices does not begin with the statements about the duties of the Christian in a civil office. Does not the obligation of kings to make provision for the spreading of the Gospel by the ministry involve a decision on the part of the kings as to what the pure Gospel is? Must not the same question be asked when Luther obligates the prince to "banish such rude people from his land" as are unwilling to learn the Catechism? (S.C. Pref., 12). Is not the acknowledgment of a definite Catechism for a country a spiritual decision in which the prince "judges doctrine"?

An essentially similar question arises from the fact that the Confessions, in spite of the principle of not mingling the two powers, do not definitely insist that the Roman bishops give up the civil office they hold. In essence they do not go beyond this statement: "In cases where bishops possess temporal authority and the sword, they possess it not as bishops by divine right, but by human, imperial right, bestowed by Roman emperors and kings for the temporal administration of their lands. Such authority has nothing at all to do with the office of the Gospel" (A.C. XXVIII, 19). Both offices are distinguished here but their personal union is not excluded. The decisive objection against the Roman bishops is not the fact but the abuse of their civil power. Above all, the complaint is made that 'they have no concern for manning the most necessary and beneficial office in the church. They care nothing for what is taught or preached, or how the Christian celebration of the sacraments is to be preserved. But they ordain crude asses, and so Christian doctrine perished because the churches were not provided with competent preachers' (Ap. XXVIII, 3). But is not also a personal union a mingling of the two authorities?

From these statements and questions it becomes clear that just as the Confessions have no obligatory teaching on the specific form of the civil and ecclesiastical powers, so they assert no definite form of their distinction, nor a definite constitution of state and church in which the relationship between the two is confessionally fixed.[28] According to the Confessions no constitution can permanently safeguard the distinction of the two powers. Just as the form of both powers must be determined and redetermined in the concrete act of obedience to .God's institution, so the actual dialogue between both will lead in each case to the concrete, constitutionally fixed form of the relationship of both, as they constantly strive to obey God's double commission. This form too is a matter of human right. Until the Last Day there is no definitive state of nonmingling but only a way of knowing about the two ordinances of God and about the obedience which the believer owes both—except in their tyrannical caricature—as divine ordinances.

9. The limit of obedience to each of the two offices is God's commandment.

The fact that obedience to the two powers is a limited obedience results from the very concept of "ordinatio Dei." Since God demands obedience through both powers, neither may be obeyed contrary to God's commandment, that is, contrary to the divine institution and authorization of the respective power.

Of civil power it is stated: "Accordingly Christians are obliged

---

[28] Thus the distinction between the two powers does not necessarily mean also separation of church and state.

to be subject to civil authority and obey its commands and laws in all that can be done without sin. But when commands of the civil authority cannot be obeyed without sin, we must obey God rather than men" (A.C. XVI, 6 f. referring to Acts 5:29). When is something not done "without sin"? This may be learned only on the basis of God's Word. Since God's Word as law and Gospel demands our obedience, disobedience to the government is commanded not only if the government were to forbid faith in the Gospel, but also if it were to demand that the Christian sin against the Ten Commandments, e.g., that he commit perjury. It would be contrary to the doctrine of law and Gospel if one were to detach obedience to God's law from faith in the Gospel. 'Except when commanded to sin' applies in the full sense of the term to the doctrine of sin and the new obedience. It must, of course, be remembered that the Confessions are here speaking only of concrete "commands and laws" of the government which cannot possibly be obeyed "without sin." Here the possibility of concrete disobedience is mentioned, not of disobedience in principle. Nothing is said of a possible situation in which a government, because of its laws and commands, may no longer be recognized as an authority ordained by God and must be removed. In view of Luther's statements on this question this silence is probably to be understood as a denial of this possibility. At least the Confessions expressly deny to the ecclesiastical office the right to depose or to establish civil government.

In basically the same manner this is true of the spiritual authority. When the bishops "teach, introduce, or institute anything contrary to the Gospel, we have God's command not to be obedient in such cases . . ." (A.C. XXVIII, 23). Nor must we follow the properly chosen bishops "if they err or if they teach or command something contrary to the divine Holy Scriptures" (A.C. XXVIII, 28). Here too Acts 5:29 is quoted (Ap. XXVIII, 21). Here too the divine commission given to the office constitutes the boundaries of the obedience due the office. Hypocrisy and vice on the part of the incumbent are not yet a reason for disobedience to pastor and church administration, nor is the mere fact that these persons also occupy a civil office. They may be opposed, however, when their doctrine and their directions contradict the Gospel as, e.g., when they require an oath to teach false doctrine as a prerequisite for ordination or installation (A.C. XXVIII, 71). Regulations which in themselves do not contradict the Gospel but are promulgated with a view to bestowing salvation as a reward for their observance can also be a reason for disobedience.

This disobedience is demanded, first, as concrete disobedience to specific anti-Gospel directions given by the spiritual authority. But the disobedience can also go beyond this and become rejection in principle of an ecclesiastical regime and disobedience in principle to all its directives. "We should forsake wicked teachers because they no longer function in the place of Christ, but are antichrists. Christ says [Matt. 7:15], 'Beware of false prophets'; Paul says [Gal. 1:9], 'If anyone is preaching to you a gospel contrary to that which you received, let him be accursed' " (Ap. VII, 48). To the extent that the excommunicated false teacher has adherents the separation from him also amounts in principle to a division in the church. But even the danger of such a schism dare not mislead men to obey an anti-Gospel church administration (cf. A.C. XXVIII, 78). The end of obedience is stated most emphatically over against the pope by the use of the anathema. The pope says "that one must be obedient to him in order to be saved. This we are unwilling to do even if we have to die for it in God's name" (S.A. II, iv, 12). We say to him, according to Zech. 3:2, " 'The Lord rebuke you, O Satan' " (S.A. II, iv, 16). Basically the same complete separation results in certain cases involving pastors and bishops. Together with the separation steps must be taken for the restoration of the proper church authority. "When the bishops are heretics or refuse to administer ordination, the churches are by divine right compelled to ordain pastors and ministers for themselves. And it is the wickedness and tyranny of the bishops that give occasion to schism and discord" (Tr. 72; cf. 66). What is here said of ordination self-evidently applies also to the preaching of the Gospel and the administration of the sacraments. The separation from a heretical church authority or even only the silence or lack of action on the part of a church authority dare never cause the end of preaching and administration of the sacraments. In such cases the congregations must act in place of the bishops and pastors and call the ecclesiastical government and thus provide for the preaching of the Gospel and the administration of the sacraments. This emergency right flows in essence from Christ's endowment of the whole church with the power of the keys.

Under what circumstances may we in practice merely disobey specific anti-Gospel directions by the church authority, and when are complete separation and repudiation of that authority demanded as a matter of principle? The Confessions give no more unambiguous and binding answers to this question than to the question regarding the form of the ministerial office. In Augsburg they still "pray" the bishops as bishops "that they may not coerce our consciences to sin" (A.C. XXVIII, 77), but that they should "relax certain unreasonable burdens" (A.C. XXVIII, 72). They are still expressly recognized as bishops: "Our churches do not ask that the bishops should restore peace and unity at the expense of their honor and dignity" (A.C. XXVIII, 71); it is "not our intention to find ways of reducing the bishops' power" (A.C. XXVIII, 77). This means that false teaching by the church authority need not at once involve separation and a split in the church. The possibility is not excluded of tolerating a church government that teaches falsely, as long as it does not suppress the preaching of the pure Gospel by force but tolerates it. But even if this is not the case, we may deduce from the manner in which the heretical bishops are addressed (A.C. XXVIII, 69-78) and, beyond this, from the whole Augsburg Confession that the church's authority is first to be recalled to the Gospel through petition and admonition before the step of separation is taken. As in dealing with all sinning members of the church, so also in dealing with the teachers of the church, excommunication is to be carried out only when their stubbornness, unteachableness, and impenitence are manifest. Until then the church must refuse obedience only *in concreto* to directives of the church government that are contrary to God's Word. The Confessions do not with casuistic exactness fix the time of separation. This is clear from the Book of Concord in so far as it contains two different judgments from the same year by Luther and by Melanchthon concerning the heretical pope; whereas Luther has declared the separation to be already accomplished, Melanchthon, in his subscription to the Smalcald Articles, thinks he can still acknowledge the pope, "if he would allow the Gospel" (B. of C., p. 316). Just as the church, without being obligated by the Confessions to specific church laws, puts church regulations into effect in the liberty of faith and in obedience to the Gospel, so the church, without casuistic directions in the Confessions but in free decision through obedience to the Gospel must also determine the moment of radical separation and must proclaim an ecclesiastical act of emergency together with the act of separation. Here too the lack of concretion in the Confessions involves a weakening of ecclesiastical action for all who know nothing about the freedom and plenary power of the believers and are therefore concerned only about preserving the minimum fixed by the Confessions. Others, however, recognize in this merely seeming deficiency of the Confessions the obligatory permission to preach the Gospel to everybody in ever-new advances, and again and again to make church order, church offices, and all people in and under these offices serve the Gospel.

Perhaps the strongest testimony to this freedom of churchly action in obedience to the Gospel and in disobedience to wrong ecclesiastical directives is to be found in the F.C. X; "The Ecclesiastical Rites that Are Called Adiaphora, or Things Indifferent." This, of course, refers to rites "which are neither commanded nor forbidden in the Word of God but which have been introduced into the church with good intentions for the sake of good order and decorum or else to preserve Christian discipline" (S.D. X, 1). Since the church has instituted these rites, "the community of God in every place and at every time has the right, authority, and power to change, to reduce, or to increase ceremonies according to its circumstances, as long as it does so without frivolity and offense but in an orderly and appropriate way, as at any time may seem to be most profitable, beneficial, and salutary for good order, Christian discipline, evangelical decorum, and the edification of the church" (S.D. X, 9). Expressly condemned is the opinion "that the community of God does not have the liberty to use one or more ceremonies at any time and place, according to its circumstances, as may in Christian liberty be most beneficial to the church" (S.D. X, 30). But the words "at any time" have one exception: The "time of confession, as when enemies of the Word of God desire to suppress the pure doctrine of the holy Gospel" (S.D. X, 10). At this moment the liberty of the church proves to be a bound liberty and it is asserted that in time of persecution, when a clear-cut confession of faith is demanded of us, "we dare not yield to the enemies in such indifferent things." For "in such a case it is no longer a question of indifferent things, but a matter which has to do with the truth of the Gospel, Christian liberty, and the sanctioning of public idolatry" (Ep. X, 6). Thus when "enemies" try to compel church decisions, the church must not submit even if it were permitted the church to arrive at the same decisions in the freedom of its own action.[29] The whole church of Christ, every Christian, especially the ministers of the Word, are obligated to "confess

---

[29] "The church knows no absolute adiaphora, just as it knows no absolute forms." Th. Harnack, *Die Kirche, ihr Amt, ihr Regiment*, p. 67.

openly, not only by words but also through their deeds and actions," the Gospel (S.D. X, 10) and also "to suffer" on that account (Ep. X, 6). By refusing to submit to coercion the church confesses the Gospel, and by refraining from the exercise of its freedom in matters of church ordinances under compulsion of the "enemies" the church confesses the freedom given to it. The command not to "yield to the enemies in such indifferent things"—even though they are indifferent things and as such are left to the freedom of ecclesiastical decision—is based on the apostolic admonition, "For liberty Christ has made us free; stand fast, therefore, and do not submit again to a yoke of slavery" (Gal. 5:1; Ep. X, 6; cf. S.D. X, 15). Because the church has been liberated by the Gospel it is bound by the Gospel to make no other use of its freedom than the proclamation of the Gospel. Every other exercise of this liberty weakens the believers, offends the weak, and confirms the idolators in their idolatry (S.D. X, 16). In freedom and because of freedom the church itself determines the front line of its resistance to tyrannical ecclesiastical or civil power and thus advances the campaign of the Gospel toward the world by testifying to the liberating power of the Gospel through disobedience and suffering.

10. In the mingling of civil authority and ecclesiastical authority the tyranny of Satan's kingdom invades both of them.

The essence of tyrannical power is the mingling of spiritual and civil authority. Therefore tyranny can arise from both. Through tyranny the civil office develops into a pseudo-spiritual office and the spiritual into a pseudo-civil office.

The Confessions direct their attention chiefly to the tyranny that arises out of the spiritual authority. It is tyranny when bishops compel priests by the power of the sword to discard and condemn their confession (Ap. XIV, 2). Above all, the papal power with its claim of total obedience backed by total force is tyranny. For the pope "roars like a lion," asserting "that no Christian can be saved unless he is obedient to the pope and submits to him in all that he desires, says, and does" (S.A. II, iv, 4) and "will not permit Christians to be saved except by his own power" (S.A. II, iv, 10). This power is to be "lord of the whole world, of all the kingdoms of the world, and of all public and private affairs. He must have plenary power in both the temporal and the spiritual realm, both swords, the temporal and the spiritual. 'Therefore the pope is a god on earth, a supreme majesty, and the most mighty lord alone in all the world.' The pope falsely derives this claim to power from the fact that the Father has subjected all things to Jesus Christ" (Ap. VII, 23).

In a basically like manner tyranny can also arise out of the civil authority when men in office try to impose on their subjects and on the whole world self-made doctrines about salvation and eternity, and do this with the claim of unlimited obedience and by force. Not the origin of tyranny, however, but its essence, the mingling of both powers, is the decisive factor. For since the mingling is at the same time a caricaturing of both powers, every tyranny, no matter whence it arose, is always also an estrangement from both of these divinely instituted offices. In contrast to them, tyranny is something essentially different, even though in it some traces of the divine ordinance are recognized.

Tyranny is something different from the ministerial and the civil office, and not simply in the sense of its being a caricature made by human words and deeds. With the same precision with which God's activity through both offices is confessed again and again, tyranny is unmasked as the work of the devil. It is "most diabolical for the pope to promote his lies . . . in contradiction to God, and to damn, slay, and plague all Christians who do not exalt and honor those abominations of his above all things" (S.A. II, iv, 14; cf. 3). Luther says this of the pope's dominion, but the same applies to every tyranny, as many statements of the Confessions show. Through tyranny the kingdom of the devil always invades both the civil and the spiritual domain with falsehood and force at the same time, in order to coerce the believers back under the devil's dominion and captivity and, beyond this, to hold all men under this devilish enslavement. Since God by the Gospel tears sinners out of the jaws of the devil, the devil constantly attacks the ministry in ever-new ways. Since God through civil government keeps the sinners alive so that the Gospel may be preached to them, the devil "would like to snatch the crown from the rulers" (L.C. IV, 62). As a liar and a murderer the devil fights in the same manner against Baptism and government, against the gift of eternal life and the preservation of earthly life, against God the Redeemer and Creator. Tyranny on earth is always a transcendent reality. For tyranny is the essence of the devil's kingdom, as liberation through the Gospel is the essence of Christ's kingdom.

VIII

THE LAST DAY

When we inquire about the eschatology of the Confessions we make the strange discovery that only one article has an expressly eschatological theme, namely, Article XVII of the Augsburg Confession and the Apology. In addition there are scattered references in other articles, above all the eschatological statements of the ancient Creeds. But even where these Creeds are explained in the Book of Concord and where one might definitely expect eschatological statements, it is notable that they are either missing altogether (as in the explanation of the second article in the Small Catechism) or are touched on only briefly (as in the explanation of the third article in the Large Catechism). Just as in view of the few doctrinal statements about creation the opinion arose that the Confessions have no sufficiently "positive position" on creation and therefore must not only be unfolded in this respect but also corrected and supplemented, so in view of the few eschatological statements the opinion has arisen that the Confessions because of a peculiar attachment to this world have remained uneschatological, or are preoccupied with a purely individual eschatology. But just as the theology which in an essential manner goes beyond the few statements of the Confessions about the Creator and the creatures must indeed be questioned seriously as to whether it has really grasped what *doctrina evangelii* means, so the same question must be directed to those who miss an eschatology of the Confessions. For they contain so few specific eschatological paragraphs because their whole doctrine in all articles is replete with eschatological expectation.

This we propose to show in the following section by going through the previous chapters of this book once more and showing the eschatological expectation in the dialectic of their statements. Besides, in advance of all individual statements, the Confessions' concept of confession is itself consciously directed to the *Eschaton*.

270

1. The church's Confession is eschatological testimony.

In the last sentences of the Book of Concord the signers confess that "in the *presence of God* and of all Christendom among both our contemporaries and our posterity, we wish to have testified that the present explanation of all the foregoing controverted articles here explained, and none other, is our teaching, belief, and confession in which by God's grace we shall appear with intrepid hearts before the judgment seat of Jesus Christ and for which we shall give an account" (S.D. XII, 40). This applies particularly to the Augsburg Confession (B. of C. Pref., p. 9), but also to the other Confessions.[1] "In these last times of this transitory world" the church here makes its confession in the expectation of the imminent return of its Lord. With its confession the church comes before his judgment seat. For as judge of the works of all men he is also the judge of all dogmatic work. But the church approaches this tribunal with "joyful and fearless hearts and consciences" (*ibid.*). For God himself has heralded the Gospel to the church which confesses the Gospel in its Creed, and this Gospel is already the decree of pardon in God's judgment for all time and eternity. Because the Gospel preached today is the *definitive* forgiveness of sins the Confession extends beyond the ages to the Last Day and is valid not only for a moment but for our whole life, and not only for those living now but also for those who shall come later. By confessing the Gospel the church is the weapon of Christ in the climactic battle against the devil's kingdom, and in joyful expectation goes forward to the revelation of Christ's kingdom, to the Last Day.

This expectation has a determining effect on all individual articles of doctrine.

2. The Last Day is expected and attested in the distinction between creatureliness and corruption.

Every man is altogether God's creature and every man is corrupted by sin in his entire nature. Since the fall the whole man is creature and sinner at the same time. His creatureliness and his corruption conceal each other in their totality from empirical observation. Nothing can be shown in man that is creation without sinful corruption. However, though we cannot separate creation and sin and can recognize neither creation nor sin empirically but only

[1] Cf. pp. 22 f.

by faith through God's Word, yet both are to be radically distinguished like God the Creator, and the devil, the seducer. In this act of distinguishing and yet refusing to separate the two, the Last Day is attested.[2] For by his distinction of creatureliness and corruption man acknowledges "that no one except God alone can separate the corruption of our nature from nature itself. This will take place wholly by way of death through the resurrection. Then the nature which we now bear will arise and live forever without original sin and completely removed . . . from it . . ." (Ep. I, 10).

3. The Last Day is expected and attested in the distinction between law and Gospel.

In the doctrine of law and Gospel too distinction and separation dare not be confused.[3] The distinction of law and Gospel by means of glorifying the Gospel is the daily and most important task of all theology in this world of sin and death. But we are forbidden to separate and tear apart law and Gospel, to preach only law to some men and only Gospel to others. In this world Christians and heathen always stand under law and Gospel at the same time; *everybody* must repent under the law and may receive forgiveness of sins by faith in the Gospel. By teaching the distinction between law and Gospel, but forbidding the separation, the Confessions acknowledge the Last Day in which Jesus Christ will separate men. Then he will condemn some on account of their sins without pardoning them, and will save others in spite of their sins without condemning them. Then he will speak the condemning word of the law to some without the proclamation of forgiveness, and by grace acquit others without the word that condemns. Then no further call to repentance will sound forth, and the separation of law and Gospel will be Christ's deed on the Last Day.

The distinction between law and Gospel is made in the Confessions by the use of the formula "law and Gospel," even though the *doctrina evangelii* must be unfolded both as proceeding from the law (Chap. 3), and as proceeding from the Gospel (Chap. 4). This preferred order, "law and Gospel,"[4] is based, first of all, on the succession of the Old and New Testaments. The time of the law

[2] Cf. pp. 44 ff.
[3] Cf. pp. 129 ff.
[4] For a critique of this order see K. Barth, *Evangelium und Gesetz* (Muenchen, 1935). It is indeed to be noted that the relationship between law and Gospel in the Confessions is so manifold and their distinction is

was followed by the time of the Gospel in Jesus Christ. But after what had to be said about the Gospel in the Old Testament and the law in the New Testament, this succession is not sufficient. We must add that the order "law and Gospel" corresponds to the direction in which the believer, commanded and questioned by the law, daily hastens to the gift of the Gospel. The act of faith in the word of forgiveness always occurs in the knowledge of the law and away from the law 'But the Gospel faces us about and directs us away from the law to the divine promises' (Ap. IV, 159). This act in which the sinner condemned by the law grasps the Gospel is an eschatologically oriented act; it is the course from time into eternity. For the gift of the Gospel is eternal life. The law remains over the regenerate only until the Last Day. But the gift of the Gospel extends into the new world of the resurrection. In the order, "law and Gospel," the believer extols the victory of the Gospel.

In the Confessions, following immediately from the distinction of law and Gospel, we find the statements about the Christian being righteous and sinner completely justified and still only partially obedient, reborn and still only partially reborn, living forever and still dying daily, freed from the devil and still daily assailed. Like the distinction between law and Gospel, this dialectic too is full of yearning expectation of the Last Day. Also the singularly quantitative assertions are understood correctly only as the expression of this waiting. Since "holiness has *begun* and is growing daily, we await the time when our flesh will be put to death, will be buried with all its uncleanness, and will come forth gloriously and arise to *complete and perfect* holiness in a new, eternal life. Now we are *only halfway* pure and holy. The Holy Spirit must continue to work in us through the Word, daily granting us forgiveness until we attain to that life where there will be no more forgiveness. In that life are only *perfectly* pure and holy people, full of goodness and righteousness, completely free from sin, death, and all evil, living in new, immortal, and glorified bodies" (L.C. II, 57 f.). Then that which can now be expressed only as contrary to fact will be a reality: "If believers and the elect children of God were perfectly renewed in this life through the indwelling Spirit in such a way that in their nature and all its powers they would be totally free from sins, they

dialectically so reciprocal that on this basis it is not possible to establish any kind of exclusive succession, either "Gospel and law" or "law and Gospel." We must see here not so much a dogma of succession as a succession in the usage of dogmatic terminology, that is, a kind of formulted shorthnd for complex relationships.

would require no law, no driver. Of themselves and altogether spontaneously, without any instruction, admonition, exhortation, or driving by the law they would do what they are obligated to do according to the will of God, just as the sun, the moon, and all the stars of heaven regularly run their courses according to the order which God instituted for them once and for all, spontaneously and unhindered, without any admonition, exhortation, compulsion, coercion, or necessity, and as the holy angels render God a completely spontaneous obedience" (S.D. VI, 6). This will be the reality of eternal life for the resurrected. The dialectic of justification and sanctification has its meaning in the abolition of this dialectic on the Last Day.

4. The Last Day is expected and attested in the distinction between the true church and external church fellowship.

The "church, which is truly the kingdom of Christ, is distinguished from the kingdom of the devil" (Ap. VII, 17), and yet members of the devil's kingdom are mingled with the church, yes, they preach and rule in the church. From this twofold fact results the obligation to distinguish between *ecclesia proprie and large dicta,* between the congregation of true believers and participation in the outward signs, between the church as Christ's kingdom and the mixture of living and dead members—members of Christ and members of the devil—collected in the church. Also, this distinction too—which for us is something given—is not to be confused with a separation which has become possible for us to make.[5] Most emphatically rejected are the attempts and opinions according to which the church in this world can and should cleanse itself from all wicked men and hypocrites. By distinguishing between the church in the real and the wider sense, and by refusing to separate them, we again testify to the returning Lord. "He will clear his threshing floor and gather his wheat into the granary, but the chaff he will burn with unquenchable fire" (Matt. 3:12; cf. Ap. VII, 19).

5. The Last Day is expected and attested in the distinction between civil and ecclesiastical power.

The power of civil government is the sword and thus it is the power over physical life and temporal death. The power of the

[5] Cf. pp. 215 f.

spiritual authority is the Word which produces eternal death and eternal life. The function of civil government is the preservation of the fallen creatures in spite of sin and under death and the devil. The function of the spiritual office is the liberation of the sinner from sin, death, and the devil; through the Gospel the sinner becomes a new creature. Thus in the midst of this old world the new creation begins, hidden under the old world, but still real. Both realms are bracketed with each other. The spiritual office proclaims the divine dignity of the civil office, and the incumbents of the civil office cannot really know this dignity without the proclamation of the spiritual office. And yet the two offices must not be mingled but kept precisely distinct, if possible even in the persons of the incumbents.[6] With this differentiation of the two offices on earth room is left for the look to Jesus Christ who in one person is king and priest, Lord and Redeemer.[7] Only on the Last Day will the distinction of the two offices come to an end. Then the gap between temporal and eternal life, temporal and eternal death, God's preservation and new creation will be closed. The returning Christ himself will then do away with the old and will before the whole world manifest his word of grace as creative and his condemnatory word as killing. Then God will no more preserve wicked men on earth and deliver the believers to suffering and death, but eternal life for which they waited by faith will be their bodily reality and they will rule forever with their Lord.

6. In the promise of the Gospel and in the distribution of the sacraments the expected eternal life is a present reality.

The expectation which fills all doctrines of the Confessions would not be an eschatological expectation if it were sure only of the future return, but not of the presence of the returning Christ. This assurance is, of course, not dependent on the contrast of the manifold distinctions already indicated, but it is dependent on the gracious superabundance with which the Gospel, in every distinction, surpasses the law. Because the Gospel by God's incomprehensible grace transcends time and even now gives us eternal life, it serves as the basis for our assurance that God's future kingdom is ours

---

[6] Cf. pp. 259 ff.
[7] It is no accident that the material in A.C. XVII follows immediately on that of XVI. Cf. Schwabach Articles, XIV, ". . . until the Lord returns for the judgment and will dissolve all power and dominion, worldly government and dominion is to be honored and obeyed. . . ." *Bek.,* p. 70.

even now. The Gospel is not only the promise of forgiveness but the sure application of forgiveness, not only the prospect of a future acquittal but the future acquittal itself. The Gospel does not merely promise eternal life but translates us into eternal life. By faith in the Gospel we have the eternal life to which we shall one day rise. In the midst of sin and death the believer is freed from sin and death. The force of the statements in the present tense is especially impressive in the doctrine of the sacraments.[8] Here too they do not involve the dissolution of eschatology, but they are the assurance that eschatology is present. For faith does not rely on the antithesis of law and Gospel but on the Gospel, not on the polarity of civil and spiritual power but on the assurance offered by the spiritual office. Nor does faith cling to the difference between the true church and external church fellowship, but on the basis of Gospel preaching and of the sacraments faith knows that in the external church fellowship the true church, Christ's kingdom on earth, is a reality. For it has pleased Christ in his incomprehensible grace to call this mixture of pious men, wicked men, and hypocrites his church, in spite of all wickedness and hypocrisy.

7. The expectation of the Last Day determines not only specific doctrinal statements but, beyond this, the general concepts and thought patterns in the Confessions.

Let us illustrate this thesis with the concept of the divine will. That concept meets us in more than one sense in the Confessions; yet they confess God's will as *one* will, indeed, as the unchangeable will of God.

a) God wills civil righteousness. "God wants this civil discipline to restrain the unspiritual, and to preserve it he has given laws, learning, teaching, governments, and penalties" (Ap. IV, 22). "God requires this civil righteousness," 'God is opposed to indecent, wild, reckless conduct and life' (Ap. XVIII, 9). Christians know this to be true from God's Word, but God desires also the civil righteousness of the pagans, and produces it through the law inscribed in their hearts. Thus it happens according to God's will that in the area of the civil order good and bad, obedience and disobedience are distinguished, and the evil man is punished while the good man is rewarded. To be sure, the obedience of civil righteousness is rare, since the devil, the enemy of civil power, constantly incites to new

---

[8] Cf. pp. 148 ff., 163 ff., 180 ff.

offenses (Ap. XVIII, 5). However, the reality of good works on the level of civil righteousness, even among the heathen, is not doubted but is constantly presupposed. And yet these works, both bad and good, remain under the spell of sin. Not only does the doer of good works in the domain of civil righteousness remain a sinner without faith, but his works too remain sins. It is not true to say "that a man does not sin if, outside the state of grace, he does the works prescribed in the commandments" (Ap. XVIII, 6). All "the good works a man may be able to do are nothing but hypocrisy and abomination before God" (Ap. II, 34 f.). Since civil righteousness at its best is an external righteousness, it is not righteousness before God. Hence also the reward of civil righteousness is not divine grace, but he who is thus rewarded remains under God's judgment like the one who is thus punished. Nevertheless, civil righteousness is God's "will": All instruction in all good arts and civil authority and honest discipline and external righteousness are the means "whereby God wills to govern and preserve this external life" (cf. preliminary draft of S.D. II; *Bek.,* p. 869). Thus God preserves mankind through civil righteousness in the sphere of death, but by it he does not save a single man from death.

b) God wills obedience to his law as revealed in the Word. "For the law is a mirror in which the will of God and what is pleasing to him is exactly portrayed. It is necessary to hold this constantly before believers' eyes and continually to urge it upon them with diligence" (S.D. VI, 4). The law "is a certain rule and norm for achieving a godly life and behavior in accord with God's eternal and immutable will" (S.D. VI, 3). God's law demands not only civil righteousness but love of God and fear of God; not only external obedience but the obedience of the heart; not only individual good deeds but the whole man. The will of God in the law demands the end of sin. Wherever God has his law preached he is not satisfied with the preservation of man. The law uncovers the sinner's sin who has been preserved by God's patience, unfolds sin, and reveals God's wrath over sin.

c) The sacraments are "signs and testimonies of God's will toward us for the purpose of awakening and strengthening our faith" (A.C. XIII). Here God's will is: forgive, save, make alive. God's will is God's "good and gracious will"; it is done "when God curbs and destroys every evil counsel and purpose . . . which would hinder us from hallowing his name and prevent the coming of his kingdom" (S.C. III, 11). God's will is God's effective grace in the Gospel. "God reveals his will in this way . . . that in those whom he thus calls he will be efficaciously active through the Word so that they may be illuminated, converted, and saved" (S.D. XI, 29). For it is "not God's will that anyone should be damned but that all men should turn themselves to him and be saved forever" (S.D. II, 49; cf. XI, 28, 32; Ep. XI, 10 f.). This is the will of the Father and the Son and the Holy Spirit (S.D. XI, 76 f.). Expressly rejected is the claim "that God does not want everybody to be saved" (Ep. XI, 19; cf. S.D. XI, 75 ff.).

The will of God, then, is attested in several respects. One might almost think it is acknowledged as a multiple, even a contradictory, will. God desires external righteousness, even though it remains sin, *and* he desires the removal of sin. God wants the removal of sin as an act of man *and* removes it himself through the act of his Son. God's will is the preservation of the sinner and it is the law which kills the sinner and the Gospel which justifies the sinner and makes him alive. It is impossible for man to remove the distinction between God's will in his preserving action and God's will in the commandments of his revealed law. This would amount to sanctifying world history and denying the revealed Word of command. Furthermore, it is impossible for man to remove the difference between God's will in the law and God's will in the Gospel. The unity of the divine will is beyond the sphere of rational solution as much as the unity of law and Gospel. Accordingly, God's will is not only revealed but also concealed. It is "contrary to the Confessions not to teach a hidden will" (Frank, *Theol. der Concordienformel,* IV, 183).

Yet it is most emphatically forbidden 'to invent contradictory wills for God,' i.e., to maintain "that God, who is the eternal Truth, contradicts himself" (S.D. XI, 35). God's will is *one* will. God's will is not to be explored by reason—and therefore not from the nature and history round about us—but it is revealed solely in God's Word (S.D. XI, 36). God's will in the Word is not an empty offer, however—such would be the law—but the efficacious action of the Holy Spirit through the Gospel. God's will is revealed and active in the Gospel. "And we should not regard this call of God . . . as a deception" (S.D. XI, 29). We may cling to this call. It is God's revealed will.

This witness to the *one* will of God in the midst of the multiplicity of the manifestations of his will is an eschatological witness. Looking away from the empirical orders of this world to the Word, and again from the Word of damnation to the Word of grace, is faith in the Gospel which creates forgiveness, new life, and new obedience; it is the expectation of the Last Day in which resurrection and acquittal, perfection and new creation will together be a reality. Then the operation of God's grace is no longer distinct from his preserving operation. Then the divine grace now promised us is also the reality of the new creature. God preserves the sinner through civil righteousness in order that God's Word may be preached to him, God places him under the law that it might be his schoolmaster to bring him to Christ, and God has the Gospel preached to the sinner so that he may arise as God's holy new creature on the Last Day.

The designation of the law as God's "immutable" will must be understood in the light of this truth (Ep. VI, 7). The terms "immutable" and "eternal" (e.g., S.D. VI, 3, 15, 17; cf. II, 50; V, 17) only seem to contradict the acknowledgment of Jesus Christ as the end of the law—and of salvation as the only divine will—and the denial of contradictory wills in God. For the same law which is preached to the sinner as a death sentence has been fulfilled by Jesus Christ; it is preached to the believer as fulfilled law, is being fulfilled more and more in the regenerate man, and is completely fulfilled in the resurrection.

8. *The aging world is approaching the Last Day as the devil unleashes his last display of power in the kingdom of Antichrist.*

'We see that these are the last times, and just as an old man is weaker than a young man, so the whole world and nature is in its last stage and is fading' (Ap. XXIII, 53). 'The world is growing old and man's nature is becoming weaker' (A.C. XXIII, 14). These statements can no more be understood biologically than those which call sin sickness and corruption. For they imply that the world is growing "worse" (*ibid.*). 'Sins and vices are not decreasing but increasing daily' (Ap. XXIII, 53). Resistance to vices is waning and offenses against divinely commanded ordinances are becoming monstrous; especially are moral excesses mentioned. Conditions before the Deluge and the vices in Sodom and other cities before their destruction are "an image" of the revolt 'of the last times . . . shortly before the end of the world' (Ap. XXIII, 54). Just as a spiteful old man who sees his end approaching, but will not bear to admit it, summons his last remaining strength and by a last brutal decision and deed shows his family once more that he nas not *yet* died, that he *still* has power, so the aging world once more rouses itself to violent deeds of its own decision, to an inconceivably horrible display of its power and falsehood in a final grandiose revolt again God. This is the kingdom of Antichrist.

"The kingdom of Antichrist is a new kind of worship of God, devised by human authority in opposition to Christ. Thus the kingdom of Mohammed has rites and works by which it seeks to be justified before God, denying that men are freely justified before God by faith for Christ's sake" (Ap. XV, 18). The kingdom of Antichrist accordingly is not atheistic but full of religion and religious rites. It does not avoid the name of God but abuses it. Yes, it does not necessarily avoid even the name of Christ but robs him of his honor (Ap. XV, 18 ff.). For it mingles law and Gospel, it teaches the sinner's justification by works and thereby distorts both the Gospel and God's law. According to Daniel, Chapter 11, the kingdom of Antichrist has religious rites and a religious ethos. All of this, however, is not based on God's authority but is 'new,' 'invented by men,' and it preaches such 'a god of whom the fathers did not know' (Ap. XV, 19). The kingdom of Antichrist in its rites, doctrine, and ethos is the satanic antitype of the adoration, proclamation, and new life in the kingdom of Christ.

The kingdom of Antichrist is further characterized by the mingling of spiritual and civil power.[9] Again Melanchthon points to Daniel, Chapter 11, when he speaks of that usurped, Christ-opposing power which claims "to have plenary power in both the temporal and the spiritual realm, both swords, the temporal and the spiritual" (Ap. VII, 23). Thus the kingdom of Antichrist is the radical personification of the essence of tyranny. In principle, it could grow out of the ecclesiastical as well as the civil office; the determining factor is that both realms are mingled in satanic distortion. The incumbent of this power is 'a god on earth' (Ap. VII, 24). Here a man had to "proclaim himself the head, and then the lord of the church, and finally of the whole world" (S.A. II, iv, 13), whereas in truth the spiritual and civil powers have their unity alone in God.

Like every tyranny, the essence of the Antichrist cannot be under-

---

[9] How much this is in the foreground is clear also from the fact that a moral indignation against the *person* of the Antichrist is lacking. The Confessions are not concerned about persons as such but about offices that have degenerated in an antichristian way.

stood only anthropologically. Rather, in the kingdom of Antichrist the kingdom of the devil invades churches and nations with inconceivable power (cf., e.g., S.A. II, iv, 14), the devil as murderer overrides the ordinances by which God the Creator preserves and protects sinful man under the office of parents and government and in marriage, and by fraudulent usurpation the devil abolishes the ministry through which God effects forgiveness and eternal life. The devil seeks to devour the church by perverting its message into antichristian religion and to seize the kingdom of God unhindered in order to destroy God's creation. This tyranny of the last times is antichristian in a pregnant sense, that is, the mimicked satanic counterpart and the presumptuous prolepsis of the reign of Jesus Christ. Whereas Jesus Christ alone is law and Gospel, here a man demands that *he* be believed, saying that "one must be obedient to him in order to be saved" (S.A. II, iv, 12). Whereas Christ's kingdom is the service of the Lord of lords and the fellowship of the brethren with him, their firstborn brother, the kingdom of Antichrist is devilish rape and enslavement. Whereas the coexistence of spiritual and civil authorities will come to its end only in the revelation of Christ's kingdom on the Last Day, here, immediately before the Last Day, man forcibly unites the power of both offices in his hand and demands of all men the acknowledgment of his total power as of a power ordained by God, as prerequisite for their continued physical existence and for the practice of their worship. Because of this he "is the real Antichrist who has raised himself over and set himself against Christ, for the pope will not permit Christians to be saved except by his own power, which amounts to nothing since it is neither established nor commanded by God" (S.A. II, iv, 10). Thus in the kingdom of Antichrist the devil deceitfully anticipates what will be a visible reality only in the returning Christ. For Christ alone is both king and priest.

The realm of Antichrist, like every mingling of the two realms, involves an impressive and mighty intensification of power. Its attack becomes ever sharper, the number of believers ever smaller. The kingdom of Antichrist will almost overwhelm the church, Christ's kingdom on earth. According to II Thess. 2:4 we are to expect 'that Antichrist will sit in the temple of God, i.e., he will rule and bear office in the church' (Ap. VII, 4). And yet this unheard-of development of power is merely a symptom of the senescence of the world, the last revolt of the world in a raving, desperate impotence. In the dominion of Antichrist the devil makes the last *futile* attempt to maintain his kingdom. For the kingdom of Antichrist can last only "until Christ comes to judge and by the glory of his coming destroys the kingdom of Antichrist" (Ap. XXIV, 98).

Who is the Antichrist? According to many statements he is the pope; according to occasional other statements, Mohammed and his followers. Going beyond this, one may say that heretics as such are antichrists (Ap. VII, 48); wherever, e.g., candles, paraments, and similar ornaments are declared to be necessary for salvation, we find 'the retinue of Antichrist' (Ap. XXIV, 51). Hence no specific person, nor a specific pope, is called Antichrist. Rather, the pope as such, the papacy, is the Antichrist, and yet it is true only that "the papacy will *also* be a part of the kingdom of Antichrist" (Ap. XV, 18). To be sure, the statements of Luther (S.A. II, iv) point to the pope with less ambiguity than do those of Melanchthon and, again, the Treatise does so more strongly than the Apology: The "marks of the Antichrist coincide with those of the pope's kingdom and his followers" (Tr. 39). It is "necessary to resist him as Antichrist" (Tr. 57).

All of these statements are made in the conviction of living in the last times and days immediately before Christ's return. This conviction may by no means be minimized; it is basic for the decisions of doctrine and practice. It is probably one of the reasons why in the age of the Reformation comparatively little effort was expended on the regulation of the church in conformity with the Confessions. Since Antichrist was recognized above all in the papal encroachment of the spiritual office on civil government, comparatively little resistance was offered to the encroachment of the civil office on the church, and the antichristian possibilities of the civil office were not in like measure taken into account. Still, no passage in the Book of Concord names the time of the Last Day. How little the confessors even toyed with an attempt to calculate this time is shown by the paradoxical advice of Melanchthon to marry in these antichristian times of devilish devastation (Ap. XXIII, 55; cf. 25). This is also shown by the fact that various statements are made about the historically present Antichrist which do not arrive at a final dogmatically fixed harmonization.[10]

---

[10] Even Luther's devastating polemic does not do this. It is true that after initial hesitation he battled the pope as the Antichrist to the end of his life, but at the same time he recognized other partners of Antichrist. His remarks concerning the pope and the Turks are largely parallel in content.

All this leads to the conclusion that the eschatological judgments of the Confessions, in spite of all distinctness, are made still in the cautious groping and questioning of the time regarding the scripturally attested signs of the Last Day.[11] Therefore we shall have to weigh carefully to what extent these historically conditioned statements about the Antichrist are to be understood as dogma or as paradigm. To understand them as paradigm would mean to regard them as a model of how to take seriously the Lord's directive that we should look in the present moment of every age for the harbingers of the end. In this case the statements about the *essence* of the Antichrist would have a more binding significance than the judgments about the *pope* as the Antichrist. At all events it must be said that the church becomes unfaithful to the Confessions if it views the pope alone as the Antichrist, instead of being ever alert in constant watchfulness for the signs of the Antichrist in each current generation.[12]

It is striking that the Confessions, except for the doctrine of the Antichrist, contain nothing about omens of the end. The silence about the other signs proclaimed in Scripture[13] is not to be understood as a denial,[14] but as an abbreviation. Like the doctrine of the

---

[11] This is overlooked when the church by means of a dogmatic positivism treats the confessional statements about the Antichrist as the definitive answer, as was done with unequivocal directness in Lutheran Orthodoxy. The confessional statements are, however, tentative answers given by the questioners themselves, and not yet the ultimate answer which God alone will provide when the Last Day comes.

[12] Thus Vilmar claimed to be loyal to the Confession even when he wrote: "Above all, one must guard against wanting to cling onesidedly to individual manifestations as though they were the real fulfillments and absolutizations of the prophecy. Evangelical exegesis was wrong in this respect and blinded itself to many, if not to most, things in that it believed itself justified in looking upon the pope and Rome as completely representing Antichrist and Babylon. Atheism and the pre-Noachite materialism, which was present already in the fifteenth century and has re-emerged in our day, are far more exact fulfillments of the antichristian kingdom as it is foretold, than Rome and the popes, even the worst of them." *Dogmatik*, II, 308 f. Beyond this, Vilmar, Kliefoth, and other Lutherans of the past century have gone counter to the Confessions and have directly combated the designation of the pope as the Antichrist.

[13] Thus, e.g., there is no mention of a conversion of the Jews at the end of history, though Luther had occupied himself with it in passing, nor of an expectation of the completion of world evangelization. Mark 13:10.

[14] The Confessions allow for an unfolding of eschatology. During the last century Vilmar, Kliefoth, Hofmann, Delitzsch, Frank, and others made marked use of this fact, in part consciously and basically going beyond the Reformers. Thus Vilmar says: "These future items of faith have not yet been experienced or lived by the church. They can be lived through only after the church will have experienced its own nature, only after it will have experienced and lived through the doctrine of the church. *Augsburg Confession*, p. 149. Neither, however, is said to have as yet happened in the age of the Reformation.

church and the two powers, so also the eschatology of the Confessions is held in thrall and is completely determined by the violent struggle between Christ's kingdom and the devil's kingdom which is rushing headlong to its finish. The drama of this war progresses cataclysmically along a single line and in breath-taking acceleration to the deceptive, fictitious triumph of the devil's kingdom and its overthrow by the triumphant returning Christ. In view of this impending catastrophe the contemporaries have little time for a comfortable contemplation of details and, above all, no time for optimistic expectations which before the end look for an upsurge of the world in increasing improvement. Therefore the opinion is rejected that "before the resurrection of the dead, saints and godly men will possess a worldly kingdom and annihilate the godless" (A.C. XVII, 5).[15]

It is also strange that the Confessions say nothing about the states of man between his departure from this world and the resurrection. We are indeed taught to pray God that "when the hour of death comes, he may grant us a blessed end and graciously take us from this world of sorrows to himself in heaven" (S.C. III, 20). But it is not explained how this prayer is related to the expectation that the decision about salvation and damnation will be made on the Last Day. Only the Roman doctrine of purgatory is rejected (Ap. XII, 13 ff, 134 ff; XXIV, 90 ff.; S.A. II, ii, 12 ff.).[16] By means of this apparent "gap in the system" [17] the Confessions most emphatically point out that everyone must *here on earth* make the decision in the final battle between God's kingdom and the devil's.

---

[15] This sentence has long experienced various interpretations. Does it reject every kind of chiliasm (so, e.g., H. H. Wendt, L. Fendt, W. Elert), or only a coarse, carnal variety as promoted in word and deed by certain Anabaptists under the influence of Jewish ideas (so, e.g., Vilmar, Zoeckler, Plitt)? Does this condemnation reject Rev. 20, or does it merely reject a brand of chiliasm which contradicts also the Apocalypse, by teaching that the pious will have a world kingdom *before* the resurrection of the dead? Even though the old Lutheran theology generally rejected every kind of chiliasm and understood the millennium (Rev. 20) not as an eschatological event but as a past epoch of church history, it must not be overlooked that the wording of A.C. XVII rejects only a definite perversion of the millennial idea. Plitt rightly observes that "it would be a mistake to turn the point of the last sentence of Article XVII against anything beyond what contemporary history suggested." *Augustana*, II, 422.

[16] Thus there are no positive assertions about the nature of the intermediate state, such as might be suggested by Luther's ideas about the sleep of the dead which is a state of being awake before God at the same time. Furthermore, nothing at all is said about the place of the dead or about further possibilities for repentance and sanctification on the part of the dead.

[17] Koellner, *Symbolik*, I, 688. This so-called "gap" is necessarily overestimated when the doctrine of the Confessions is regarded as a system rather than as summary of proclamation.

9. The Last Day is the glorious return of our Lord Jesus Christ who will raise the dead, judge all men, give eternal life to all believers, and condemn the ungodly to eternal death. His kingdom shall have no end.

The return of Jesus Christ is the public manifestation of his reign. Christ's kingdom does not come into being only on the Last Day. Sitting on the right hand of the Father, he has dominion over all creatures even now (A.C. III, 4). His kingdom is real even now on this earth in his church. Through Word and sacrament he is even now present on earth for his believers and has never left them. But "the kingdom of Christ has not yet been revealed" (Ap. VII, 17); it is still hidden among sinners. His presence is still concealed in human word and earthly elements. Only on the Last Day will his dominion become visible before all eyes. Then he will come "openly" (A.C. III, 6) and will "condemn ungodly men and the devil to hell and eternal punishment" (A.C. XVII, 3). But also Christ's victory over the devil will not be won only on the Last Day. Even now he is plucking his own out of the jaws of the vanquished devil and protecting them against his cunning assaults. He who descended into hell already "conquered the devil, destroyed hell's power, and took from the devil all his might" (S.D. IX, 2). But Christ's kingdom, the church, is still afflicted and pervaded by the members of Satan's kingdom. Only on the Last Day will the battle line between the two kingdoms become finally visible. Then the communion of saints will visibly step forth from the external church fellowship. "It is our solace . . . that the . . . devil and . . . our enemies shall . . . come to naught, no matter how proud, secure, and powerful they think they are" (L.C. III, 70; cf. 54).

The unveiling of Christ's kingdom is the act of the returning Christ affecting not only angels and men but the whole world. The Last Day is 'the consummation of the world' (A.C. XVII, 1). The Last Day is also the *end* of this world; then Christ will "completely divide and separate us from the wicked world" (L.C. II, 31). The Last Day is the end of the world with respect to its corruption and demonic possession, but is its consummation as the creation of God. Together with the 'consummation of the world' the identity of the present and future creation is affirmed[18] without, however, over-

---

[18] The so-called Lutheran enjoyment of this world may not be dissociated from the expectation of the world's consummation. Only because we look for a new earth and a new heaven is an ingenuous, childlike affirmation of this world possible in spite of its corruption, and hence in spite of its denial.

looking in unbroken teleology the difference between the present and the future creation. This distinction finds expression, furthermore, in all the temporal qualifications of the statements about the course of the world up to the Last Day—the "last times" precede the "end." But the remarks about the actions of Christ on the Last Day are not qualified by time. In a totally unique manner they are simultaneous, less in a temporal sense than as being beyond any further succession in time. The consummation of the world is also the raising of the dead and the Last Judgment. The Holy Spirit will accomplish[19] resurrection, purification, and sanctification "instantly . . . and will eternally preserve us in it . . ." (L.C. II, 59). Christ's decisions are "eternal," i.e., 'without end' (A.C. XVII, 3).

At the coming of Christ "all men shall rise with their bodies" (Athan. 38). We await the time "when our flesh will be put to death, will be buried with all its uncleanness, and will come forth gloriously and arise to complete and perfect holiness in a new, eternal life" (L.C. II, 57). Though Luther criticizes the term "resurrection of the flesh" (L.C. II, 60), the whole anti-Gnostic precision of this expression is preserved and the identity of our present and future body is unequivocally avowed. To be sure, in distinction from our perishable old body, the body of the resurrected will be new, immortal, and glorified (L.C. II, 58), but a denial of the identity of the two bodies, because they will be inconceivably and immeasurably different, would be—to use the terminology of the Formula of Concord—equivalent to the claim that sin is the substance and creatureliness is the *accidens* of man. It is noteworthy that the Confessions indeed teach the resurrection of *all* the dead but define more closely only the corporeality of the risen *believers*.

The returning Christ will "judge the quick and the dead" (Nic.; Apost.; Athan.; A.C. III, 6). The Athanasian Creed mentions works as the criterion of judgment: ". . . and give an account of their own deeds. Those *who have done good* will enter eternal life, and those who have done evil will go into everlasting fire" (Athan., 38 f.). The Augsburg Confession puts it differently: He will "give eternal life and everlasting joy to *believers and the elect,* but . . . condemn ungodly men and the devil to hell and eternal punishment" (A.C. XVII, 2 f.). Thus, within the total content of the Book of Concord, faith and works are both named as criteria of the Last

---

[19] Calling the resurrection of the dead the work of Christ (A.C. XVII) and also the work of the Holy Spirit (L.C. II, 59) can, of course, not be a contradiction within the frame of the trinitarian confession.

Judgment, and yet no rational harmonization of the two is offered; and in just this way the Confessions correspond to the New Testament expressions concerning judgment and thus preserve to the end the dialectic of law and Gospel which men cannot solve. This is also true of what the Apology teaches when, with reference to I Cor. 3:8, it says that one day the rewards of the believers will differ according to their works (Ap. IV, 194; cf. 356 ff.). The Last Judgment is twofold in the strict sense. Both eternal life and eternal damnation are everlasting; the doctrine of apocatastasis is expressly rejected, 'that there will be an end to the punishments of condemned men and devils' (A.C. XVII, 4).[20] However, unlike the salvation of the elect, the status of the condemned is not further described.[21] Here again it is evident that the sum total of all churchly proclamation is the salvation, not the rejection, of the sinners. The church cannot show an independent interest in damnation, divorced from the call to repentance issued by the Gospel.

Eternal life and eternal joy (*"vita aeterna et perpetua gaudia,"* A.C. XVII, 2) for the perfected elect means life in the manifest eternal kingdom of Christ. We shall then live in unconcealed reality and Spirit-created corporeality, "even as he is risen from the dead and lives and reigns to all eternity" (S.C. II, 4). Then man is no longer creature and sinner at once. The "flesh of sin is put off entirely and man is completely renewed in the resurrection" (S.D. VI, 24). Men are now God's creatures without corruption in "new, immortal, and glorified bodies" (L.C. II, 58). Then man is also no longer righteous and sinner at once. Having begun sanctification, on earth, God's Spirit has now completed it "instantly" (L.C. II, 59). The dialectic of a new birth which is still only a partial renewal, of new obedience and continuing sinfulness, of the liberated and enslaved will—the dialectic from which no believer on earth was exempt—is then at an end. All quantitative concepts have then run their course. We are then completely renewed and perfected. We shall live under Christ completely righteous, completely

---

[20] "The view that the punishments imposed at Judgment have a term rests . . . on a confusion of the cosmic judgment with the punitive judgment. . . . Not the fact that God punishes us without ceasing is dreadful but that God breaks his rod of affliction, that *he stops punishing.*" Vilmar, *Augsburg Confession,* p. 151.

[21] The same is true of Luther's sermons and books. "With great warmth Luther on the basis of Scripture depicts and elaborates for his hearers and readers this blessed state to which God's love and grace wants to bring the faithful in order to console and encourage. In spite of the gravity with which Luther reminds his audiences of the terrors of damnation he is reticent about elaborating on the details." J. Koestlin, *Luthers Theologie,* II, 349.

holy, completely obedient, and yet free. Then man is no longer both living and dying, by faith living in this world of death, and in daily repentance dying as one who lives forever. For all eternity we are then completely divided and separated "from the wicked world, the devil, death, sin, etc." (L.C. II, 31). Neither spiritual nor temporal death is then in prospect; what Baptism signified is fulfilled—"body and soul shall be saved and live forever" (L.C. IV, 46).

The distinction between law and Gospel thus comes to an end on the Last Day. The risen believers no longer need the law. They do "of themselves and altogether spontaneously, without any instruction, admonition, exhortation, or driving by the law . . . what they are obligated to do according to the will of God" (S.D. VI, 6). Through "God's indwelling Spirit they will do his will spontaneously, without coercion, unhindered, perfectly, completely, and with sheer joy, and will rejoice therein forever" (S.D. VI, 25). Nor do they need then the promise of the Gospel any more. Only "until we attain to that life where there will be no more forgiveness" (L.C. II, 58) does the Holy Spirit work in us through the word of forgiveness. For the risen believers are rid of all sin. In the resurrection of the believers on the Last Day it becomes a reality that man "will no longer require either the preaching of the law or its threats and punishments, just as he will no longer require the Gospel. They belong to this imperfect life" (S.D. VI, 24). The law is no longer in force for those who are risen in Christ because it finds in them nothing more to judge and to punish. The word of forgiveness is no longer preached to those who are risen in Christ because in the meantime his promise has become a visible reality. They no longer *believe* the Word of life but they *see* the life which the Word had once promised them. They "see God face to face" (S.D. VI, 25).

Thus in the expectation of the end the Confessions are aware of their own transitoriness also. Through the summary of Holy Scripture God had given them the distinction between law and Gospel as their theme. On the Last Day God takes back this theme by revealing before all the reality that was promised and bestowed in the Word. This awareness of the end of our theology is filled with joy.

10. Before the creation of the world God elected his children to eternal life in Christ.

The Confessions look beyond this world to the future, but they finally also look backward before this world. The believers are not only awaiting God's act at the end of the world but they may also know about the fundamental election of the children of God before the creation of the world. Embraced by God's election and act at the beginning and at the end, the believer is completely secure. The Confessions, however, look backward far more timidly and mutely than they look forward.

According to A.C. V, the Holy Spirit works faith "when and where he pleases" (*"ubi et quando visum est Deo"*). This "when and where" is not simply the place and hour of the proclamation of the Word and the distribution of the sacraments, but through Word and sacraments faith comes into being where and when it pleases God. There are times and places in which and at which the Gospel is not received by faith, yes, in which and at which the Holy Spirit does not work faith through Word and sacraments. The little clause quoted above is to be understood in a predestinarian sense even though it speaks only of God's volition and not of his nonvolition.[22] According to A.C. XVII, the returning Christ will give eternal life to the "elect." This concept must not be toned down, since the "believers" are also described as the "elect." It must be noted further that, according to A.C. XIX, the human will turns away from God "as soon as God withdraws his support" (*"non adjuvante Deo"*). This does not, of course, admit the conclusion that God is the cause of sin,[23] but it must not be overlooked that God's nonassistance is a divine act, as the German text states more clearly, "God withdraws his hand" (A.C. XIX). This article does not attempt to clear up the mystery of the relationship between the two facts that only the devil and man are the cause of sin, and that sin came into existence in the moment of being forsaken by God. This refusal to offer a rational solution has been largely overlooked by the commentators on the Augsburg Confession.

Such "predestinarian splinters" in the Augsburg Confession must "not be taken to mean too much"; they are not yet a doctrine of predestination. But they are more than mere "predestinarian arabesques" (K. Thieme, *Augsburgische Konfession*, pp. 72, 74)

---

[22] This is now generally acknowledged, though formerly it was widely denied. Cf. H. Engelland, *Melanchthon*, pp. 568 ff., for a resume of the various interpretations.

[23] Schleiermacher approaches this conclusion when he says, "This sentence, 'as soon as God withdraws his support,' declares that sin is ordained by God, even though it is not possible to assert specific divine causality for any single sinful act. This must be maintained, or else redemption could not have been ordained by God. Hence, not sin of and by itself is ordained but only sin with reference to redemption." *Der christliche Glaube* (2nd ed.), Sec. 81, 3. Cf. the similar view in J. Muller, *Die christliche Lehre von der Sünde*, I, 361 ff.

since they are set off against the background of an unexpressed doctrine of predestination. Since the sinner cannot believe by his own power but, on the contrary, faith is created by the Holy Spirit through Word and sacrament; since, moreover, not all who hear the Gospel and receive the sacraments are saved but only those who believe, no solution remains in the final analysis but to find the difference between the saved and lost sinners in God's action and therefore also in God's counsel. Nevertheless it is striking that the twofold predestination, though never denied in the Augsburg Confession, is peculiarly passed over in silence, and the same is true of the Apology, the two Catechisms, and the Smalcald Articles.

Not until the Formula of Concord is there a separate article (XI), "Eternal foreknowledge and election." But it does not teach the twofold predestination.

"The eternal election" is "God's predestination to salvation"; it "does not extend over both the godly and the ungodly, but only over the children of God who have been elected and predestined to eternal life 'before the foundations of the world were laid' . . ." (S.D. XI, 5). ". . . by God's gracious will and pleasure in Christ Jesus it is also a cause which creates, effects, helps, and furthers our salvation and whatever pertains to it" (S.D. XI, 8; cf. Ep. XI, 5). Predestination is only the cause of salvation but not the cause of damnation; it predestines only to eternal life, not to eternal death.

"The passage, 'Many are called, but few are chosen,' does not mean that God does not desire to save everyone. The cause of condemnation is that men either do not hear the Word of God at all but wilfully despise it, harden their ears and their hearts, and thus bar the ordinary way for the Holy Spirit, so that he cannot perform work in them, or, if they do hear the Word, they cast it to the wind and pay no attention to it. The fault does not lie in God or his election, but in their own wickedness" (Ep. XI, 12; cf. 17-19). Not God's election but the sin of men is the cause of their damnation; and in this connection there is no reference to original sin in general, but again and again to actual offenses against the Gospel which they hear, and against the Holy Spirit working through the Gospel (cf. S.D. XI, 40-42, 58-62, 78, 83, 85).

These offenses are not produced by God's election and will but are merely foreknown by God. "God's foreknowledge is nothing else than that God knows all things before they happen. . . . This foreknowledge extends alike over good people and evil people. But it is not a cause of evil or sin which compels anyone to do something wrong; the original source of this is the devil and man's wicked and perverse will. Neither is it the cause of man's perdition; for this man himself is responsible" (Ep. XI, 3 f.). "Thus there is no doubt that before the world began God foresaw right well with utter certainty, and that he still knows who of those who are called will believe and who will not; likewise, who of the converted will persevere and who will not; and who after falling away will return and who will become obdurate. God is also aware and knows exactly how many there will be on either side" (S.D. XI, 54).

To be sure, the "foreknowledge of God" is not merely a foreknowing but also an action by which God governs everything, even what is evil; God "controls the evil and imposes a limit on its duration, so that in spite of its intrinsic wickedness it must minister to the salvation of his elect" (Ep. XI, 4; cf. S.D. XI, 6 f.). But also the action of divine foreknowledge remains strictly separate from God's predestination. God's election is the cause of salvation but God's foreknowledge is not the cause of evil, neither of the first sin of Adam nor of the resulting enmity of fallen man against the Gospel. Neither is it the cause of damnation.

It is not indeed denied "that God gives his Word at one place and not at another; that he removes it from one place but lets it remain at another; or that one becomes hardened, blinded, and is given over to a perverse mind while another in equal guilt is again converted" (S.D. XI, 57). However, the cause of such hardening is not God but the sin of man. Through hardening and blinding, God *punishes* preceding sins and especially the impenitent security of those who had already been converted through the Gospel. God here "punishes sin with sin" (S.D. XI, 83; cf. 78-83).

In this distinction of foreknowledge and election F.C. XI is not "restatement and exposition" of an article of the Augsburg Confession. For the latter contains neither a special article about predestination nor this distinction. Beyond this, it must be asked whether the doctrine of predestination in the Formula of Concord agrees with the earlier Lutheran Confessions or contradicts them. Does it not seem that in this doctrine of obduracy and damnation concrete actual sins receive an isolated preponderance which causes the horrible reality of being a sinner to recede into the background? Do not these statements about willfully incurring damnation create the impression that here a possibility is presupposed for man to make and keep himself receptive to the Gospel? What can it mean that sinners "bar the ordinary way for the Holy Spirit, so that he *cannot* work in them?" (Ep. XI, 12). Does not the Holy Spirit *always* work *in spite of* the resistance of men? *Must* not enslaved man always contradict the Holy Spirit until He overcomes him and finally renews him completely on the Last Day? Man is never lord over the ability or nonability of the Spirit of God, neither before nor after conversion! We could at once ask the further question: Is not perhaps this rejection of a twofold predestination in the distinction of election and foreknowledge, in spite of all reverence for the mystery, the beginning of a rational resolution of the mystery of divine election as it became manifest in Lutheran Orthodoxy? [24] Does this rejection still correspond to the mystery of the unity and difference of law and Gospel in the revelation of the triune God who, through the Gospel, both saves and judges? After all, is not the cross of his Son the revelation of salvation as well as the revelation of his anger? By contrast, does not the doctrine of the Formula of Concord regarding the call change the incomprehensibility and freedom of divine mercy into a necessity of divine deliverance through the proclaimed Word? Does not this doctrine lead into the danger of a false security? [25]

These questions may not simply be disregarded. It is to be expected as a matter of fact that a twofold, rather than single, predestination[26] will be taught if the doctrine of sin and grace, as

[24] Here the eternal election follows from the *voluntas Dei universalis (antecedens)*, that is, the will of God manifest in the Gospel to save all men, and from the *voluntas Dei specialis (consequens)*, that is, the will to save those whose faith in the Gospel God foresaw from eternity. Correspondingly, the eternal reprobation follows from the fact that God knows in advance those people who will not believe. Here the structure of the doctrine of election and of reprobation is no longer basically differentiated, as in F.C. XI, but the elements of the doctrine of obduration are interwoven with the doctrine of election to produce a rational system made up of mutually supporting statements concerning God's offer, knowledge, and election, in which man's attitude toward God's offer peculiarly motivates God's reprobating and electing action. Cf. J. Gerhard, *Loci*, VII; H. Schmid, *Die Dogmatik der ev. luth. Kirche* (6th ed., 1876) par. 30.

[25] It could also be asked whether this relationship between Word and Spirit in the Formula's doctrine concerning God's call does not create the danger of letting the election disappear in the general call, and thus be misunderstood in a universalistic sense. The Formula of Concord certainly does not teach a universal election. Cf. Frank, IV, 162 ff. Yet it is noteworthy how obstinately Sam. Huber insisted that his universalism agreed with this doctrine. On the Huber controversy over predestination see A. Schweizer, *Zentraldogmen*, I, 504 ff.

[26] In any case we must guard against oversimplifying the simple predestination of the Formula of Concord. The *Apologia oder Verantwortung des christl. Concordienbuches* (Dresden, 1584) insists that it can claim Luther's support: "The Christian Book of Concord does not deny that there is no reprobation on God's part, or that God could not reject some. Hence it does not contradict

well as the predestinarian sprouts of the Augsburg Confession and the other earlier Confessions are to be developed into a doctrine of predestination. The predestinarian theology of Luther and the younger Melanchthon, from which these Confessions cannot be separated, point in this direction.[27]

Nevertheless, we dare not fail to recognize that F.C. XI develops statements of the earlier Confessions in a very special direction, and perhaps we can do justice to this article only if we do not look for an extensive doctrine of predestination,[28] but for special guidance on how a person should be comforted who is disturbed by the knowledge of God's twofold predestination. Not in the deductions which may result from this article for the preaching of repentance and grace but in the line of thought of a very special pastoral consolation for one who in repentance is despondent about grace, a genuine theological connection between F.C. XI and the Augsburg Confession may be established.

If you are without hope and in doubt whether you will be saved on the Last Day, then listen: Before the foundation of the world God has elected you to salvation by grace in Christ. Before you

---

Luther's dictum in *De servo arbitrio* against Erasmus that this is the highest degree of faith to believe that God would remain gracious, even though he saved so few people. On the contrary, this book desires to avoid ascribing to God the true cause of reprobation or condemnation, as our opponents teach. Furthermore, in this disputation all men must place a finger on their mouth and say with the apostle Paul (Rom. 11), 'they were broken off because of unbelief,' and (Rom. 6), 'the wages of sin is death.' Again, when the question is asked why God the Lord does not convert and save all people through the Holy Spirit (as he well could), we should say further with the apostle, 'How unsearchable are his judgments, and his ways past finding out.' By no means, however, dare we ascribe to God the Lord himself the full and real cause of the reprobation or damnation of the impenitent." "Furthermore, following Luther, we do not wish to investigate those matters concerning God which are hidden and have not been revealed." *Ibid.*, p. 206.

[27] The best recent study of the problems involved in double and single election is that of H. Vogel, which introduces a distinction between *praedestinatio gemina* and *praedestinatio dialectica. Theol. Aufsaetze* (Muenchen, 1936), pp. 222 ff.

[28] Frank's entire commentary on F.C. XI points in the same direction. It is determined by the conviction "that it was not the intention of the confessors on the basis of Scripture to define the concept of the predestination and selection of God or to embrace this whole area confessionally according to the teaching of Scripture." The concern is said to have been merely an unfolding of "the faith consciousness of the church." This phrase certainly sounds highly dubious today. Yet its aim is to emphasize the grace that is to be preached to the believing sinner. This is also supported by the observation that F.C. XI has no interest in statements concerning those who did not hear the Gospel but only in the obduration and judgment which will befall those who heard the Gospel and despised it. The point at issue is the word that concerns the man beneath the pulpit and tells him only what he should know about himself.

existed he has well and safely guarded your salvation in Christ. He "ordained my salvation in his eternal purpose, which cannot fail or be overthrown, and put it for safekeeping into the almighty hand of our Saviour, Jesus Christ, out of which no one can pluck us" since he knows that "due to the weakness and wickedness of our flesh it could easily slip from our fingers, and through the deceit and power of the devil and the world it could easily be snatched and taken from our hands" (S.D. XI, 45 ff.).

But if you doubt and brood about whether you are elected by God in Christ, if you reason thus: " 'If God has elected me to salvation I cannot be damned, do as I will.' Or, 'If I am not elected to eternal life whatever good I do is of no avail; everything is in vain in that case' " (Ep. XI, 8), then hear this: "We are not to investigate this predestination in the secret counsel of God, but it is to be looked for in his Word, where he has revealed it" (Ep. XI, 6). You may not judge concerning election on the basis "either of reason or of God's law. This would either lead us into a reckless, dissolute, Epicurean life, or drive men to despair and waken dangerous thoughts in their hearts" (Ep. XI, 9). "We must learn about Christ from the holy Gospel alone, which clearly testifies that 'God has consigned all men to disobedience, that he may have mercy upon all,' . . . and that he does not want anyone to perish . . ., but that everyone should repent and believe on the Lord Christ" (Ep. XI, 10). The revealed Christ is the open book of life (Ep. XI, 7). Hearing the Gospel of Christ and receiving the sacrament, you may be fully assured that your name is entered in this book of life (cf. S.D. XI, 9 ff., 22 ff.). Only in the Gospel is God's will revealed.

But has not God's decree also ordained men to damnation, even such as hear the Gospel and receive the sacraments on earth? Are not these too lost? God's election and decree ordains nobody to damnation. The damnation of a man always has its cause in man himself, in his willful rebellion, in his impenitence, his unbelief, and his apostasy from the Gospel. God is not willing "that any should perish, but that all should reach repentance" (II Pet. 3:9).

But if you continue to pine away in unconsolable fear whether you will remain faithful, whether you will not fall away, then hear this: God has ordained that "he would be effective and active in us by his Holy Spirit through the Word when it is preached, heard, and meditated on, would convert hearts to true repentance, and would enlighten them in the true faith" (S.D. XI, 17). The

Gospel is no empty word but through the Gospel the Holy Spirit is active in us and "gives grace, power, and ability" (S.D. XI, 33). The Gospel is God's true, serious, and effective will of grace. Through the Gospel you receive everything—strengthening of faith, eternal salvation, and the sure promise that God has already ordained you to eternal life before the foundation of the world. Believing in the Gospel you may be sure that you are firmly embraced by the gracious purpose of God in Christ before the creation of the world and by the gracious act of the returning Christ at the end of the world.

Knowing about the election, then, is to be an excellent, glorious consolation (S.D. XI, 45) to you, and the correct doctrine of the eternal election of God "a useful, salutary, and comforting doctrine, for it mightily substantiates the article that we are justified and saved without our works and merit, purely by grace and solely for Christ's sake" (S.D. XI, 43). We may be sure of eternal salvation because we may be sure of our election in Christ. For the Lord "assures us of this gracious election not only in mere words, but also with his oath, and has sealed it with his holy sacraments, of which we can remind ourselves and with which we can comfort ourselves in our greatest temptations and thus extinguish the flaming darts of the devil" (Ep. XI, 13).

Appendix

GUIDELINES FOR DOGMATICS

It is not yet work in dogmatics when the Confessions are quoted, not even when inferences are drawn from the quotations for the church's proclamation and activity. Nor is it dogmatics, though the theology of the Lutheran Confessions is compared a thousand times with Reformed doctrine and the latter is measured by the former. Again, it is not yet dogmatics to view and judge the Lutheran Confessions in the light, say, of Luther's theology. Nor yet is it dogmatics in the strict sense to compare one Lutheran Confession with another and so establish their agreement or disagreement with each other—for example, to subject the Formula of Concord to the norm of the Augsburg Confession and its Apology. It is, of course, of the essence of a Confession that the simultaneously valid creeds of a church may not contradict each other in their witness to the Gospel. It is, therefore, a very important task to investigate whether and to what extent the Formula of Concord may actually be regarded as an exposition of the Augsburg Confession. However, even such critical investigations remain in the realm of a comparative study in the history of dogma and are preliminary to dogmatics proper as long as in such studies the Holy Scriptures are not given their due place as the overarching unique rule and norm of all theological assertions. Dogmatic work in the Confessions begins only in the act of listening to them as exposition of Scripture, that is, in the act of repeating the Scripture exposition of the Confessions by means of scriptural exegesis. We may speak of dogmatic judgments only when the judgment is made on the basis of Scripture that certain statements of the Confessions are correct or incorrect, that is to say, scriptural or antiscriptural.

This retracing of the Scripture exposition of the Confessions by means of biblical exegesis must proceed in a twofold way:

1. The Scripture references of the Confessions must be re-examined by means of biblical exegesis. This presupposes a careful recapture of the exegesis applied to the respective Bible passage in the Confessions (especially when the same passage is used a number of times). We must investigate which aspects of the text are applied in the Confessions, and which are passed over.

2. Every doctrine of the Confessions must be subjected to *all* pertinent Scripture texts, even though they are not cited in the Confessions. For example, the Lutheran doctrine of the civil government must be re-examined in the light of the exegesis of *all* biblical utterances concerning

297

government. Every statement of Scripture, even though not used in the Confessions, is of normative significance for their doctrine. The Confessions themselves claim to be the summary of Scripture, not just an exposition of individual texts.

Both kinds of examination must constantly overlap each other. The first cannot suffice because the Scripture quotations of a creedal statement necessarily remain incomplete, yes, in essence relatively incidental. The second method must be added in the study of each doctrine. In every case, the conduct of this dogmatic conversation between Scripture and Confession calls for the observance of the following rules:

a) The assertions of the Confessions to be examined must be understood from their center, the doctrine of justification. Otherwise the examination will miss the real content. It is possible to discover that a statement viewed in isolation is false, while in the total context of the Confession it proves itself to be true.

b) The Scripture passages that are important for the examination must be interpreted each in its own scriptural context, not only in its immediate textual setting but also in the context of its author's message and in its place in the history of salvation, either in the Old or the New Testament. Only in this concrete connection can these texts be correctly seen as words of the one scriptural witness. It will not do to ignore the hermeneutic rules of modern exegesis and to isolate Scripture texts as *loci classici* of dogmatics. It is just as wrong to isolate the theology of Paul or the words of the Synoptics for the purpose of measuring the statements of the Confessions by them alone. Every text must be interpreted in its context as a word of the entire Scriptures of both testaments.

c) The exegetical analysis must be made in concert with the fathers and the brethren, that is, with careful consideration of the older and the more recent exegesis of the respective passages. It is not yet a proper investigation if an individual should place his personal exegetical ideas above the Confession. Just as the Confession itself was formulated as Scripture exposition in the consensus of the church, so any further conversation between Scripture and Confession will be carried on in the right way only by someone who listens to the interpretation of the fathers and brethren, either to adopt it or to correct it. And this willingness to listen must not be limited to the exegesis of one's own denomination.

d) The exegetical investigation must clearly understand from the start that in line with the nature of a Confession the criterion of its scripturalness does not consist in its verbatim agreement with the Scriptures. The Confession is a witness to the sum of Scripture in the words of the confessor, and that with adverse reference to heresies. A scriptural Confession may be made in nonbiblical terms (cf. the concepts in the doctrine of the Trinity). A Confession may be scriptural even when for the purpose of comprehending the fullness of the scriptural statements biblical concepts are broadened and given a content beyond their original meaning. A Confession, it must be remembered, can never take up the fullness of biblical concepts word for word, but must select some aspects in order to witness to the whole. Thus from the start we must reckon with the fact that the decision concerning the scripturalness of a statement in the Confessions will in many cases be by no means a simple one,[1] yes, will appear to be an act of presumption. It will here be highly important for the dogmatician to be granted an insight, by the multiplicity of witnesses who speak in the Scriptures, into the greater or lesser importance of the divergences of the Confessions from the Holy Scriptures. A clear understanding of the differences in the unity of the biblical witness—for example, the differences between the Johannine and Pauline theology—is the most reliable aid in answering the question whether certain differences between Scripture and Confession must be labeled scriptural or antiscriptural.

A few examples may illustrate these methodological principles. We add them as questions, since at this point they are merely to serve the purpose of guidelines to stimulate a conversation between Scripture and Confession with respect to certain individual matters. These examples were selected *purely from the viewpoint of method* and are in no wise comprehensive. It will remain the task of dogmatics itself to answer these and numerous other questions that need to be asked.

Thus, for example, as the exegetical process of the Confessions is repeated we might put the following questions *in view of individual Scripture quotations:*

CHAPTER 3/4: *Rom. 3:21-30* (see B. of C., pp. 643, 644). In the exegetical restudy of the Lutheran commentary on the Pauline statements regarding the redemption in Christ Jesus, justification, and faith our attention must be directed primarily to the explanation of statements concerning the *dikaiosunē theou* in verses 21 f. and 25 f. They are explained either as *justitia coram ipso (Deo),* "the righteousness that avails before God" (A. C. IV, 3; Ap. IV, 41), or they are passed over (this is true of verse 25 f., but also of verse 1:17a). Is this interpretation tenable in verse 25 f.? Does not the manifestation of the *dikaiosunē theou* also include the fact that God is righteous (v. 26), the righteousness by which God is righteous and makes righteous? Is this only justifying grace, and not also judgment—a judgment, that is, that descended on Christ Jesus, and grace for us, but grace that justifies because the divine judgment struck Christ Jesus in his atoning death? Hence does not *dikaiosunē theou* also in verse 21 f. mean the revelation of the judging-saving action of God, where the genitive (*theou*) must be taken as *subjectivus* and *auctoris?* Do we find the same shift in the Lutheran, as against the Pauline, statements in the interpretation of the remaining Pauline and other biblical utterances about the righteousness of God?

---

[1] Thus, among other things, we must note that even when a Scripture text is incorrectly explained in the Confessions the respective doctrinal statement of the Confession may be correct, namely, if it is based on other texts which perhaps are not even quoted. On the contrary, a word of Scripture in the Confessions which in itself is used correctly may, through inadmissible generalizations and deductions (in themselves perhaps entirely logical), lead to an antiscriptural statement of doctrine.

Is this shift conditioned by a stand against a specific heresy or is it determined anthropologically, that is, by man's need and yearning, which through a sort of synergism reshapes the Pauline concept of God's righteousness so that this very yearning finds appeasement through God's merciful forgiveness? (A. Schlatter). But is God's righteousness—this righteousness which is manifest in God's wrath and in his mercy, which judges and at the same time creates righteousness—actually overlooked? Do perhaps other statements of the Confessions counterbalance the shift in emphasis at this point?

CHAPTER 5: *Rom. 6:1-11* (see B. of C., p. 644). Verse 4 is cited in the section on Baptism in the Small Catechism as proof for the answer to the fourth question: Baptism with water "signifies that the old Adam in us, together with all sins and evil lusts, should be drowned by daily sorrow and repentance and be put to death. . . ." Does this do justice to Rom. 6:4? This passage testifies most emphatically to the fact of our death and burial as *accomplished* in Baptism. Our resurrection is still to come but our death is past, since through Baptism we have been given into Christ's death, we have been sunk into Christ's grave. Buried in Christ's death through Baptism, we have died to sin. *Having died* with Christ, let us also walk in a new life! Furthermore, because we, as having died with Christ, shall also be like unto Christ's resurrection, therefore let us walk in a new life! On the basis of Christ's death and resurrection we are living between the fact of our death from which we come and our resurrection toward which we are going. This suggests the question: Do not the statements of Rom. 6:1 ff. belong already in the answer to the question concerning the benefit of Baptism? May we speak of the benefits or even the essence of Baptism without speaking of Christ's death and resurrection? On the other hand, is Rom. 6:4 a proof for the necessity of our daily dying? Is our death which took place in Baptism equivalent to the *veri terrores* (*conscientiae*) which the baptized person too experiences in his repentance again and again? (Ap. XII, 46). Strangely enough in the Apology too the decisive reference to Christ's death in all statements from Rom. 6:1-11 is passed over. In the Large Catechism the reference to Romans 6 is missing entirely.

CHAPTER 7: *Matt. 16:18 f.* Is the exegesis (Tr. 22 ff.) tenable according to which Jesus is here addressing not the person of Peter, but in the person of Peter all apostles (indeed, the whole church, all believers); and according to which it is not the person of Peter that is called the rock on which Jesus builds his church, but rather the apostolic office (indeed, the office of the ministry), the confession concerning Christ, faith (finally the eternal election of God, Ep. XI, 5; S. D. XI, 8)? Or is Jesus here emphasizing also the person of the confessing Peter? Must we correct the Lutheran doctrine of the ministry, especially the statements about the relationship between office and person, in view of the fact that Matt. 16:18 does not separate office, confession, and person, and singles out Peter also as the *person* active in his office, a person distinct from the rest of the contemporary disciples and witnesses of Christ?

Rom. 13:1-7 is quoted especially to support the assertion that the government is God's institution, and its activity in judgments, penalties, and wars is God's work (Ap. XVI, 7); therefore it is to be obeyed. Hence the Lutheran doctrine of the *justitia civilis* rests essentially on this text. For the purpose of exegesis we would have to ask: Are the concepts "good" and "bad" theological—or do they remain in the realm of human relations, like "beneficial" and "harmful"? Is the context of these concepts determined by the government itself, or is it predetermined? Are "good" and "bad" in the laws and verdicts of the government identical with "good" and "bad" as used in the apostolic exhortations to the church? (Rom. 12:2, 9, 21; 13:10). Are the good works for which the doer receives the government's praise identical with the fulfillment of God's law through love? (Rom. 13:8-10). Is the admonition of Rom. 13:1 ff. directed only to the doers of good or evil within the church, or does it distinguish also between the doers of good and evil outside the church, that is, in the actions of the unbelievers, the sinners? What then is the scope of the identity of the distinction between good and evil within the church and outside the church and, again, in the laws and judgments of the pagan government and in the admonitions to, and the obedience of, faith by the church? (cf. also Titus 3:1 ff.; I Pet. 2:14 ff.). To what extent do the heathen *know* about the good or evil they do? Whence do they know it? Corresponding questions arise with respect to the terms *exousia, diatagē (tassesthai, hupotassesthai), diakonos, leitourgos.* Does the government act in the service of God and does God operate through it even when it judges and condemns arbitrarily and unjustly? Does God through the government praise the doer of good even when he is unjustly condemned by the government and has to suffer injury ("the glory of suffering")? To sum up, can the Lutheran doctrine of the *justitia civilis* be based on Rom. 13:1 ff.? Are not perhaps the New Testament exhortations more concerned with the necessary event of obedience on the part of the believers and less with the phenomenon of civil righteousness as such than is the case with the Confessions? May we perhaps find in the Confessions the beginnings of an attempt to make "civil righteousness" independent of faith and perhaps even contrary to faith, the object of independent interest in a way that is different from the slant of the New Testament statements?

CHAPTER 8: *Ex. 4-14 (The Hardening of Pharaoh's Heart*, S. D. XI, 84 ff.). Does the Old Testament text say that Pharaoh's hardening by God is conditioned by Pharaoh's attitude toward Israel? Or is it not rather true that Pharaoh's hardening by God conditions his obduracy against the commission given to Moses, and hence Pharaoh's refusal to obey? In God's instructions to Moses is God's intention to harden Pharaoh's heart based on human attitudes at all? Does not God rather designate as his only goal that Pharaoh is not to let Israel go? God wants to do wonders in the sight of all, so that both Egyptians and the children of Israel may know that Yahweh is the Lord (Ex. 4:21; 7:3 ff.; 10:1 f.). Does not Paul too refer to Pharaoh (Rom. 9:17) in a sense different from that of the Formula of Concord? (S.D. XI, 86). Does the Pharaoh narrative itself undermine the doctrine of reprobation in the Formula of Concord?

Rom. 9:10 ff. (S.D. XI, 43, 88). Is it permissible to deduce from this text only that God has elected men to *eternal life* before their birth or their deeds? Does not this text also teach that God hates and rejects men before they are born and have done no good or evil? Furthermore, in the exegesis of Rom. 9:21 ff. (S.D. XI, 79) may we overlook the fact that God, like a potter, prepares not only vessels of honor but also vessels of dishonor, not only vessels of mercy but also vessels of wrath? In all this, may the basic axiom of verse 18 be passed by? Dogmatics indeed cannot avoid selective quotation of individual texts from the whole of Scripture, or emphasis on *one* specific aspect from among the fullness of an individual quotation. But where are the required limits?

In re-examining the use of *certain biblical concepts* in the Confessions, questions such as these suggest themselves:

CHAPTER 3/4: *"Nomos" and admonition in Paul's letters.* Do the admonitions addressed to the Christian congregation belong into the category of *nomos* (as in the Lutheran concept of the *tertius usus legis*)? Are they based on the authority of the Mosaic law (what, for example, is the meaning of Rom. 12:1, "I beseech you by the mercies of God")? Is it proper to base the idea of the *tertius usus legis* on Rom. 8:2, "the law of the spirit of life in Christ Jesus"; Gal. 6:2, "the law of Christ"; Rom. 3:27, "the law of faith"; and on passages like Rom. 3:31; 13:10 and Gal. 5:14? Is Paul concerned about the identity of the content of his admonitions with the Old Testament law, especially the Decalogue? Does Paul not rather regard the law as having been abrogated by Christ in such a way that he even distinguishes in principle between the law and his apostolic admonitions and no longer calls them law though in content they agree with Mosaic commandments?

"Nomos" and "entolē" in the Johannine writings: Are the *entolai* addressed to the disciples or the Christian community called law? Is the *entolē* in which the commandments are summed up, namely, the law of love, so designated? Is John interested in demonstrating the identity of the commandment to be addressed to the church with the Old Testament law, or even in deriving the authority of these New Testament *entolai* from the Mosaic commandments, particularly the Decalogue? (The Synoptics, Paul, and Hebrews use *entolē* with special reference to the Mosaic law.) Or is the *entolē* addressed to the church a basically new word distinct from the law, precisely not "given by Moses," but "through Jesus Christ" (John 1:17), namely, the commandment of love given by the loving and serving Christ, whose self-imparting turns also the individual *entolai* into a new commandment? What is the meaning of "old" and "new" commandment in John 13:34; I John 2:7 f.; II John 5? Is this the basis for subsuming the New Testament admonitions under the concept of *tertius usus legis*?

Euaggelion: Have the Confessions taken over the full significance of the New Testament term? Or is there a shift from message to doctrine;

from the oral call to written sentences which must then be explained; from the event of proclamation to a conscious possession of what is to be proclaimed; from the tidings of joy through whose proclamation God's rule draws near to the mere announcement that it is drawing near; from the call in which God reveals himself to instruction about God's revelation; from the Word in which the living Christ acts to a report concerning that which Jesus once did for us; from the herald's cry, which is an eschatological event to an announcement which stirs hope by treating of coming events?

Pistis: Is the criticism justified that, in Lutheran doctrine, faith is not created through an act of God, but is related to a doctrine of justification revealed by God? (A. Schlatter, *Gottes Gerechtigkeit*, pp. 42 f.).

Are we to understand the concern of the Lutheran concept of faith for the word *sola* and the *particulae exclusivae* as a *via negationis*—remaining ultimately in the domain of the psychological—as "that foreshortening of life, which excludes activity and leaves nothing but faith"? (*ibid.*, p. 153). Does the concept of faith in the Confessions do full justice to what Paul means by *pistis Iēsou Christou?* This genitive is certainly not only objective—it is that too, of course—"But this is not the only relationship between these two entities. On the contrary, Christ (like God) is for Paul never the Object in the sense that He does not at once make him (Paul) the object in this way that he (Paul) with his subjectivity thereby becomes partaker in the objectivity of this Subject (Christ). More concretely, whoever believes in Christ is thereby 'in Christ' " (O. Schmitz, *Die Christus-Gemeinschaft des Paulus im Lichte seines Genitivgebrauchs,* [Gütersloh, 1924], p. 132). Do the Confessions take up the full witness of the Synoptics concerning faith, which not only clings to Jesus as the one who bestows forgiveness, but is directed to him also as the one who hears *every* plea for help, and who not only cures the sickness of believers, but also responds to the believing parents of the sick by healing the disease? Do the Confessions restrict the concept of faith to the reception of forgiveness and thus abridge the all-inclusive promise (e.g., Mark 11:22-24) which Jesus makes to faith? The Confessions should be examined further on the basis of the statements of Isaiah and John about faith, as well as the concept of faith in Hebrews, etc. Which of these particular biblical concepts of faith finds fullest expression in the Confessions?

CHAPTER 5: *"Eis to onoma tou kuriou Iēsou," ". . . tou patros kai tou huiou kai tou hagiou pneumatos," and "en tō onomati Iēsou Christou"* in the New Testament baptismal texts: The Confessions use the baptismal formula only in the wording, "In the name [*in nomine*] of the Father and of the Son, and of the Holy Ghost." This follows the Vulgate rather than the text of Matt. 28:19 unanimously attested in the Greek manuscripts: *eis to onoma* ("into the name"). The formula is explained to mean that Baptism was not invented by men, but instituted by God; it is not performed by men, but by God. Even though men administer Baptism, it remains God's own work (L.C. IV, 6-13). The Confessions speak only of *God's* name in general, not of God's *trinitarian* name. The latter is neither mentioned nor unfolded in the explanation. Besides, there is reference only to *God's* institution in general, there is no consideration of the fact that *Christ as the Risen One*, that is, Christ, who had just come from his death and his grave, instituted Baptism. Is this treatment in the Confessions adequate? May the Confessions ignore the formula *eis to onoma* by means of which the baptized person becomes the property of him in whose name he was baptized? It is true, the formulas *en* and *epi tō onomati* and *eis to onoma* have this in common that a person is placed under another; yet the formula *eis to onoma* adds something essential to *en tō onomati* in Baptism. Furthermore, may the Lutheran doctrine of Baptism ignore the formula *eis to onoma tou kuriou Iēsou*, through which the baptized person is assigned to the crucified and risen Lord and inserted into the event of the dying and rising of Jesus? Is not this christological aspect present also in the trinitarian formula? Must we not here speak of God christologically, in witness to the triune God who is manifest and active in the crucified and risen Christ? Must not the doctrine of Baptism voice the one name of Father, Son, and Holy Spirit in its threefold unfolding? [2]

CHAPTER 7: *Body and soul in the doctrine of the two offices.* Is it correct to define the function of the two offices in such a way that the civil office is charged with the protection of the *"body"* (the care for the "outward and temporal . . . mode of existence and righteousness"), and the spiritual office with the protection of the *"soul"* (the care for the "inward and eternal mode of existence and righteousness of the heart," A.C. XXVIII, 11; XVI, 4)? Does not this formulation create for the church and her obedience of faith the danger of an escape into an otherworldliness of mere inwardness? The injunction of the spiritual office is addressed not only to the soul but to the whole man, including his body: "Present your *members* to God as instruments of righteousness" (Rom. 6:13). And the apostle exhorts, "Present your *bodies* a living sacrifice, holy, acceptable to God, which is your reasonable service" (Rom. 12:1). Indeed the promise of the Gospel too embraces the whole man, including his body. On the other hand, is it true that the protection and authority of the civil office is limited to the body of its subjects? Is not more implied in the fact that fear and honor are due the government "for conscience sake"? (Rom. 13:7, 5). Beyond this, we should ask the Confessions, especially the Apology and the Formula of Concord, whether their statements about soul and body are influenced more strongly by the biblical or the Greek humanistic anthropology.

CHAPTER 8: *Yada* (Jer. 1:5), *proginōskein, prognōsis, proorizein, protithesthai, prothesis, pronoein, pronoia, prooran, eklegesthai, eklogē:* Does the biblical use of these terms allow the separation of *praedestinatio*

[2] Cf. G. Bornkamm's exegesis of the baptismal command with special reference to the baptism of Jesus: "The Father reveals himself as Father in the sending of the Spirit and the Messianic proclamation of the Son; the Son reveals himself as Son in that he is the one designated by the Father through the sending of the Spirit, the one crucified and exalted to be Lord of heaven and earth; and the Spirit reveals himself as Spirit in that he is the mediator of the theophany who descends upon Jesus and makes him the Son of God." "Die neutestamentliche Lehre von der Taufe," *Theol. Blaetter* (1938), p. 47.

APPENDIX

(*electio*) and *praescientia* (*praevisio*) in the sense of F.C. XI? Does the Scripture anywhere present divine knowledge separate from divine action?

Regarding *biblical texts and concepts that are missing in the Confessions, or receive very little attention,* we should like to ask:

CHAPTER 2: *The New Testament statements concerning the revelation of God in his works.* Rom. 1:19 ff. is quoted only in support of the assertion that man has only "a faint spark" of the knowledge of God. Nothing is said about the basis for this spark, namely, the statement concerning the revelation of the invisible nature of God in his works. Rom. 2:14 ff. and Acts 14:15 ff. are not cited at all, and Acts 17 is introduced only to show that the human nature is God's creature even after the fall (Acts 17:25, 28) and that God commands all men to repent (Acts 17:30). Is it permissible to pass over the New Testament declaration concerning the self-witness of God in his work of creation, or is this arbitrariness? What is legitimately "permissible"? Is the absence of a particular chapter on God's revelation in his works alongside a chapter on God's revelation in his Word a denial of the former? Is it not rather a necessary recognition of the well-attested fact that the witness of God in his works does, in fact, *not* lead one who fails to hear the Word to a true knowledge of the God who is manifest in his works? And that for this reason the God who is revealed in his works has himself *proclaimed* by Paul and is known in truth only through the Word? And that he who has come to a knowledge of God through the *Word* receives through the witness of God in his works no knowledge beyond that given in God's revelation in his Word?

CHAPTER 3/4: Have the Confessions taken seriously *the statements of the Psalms and of the Synoptic Jesus concerning the righteous man,* or have they passed it by? Does the distinction between *justitia civilis* and imputed righteousness, that is, work-righteousness and faith-righteousness, suffice for the understanding of these statements?

En Christō, en Christō Iēsou, en kuriō: These frequent formulas of Pauline theology receive remarkably little consideration in the Confessions. On the contrary, the phrase *"propter Christum"* plays a big role, though it has a very slender basis in Paul's writings. Can *propter Christum* convey the content of *en Christō* or is *propter Christum,* as contrasted with *en Christō,* restricted to a foundational context, indeed to the designation of Christ's death as the foundational event of the past? Or do the Confessions perhaps include *en Christō* at another place, such as the doctrine of the sacraments, by the admonition to make daily use of the sacraments, specifically: in the daily *event* of entering into our Baptism and of our receptive hastening to the Lord's Supper? Or, if not in the doctrine of Baptism, then at any rate in the doctrine of the Lord's Supper? Are the essential aspects of the Pauline formulas incorporated in the doctrine of Christ's body and blood in the Lord's Supper as the body and blood of the crucified and risen, as the body and blood given on the cross and proffered today from heaven; and does faith in the living presence in the Lord's Supper of the Christ who once died on the

305

cross do full justice to the Pauline formulas? Or do these formulas find neither explicit nor implicit expression in the Confessions? Is the Lutheran attitude against the false, mystical categories of scholastic theology sufficient warrant for avoiding the Pauline formulas?

CHAPTER 5: *Col. 2:11 ff. and 3:1 ff.* The first reference is used by the Apology in connection with justification and repentance, but both texts are missing in the doctrine of Baptism. Is the *content* of these important passages included in the Lutheran doctrine of Baptism, which should be in essence the sum of *all* biblical statements about Baptism even though they are not all quoted; or do these texts correct the Lutheran view? Here too we should ask whether the aspect of becoming contemporary with Christ's burial and resurrection (*"suntaphentes auto* . . . , *en hō kai sunegerthete"*) is really given due consideration. Is there sufficient clear testimony to the *baptismal act* as a dying of the baptized, and to the *fact* of the death of the baptized; as well as to the event of resurrection in the *administration* of Baptism, to the *fact* of the baptized person's having risen? (here Colossians goes beyond Rom. 6). Do the Lutheran statements concerning *vivificatio* and *vita aeterna* make sufficiently clear that we are here concerned with the eschatological event of the resurrection of the dead, toward which the baptized—the one buried in Christ's death—is proceeding in that he is coming from it?

Matt. 26:29; Mark 14:25; Luke 22:15-18. The Confessions nowhere quote the eschatological words which Jesus spoke at the institution of the Holy Supper, not even in the harmonizing reproduction of the four New Testament reports in the Small and Large Catechisms. The quotations of I Cor. 11:26 too stop short of *achri hou elthē.* What is the reason for this silence? Are these eschatological words only formally absent, or is their content too (the tentativeness of the celebration, the reference to the future messianic meal in the kingdom of God) overlooked? Must these eschatological words apply a correction to the Lutheran doctrine?

CHAPTER 7: *The Passion story.* What the Confessions say about government is supported mainly by references to the epistles and a few words of Jesus (see, e.g., B. of C., p. 355). But in a peculiar way there is no reference to the Passion story in this connection, even though at the trial of Jesus we have the most elementary contact between the ministry of the Word—in the person of the incarnate Word himself—and the civil government in its three different forms, the council, Pilate, and Herod. Not the *events* of the trial and execution, but only the words of the prisoner are quoted in this connection, "My kingdom is not of this world" (John 18:36), without even safeguarding this statement against a false otherworldly conception. In the Passion story Jesus acknowledges the government (not only the Jewish, but also the foreign, hostile power). Jesus obeys the government in his answers during the trial; he forgoes further answers and self-defense at certain moments of the interrogation; he refuses to make use of any external force at his disposal (Peter's sword, the legions of angels). The government does not deal with him without revealing in its own words Christ's innocence and therewith the injustice of its own judicial proceeding. Finally, there is the paradoxical state of affairs that God himself gives up his Son to the cross, while the government unjustly crucifies him. Now, what conclusions may be drawn from this account for the doctrine of government? Do these facts supplement the epistolary references to government and correct the statements of the Confessions? Does Jesus in the Passion story prove himself to be the Lord of government in such a way that the doctrine of government is pushed from the sphere of the first article to that of the second?

Matt. 28:19: Reference is made to this command of the Risen One in the doctrine of Baptism, but only incidentally in the doctrine of the ministry. It must be noted that this command is issued in the moment in which Jesus experiences the fulfillment of being exalted as Lord of all lords, powers, and dominions. This command which sends the message to "all nations" gives the preaching office the permanent structure of an ever-progressing missionary assault which is constantly on the move toward those who are still far off. Does the Lutheran concept of the ministry express this aspect clearly enough?

1 Cor. 12:28 and Eph. 4:11: These expressions concerning the variety of offices in the church are either not cited in the Confessions or are only partially used, without being interpreted. From Eph. 4 only this is drawn, that Paul lists *"pastores et doctores"* among the gifts given to the church (Tr. 67). These shepherds and teachers, though distinguished in Eph. 4:11, are fused into one in the Lutheran view, which regards the ministry as a continuation of the New Testament offices of *presbuteroi* and *episkopoi* (e.g., Tr. 61 ff.), while it sees its origin in the apostolate. Do the Confessions have a biblical basis for teaching only one ecclesiastical office and concentrating in it the multiplicity of the New Testament offices? In addition to the apostolate, were also the offices of prophet and evangelist confined to the founding of the church and therefore transitory, and may the office of deacon be relegated to the status of an office that served only transitory, temporary needs?

Rom. 12:6 ff. and 1 Cor. 12:4 ff.: These most important passages concerning the *charismata* (as also I Cor. 14:26 ff.) receive no consideration in the Confessions. The Confessions do not enlarge upon the variety of the spiritual gifts. Repeatedly they emphasize enlightenment, repentance, regeneration, new life, and new obedience as the one work of the Spirit. All this the Holy Spirit does by means of Word and sacrament in *every* Christian, whereas, according to the New Testament, beyond this the one receives the gift of prophecy, another the gift of healing, etc., for the benefit of the entire congregation. May this New Testament witness concerning the variety of spiritual gifts be ignored? Here it must be observed that the variety of offices is not isolated from the variety of spiritual gifts, but is produced by the Holy Spirit. Essentially, "services" and "gifts of grace" are parallel expressions (though not every charism refers to a specific office). Office and charism are connected also in the sense that in the New Testament the charism is named both as presupposition for, and as

307

effect of, the investiture into office. This leads to the question: Is the doctrine of the *one* church office of preaching the Word and administering the sacraments perhaps a human arrangement which overlooks the wealth of spiritual gifts? Or, was the wealth of spiritual gifts intended only for the time of the founding of the church?

CHAPTER 8: Does the doctrine of predestination in the Formula of Concord allow room for *the predestinarian statements of John's Gospel*, which are either ignored (e.g., John 6:64 f.; cf. 6:44; 8:43-47; 12:37-41; 17:2, 6, 9, 11, 12, 24) or used only incompletely (10:26-29)? "Room" in what sense? Would it suffice to say, "These statements do not contradict what is said in the Confessions"? Or, going beyond that, would we have to say, "These statements are attested in the Confession, not by means of direct quotations but in substance"?

Concepts which may appear in the Confessions, but *not in the Bible, or at least not in the same connection*, would have to be investigated as to the extent to which they reproduce biblical truths.

CHAPTER 2: *"Substantia" and "accidens" in Formula of Concord, I:* Only in the debate against divergent teachings that employ them do these two terms here receive a certain significance for the doctrine of creation and sin. Here the Aristotelian significance of both terms is decisively broken through (see p. 46, n. 7). Yet the question remains as to the suitability of these terms, even as theologically transmuted in the Confessions, for a comprehension of the truths they were meant to convey. One could begin by pointing out the difference between the New Testament concepts of *ktisis* (*ktisma*) and *kosmos*. *Ktisis* is creation as the result of God's creative act; *kosmos* (according to the predominant usage of Paul and John) represents the world as the creation which is corrupted by sin, inimical to God, and doomed to judgment. The believers are *ktisis*, yes, *"kainē ktisis"* (II Cor. 5:17; Gal. 6:15). But they are not of the world. Placed in opposition are: To be of the world and to be of God (I John 4, 5), "the spirit of the world" and "the spirit which is from God" (I Cor. 2:12). As *"kainē ktisis,"* the believers are the first fruits of the new creation, the beginning of the eschatological event in which "the first heaven and the first earth" will pass away and "a new heaven and a new earth" will come into being (Rev. 21:1). These, together with the believers, may also be designated as *kainē ktisis*. There is, however, no teaching of a *kainos kosmos*. The redeemed creation is no longer *kosmos*, and is not so called in the New Testament. *Kosmos* is then left behind as the essence of the sinful, moribund world. Now we might ask whether these terms, *ktisis* and *kosmos*, in their divergence signify the same thing as the distinction of substance and accident in the Confessions. Is this what the Confessions mean to say when they speak of the coming separation between creatureliness and corruption? In that case, substance would correspond to *ktisis*, and substance and accident together would correspond to *kosmos*. But does not *kosmos* in a higher degree signify the *final* mortal decline of the ungodly world, and is not *kainē ktisis* something quite different from *kosmos* minus sin?

CHAPTER 3/4: M. Kähler has raised the decisive biblical-theological objection against the concepts *"satisfactio" and "meritum" in the doctrine of the atonement.* Can they serve as summary of the biblical statements in spite of their divergences from Scripture in both wording and content? (See p. 83, n. 9).

To "cut," "separate," "distinguish" the Word of God; law and Gospel as the two "parts" of the Word of God. These frequent terms in the Confessions presuppose the unity of the Word of God and the one atoning event of Christ's death on the cross. In the last analysis these terms are intended only to bear witness to this event and its double significance of judgment and grace. And the "distinguishing," "cutting," and "separating" is designated not as a deed of men, but as the deed of God, namely, as the work of the Holy Spirit in repentance and faith. For the distinction takes place in receiving the benefits of Christ in repentance through faith. One could ask whether and to what extent at another place and from another point of view the Pauline expressions concerning the revelation of the *dikaiosunē theou* are given their due—expressions which elsewhere in the Confessions experience a singular shift, if not even an abridgment (see p. 299 f.). Does the real theme of the Confessions, the distinction between law and Gospel—that is, in the last analysis, the distinction between law and Gospel in the act of the cross—does this really bear witness to the *dikaiosunē theou* which is operative in all divine utterances, which judges and saves, in that God is righteous and makes righteous? Does the distinction between law and Gospel acknowledge the righteousness of God who saves us through Christ's atoning death?

The quantitative concepts in the doctrine of regeneration and the new obedience. Do the New Testament statements permit making these judgments regarding the Christian with so much emphasis? Does the New Testament permit designating the regeneration of the believers until the Last Day as imperfect and only partial? As for the New Testament words about growth in grace and knowledge, growth in faith, about God letting the plant of righteousness grow, about the minors and the perfect, about milk and solid food—do not these expressions stand more in the service of the forward-pressing admonition and of that hope which is hastening toward the end, rather than merely indicating an interest in declarative judgments concerning the status of the more or less pious man? Are such judgments already a shift of focus for faith which should be directed exclusively to God and his crucified, risen, and returning Christ in whom our life is hidden? Does, then, the Lutheran doctrine of repentance give the law a significance which it does not have in the apostolic statements about the Christian and his sin? As a result, is there not perhaps also a weakening of the witness to the unity of that gracious act which God performs now and at the Last Day? Despite all safeguards, is not the way opened for making justification, regeneration, and new obedience into separate matters which stand alongside one another and in succession? In this connection one should examine, e.g., the relationship of *katallassein, dikaioun, sōzein, anakainōsis,* and *hagiazein,* in the writings of Paul, and on this basis one should subject to review the material in the Confessions (especially what is said about justification and regeneration in the Formula of Concord).

CHAPTER 5: *"Signum" in the doctrine of the sacraments.* This term plays a negligible role in the Catechisms, but looms large in Melanchthon's commentary on the New Testament doctrine of Baptism and the Lord's Supper in the Augsburg Confession and the Apology. This use was obviously less influenced by the New Testament concept of "sign" than by the historic past of this term within the doctrine of the sacraments, especially since Augustine. It is to be questioned to what extent the term really serves in the exegesis of the Baptism and Lord's Supper texts. Does not the word "sign" in every case imply a separation and then the urge to establish relations in which the New Testament texts have little or no interest? There is, for example, the separation between the washing of water and regeneration, between immersion and surrender into Christ's death, between bread and wine and body and blood, between distribution of bread and wine and the gift of Christ's body and blood on the cross, between Christ's body and blood and the forgiveness of sins. The Confessions are not clear on what they mean by "sign" (see p. 186). It is, in fact, impossible to co-ordinate consistently "sign" and the "thing signified" in the Lord's Supper. What, precisely, is the sign? Is it bread and wine, or the meal, or Christ's body and blood? Is the "thing signified" Christ's body and blood, or the event of the cross, or forgiveness? Nor can a parallel co-ordination of "sign" and "thing signified" in Baptism and Lord's Supper be carried through. And even if after the distinction of "sign" and "thing signified" the two are rejoined by *"est"* ("in, with, and under,"), there remains a shift from the New Testament statements which are concerned in Baptism—certainly in the Pauline texts—entirely with the event of the death and resurrection of Christ, and in the Lord's Supper entirely with the event of Christ's giving his body and blood, of which we partake. Is the theme the co-ordination of *two* different things or processes, or is it our receptive involvement in the *one* event? To what extent was it necessary for the Confessions, on the basis of the history of dogma, to employ this "sign" concept in this connection?

CHAPTER 7: *Jus humanum.* Is not this term misleading? Is not man's freedom to order the affairs of the church the freedom of Christ who rules the church, and the governance of the Holy Spirit who does not leave the church destitute of spiritual gifts and, hence, of offices? Does the term *"jus humanum"* take seriously the revelations of the ascended and exalted Christ and the directives of the Holy Spirit, as reported by the Acts and the epistles even with respect to questions of church organization and especially of mission and service? (e.g.,

Acts 9:3 ff., 10 ff.; 22:17 ff.; 13:2 ff.; 15:28; 16:6 ff.). Is not the choice of the term *"jus humanum"* unfortunate also because it is applied only to the rights of *believers?*

In the context of such limited questions about details, and on the presupposition of their answer, we should then examine *the principal doctrines of the Confessions* with a view to determining whether they summarize and witness the statements of the *entire* Scriptures. We shall have to be content here simply to summarize a few of the questions already indicated above.

The doctrine of the law. On the basis of the Pauline distinction between *nomos* and admonition, and the Johannine distinction between *nomos* and *entolē*, we ask whether the distinction between the Old Testament law and New Testament admonitions is sufficiently safeguarded merely by distinguishing the three uses of the one eternal, immutable law? What is meant by the statement that "the office of the law remains in the church"? Does this so expand the concept of law and estrange it from the Old Testament meaning that it makes room for the New Testament admonition, or is the latter so much equated with the former as to make the idea of law possible? If the first is true, we ask whether such expansions of biblical concepts beyond their original biblical import are permissible in dogmatics, and, if so, where are the limits? Are they to be used merely as abstract dogmatic shorthand, or, if we go beyond this, may they be used as a starting point for further dogmatic conclusions and as a basis for further theological insights? The subordination of the New Testament admonition under the concept "law" is further accented by the Confessions when they teach the commands of God addressed to the church by way of an explanation of the Decalogue revealed on Mount Sinai. It is true, the Confessions appeal to Christ's explanation of the law in the Sermon on the Mount, but the epistles appeal obviously less to the Old Testament *law* which Jesus expounded in the Sermon, than to the *exposition* which Jesus gave this law in that he fulfilled it. The humiliation of Jesus is the decisive basis for the apostolic admonition. Do the Confessions make clear that the Decalogue is preached not as Mosaic law but as New Testament admonition, not in the Old Testament expectation of the coming Christ, even when it is preaching of repentance, but as proceeding from Christ's death and resurrection? Do the Confessions present the law in such a way that here the church, as the community of those who have been liberated by Christ from the curse of the law, chooses the words of the Decalogue in the *free* decision of faith for the purpose of teaching the new commandment of Christ? Here belongs also the question concerning the exegetical foundation for the distinction of moral, ceremonial, and judicial law. Does this distinction perhaps go only halfway, in spite of all assertions that the animal sacrifices have been abrogated by Christ's death? Is there, then, a dislocation in the confessional doctrine of the law over against the New Testament statements—a dislocation which affects also the remarks about the sin of the Christian and his experience of the divine wrath? May the believer, fixing his eyes on Jesus Christ, perhaps be freed even more fully from looking at himself—and hence from contemplating the old man, which is a demand and function of the law—than the Confessions imply?

The distinction of law and Gospel in the Old and New Testament. Do the Confessions sufficiently clarify the distinction between the two testaments when they say that law and Gospel must be distinguished as the two "parts" in both the Old and the New Testaments? It is to be noted in any case that in the letter to the Galatians Paul is demonstrating the distinction in the Old Testament between *epanggelia* and *nomos,* not *euaggelion* and *nomos,* and that as a servant of the New Testament he does not preach law and Gospel, but rather the Gospel, to the accompaniment of pleading, consoling, and exhorting. May dogmatic language undertake formulated expansions of biblical concepts which forsake important differentiations of biblical terms in favor of abstract gradations and abbreviations? What about the dogmatic conception of Scripture? The Old and New Testaments are not simply the two "parts" of Scripture. Rather, the Word of the Old Testament is essentially Scripture, whereas the Word of the New Testament is oral proclamation, the cry of the herald. The service of the Old Testament is that of the letter, while the service of the New Testament is that of the spirit. And even though its good news was soon put in writing—in the first instance, through letters—and was thus addressed to men, yet these writings remain for all time basically different from the Old Testament Scripture. Is there a permissible or impermissible abbreviation in the confessional formula that the entire Scriptures of Old and New Testaments teach law and Gospel? Does this formula serve the Gospel, or does it again draw the Gospel close to the letter? Are the Confessions aware of the limits of such ultimate formulated abstractions, or do such formulas assert their independence in order to set themselves up as norm over against Scripture and to judge Scripture, inasmuch as they hinder the exegetical perspective for the peculiarities of the Old and New Testament witness?

The doctrine of Baptism. On the basis of observations and questions regarding the exegesis of Rom. 6; Matt. 28:19; Col. 2:11 ff. and 3:11 ff., as well as the "sign" concept, we should ask whether the Confessions give a scriptural witness to Christ's death and resurrection as the event into which the sinner is placed through his Baptism. For in the doctrine of Baptism the forgiveness of sins, deliverance from death and devil, and the gift of life can be separated as little from the very real joint burial and resurrection with Christ as in the Lord's Supper forgiveness of sins, life, and salvation can be separated from the event of the surrender of Christ's true body and blood on the cross.

Accordingly, Scripture in its references to Baptism speaks more strongly than the Confessions of the fact of the baptized person's death and resurrection, both in the perfect tense and in the expectancy of the day of the Lord. In this way do not the imperatives of the New Testament admonition to walk in a new life become even stronger and more urgent, that is to say, more consoling and more winsome than they already are in the Lutheran doctrine? From the same starting point the further question suggests itself as to whether it is advisable to begin with the element in defining Baptism rather than with the event, the water rather than the baptizing with water, that is, a burial in Christ's death and burial, or rather, Christ's death and burial itself. Is perhaps the full comprehension of Baptism impeded by starting the discussion of the nature of Baptism with the water (even though the Catechisms speak of the water only in so far as it is connected with God's Word *in actu*)? As we try to answer these questions we must, of course, take into consideration the stand of the Confessions over against a false realization of the eschatological event on the part of the scholastic doctrine of Baptism and over against a disparagement of the external element in the part of the Enthusiasts, and the extent to which the Lutheran shift from the New Testament material may have been conditioned by these antitheses.

The doctrine of the two offices. What was said before about the doctrine of the *ministry* in connection with Matt. 28:19; Rom. 12; I Cor. 12; Eph. 4; as well as the discussion of the concept *"jus humanum"* with reference to ecclesiastical order suggest the question whether Scripture permits speaking of the civil and spiritual offices in so far-reaching a parallelism as the Confessions do. Perhaps the fact that the exalted Christ is given "all power in heaven and earth" and that he is exalted to be the "Prince of the kings of the earth" (Rev. 1:5) already shatters and surpasses the distinction of assigning the civil office to the preserving activity of God the Creator and the ministry to the redeeming lordship of Jesus Christ. The New Testament presents the living Christ as ordering and guiding his church by means of ever-new concrete directives in that his Spirit creates the concrete wealth of spiritual gifts and offices in the church and leads it through every danger into all truth. Is not this even more incomparably distinct from the civil office and its precepts, laws, and judgments, than is expressed in the far-reaching adaptation of both sets of statements in the Lutheran doctrine of the two offices? As to the *civil* office, are the New Testament remarks about government perhaps in an even stronger eschatological motion and expectation than the Confessions so that, on the one hand, they are less interested in *justitia civilis* as such and, on the other hand, give a more positive witness to the total lordship of Christ as King of all kings and kingdoms? And this precisely in the slave's obedience to an arbitrary master and the subjects' obedience to a pagan government—as rendered to the Lord Christ and not to men—and above all—in Christ's own Passion. In such a context, can there possibly remain an *independent* interest in God's work of preservation through government? Is the schematic parallelism in the Confessions' doctrine of the two offices so independent that it no longer functions as a servant in summarizing the multiplicity of Scripture statements, but rather joins itself to them as a regulating principle of dogmatic judgments, that is, as a hidden additional source of knowledge?

Can the *doctrine of predestination* in the Formula of Concord avail as the doctrine of the church, in view of its scriptural documentation and its basic theological concepts (*praedestinatio, praescientia*)? Is the criticism of the exegesis of individual texts, such as Exod. 4 ff. and Rom. 9:10 ff., sufficient ground of itself to reject this article as doctrine of the church? Beyond this, F.C. XI gives rise to the basic question as to whether it is proper in a Confession to elevate a very special pastoral assurance to the position of an article of that doctrine which must in essence be the type and model of *all* proclamation?

Finally the question should be asked whether Scripture itself places the sinner's justification, or the distinction between law and Gospel, into the *center* and regards it as the *summary* of its witness. Is the church justified in thus giving preference to the Pauline concepts as the Lutheran Confessions are actually doing?

What may we expect from undertaking this kind of conversation between Confession and Scripture? In the first place we are compelled to ask the basic question, "What does 'scriptural' mean?" Does this mean that there are Scripture passages which teach the respective assertion of dogmatics? Or that there are no Scripture texts that contradict this dogmatic expression? Obviously the understanding of dogma as summary of Scripture is to be found between these two extremes—but where and in what respect is it different from them? Scripture proof consists neither in the isolating emphasis of certain *loci classici*, as became customary in orthodox dogmatics to the neglect of the contexts and the historical connection of the texts quoted, nor in the uncommitted, general reference to the whole of Scripture, as is promised in many a neo-Protestant dogmatics to the exclusion of explaining individual texts. But which point of view determines the selection of the texts? Which passages reveal the sum of Scripture? The discussion of this question is already made difficult by the fact that with respect to the methodological principles of biblical exegesis there is no adequate clarity in the area of New Testament studies, and no agreement or clarity at all in the area of Old Testament studies. But even if there were, dogmatics has a task that transcends the construction of an Old or New Testament theology. We must ask further which biblical statements are to be preferred in summarizing their fulness, and which extrabiblical concepts should be included for the purpose of attesting the fulness of the biblical witness. To what extent may biblical concepts be expanded beyond their original meaning, and logical deductions from biblical statements be employed for broadening and rounding out dogmatic perception? The answer to each of these questions is already a dogmatic decision which can result only from completing the process of forming dogmatic judgments. Therefore this matter properly belongs in dogmatics. Here we merely wish to call attention to the truth that the church's dogmatics is never an end in itself but only serves the church's proclamation. Confession presupposes preaching and, again, leads to preaching. Just so, dogmatics proceeds from the church's proclamation and leads back to it. The scripturalness of dogmatic sentences can ultimately not be demonstrated in theory at all, but only in the event of the church's proclamation which hastens from text to text and thus interprets Scripture.

What will be the result of such conversations between Confession and Scripture as are carried through to clarity in awareness of the problems surrounding dogmatic Scripture proof? In every case, perceptions gained from the history of dogma will become dogmatic insights, and out of assertions about an existing doctrine will grow the event of doctrine. This will, of course, be true only when these conversations are carried on in recognition of the Holy Scriptures as the sole norm, that is to say, when at the start the result of these conversations is in no way anticipated but is left open in principle and is awaited as *result* of the conversation. Such a conversation between Scripture and Confession will be fruitful for dogmatics only when, from the start, three possible results are kept in view:

a) The biblical-exegetical review will result in establishing the scripturalness of the confessional statements in question. In this case, the conversation between Confession and Scripture does not simply produce some kind of dogmatic insight, rather, the confessional statement has itself become a dogmatic insight and has demonstrated its dogmatic correctness also to me. The confessional statement has become my confession. This would happen, for example, if the doctrine of justification in the Confessions should prove itself for me to be biblical in spite of A. Schlatter's noteworthy objections, or the doctrine of the Lord's Supper in the Confessions should show itself to be for me the right explanation of the New Testament words of institution in spite of the dissenting judgments of almost all newer exegetes.

b) We discover that the examined statements of the Confessions, while not wrong, are nevertheless not the complete exposition of Scripture; or, though possible, are not compelling; or that they are based on individual texts, but not on all of them together; or that the Confessions interpret texts out of context and subordinate them to points of view that are foreign to the text, say, by abbreviating the content in the interest of a one-sided polemic. Such discoveries too are extremely important for the function of dogmatic judgments and may prove to be profitable. They need not lead at once to a rejection of the confessional statements concerned. They do help us, however, in such statements to see a particular, more or less supported and interesting exegesis of Scripture rather than the clear expressions of Scripture itself. This would indeed mean that such statements may not without further ado provide sufficient grounds for separation among churches, that is, for refusing church fellowship to those who do not accept such propositions. The unity of the church is determined by the unity of the Gospel as witnessed in the clear statements of Scripture. The church is not a society for the preservation of confessional idiosyncrasies for the sake of these peculiarities themselves.

c) The possibility must also be frankly acknowledged, however, that a biblical-exegetical review may lead to the conclusion that certain, perhaps even decisive, declarations of the confessions are contrary to Scripture. Dogmatics owes the church a public accounting concerning such judgments. A member of the church has the duty to state such judgments and submit them to the arbitration of the church, even though he does so in the modesty of a pupil of the Confession and in awareness of the fact that he is a son of the confessing church, his mother. The dogmatic judgments of the individual must be inserted and absorbed into the ongoing theological conversation of the church, and must be taken up, processed exegetically, and answered particularly by those members of the church who have been called into the office of the church. No individual is empowered to repeal confessional statements. This the church alone may do in the consensus of faith. Nor may an individual elevate new formulations to the status of a confession, for this too is the prerogative of the church. The individual will not even act wisely if he tries to decide for himself whether his theological knowledge separates him only from individual propositions or from the Confession as a whole. Only the consensus of faith can determine the boundary at which the variety of witnesses and theological trends within the same church ends and the "outside" of the church begins. But where the consensus in the church really exists as the ever-new event of the Holy Spirit who creates the unity of the church, there in the course of fraternal conversation the exegetical insights of the one result in the enrichment and correction of the insights of the other, and the replies of others again redound to the correction and enrichment of the perception of the individual. In the course of such fraternal exchange under the Scriptures as the norm, and in the process of restatement by means of this exchange, the dogmatic insight of the individual becomes the doctrine of the church.

But whatever may result for the individual from the conversation between Confession and Scripture, this conversation continues throughout life, and its results at any point furnish the start for a continuance of this conversation. The Scripture must be heard ever anew. Ever again we must surrender our dogmatic insights to the Scriptures, because we never stop placing ourselves under the Word of Scripture as people who have been instructed by the church. Whether the results of such conversations are now affirmative, now limiting, now negative, in every case they are for dogmatic endeavor *stages* along the way of life.

In the midst of present-day confusion in the church's doctrine and practice many a person may discover that he will hungrily and avidly take the Confessions to himself and be filled with the superabundant comfort which they offer the afflicted conscience, and with the clear wealth they afford to theological thought. But then he will in growing measure become aware of a poverty in the Confessions over against the riches of Scripture. He will discover that the Confessions seem to have overlooked or abridged certain important truths of Scripture and that they seem to provide no answer to urgent concrete questions of the hour. Penetrating farther into the Confessions, he will recognize the boundary which dogma has by its very nature. Dogma is not proclamation but is in the service of proclamation. It does not substitute for the riches of Scripture but only guards the knowledge of these riches from perversion. And now even gaps, contradictions, and shifts in the Confessions over against the Scriptures begin to speak. There is such a thing as an omission of Scripture passages which is at the same time a confession of them, and a contraction of biblical concepts which at the same time attests their full measure. All statements of the Confessions are directed against the fact of a usurpation of certain biblical concepts and expressions by concrete heresy. The exegesis of the Lutheran Confessions is to a certain extent concentrated in the Lutheran position against the doctrine of grace as taught by the Roman church of the late Middle Ages. The correction of the opponents' false interpretations had to be undertaken in connection with certain specific texts, and especially in the exegesis of those Scripture statements which the opponents had distorted or omitted. In the process of witnessing to that which Scripture says here in *opposition* to false doctrine, the correct understanding of Scripture *in general* had to be determined. Thus the further study of the Confessions leads again to a fuller confidence in their model. The knowledge that the Confessions bore witness to the summary of Scripture in the face of a specific heresy of their time leads to the recognition of what the church of the present must affirm in the interpretation of Scripture in the face of the new heresies of today.

INTRODUCTION TO THE LITERATURE

None of the bibliographies here offered* aims at completeness. Principally those writings are mentioned which either represent an important contribution, significant for research in the history of theology, or which point the reader to other sources not mentioned here. At the same time, the listing of the chief older works serves the purpose of calling attention to the extremely interesting history of the interpretation of the Confessions. Unfortunately, this history is beyond the scope of this book.

* Three bibliographies are here provided in this English edition: (1) the general bibliography which Schlink originally appended to his book, listing only such works as treat either the whole Book of Concord or one of the Confessions as a whole; (2) a selection of the special bibliographies which Schlink originally introduced as footnotes in connection with the particular chapters or specific topics to which they have reference; (3) a list of relevant works in English to supplement the Schlink bibliographies, which are largely confined to European sources. Schlink's bibliographies are cited here in form exactly as he gave them; no attempt has been made to supply such detailed facts of publication as are customary in American bibliographies.—H.J.A.B.

I GENERAL BIBLIOGRAPHY

THE BOOK OF CONCORD AS A WHOLE

Hutterus, Leonhard. *Libri Christianae Concordiae: Symboli ecclesiarum* GNESIOS *Lutheranarum.* Wittenberg, 1609.

Rechtenbach, Leonhard. "Encyclopaedia symbolica vel analysis Confessionis August.," *Artic. Schm* . . . . Leipzig, 1612.

Carpzov, Jo. Benedict. *Isagoge in libros ecclesiarum Lutheranarum symbolicos.* Leipzig, 1665 *et seq.*

Walch, Joh. Georg. *Introductio in libros ecclesiae Lutheranae symbolicos, observationibus historicis et theologicis illustrata.* Jena, 1732.

———. *Bibliotheca theologica selecta litterariis annotationibus instructa.* Jena, 1757-65.

Feuerlin, Jac. Guil. *Bibliotheca symbolica evangelica Lutherana, Goettingen, 1752; aucta et locupleta,* ed. J. B. Riederer. Nuernberg, 1768, esp. I, 17 ff.

Walch, Christian W. F. *Breviarium theologiae symbolicae ecclesiae Lutheranae.* Goettingen, 1781.

Baumgarten, Sieg. Jac. *Erleuterungen der im chr. Concordienbuch enthaltenen symb. Schriften der ev. luth. Kirche nebst einem Anhange von den uebr. Bekenntnissen und feierlichen Lehrbuechern in gedachter Kirche.* Halle, 1747.

Semmler, Joh. Salomo. *Apparatus ad libros symbolicos ecclesiae Lutheranae.* Halle, 1775.

Planck, Gottlieb Jacob. *Abriss einer historischen und vergleichenden Darstellung der dogmatischen Systeme unserer verschiedenen christlichen Hauptpartheien nach ihren Grundbegriffen . . . .* Goettingen, 1797 et seq.

Marheinecke, Phil. Kon. *Institutiones theologiae symbolicae.* Berlin, 1814.

Winer, G. B. *Comparative Darstellung des Lehrbegriffs der verschiedenen christl. Kirchenparteien.* Berlin, 1824; 4. Aufl., hrsg. P. Ewald, 1882.

Koellner, Eduard. *Symbolik der lutherischen Kirche, I. Teil* ("Symbolik aller christlichen Konfessionen.") Hamburg, 1837.

v. Scheele, K. H. G. *Theologische Symbolik, II. Teil.* Gotha, 1881.

Plitt, Gustav. *Grundriss der Symbolik.* Leipzig, 1875; 5. Aufl. hrg. Victor Schultze, 1911.

Schmidt, H. *Handbuch der Symbolik.* (2nd ed.). Berlin, 1895.

Mueller, E. F. Karl. *Symbolik.* Erlangen-Leipzig, 1896.

Tschackert, Paul. *Die Entstehung der lutherischen und der reformierten Kirchenlehre samt ihren innerprotestantischen Gegensaetzen.* Göttingen, 1910.

Wernle, Paul. *Luther, I* ("Der evangelische Glauben nach den Hauptschriften der Reformatoren.") Tuebingen, 1918.

Elert, Werner. *Morphologie des Luthertums,* I, Muenchen, 1931; II, 1932.

Cf. also the introductions and notes in the editions of the Book of Concord by Rechenberg, Adam., Leipzig, 1678 *et seq.;* Walch, Joh. Georg., Jena, 1750; Hase, Carl August., Leipzig, 1827.

Also, cf. especially, Kolde, Theodor. zur 10 Aufl. der Ausgabe von Joh. Tobias Mueller, Guetersloh, 1907, auch separat., (3rd ed.), Guetersloh, 1913; Lietzmann, Hans. Heinrich Bornkamm, Hans Volz, and Ernst Wolf, in *der Ausgabe des deutschen Evangelischen Kirchenausschusses,* Goettingen, 1930 (hereinafter referred to as *Bekenntnisschriften*).

The Three Ancient Creeds

The older literature is listed in Feuerlin, I, 29 ff.; and Koellner, pp. 1, 6 f., 28 f., 53 f.

Hahn, August. *Bibliothek der Symbole und Glaubensregeln der alten Kirche,* 3. Aufl. Ludwig Hahn mit Anhang von Adolf Harnack. Breslau, 1897.

Kattenbusch, Ferd. *Luthers Stellung zu den oekumenischen Symbolen.* Giessen, 1883.

———. *Das apostolische Symbol,* I, Leipzig, 1894; II, 1900.

Harnack, Adolf. *Das apostolische Glaubensbekenntnis.* Berlin, 1892.

Zahn, Theodor. *Das apostolische Symbolum.* Erlangen-Leipzig, 1893.

Kunze, Johannes. *Glaubensregel, Heilige Schrift und Taufbekenntnis.* Leipzig, 1899.

Loofs, Friedrich. *Symbolik*. Tuebingen-Leipzig, 1902, pp. 1-65.

Seeberg, Alfred. *Der Katechismus der Urchristenheit*. Leipzig, 1903.

Feine, Paul. *Die Gestalt des Apostolischen Glaubensbekenntnisses in der Zeit des Neuen Testamentes*. Leipzig, 1925.

Lietzmann, Hans. "Symbolstudien I-XIV," *Zeitschrift fuer neutestamentliche Wissenschaft* (1922, 1923, 1925, 1927).

For further literature see Loofs and *Bekenntnisschriften*, pp. XIV f.

Augsburg Confession and Apology

Schmidt, W. F. and K. Schornbaum, (eds.). *Die fraenkischen Bekenntnisse, eine Vorstufe der Augsburgischen Konfession*. Muenchen, 1930.

Foerstemann, K. E. *Urkundenbuch zu der Geschichte des Reichstages in Augsburg im Jahre 1530*. Halle, 1833, 35.

Schirrmacher, F. W. *Briefe und Akten zu der Geschichte des Religionsgespraeches zu Marburg, 1529 und des Reichstages zu Augsburg, 1530*. Gotha, 1876.

Ficker, Johannes (ed.). *Die Konfutation des Augsburgischen Bekenntnisses in ihrer ersten Gestalt*. Leipzig, 1891.

Chytraeus, David. *Historia der Augsb. Conf*. Rostock, 1576 et seq.

Coelestin, G. *Historia Comitiorum A. MDXXX Augustae celebratorum*. Frankfurt a.O., 1577 ff. et seq.

Mylius, Georg. *Augustanae Confessionis explicatio*. Jena, 1596.

Hutterus, Leonhard. *Augustanae Confessionis Analysis Methodica*. Wittenberg, 1602.

Hunnius, Aegidius. *Theses de Augustana Confessione, Ecclesiarum Evangelicarum Symbolo Augustissimo*. Rostock, 1622.

Huelsemann, Johannes. *Manuale Confessionis Augustanae*. Wittenberg, 1624 et seq.

Mentzer, Balthasar. *Exegesis Augustanae Confessionis*. Giessen, 1613 et seq.

Calovius, Abraham. *Criticus sacer vel Commentarius apodicticoelenchticus super Augustanam Confessionem*. Leipzig, 1646.

Crocius, Johannes. *Commentarius de Augustanae Confessionis societate*. Kassel, 1647.

Alting, Henricus. *Exegesis Logica et Theologica Augustanae Confessionis*. Amsterdam, 1647.

Mueller, J. J. *Historia von der evangelischen Staende Protestation*. Jena, 1705.

Salig, Christian Aug. *Historia der Augsb. Konfession und ders. Apologie*. Halle, 1733-35.

Cyprian, E. S. *Historia der Augsb. Conf*. Gotha, 1730.

Reinbeck, Johann Gust. *Betrachtungen ueber die in der Augspurgischen Confession enthaltene und damit verknuepfte goettliche Wahrheiten, welche theils aus vernuenftigen Gruenden, allesamt aber aus Heiliger Goettlicher Schrift hergeleitet und zur Uebung der wahren Gottseeligkeit angewendet werden*. Berlin-Leipzig, 1733, continued by J. G. Cranz, 1745 f.

Buesching, Anton Friedrich. *Allgemeine Anmerkungen ueber die symbolischen Schriften der ev.-luth. Kirche und bes. Erlaeuterungen der Augsburgischen Confession.* Hamburg, 1770.

Bertram, J. C. "Von der Apologie der Augsburgischen Konfession und ihren verschiedenen Abfassungen," *literar. Abhandlungen*, III, IV (Halle, 1782-83).

Weberus, Michael. *Confessio Augustana.* Wittenberg, 1807.

Rudelbach, A. G. *Historisch-kritische Einleitung in die Augsburgische Confession.* Dresden, 1841.

Knaake, J. K. F. *Luthers Anteil an der Augsburgischen Konfession.* Berlin, 1863.

Kalinich, R. *Luther und die Augsburgische Konfession.* Leipzig, 1861.

Plitt, Gustav. *Einleitung in die Augustana.* Erlangen, I, 1867; II, 1868.

————. *Die Apologie der Augustana geschichtlich erklaert.* Erlangen, 1873.

Zoeckler, O. *Die Augsburgische Konfession als symbolische Lehrgrundlage der deutschen Reformationskirche.* Frankfurt, 1870.

Vilmar, August F. C. *Die Augsburgische Confession,* hrg. Piderit. Guetersloh, 1870.

Brieger, Th. *Die Torgauer Artikel.* Leipzig, 1890.

Kolde, Theodor. *Die aelteste Redaktion der Augsburger Konfession mit Melanchthons Einleitung zum erstenmal herausgegeben und geschichtlich gewuerdigt.* Guetersloh, 1906.

————. "Neue Augustanastudien," *Neue kirchliche Zeitschrift* (1906), pp. 729 ff.

————. *Die Augsburgische Konfession lateinisch und deutsch, kurz erlaeutert* (2nd ed.). Gotha, 1911.

Gussmann, W. *Quellen und Forschungen zur Geschichte des Augsburgischen Glaubensbekenntnisses,* I, vols. 1-2. Leipzig, 1911.

Wendt, Hans Hinrich. *Die Augsburgische Konfession im deutschen und lateinischen Text mit Erklaerung des Inhalts und Beifuegung der Hauptquellen.* Halle, 1927.

v. Schubert, Hans. *Bekenntnisbildung und Religionspolitik, 1529-1530.* Gotha, 1910.

————. "Der Reichstag zu Augsburg im Zusammenhang der Reformationsgeschichte," *Schriften des Vereins fuer Reformationsgeschichte* (Leipzig, 1930), No. 150.

Thieme, Karl. *Die Augsburgische Konfession und Luthers Katechismen auf theologische Gegenwartswerte untersucht.* Giessen, 1930.

Hermann, Rudolf. "Zur theologischen Wuerdigung der Augustana," *Luther-Jahrbuch.* Muenchen, 1930, pp. 162 ff.

Nagel, William Ernst. *Luthers Anteil an der Confessio Augustana, Beitraege zur Foerderung christlicher Theologie.* Guetersloh, 1930.

For further references see Feuerlin, I, 37 ff., 124 ff.; Koellner, pp. 150 ff., 397 f.; Vilmar, pp. 22 ff.; Kolde, *Histor. Einl.*, pp. III, XXXIII; *Bekenntnisschriften,* pp. XXI, XXIII.

SMALCALD ARTICLES AND THE TREATISE ON THE POWER AND PRIMACY OF THE POPE

Luther, Martin. *Weimar Ed.*, 50, 160 ff.

Volz, Hans (ed.). *Corpus Catholicorum 18: Drei Schriften gegen Luthers Schmalkaldische Artikel von Cochlaeus, Witzel und Hoffmeister.* Muenster, 1932.

Bertram, J. Chr. *Geschichte des symbolischen Anhangs der Schmalkald. Artikel,* hrg. Riederer. Altdorf, 1770.

Plitt, G. *De autoritate articulorum Smalcaldicorum.* Erlangen, 1862.

Thieme, Karl. *Luthers Testament wider Rom.* Leipzig, 1900.

Volz, Hans. "Luthers Schmalkaldische Artikel und Melanchthons Tractatus de potestate papae," *Theol. Studien und Krit.* (1931), pp. 1 ff.

Merz, Georg. *Schmalkaldische Artikel, herausgegeben und erlaeutert.* Muenchen, 1937, pp. 36 ff.

For further references see Feuerlin, I, 153 ff.; Koellner, p. 439; *Realenzyklopaedie fuer prot. Theol. und Kirche* (3rd ed.), XVII, 640 (hereinafter referred to as *RE³*).

LUTHER'S CATECHISMS

Luther, Martin. *Weimar Ed.*, 30¹, 123 ff. hrg. mit wichtigen Einleitungen von O. Albrecht, u.A.

———. "Katechismuspredigten," *ibid.*, pp. 1 ff.

Dieterici, Conradi. *Institutiones catecheticae depromptae e B. Lutheri catechesi et variis notis illustratae annexis quatuor symbolis oecumenicis et Augustana confessione.* Ulm, 1613 *et seq.*

Spener, Philipp Jakob. *Tabulae catecheticae.* Frankfurt, 1683 *et seq.*

Augusti, J. Chr. Wilh. *Versuch einer historisch-kritischen Einleitung in die beyden Haupt-Katechismen der ev. Kirche.* Elberfeld, 1824.

Loehe, Wilhelm. *Haus-, Kirchen- und Schulbuch,* I. Guetersloh, 1845 *et seq.*

v. Zezschwitz, C. A. G. *System der christlich kirchlichen Katechetik,* II, 1., Abt. "Der Katechismus." Leipzig, 1864.

Harnack, Theodosius. *Erklaerung des Kleinen Katechismus* ("Katechetik," II.) Erlangen, 1882.

Hardeland, Th. *Der kleine Katechismus nach Luthers Schriften ausgelegt.* Goettingen, 1889.

Goepfert, E. *Woerterbuch zum kleinen Katechismus Martin Luthers.* Leipzig, 1889.

Nebe. *Der Kleine Katechismus Luthers ausgelegt aus Luthers Werken.* Stuttgart, 1891.

Kaftan, Theodor. *Auslegung des Lutherschen Katechismus.* Schleswig, 1892. (7th ed.), 1926.

Doerries, Bernhard. *Erklaerung des kleinen Katechismus,* I-III, 1891-1926.

Buchwald, Georg. *Die Entstehung der Katechismen Luthers und die Grundlage des grossen Katechismus.* Leipzig, 1894.

Fricke, Friederike. *Luthers kleiner Katechismus in seiner Einwirkung auf die katechetische Literatur des Reformationsjahrhunderts.* Goettingen, 1898.

Cohrs, Ferd. "Die evangelischen Katechismusversuche vor Luthers *Enchiridion* I-V," *Monumenta Germaniae Paedagogica*, XX ff. Berlin, 1900-07.

Ebeling, August. *Historisch-kritische Ausgabe von Luthers kleinem Katechismus* (2nd ed.). Hannover, 1901.

Albrecht, Otto. "Luthers Katechismen," *Schriften des Vereins fuer Reformationsgeschichte* (Leipzig, 1915) pp. 121-22.

Reu, Joh. Michael. *Quellen zur Geschichte des kirchlichen Unterrichts im ev. Deutschland zwischen 1530 und 1600.* 8 vols. Guetersloh, 1904-27.

————. *Dr. M. Luthers Kleiner Katechismus, Die Geschichte seiner Entstehung, seiner Verbreitung und seines Gebrauchs.* Muenchen, 1929.

Meyer, Johannes. *Historischer Kommentar zu Luthers Kleinem Katechismus.* Guetersloh, 1929.

Thieme, Karl. *Die Augsburgische Konfession.*

Bornhaeuser, Karl. *Der Ursinn des Kleinen Katechismus D. Martin Luthers.* Guetersloh, 1933.

For further references see Feuerlin, I, 160 ff.; Koellner, pp. 473 ff.; *RE³* X, 130; Kolde, *Histor. Einl.*, p. LIV; Meyer, pp. 490 ff., 530 ff.

THE FORMULA OF CONCORD

Andreae, Jacob. *Funff Predigen von dem Wercke der Concordien und endlicher Vergleichung der vorgefallenen streitigen Religionsartickeln* . . . Dresden, 1580.

————. *Theologorum et Ministrorum Ecclesiarum in ditione Jo. Casimiri Palatini Admonitio Christiana de libro Concordiae.* Neustadt, 1581.

————. *Acta und Schriften zum Concordi Buch gehoerig und noetig, darinnen zwischen den Fuerstlichen Braunschweigischen und Wuerttembergischen Theologen gestritten wird.* 1589.

————. *Apologia oder Verantwortung des christl. Concordienbuches, gestellet durch etliche hierzu verordnete Theologen im Jahr 1583.* Dresden, 1584.

Hospinian, Rud. *Concordia Discors, h.e. de origine et progressu Formulae Concordiae Bergensis liber unus.* Zuerich, 1607.

Hutterus, Leonhard. *Libri Christianae Concordiae Explicatio plana et perspicua.* Wittenberg, 1608 *et seq.*

————. *Concordia Concors, de origine et progressu Formulae Concordiae ecclesiarum Conf. Aug.* Wittenberg, 1614 *et seq.*

Musaeus, Joh. *Praelectiones in Epitomen Formulae Concordiae.* Jena, 1707.

Balthasar, J. H. *Historie des Torgauer Buches.* Greifswald, 1742.

Anton, Joh. Nic. *Geschichte der Concordienformel der ev. luth. Kirche.* Leipzig, 1779.

Thomasius, Gottfried. *Das Bekenntnis der evangelisch-lutherischen Kirche in der Konsequenz seines Prinzips.* Nuernberg, 1848.

Heppe, Heinrich. *Geschichte des deutschen Protestantismus in den Jahren 1555-1581*, I-IV. Marburg, 1852-1859.

Goeschel, K. Fr. *Die Concordien-Formel nach ihrer Geschichte, Lehre und kirchlicher Bedeutung*. Leipzig, 1858.

Frank, Fr. H. R. *Die Theologie der Concordienformel*. Erlangen, 1858-65.

    For further references see Feuerlin, I, 168 ff.; Koellner, pp. 523 ff.; Kolde, *Hist. Einl.*, pp. LXXV ff.; *RE³*, X, 732; *Bekenntnisschriften*, p. 738.

    For the total area consult also the presentations in the history of dogma, especially:

Planck, Gottlieb Jacob. *Geschichte der Entstehung, der Veraenderungen und der Bildung unseres protestantischen Lehrbegriffs vom Anfang der Reformation bis zu der Einfuehrung der Konkordienformel*. Leipzig, 1781-1800.

Thomasius, Gottfried. *Die christliche Dogmengeschichte als Entwickelungsgeschichte des kirchlichen Lehrbegriffs dargestellt*. 2 Aufl. hrg. N. Bonwetsch und R. Seeberg. Erlangen-Leipzig, 1889, Vol. II.

Loofs, Friedrich. *Leitfaden zum Studium der Dogmengeschichte* (4th ed.). Halle, 1906.

Seeberg, Reinhold. *Lehrbuch der Dogmengeschichte*, IV, 2²⋅³, Erlangen-Leipzig, 1920. Translated by Charles E. Hay. *Textbook of the History of Doctrines*. Grand Rapids: Baker Book House, 1954.

Ritschl, Otto. *Dogmengeschichte des Protestantismus*, I-IV. Leipzig, 1908, 1912; Goettingen, 1926, 1927.

Weber, H. E. *Reformation, Orthodoxie und Rationalismus*. Guetersloh, I¹, 1939; I², 1940.

II SPECIAL BIBLIOGRAPHY

CHAPTER AND TOPIC REFERENCES

CHAPTER I

1. THE DOCTRINE OF THE CONFESSIONS CONCERNING SCRIPTURE

Koellner, E. *Symbolik*. Hamburg, 1837, I, 610 ff.

Tschackert, P. *Entstehung*. Goettingen, 1910, pp. 306 ff.

Noesgen. "Die Lehre der lutherischen Symbole von der Heiligen Schrift," *Neue kirchl. Zeitschrijt* (1895), pp. 887 ff.

Elert, Werner. *Morphologie des Luthertums*. Muenchen, 1931, I, 159 ff.

Stange, C. "Das Problem der dogmatischen Autoritaet im Augsburger Bekenntnis," *Zeitschrift fuer systematische Theologie* (1933), pp. 613 ff.

Kropatscheck, Fr. *Das Schriftprinzip der lutherischen Kirche*. Leipzig, 1904.

2. LUTHER'S DOCTRINE CONCERNING SCRIPTURE

Preuss, H. *Die Entwickelung des Schriftprinzips bei Luther bis zur Leipziger Disputation*. Leipzig, 1901.

Scheel, O. *Luthers Stellung zur Heiligen Schrift*. Tuebingen, 1902.

Thimme, K. *Luthers Stellung zur Heiligen Schrift.* Guetersloh, 1903.

Schempp, P. *Luthers Stellung zur Heiligen Schrift.* Muenchen, 1929.

Bornkamm, H. *Das Wort Gottes bei Luther.* Muenchen, 1933.

Holl, Karl. "Luthers Bedeutung fuer den Fortschritt der Auslegungskunst," *Ges. Aufsaetze* (6th ed.). Tuebingen, 1932, I, 544 ff.

Hahn, F. "Luthers Auslegungsgrundsaetze und ihre theologischen Voraussetzungen," *Zeitschrift fuer syst. Theol.,* XII (1935), 165 ff.

3. THE NATURE OF A CONFESSION

Hoefling, F. *De symbolorum natura, necessitate, auctoritate atque usu.* Erlangen, 1841.

Kahnis, K. F. A. *Christentum und Luthertum.* Leipzig, 1871, pp. 90 ff.

Kattenbusch, F. "Bekennen und Bekenntnis," *Christliche Welt* (1930), pp. 571 ff.

Sasse, Herman. "Das Bekenntnis der Kirche," *Christentum und Wissenschaft* (1930), pp. 321 ff.

Elert, Werner. *Schrift und Bekenntnis.* Leipzig, 1936.

Gogarten, F. *Das Bekenntniss der Kirche.* Jena, 1934.

Asmussen, Hans. *Barmen.* Muenchen, 1935.

Schlink, Edmund. *Pflicht und Versuchung christlichen Bekennens.* Muenchen, 1935.

Lilje, Hans. "Bekenntnis und Bekennen," *Bekennende Kirche,* 32 (Muenchen, 1935).

Gollwitzer, H. "Die Bedeutung der Bekenntnisbewegung und der Bekenntnissynoden fuer die Kirche," *Ev. Theol.* (1936), pp. 234 ff.

4. THE LEGAL ASPECTS OF CONFESSIONAL OBLIGATION

Schleiermacher, F. "Ueber den eigenthuemlichen Werth und das bindende Ansehen der symbolischen Buecher," *Reformationsalmanach* (1819), pp. 335 ff.

Johannsen. *Allseitige wissenschaftl. und histor. Untersuchung der Rechtmaessigkeit der Verpflichtung auf symbolische Buecher ueberhaupt und der Augsburgischen Konfession insbesondere.* Altona, 1833.

Rudelbach, A. G. *Historisch-kritische Einleitung in die Augsburgische Confession.* Dresden, 1841, pp. 169 ff.

v. Scheurl, A. "Die Rechtsgeltung der Symbole," *Kirchenrechtliche Abhandlungen.* Erlangen, 1873, pp. 149 ff.

Hoffmann, G. "Lehrzucht und Glaubensduldung bei Luther und im Luthertum," *Luthertum* (1939), pp. 40, 161 ff., 193 ff.

CHAPTER II

1. THE DOCTRINE OF SIN

Vilmar, A. F. C. *Dogmatik* (repr. of 1st ed.). Guetersloh, 1937, I, pars. 36 ff.

Moehler, J. A. *Symbolik.* Muenchen-Regensburg (5th ed.), 1894, pars. 6.

Warko, A. "Die Erbsuenden- und Rechtfertigungslehre der Apologie in ihrem geschichtlichen Gegensatze zur mittelalterlichen und gleichzeitigen katholischen Theologie," *Theol. Studien und Krit.* (1906), pp. 86 ff., 200 ff.

Niemeier, G. "Die Lehre von der Suende und Erbsuende in den Bekenntnisschriften der Evangelisch-Lutherischen Kirche," *Ev. Theol.* (1938), pp. 183 ff.

Hof, O. "Die Erbsuendenlehre der luth. Bekenntnisschriften," *Kirchl. posit. Blaetter Badens* (1937).

2. LUTHER'S DOCTRINE OF SIN

Harnack, Th. *Luthers Theologie,* Neuausg. Muenchen, 1927, I, 193 ff.

Koestlin, J. *Luthers Theologie* (2nd ed.). Stuttgart, 1901, II, 116 ff.

Braun, W. *Die Bedeutung der Concupiszenz in Luthers Leben und Lehre.* Berlin, 1908.

Titius, A. "Die kirchliche Lehre von der Konkupiszenz," *Festgabe fuer A. v. Harnack.* Tuebingen, 1921, pp. 331 ff.

Schott, E. *Fleisch und Geist nach Luthers Lehre unter besonderer Beruecksichtigung des Begriffes "totus homo."* Leipzig, 1928.

Seeberg, R. *Textbook . . . Doctrines.* Book III, 242 ff.

Ljunggren, Gustav. *Synd och skuld i Luthers teologi.* Stockholm, 1927.

Noejgaard, Niels. *Om Begrebet Synd hos Luther.* Copenhagen, 1929.

For Melanchthon's doctrine of sin see H. Engelland, *Melanchthon, Glauben und Handeln.* Muenchen, 1931, pp. 13 ff., 80 ff., 237 ff.

3. LUTHER'S VIEW OF THE NATURAL KNOWLEDGE OF GOD AND OF THE LAW

Vossberg, H. *Luthers Kritik aller Religion.* Leipzig, 1922.

Holl, K. "Luther und die Mission," *Neue Allg. Miss.-Zeitschrift* (1924).

Holsten, W. *Christentum und nichtchristliche Religionen nach der Auffassung Luthers.* Guetersloh, 1932.

Wolf, E. *Martin Luther.* Muenchen, 1934.

———. "Glaube, Religion, Evangelium im Verstaendnis reformatorischer Theologie," *Ev. Theol.* (1934), pp. 226 ff.

———. " 'Natuerliches Gesetz' und 'Gesetz Christi' bei Luther," *Ev. Theol.* (1935), pp. 305 ff.

———. "Vom Problem des Gewissens in reformatorischer Sicht," *Der alte und der neue Mensch.* Muenchen, 1942.

Merz, G. "Gesetz Gottes und Volksnomos bei Martin Luther," *Jahrbuch der Luthergesellschaft* (1934).

Lau, F. *"Aeusserlich Ordnung" und "Weltlich Ding" in Luthers Theologie.* Goettingen, 1933.

Grobmann, A. *Das Naturrecht bei Luther und Calvin, eine politische Untersuchung.* Phil. Dissertation. Hamburg, 1935.

Schlink, E. *Der Mensch in der Verkuendigung der Kirche.* Muenchen, 1936, pp. 140 ff.

———. "Die Offenbarung Gottes in seinen Werken und die Ablehnung der natuerlichen Theologie," *Theol. Blaetter* (1941), p. 1.

Arnold, F. *Zur Frage des Naturrechtes bei Martin Luther, ein Beitrag zum Problem der natuerlichen Theologie auf reformatorischer Grundlage.* Muenchen, 1937.

Josefson, Ruben. *Den naturlige teologiens problem hos Luther.* Uppsala, 1943.

INTRODUCTION TO LITERATURE

For Melanchthon see E. Troeltsch, *Vernunft und Offenbarung bei Johann Gerhard und Melanchthon,* Goettingen, 1891; F. Huebner, *Natuerliche Theologie und theokratische Schwaermerei bei Melanchthon,* Guetersloh, 1936.

4. THE CATECHISMS' DOCTRINE OF GOD

Wobbermin, G. "Die Frage nach Gott in Luthers Grossem Katechismus," *Festgabe fuer J. Kaftan.* Tuebingen, 1920, pp. 418 ff.

Thieme, Karl. "Der Gott der Katechismen," *Zeitschr. fuer Theol. und Kirche* (1929), pp. 183 ff.

Schmidt, F. W. "Die Frage nach Gott in Luthers Grossem Katechismus," *ibid.,* pp. 357 ff.

Thieme, Karl. "Gott und Glaube nach den Katechismen," *Die Augsburgische Konfession,* pp. 98 ff.

5. LUTHER'S DOCTRINE OF GOD

Schultz, H. "Luthers Ansicht von der Methode und der Grenze der dogmatischen Aussagen ueber Gott." *Zeitschrf. fuer Kirchengesch.,* IV (1880), 77 ff.

Hirsch, E. *Luthers Gottesanschauung.* Goettingen, 1918.

Seeberg, E. *Luthers Theologie,* I. Goettingen, 1929.

CHAPTER III

1. LUTHER'S DOCTRINE OF THE LAW

Gottschick, J. "Die Seligkeit und der Dekalog, Katechetische Lutherstudien," *Zeitsch. fuer Theol. und Kirche* (1892), pp. 171 ff., 438 ff.

Thieme, K. and A. Hardeland. "Zum ersten Hauptstueck des Kleinen Katechismus," *Neues saechsisches Kirchenblatt* (1917).

Meyer, J. "Luthers Dekalogerklaerung 1528 unter dem Einfluss der saechsischen Kirchenvisitation," *Neue kirchliche Zeitschrift* (1915), pp. 546 ff.

Harnack, Th. *Luthers Theologie* (2nd ed.), I, 365 ff.

Seeberg, R. *Textbook . . . Doctrines.* Book III, 246 ff.

Jacob, G. *Der Gewissensbegriff in der Theologie Luthers.* Tuebingen, 1929.

Elert, W. *Morphologie des Luthertums,* I, 13 ff.

Bornkamm, H. "Gesetz und Evangelium in Luthers Auslegung des Alten Testaments," *Zeitschrift fuer systematische Theologie* (1943), 20, 68 ff.

2. THE FIRST COMMANDMENT IN LUTHER'S CATECHISMS

Hardeland, A. *Der Begriff der Gottesfurcht in Luthers Katechismen.* Guetersloh, 1914.

―――. *Das erste Gebot in den Katechismen Luthers.* Leipzig, 1916.

―――. "Luthers Erklaerung des ersten Gebots im Lichte seiner Rechtfertigungslehre," *Theol. Studien und Krit.* (1919), pp. 201 ff.

Albrecht, O. "Streiflichter auf Luthers Erklaerung des ersten Gebots im

Kleinen Katechismus," *Theol. Studien und Krit.* (1917), pp. 421 ff.

Meyer, J. *Historischer Kommentar*, pp. 170 ff.

Mueller, H. M. and H. Bornkamm. "Diskussion ueber das 1. Gebot bei Luther," *Theol. Bl.* (1927), cols. 269 ff. (1928), cols. 37 ff.; *Zeitschr. fuer systematische Theol.*, V, 453 ff.

3. THE DOCTRINE OF THE FREEDOM OF THE WILL

Luthardt, Chr. E. *Die Lehre vom freien Willen*. Leipzig, 1863, pp. 162 ff., 261 ff.

Stange, C. "Die reformatorische Lehre von der Freiheit des Handelns," *Neue kirchl. Zeitschr.* (1903), pp. 214 ff.

Kattenbusch, F. *Luthers Lehre vom unfreien Willen und von der Praedestination nach ihren Entstehungsgruenden untersucht*. Goettingen, 1905.

Zickendraht, K. *Der Streit zwischen Erasmus und Luther ueber die Willensfreiheit*. Leipzig, 1909.

Schott, E. "Luthers Lehre vom *servum arbitrium* in ihrer theol. Bedeutung," *Zeitschr. fuer syst. Theol.* (1930), pp. 399 ff.

Iwand, H. J. "Studien zum Problem des unfreien Willens," *Zeitschr. fuer syst. Theol.* (1930), pp. 216 ff.

————. *Erlaeuterungen zu Luthers "de servo arbitrio" in der Muenchener Lutherausgabe*, 1939.

Hermann, R. "Zu Luthers Lehre vom unfreien Willen," *Schriften der Greifswalder Luthergesellschaft* (Berlin, 1931).

Lammers, H. *Luthers Anschauung vom Willen*. Berlin, 1935.

4. THE DOCTRINE OF THE CONFESSIONS CONCERNING THE ATONEMENT

Koellner, E. *Symbolik*. Hamburg, 1837, I, 636 ff.

Thomasius, G. *Das Bekenntnis der luth. Kirche von der Versoehnung*. Erlangen, 1857.

————. *Christi Person und Werk*, II (3rd ed.). Erlangen, 1888.

Knoke, K. "Zur Sicherstellung des urspruenglichen Sinns der lutherischen Erklaerung des 2. Artikels," *Neue kirchl. Zeitschr.* (1891), pp. 93 ff.

Kaehler, M. "Zur Lehre von der Versoehnung, *Dogmat. Zeitfragen*, II (Leipzig, 1898; reprint, Guetersloh, 1937), 11 ff.

Tschackert, P. *Entstehung*. Goettingen, 1910, pp. 320 ff.

Meyer, J. *Historischer Kommentar zu Luthers kleinem Katechismus*. Guetersloh, 1929, pp. 257 ff., 295 ff.

Bachmann, Ph. "Christus der Gekreuzigte in der Augsburgischen Konfession," *Monatschr. fuer Pastoral-Theologie* (1930), pp. 45 ff.

Stange, C. "Die Christusfrage in der Augsburgischen Konfession," *Zeitschr. fuer syst. Theol.* (1931), pp. 293 ff.

Elert, W. *Morphologie des Luthertums*, I, 101 ff., 111 ff.

Seeberg, E. "Christus, Wirklichkeit und Urbild," *Luthers Theologie*, II. Stuttgart, 1937, 378 ff.

5. LUTHER'S CHRISTOLOGY

Dorner, J. A. *Entwicklungsgeschichte der Lehre von der Person Christi* (2nd ed.), Berlin, 1853, II, 510 ff.

Ritschl, A. *Rechtfertigung und Versoehnung* (3rd ed.). Bonn, 1889, I, 217 ff. English Trans.: *The Christian Doctrine of Justification and Reconciliation*, eds. H. R. MacKintosh and A. B. Macaulay. Edinburgh: T. & T. Clark, 1900.

Harnack, Th. *Luthers Theologie*, II.

Seeberg, R. *Textbook . . . Doctrines*. Book III, 266 ff.

Stange, C. "Die Person Jesu Christi in der Theologie Luthers," *Zeitschr. fuer syst. Theol.* (1929), pp. 449 ff.

Vogelsang, E. *Christusglaube und Christusbekenntnis bei Luther*. Bonn, 1935.

Wolf, E. "Die Christusverkuendigung bei Luther," *Jesus Christus im Zeugnis der Hl. Schrift und der Kirche* (Muenchen, 1936), pp. 179 ff.

Seeberg, E. *Luthers Theologie*, II.

Tiililä, Osmo. *Das Strafleiden Christi*. Helsinki, 1941.

For Melanchthon's Christology see Herrlinger, *die Theologie Melanchthons in ihrer geschichtlichen Entwicklung*, Gotha, 1879, pp. 174 ff.

Bring, Ragnar. *Dualismen hos Luther*. Stockholm, 1929.

6. THE DOCTRINE OF JUSTIFICATION IN THE CONFESSIONS

Ritschl, A. *Rechtfertigung und Versoehnung* (3rd ed.), II, 62 ff.

Loofs, F. "Die Bedeutung der Rechtfertigungslehre der Apologie fuer die Symbolik der lutherischen Kirchen," *Theol. Studien und Krit.* (1884), pp. 613 ff.

———. *Leitfaden zum Studium der Dogmengeschichte* (4th ed.). Halle, 1906, pp. 824 ff.

———. "Die Rechtfertigung nach den lutherischen Gedanken in den Bekenntnisschriften," *Theol. Studien und Krit.* (1922), pp. 307 ff.

Eichhorn, A. "Die Rechtfertigungslehre der Apologie," *Theol. Studien und Krit.* (1887), pp. 415 ff.

Oehler, G. F. *Lehrbuch der Symbolik*. Stuttgart, 1891, pp. 532 ff.

Frank. "Rechtfertigung und Wiedergeburt," *Neue kirchl. Zeitschr.* (1892), pp. 846 ff.

Stange, C. "Ueber eine Stelle in der Apologie," *Neue kirchl. Zeitschr.* (1899), pp. 169 ff.

———. "Zum Sprachgebrauch in der Apologie," *ibid.*, pp. 543 ff. Repr. in *Studien zur Theologie Luthers*, I (Guetersloh, 1928), 453 ff., 476 ff.

Warko, A. "Die Erbsuenden- und Rechtfertigungs-lehre der Apologie," *Theol. Studien und Krit.* (1906), pp. 86 ff., 200 ff.

Thieme, K. "Zur Rechtfertigungslehre der Apologie," *Theol. Studien und Krit.* (1907), pp. 363 ff.

———. *Augsburgische Konfession*, pp. 57 ff.

Fischer, E. F. *Autoritaet und Erfahrung in der Begruendung der Heilsgewissheit nach den Bekenntnisschriften der ev. luth. Kirche*. Leipzig, 1907.

Kunze, J. "Die Rechtfertigungslehre in der Apologie," *Beitr. zur Foerderg. christl. Theol.* (1908), pp. 353 ff.

Ritschl, O. "Der doppelte Rechfertigungsbegriff in der Apologie," *Zeitschr. fuer Theol. und Kirche* (1910), pp. 292 ff.

Seeberg, R. *Textbook . . . Doctrines*. Book III, 336 ff.
Engelland, H. *Melanchthon, Glauben und Handeln*, pp. 541 ff.
Elert, W. *Morphologie des Luthertums*, I, 79 ff.
Weber, H. E. *Reformation, Orthodoxie und Rationalismus*, I[1]. Guetersloh, 1937, 65 ff.

7. LUTHER'S DOCTRINE OF JUSTIFICATION

Ritschl, A. *Rechtfertigung und Versoehnung* (3rd ed.), I, 141 ff.
Harnack, Th. *Luthers Theologie* (2nd ed.), II, 321 ff.
Koestlin, J. *Luthers Theologie* (2nd ed.), II, 173 ff.
Ritschl, O. *Dogmengeschichte des Protestantismus*, II, 85 ff.
Seeberg, R. *Textbook . . . Doctrines*, III, 260 ff.
———. "Die Rechtfertigungslehre in Luthers Vorlesung ueber den Roemerbrief," *Ges. Aufs.* (6th ed.), I, 111 ff.
———. "Die Rechtfertigungslehre im Licht der Geschichte des Protestantismus," *Ges. Aufs.* (2nd ed.). Tuebingen, 1922, III, 525 ff.
———. "Zur Verstaendigung ueber Luthers Rechtfertigungslehre," *Neue kirchliche Zeitschrift* (1923), pp. 165 ff.; cf. 1924, pp. 47 f.
Holl, K. "Zu den neuesten Problemen der lutherischen Rechtfertigungslehre," *Zeitschr. fuer Theol. und Kirche* (1925), pp. 351 ff.
Walther, W. "Neue Konstruktionen der Rechtfertigungslehre Luthers," *Neue kirchl. Zeitschr.* (1923), pp. 50 ff.; cf. 668 ff.
Althaus, P. *Theol. Aufsaetze*, II. Guetersloh, 1935, pp. 1 ff., 31 ff.
Hermann, R. "Das Verhaeltnis von Rechtfertigung und Gebet nach Luthers Auslegung von Roem. 3 in der Roemerbriefvorlesung," *Zeitschr. fuer syst. Theol.* (1926), pp. 601 ff.
———. "Beobachtungen zu Luthers Rechtfertigungslehre," *Seeberg-Festschrift*, I. Leipzig, 1929, 239 ff.
———. *Luthers These "Gerecht und Suender zugleich."* Guetersloh, 1930.
Kattenbusch, F. "Die vier Formen des Rechtfertigungsgedankens," *Zeitschr. fuer syst. Theol.* (1933), pp. 28 ff., 203 ff.
Elert, W. "Deutschrechtliche Zuege in Luthers Rechtfertigungslehre," *Zeitschr. fuer syst. Theol.*, XII (1935), 22 ff.
v. Walther, J. *Mystik und Rechtfertigung beim jungen Luther*. Guetersloh, 1937.
Seeberg, E. *Luthers Theologie*, II.
Link, W. *Das Ringen Luthers um die Freiheit der Theologie von der Philosophie*. Muenchen, 1940.
Iwand, H. J. *Rechtfertigungslehre und Christusglaube*. Leipzig, 1930.
———. *Glaubensgerechtigkeit nach Luthers Lehre*. Muenchen, 1941.

8. MELANCHTHON'S DOCTRINE OF JUSTIFICATION

Herrlinger. *Die Theologie Melanchthons in ihrer geschichtlichen Entwicklung*. Gotha, 1879, pp. 4 ff.
Fischer, E. F. *Melanchthons Lehre von der Bekehrung*. Tuebingen, 1905.
Ritschl, O. *Dogmengeschichte des Protestantismus*, II, 226 ff.
Engelland, H. *Melanchthon, Glauben und Handeln*.

9. LUTHER'S CONCEPT OF FAITH

v. Loewenich, W. *Luthers theologia crucis.* Muenchen, 1929 (3rd ed., 1939).

Mueller, H. M. *Erfahrung und Glaube bei Luther.* Leipzig, 1929.

Kattenbusch, F. "Erfahrung und Glauben bei Luther," *Theol. Blaetter* (1929), pp. 305 ff.

Frey, F. *Luthers Glaubensbegriff.* Leipzig, 1939.

Bohlin, Torsten. *Gudstro och Kristustro hos Luther.* Stockholm, 1927.

Bring, Ragnar. *Foerhaalandet mellan tro och gaerningar inom luthersk teologi.* Stockholm, 1929.

Pinnoma, Lennart. *Der existentielle Charakter der Theologie Luthers.* Helsinki, 1940.

Prenter, Regin. *Spiritus Creator.* Kopenhagen, 1944; English ed., Philadelphia: Muhlenberg Press, 1953.

For Melanchthon see H. Roemer, *Die Entwicklung des Glaubensbegriffs bei Melanchthon nach dessen dogmatischen Schriften.* Bonn, 1902.

CHAPTER IV

1. JUSTIFICATION AND THE NEW OBEDIENCE

Schneckenburger, M. *Vergleichende Darstellung des luth. und ref. Lehrbegriffs.* Stuttgart, 1855.

Ritschl, A. *Geschichte des Pietismus,* I. Bonn, 1880, 36 ff.

Luthardt, Ch. E. *Geschichte der christlichen Ethik,* II. Leipzig, 1893, 53 ff., 9 ff.

Coelle, R. *Die guten Werke oder der VI. Artikel der Augsburgischen Konfession.* Goettingen, 1896.

Thieme, K. *Die sittliche Triebkraft des Glaubens.* Leipzig, 1895.

————. *Der Geist der lutherischen Ethik in Melanchthons Apologie.* Giessen, 1931.

Stange, C. "Die Heilsbedeutung des Gesetzes," *Studien zur Theologie Luthers* (Leipzig, 1904), I, 53 ff.

————. "Die Entstehung eines Christenmenschen nach dem Augsburger Bekenntnis," *Allg. ev. luth. Kirchenzeitung* (1930), pp. 413 ff.

Ritschl, O. *Dogmengeschichte des Protestantismus,* II, 184 ff., 274 ff.

Hermann, R. "Willensfreiheit und gute Werke im Sinne der Reformation," *Studien des Apol. Sem.,* hrg. C. Stange, Vol. 23 (1928).

Althaus, P. *Der Geist der luth. Ethik im Augsburgischen Bekenntnis.* Muenchen, 1930.

Koeberle, A. *Rechtfertigung und Heiligung* (4th ed.). Leipzig, 1938. Translated by John C. Mattes. *The Quest for Holiness* (3rd German ed.). Minneapolis: Augsburg, 1938.

Dietrich, O. *Luthers Ethik in ihren Gliederungen.* Leipzig, 1930.

Dehn, G. "Der neue Mensch," *Theologia Viatorum.* Muenchen, 1939, pp. 67 ff.

Haar, J. *Initium creaturae Dei.* Guetersloh, 1939.

Olsson, Herbert. *Grundproblemet i Luthers sozialetik.* Lund, 1934.

Wingren, Gustav. *Luthers laera om kallelsen.* Lund, 1942. Translated by Carl C. Rasmussen. *Luther on Vocation.* Philadelphia: Muhlenberg, 1957.

2. LUTHER'S DISTINCTION BETWEEN LAW AND GOSPEL

Harnack, Th. *Luthers Theologie* (2nd ed.), I, 444 ff.

Loofs, F. *Leitfaden zum Studium der Dogmengeschichte*, pp. 770 ff.

Seeberg, R. *Textbook . . . Doctrines*, Book III, 246 ff.

Seeberg, E. *Luthers Theologie*, II, 205 ff., 411 ff., 447 ff.

Schempp, P. *Luthers Stellung zur Heiligen Schrift*, para. 7.

Diem, Har. *Luthers Lehre von den zwei Reichen.* Muenchen, 1938, pp. 162 ff.

Wolf, E. "Gesetz und Evangelium in Luthers Auseinandersetzung mit den Schwaermern," *Ev. Theol.* (1938), pp. 96 ff.

Walther, C. F. W. *Gesetz und Evangelium.* St. Louis: Concordia, 1897; reissued, 1946. Translated by W. H. T. Dau. *The Proper Distinction of Law and Gospel.* St. Louis: Concordia, 1929.

v. Engestroem, Sigfrid. *Luthers Trosbegrepp.* Uppsala, 1933.

Barth, K. *Evangelium und Gesetz.* Muenchen, 1935.

CHAPTER V

1. REPENTANCE

Steitz, G. E. *Die Privatbeichte und Privatabsolution der lutherischen Kirche aus den Quellen des 16. Jahrhunderts.* Frankfurt, 1854.

Kliefoth, Th. "Die Beichte und Absolution," *Liturgische Abhandlungen*, II. Schwerin, 1856.

Pfisterer, G. F. *Luthers Lehre von der Beichte.* Stuttgart, 1857.

Vilmar, A. F. C. *Von der christlichen Kirchenzucht.* Marburg, 1872, pp. 30 ff.

Herrmann, W. "Die Busse des evangelischen Christen," *Zeitschr. fuer Theologie und Kirche* (1891), pp. 28 ff.

Lipsius, R. A. *Luthers Lehre von der Busse.* Braunschweig, 1892.

Fischer, E. "Zur Geschichte der evangelischen Beichte," *Studien zur Geschichte der Theologie und Kirche*, hrg. von Bonwetsch-Seeberg. Leipzig, 1903.

Galley, A. *Die Busslehre Luthers und ihre Darstellung in neuester Zeit.* Guetersloh, 1900.

Rietschel, G. *Lehrbuch der Liturgik*, II. Berlin, 1909, 345 ff.

Tschackert, P. *Entstehung*, pp. 71 ff.

Seeberg, R. *Textbook . . . Doctrines*, Book III, 235 ff.

Bartels, F. "Die Beichte in der lutherischen Kirche," *Junge Kirche* (1936), pp. 976 ff.

2. BAPTISM

Hoefling, J. W. F. *Das Sakrament der Taufe*, I, II. Erlangen, 1859.

Kawerau, G. "Liturgische Studien zu Luthers Taufbuechlein von 1523," *Zeitschr. fuer kirchl. Wissenschaft und kirchl. Leben* (1889), pp. 407 ff.

Hering, H. "Luthers Taufbuechlein von 1523, besonders das typologische Gebet," *Theol. Studien und Krit.* (1892), pp. 282 ff.

Althaus, Paul, Sr. *Die historischen und dogmatischen Grundlagen der lutherischen Taufliturgie.* Hannover, 1893.

Rietschel, G. "Luthers Lehre von der Kindertaufe und das lutherische Taufformular," *Beitraege zur Ref.-Gesch., Festschrift fuer Koestlin.* Gotha, 1896.

Rietschel, G. *Lehrbuch der Liturgik,* II, 63 ff.

Gottschick, J. "Die Lehre der Reformation von der Taufe," *Hefte zur christl. Welt, 56.* Tuebingen, 1906.

Lauerer, H. *Luthers Anschauung von der Taufe.* Leipzig, 1907.

Schulze, L. *Die Lehre von der Taufe in der lutherischen Kirche nach ihrer biblischen Grundlage.* Guetersloh, 1911.

Stange, C. "Der Todesgedanke in Luthers Tauflehre," *Studien zur Theologie Luthers,* I, 348 ff.

Elert, W. *Morphologie des Luthertums,* I, 255 ff.

Diem, Har. "Zum Verstaendnis der Taufe bei Luther," *Ev. Theol.* (1935), pp. 403 ff.

Josefson, Ruben. *Luthers Laera om dopet.* Stockholm, 1944.

Schroeter, F. "Taufe und Kindertaufe in den lutherischen Bekenntnisschriften," *Kirche und Amt,* I. Muenchen, 1940.

Koestlin, J. *Luthers Theologie* (2nd ed.), I, 405 ff.; II, 237 f.

Lutterjohann, J. "Die Stellung Luthers zur Kindertaufe," *Zeitschr. fuer syst. Theol.* (1933), pp. 188 ff.

3. THE DOCTRINE OF THE LORD'S SUPPER IN THE LUTHERAN CHURCH

Ebrard, Aug. *Das Dogma vom heiligen Abendmahl und seine Geschichte,* II. Frankfurt a.M., 1846.

Schmid, H. *Der Kampf der lutherischen Kirche um Luthers Lehre vom Abendmahl im Reformationszeitalter.* Leipzig, 1868 (2nd ed., 1873).

Fricke, O. *Die Christologie des Johannes Brenz.* Muenchen, pp. 258 ff.

Althaus, P. *Die lutherische Abendmahlslehre in der Gegenwart.* Muenchen, 1931.

Elert, W. *Morphologie des Luthertums,* I, 263 ff.

Stoll, Chr. *Vom Abendmahl Christi.* Muenchen, 1935.

Hopf, F. W. "Die Abendmahlslehre der evangelisch-lutherischen Kirche," *Abendmahlsgemeinschaft?* Muenchen, 1937, pp. 122 ff.

Gollwitzer, H. *Coena Domini, Die altlutherische Abendmahlslehre in ihrer Auseinandersetzung mit dem Calvinismus, dargestellt an der lutherischen Fruehorthodoxie.* Muenchen, 1937.

Sasse, H. *Kirche und Herrenmahl.* Muenchen, 1938.

Bizer, E. *Studien zur Geschichte des Abendmahlsstreites im 16. Jahrhundert.* Guetersloh, 1940.

4. LUTHER'S DOCTRINE OF THE LORD'S SUPPER

Dieckhoff, A. W. *Die evangelische Abendmahlslehre im Reformationszeitalter,* I. Goettingen, 1854.

Graebke, F. *Die Konstruktion der Abendmahlslehre Luthers in ihrer Entwicklung.* Leipzig, 1908.

Koehler, W. *Zwingli und Luther,* I. Leipzig, 1924.

———. *Das Marburger Religionsgespraech 1529, Versuch einer Rekonstruktion.* Leipzig, 1929.

Ritschl, O. *Dogmengeschichte des Protestantismus,* III, 76 ff.

Barth, Karl. "Ansatz und Absicht in Luthers Abendmahlslehre," *Die Theologie und die Kirche.* Muenchen, 1928, pp. 26 ff.

Sommerlath, E. *Der Sinn des Abendmahls nach Luthers Gedanken 1527-1529.* Leipzig, 1930.

Hildebrandt, F. *"EST," Das lutherische Prinzip.* Goettingen, 1931.

Kattenbusch, F. "Luthers Idee der Consubstantiation im Abendmahl," *Festschrift fuer J. Ficker* ("Forschungen zur Kirchengeschichte und zur christlichen Kunst.") Leipzig, 1931, pp. 62 ff.

Schott, E. "Luthers Anthropologie und seine Lehre von der *manducatio oralis* in wechselseitiger Beleuchtung," *Zeitschr. fuer syst. Theol.* (1932), pp. 585 ff.

Schempp, P. "Das Abendmahl bei Luther," *Ev. Theol.* (1935), pp. 248 ff.

Gollwitzer, H. "Luthers Abendmahlslehre," *Abendmahlsgemeinschaft?* pp. 94 ff.

Gass, H. *Die Abendmahlslehre bei Luther und Calvin.* Guetersloh, 1940.

5. MELANCHTHON'S DOCTRINE OF THE LORD'S SUPPER

Plitt, G. "Melanchthons Wandlung in der Abendmahlslehre," *Zeitschr. fuer Prot. und Kirche* (1868), pp. 65 ff.

Diestelmann, Th. *Die lezte Unterredung Luthers und Melanchthons ueber den Abendmahlsstreit.* Goettingen, 1874.

Herrlinger. *Die Theologie Melanchthons in ihrer geschichtlichen Entwicklung,* pp. 123 ff.

Haussleiter, J. "Die geschichtliche Grundlage der letzten Unterredung Luthers und Melanchthons ueber den Abendmahlsstreit (1546)," *Neue kirchl. Zeitschr.* (1898), pp. 831 ff.

Seeberg, R. *Textbook . . . Doctrines,* Book III, 285 ff., 322 ff.

Ritschl, O. *Dogmengeschichte des Protestantismus,* IV, 1 ff.

6. SACRAMENT

Thimme, K. "Entwicklung und Bedeutung der Sakramentslehre Luthers," *Neue kirchl. Zeitschr.* (1901), pp. 749 ff., 876 ff.

Kaehler, M. *Die Sakramente als Gnadenmittel.* Leipzig, 1903.

Tschackert, P. *Entstehung,* pp. 348 ff.

Harnack, A. *Lehrbuch der Dogmengeschichte* (5th ed.), III, 851 ff., 880 ff.

Seeberg, R. *Textbook . . . Doctrines,* Book III, 341 ff.

Stange, C. *Die Lehre von den Sakramenten.* Guetersloh, 1920.

Bornkamm, H. "Die Sakramentsfrage bei Luther," *Deutsche Theol.* (1934), pp. 301 ff.

Koeberle, A. *Wort, Sakrament und Kirche im Luthertum.* Guetersloh, 1934.

Gerke, F. "Anfechtung und Sakrament in Martin Luthers Sermon vom Sterben," *Theol. Blaetter* (1937), pp. 81 ff.

Weber, H. E. "Wort und Sakrament," *Theol. Blaetter* (1937), pp. 81 ff.

7. CHRISTOLOGY AND THE LORD'S SUPPER

Luther, Martin. *Vom Abendmahl Christi. Bekenntnis*, 1528.

Brenz, J. *De personali unione duarum naturarum in Christo.* Tuebingen, 1561.

———. *De majestate Domini nostri Jesu Christi ad dextram Dei Patris et de vera praesentia corporis et sanguinis ejus in coena.* Frankfurt, 1563.

Chemnitz, Martin. *De duabus naturis in Christo.* Jena, 1570 (2nd ed., 1578).

Dorner, J. A. *Entwicklungsgeschichte der Lehre von der Person Christi* (2nd ed.). Berlin, 1853, II, 706 ff.

Thomasius, G. *Christi Person und Werk.* Erlangen, 1857, II, 405 ff.

Frank, F. H. R. *Theologie der Concordienformel*, III, 165 ff.

Loofs, F. *Leitfaden zum Studium der Dogmengeschichte* (4th ed.), pp. 920 ff.

Ritschl, O. *Dogmengeschichte des Protestantismus*, IV, 102 ff.; cf., 70 ff.

Fricke, O. *Die Christologie des Johannes Brenz.* Muenchen, 1927, pp. 264 ff.

Noth, G. *Grundlinien der Theologie des Martin Chemnitz*, 1930.

Weber, H. E. *Reformation, Orthodoxie und Rationalismus*, I², 115-185.

Jaeger, K. *Luthers religioeses Interesse an seiner Lehre von der Realpraesenz.* Giessen, 1900.

Gennrich, P. W. *Die Christologie Luthers im Abendmahlsstreit 1524-1529.* Goettingen, 1929.

CHAPTER VI

1. THE DOCTRINE OF THE CHURCH IN THE CONFESSIONS

Plitt, G. *Einleitung in die Augustana*, II, 206 ff.

———. *Die Apologie der Augustana geschichtlich erklaert.* Erlangen, 1873, pp. 136 ff.

Zoeckler, O. *Die Augsburgische Konfession als symbolische Lehrgrundlage der deutschen Reformationskirche.* Frankfurt, 1870, pp. 200 ff.

Vilmar, A. F. C. *Die Augsburgische Confession*, pp. 84 ff.

Trebitz, K. *Das Wesen der Kirche nach heiliger Schrift, Geschichte, und Bekenntnis, insbesondere Art. VII der "CA".* Leipzig, 1870.

Wangemann. "Die lutherische Kirche der Gegenwart in ihrem Verhaeltnis zur *Una sancta*," Book I, Berlin, 1883: *Der siebente Artikel der Augsb. Konfession*, pp. 12 ff.

Mullert, H. *Congregatio sanctorum, in qua evangelium recte docetur.* Harnack-Ehrung. Leipzig, 1921, pp. 292 ff.

Haack. "Zeitgemaesse Randbemerkungen zu den Artikeln VII und VIII der Augustana ueber die Kirche," *Neue kirchl. Zeitschr.* (1924), pp. 138 ff., 224 ff., 517 ff., 577 ff.

Elert, W. "Die Botschaft des VII. Artikels der Augsb. Konf.," *Allg. Ev.-luth. Kirchenzeitung* (1927), pp. 1011 ff.

Thieme, K. *Die Augsburgische Konfession*, pp. 191 ff.

Bornkamm, H. "Die Kirche in der Augustana," *Monatsschrift fuer Pastoraltheologie* (1930), pp. 191 ff.

Leonhard, W. "Was die Kirche sei, Bemerkungen zu Artikel VIII der Augustana," *Hochkirche* (1930), pp. 237 ff.

Asmussen, H. *Kirche Augsburgischer Konfession.* Muenchen, 1934.

Diem, Herman. "Est autem ecclesia congregatio sanctorum . . .," *Theol. Aufsaetze.* Muenchen, 1936, pp. 320 ff.

Wehrung, G. "Zu Augustana VIII," *Zeitschr. fuer syst. Theol.* (1937), pp. 3 ff.

Braun, H. "Die Begrenzung und die Offenheit der Kirche nach *CA* VII und VIII," *Kirche und Amt,* I. Muenchen, 1940.

Meyer, J. *Historischer Kommentar,* pp. 340 ff.

Thurneysen, E. *Die Kirche in Luthers Auslegung des Glaubens.* Muenchen, 1938.

Loehe, W. *Drei Buecher von der Kirche.* Guetersloh, 1847.

Delitzsch, Fr. *Vier Buecher von der Kirche.* Dresden, 1847.

Kliefoth, Th. *Acht Buecher von der Kirche.* Halle, 1854.

Vilmar, A. F. C. *Dogmatik,* pars. 60 f.

Koehler. "Die Lehre der lutherischen Bekenntnisschriften ueber Kirche, Kirchenamt und Kirchenregiment," *Jahrbuecher fuer deutsche Theol.,* XVI, 1871, 381 ff.

Seeberg, R. *Der Begriff der christlichen Kirche,* I. Erlangen, 1885.

Coelle, R. *Die genuine Lehre von der Kirche nach den Symbolen der ev.-luth. Confession.* Leipzig, 1894.

Sohm, R. *Kirchenrecht,* I. Leipzig, 1892, 482 ff.; II, 1923, 130 ff.

Schilling, O. "Der Gemeinschaftsgedanke in den luth. Bekenntnisschriften," *Theol. Studien und Krit.* (1929), pp. 233 ff.

Winter, K. "Die Lehre von der Kirche in den ev.-luth. Bekenntnisschriften," *Festgabe fuer W. Zoellner,* "Credo ecclesiam." Guetersloh, 1930, pp. 3 ff.

Elert, W. *Morphologie des Luthertums,* I, 224 ff.

Hoffmann, G. "Wer gehoert nach dem Urteil der Bekenntnisschriften zum 'Kirchenvolk'?" *Junge Kirche* (1937), pp. 218 ff.

2. LUTHER'S DOCTRINE OF THE CHURCH

Koestlin, J. *Luthers Lehre von der Kirche.* Stuttgart, 1853.

Kolde, Th. *Luthers Stellung zu Konzil und Kirche.* Guetersloh, 1876.

Gottschick, J. "Hus', Luthers, und Zwinglis Lehre von der Kirche," *Zeitschr. fuer Kirchengeschichte* (1886), pp. 543 ff.

Holl, K. "Die Entstehung von Luthers Kirchenbegriff," *Ges. Aufs.* (6th ed.), I, 288 ff.

Kattenbusch, F. *Die Doppelschichtigkeit in Luthers Kirchenbegriff.* Gotha, 1928.

Kohlmeier, E. "Die Bedeutung der Kirche fuer Luther," *Zeitschr. fuer Kirchengeschichte* (1928). pp. 466 ff.

Althaus, P. "Communio sanctorum," *Die Gemeinde im luth. Kirchengedanken,* I. Muenchen, 1929.

Jacob, G. "Luthers Kirchenbegriff," *Zeitschr. fuer Theol. und Kirche* (1934), pp. 16 ff.

For Melanchthon see H. Busch, "Melanchthons Kirchenbegriff." Dissertation. Bonn, 1918; and W. Elert, *Societas bei Melanchthon*, *Das Erbe Martin Luthers und die gegenwaertige theol. Forschung, Festschrift fuer Ludwig Ihmels.* Leipzig, 1928, pp. 101 ff.

3. CHURCH DISCIPLINE

Richter, Aem. L. *Geschichte der evangelischen Kirchenverfassung in Deutschland.* Leipzig, 1851, pp. 36 ff.

v. Scheurl, A. "Ueber Wiederherstellung der Kirchenzucht und der alten Gottesdienstordnung," *Fliegende Blaetter fuer kirchliche Fragen der Gegenwart,* III. Erlangen, 1857.

Goeschen, O. *Doctrina de disciplina ecclesiastica ex ordinationibus ecclesiae evangelicae saeculi decimi sexti adumbrata.* Halle, 1859.

Vilmar, A. F. C. *Von der christlichen Kirchenzucht, ein Beitrag zur Pastoraltheologie.* Marburg, 1872.

Kolde, Th. "Zur Geschichte der Ordination und der Kirchenzucht," *Theol. Studien und Krit.* (1894), pp. 217 ff.

Kahl, W. *Der Rechtsinhalt des Konkordienbuches,* pp. 36 ff.

Stoll, Chr. *Kirchenzucht.* Muenchen, 1937.

v. Campenhausen, H. "Die Schluesselgewalt der Kirche," *Ev. Theol.* (1937), pp. 143 ff.

Besch, Joh. "Fragen und Wuensche betr. die Kirchenzucht in evangelischen Gemeinden," *Past.-Theol.* (1938), pp. 29 ff.

Dollinger, R. "Kirche ohne Kirchenzucht?" *Junge Kirche* (1936), pp. 50 ff.

———. "Jesus und die Kirchenzucht," *Deutsches Pfarrerblatt* (1938), pp. 408 f., 424 ff.

Hartenstein, K. *Pflicht und Weg evangelischer Kirchenzucht* ("Rechtglaeubigkeit, und Froemmigkeit," III.) Berlin, 1938, 119 ff.

4. VISIBLE AND INVISIBLE CHURCH

Muenchmeyer, A. F. O. *Das Dogma von der sichtbaren und unsichtbaren Kirche.* Goettingen, 1854.

Ritschl, A. "Ueber die Begriffe: sichtbare und unsichtbare Kirche," *Ges. Aufsaetze,* pp. 68 ff.

Gottschick, J. "Die sichtbare und die unsichtbare Kirche," *Theol. Studien und Krit.* (1873), pp. 3 ff.

Rietschel, E. "Luthers Anschauung von der Unsichtbarkeit und Sichtbarkeit der Kirche," *Theol. Studien und Krit.* (1900), pp. 404 ff.

———. *Das Problem der unsichtbar-sichtbaren Kirche bei Luther.* Leipzig, 1932.

Laurer, H. "Die Sichtbarkeit der Kirche," *Luthertum* (1939), pp. 65 ff.

CHAPTER VII

1. CIVIL GOVERNMENT

Vilmar, A. F. C. "Die Lehre von der Obrigkeit," *Kirche und Welt, Ges. pastoral-theol. Aufsaetze,* I. Guetersloh, 1872, 228 ff.

v. Gierke, O. *Das Deutsche Genossenschaftsrecht*, III, Berlin, 1881; IV, 1913.

Hopf, F. W. *Vom weltlichen Regiment nach evangelisch-lutherischer Lehre.* Muenchen, 1937.

Brandenburg, E. *Martin Luthers Anschauung vom Staate und von der Gesellschaft.* ("Schriften des Vereins fuer Ref.-Gesch."). Halle, 1901.

Jordan, H. *Luthers Staatsauffassung.* Muenchen, 1917.

Holstein, G. *Luther und die deutsche Staatsidee.* Tuebingen, 1926.

Joachimsen, P. *Sozialethik des Luthertums.* Muenchen, 1927.

Pauls, Th. *Luthers Auffassung vom Staat und Volk* (2nd ed.). Halle, 1927.

v. Loewenich, W. "Das Neue in Luthers Gedanken ueber den Staat," *Lutherjahrbuch*, 1932, pp. 110 ff.

Merz, G. *Glaube und Politik im Handeln Luthers.* Muenchen, 1933.

Matthes, K. *Luther und die Obrigkeit.* Muenchen, 1937.

Deutelmoser, A. *Luther, Staat und Glaube.* Jena, 1937.

Diem, Har. *Luthers Lehre von den zwei Reichen.* Muenchen, 1938.

Lamparter, H. *Luther und der Tuerkenkrieg.* Muenchen, 1940.

Toernvall, Gustav. *Geistliches und weltliches Regiment bei Luther.* Muenchen, 1947.

Mueller, K. "Luther und Melanchthon ueber das *jus gladii* 1521," *Geschichtliche Studien fuer A. Hauck.* Leipzig, 1916, pp. 235 ff.

Sohm, W. "Die Soziallehren Melanchthons," *Hist Zeitschr.*, Vol. 115 (1916), pp. 64 ff.

Elert, W. *Morphologie des Luthertums*, II, 291 ff.

2. CHURCH GOVERNMENT

Richter, Aem. L. "Grundlagen der Kirchenverfassung nach den Ansichten der saechsischen Reformatoren," *Zeitschr. fuer deutsches Recht und deutsche Rechtswissenschaft*, IV (1840).

Loehe, W. *Kirche und Amt.* Leipzig, 1851.

Hoefling, J. W. F. *Grundsaetze evangelisch-lutherischer Kirchenverfassung* (2nd ed.), Erlangen, 1851; (3rd ed.), 1853.

Harless, G. Chr. A. *Kirche und Amt nach lutherischer Lehre.* Stuttgart, 1853.

Muenchmeyer, A. F. O. *Das Amt des Neuen Testamentes nach der Lehre der Schrift und der lutherischen Bekenntnisse.* Osterode, 1853.

Stahl, *Die Kirchenverfassung nach Lehre und Recht der Protestanten* (2nd ed.), Erlangen, 1862.

Harnack, Th. *Die Kirche, ihr Amt. ihr Regiment.* Nuernberg, 1862; repr., Guetersloh, 1934.

v. Scheurl, A. *Die Lehre vom Kirchenregiment.* Erlangen, 1862.

Huschke, E. *Die streitigen Lehren von der Kirche, dem Kirchenamt, dem Kirchenregiment und den Kirchenordnungen.* Leipzig, 1863.

Mejer, O. *Die Grundlagen des lutherischen Kirchenregiments.* Rostock, 1864.

Dieckhoff, A. W. *Luthers Lehre von der kirchlichen Gewalt.* Berlin, 1865.

Vilmar, A. F. C. *Die Lehre vom geistlichen Amt.* Marburg-Leipzig, 1870.

———. "Einige Gesichtspunkte zur Eroerterung der Lehre von der Kirche, vom geistlichen Amt und vom Kirchenregiment," *Kirche und Welt,* I, 192 ff.

Koehler, "Die Lehre der lutherischen Bekenntnisschriften ueber Kirche, Kirchenamt und Kirchenregiment," *Jahrbuecher fuer deutsche Theologie,* 1871, pp. 403 ff.

Riecker, K. *Die rechtliche Natur des evangelischen Pfarramts.* Leipzig, 1891.

Sohm, R. *Kirchenrecht.* I, Leipzig, 1892; II, 1923.

Kahl, W. *Der Rechtsinhalt des Konkordienbuchs, Sonder-Abdr, a.d Festgabe fuer O. Gierke.* Breslau, 1910.

Oeschey, R. "Augustana und Kirchenverfassung," *Allg. Ev.-luth. Kirchenzeitung* (1930), pp. 1082 ff., 1106 ff., 1130 ff.

———. *Fragen der Kirchenordnung in den Schmalkaldischen Artikeln und dem Tractatus.* Leipzig, 1937.

Trillhaas, W. "Die lutherische Lehre *"De potestate ecclesiastica,"* Zwischen den Zeiten* (1933), pp. 497 ff.

Hopf, F. W. *Lutherische Kirchenordnung.* Muenchen, 1935.

Gronau, "die Ordnung der Kirche nach den Schmalkaldischen Artikeln und Melanchthons *Tractatus,*" *Pastoraltheologie* (1935), pp. 170 ff.

Wolf, E. "Zur Verwaltung der Sakramente nach Luther und den lutherischen Bekenntnisschriften," *Kirche und Amt,* I, Muenchen, 1940.

Muenter, W. O. *Kirche und Amt,* II. Muenchen, 1941.

3. CHURCH AND STATE

Brieger, Th. "Die kirchliche Gewalt der Obrigkeit nach der Anschauung Luthers," *Zeitschr. fuer Theol. und Kirche* (1892), pp. 513 ff.

Bess, L. *Luther und das landesherrliche Kirchenregiment.* Marburg, 1894.

Riecker, K. *Sinn und Bedeutung des landesherrlichen Kirchenregiments.* Leipzig, 1902.

Drews, P. "Entsprach das Staatskirchentum dem Ideale Luthers?" *Zeitschr. fuer Theol. und Kirche* (1908), Erg.-Heft.

Mueller, K. "Anfaenge der Konsistorialverfassung im lutherischen Deutschland," *Hist. Zeitschr.* (1909), 102, 1 ff.

Holl, K. "Luther und das Landesherrliche Kirchenregiment," *Ges. Aufs.* (6th ed.), I, 326 ff.

Eger, K. "Grundsaetze ev. Kirchenverfassung bei Luther," *Theol. Studien und Krit.* (1934-35), pp. 77 ff.

v. Harless, A. *Staat und Kirche.* Leipzig, 1870.

v. Hofmann, J. Chr. K. *Das Verhaeltnis von Kirche und Staat, Vermischte Aufsaetze,* hrsg. Schmid. Erlangen, 1878, pp. 141 ff.

Rieker, K. *Die rechtliche Stellung der evangelischen Kirche Deutschlands.* Leipzig, 1893.

"Staat und Kirche nach lutherischer, reformierter und moderner Anschauung," *Hist. Vierteljahrschr.* (Leipzig, 1898).

Mueller, K. *Kirche, Gemeinde und Obrigkeit nach Luther.* Tuebingen, 1910.

Hashagen, J. *Staat und Kirche vor der Reformation*. Essen, 1931.

Schmidt, W. F. "Kirche und Staat nach lutherischem Bekenntnis," *Junge Kirche* (1935), pp. 186 ff.

Althaus, P. "Kirche und Staat nach lutherischer Lehre," *Allg. Ev.-luth. Kirchenzeitung* (1935), pp. 745 ff.

Sasse, H. *Kirchenregiment und weltliche Obrigkeit nach lutherischer Lehre*. Muenchen, 1935.

———. *Die Kirche und das Staatsproblem in der Gegenwart* ("Kirche und Welt," Vol. 3) Geneva, 1934 (2nd ed., Berlin, 1935).

CHAPTER VIII

1. ESCHATOLOGY

Vilmar, A. F. C. *Dogmatik*, pars. 69 ff.

Koestlin, J. "Ein Beitrag zur Eschatologie der Reformatoren," *Theol. Studien und Krit.* (1878), pp. 125 ff.

Kliefoth, Th. *Christliche Eschatologie*. Leipzig, 1886.

Althaus, P. *Die letzten Dinge* (4th ed.). Guetersloh, 1933.

2. PREDESTINATION

Harnack, Th. *Luthers Theologie*, I, 113 ff.

Ritschl, O. *Dogmengeschichte des Protestantismus*, III, 1 ff.

Seeberg, E. *Luthers Theologie*, I, 140 ff.

Engelland, H. *Melanchthon, Glauben und Handeln*, pp. 18 ff., 145 ff.

Vogelsang, E. *Der angefochtene Christus bei Luther*. Berlin-Leipzig, 1932.

Schweizer, Alex. *Die protestantischen Zentraldogmen in ihrer Entwicklung innerhalb der ref. Kirche*, I Hälfte. Zuerich, 1854, pp. 477 ff.; cf. 380-585.

Frank, Fr. H. R. *Die Theologie der Concordienformel*, IV, 121 ff.

Thomasius, G. *Das Bekenntnis der evangelisch-lutherischen Kirche*, pp. 216 ff.

Tschackert, P. *Entstehung*, pp. 559 ff.

Seeberg, R. *Textbook . . . Doctrines*, Book III, 388 f.

Elert, W. *Morphologie des Luthertums*, I, 116 ff.

Weber, H. E. *Reformation, Orthodoxie und Rationalismus*, I^1, 151 ff.; I^2, 93 ff.

III ENGLISH BIBLIOGRAPHY

1. EDITIONS OF THE LUTHERAN CONFESSIONS

The Christian Book of Concord, or Symbolical Books of the Evangelical Lutheran Church. Newmarket, Va.: Solomon D. Henkel and Bros., 1851.

The Book of Concord, or The Symbolical Books of the Evangelical Lutheran Church, ed. Henry Eyster Jacobs. Philadelphia: General Council Publication Board, MCMXIX, first edition, 1882.

Triglot Concordia: The Symbolical Books of the Ev. Lutheran Church, German-Latin-English, eds. F. Bente and W. H. T. Dau. Published as a Memorial of the Quadricentenary Jubilee of the Reformation, anno Domini 1917, by resolution of the Evangelical Lutheran Synod of Missouri, Ohio, and Other States. St. Louis: Concordia, 1921.

The Book of Concord: The Confessions of the Evangelical Lutheran Church, trans. and ed. Theodore G. Tappert in collaboration with Jaroslav Pelikan, Robert H. Fischer, Arthur C. Piepkorn. Philadelphia: Muhlenberg, 1959.

2. THE CONFESSIONS AS A WHOLE

Allbeck, W. D. *Studies in the Lutheran Confessions.* Philadelphia: Muhlenberg, 1952.

Arndt, W. F. The Pertinency and Adequacy of the Lutheran Confessions," *Concordia Theological Monthly* (hereinafter cited as *CTM*), XX, 674 ff.

Bretscher, P. M. "Theses on the Lutheran Confessions," *CTM*, XXIV, 216 ff.

Brunner, Peter. "The Present Significance of the Lutheran Confessions," *The Unity of the Church, a Symposium.* Rock Island: Augustana, 1957.

Bente, F. "Historical Introductions," *Triglot Concordia.*

Elert, Werner. The Church's Faith and Confession, *Lutheran Church Quarterly* (hereinafter cited as *LCQ*), 2, 409 ff.

Heick, O. W. "The Meaning of the Lutheran Symbols," *LCQ*, 19, 348 ff.

Kinder, Ernst. "The Confession as Gift and as Task," *The Unity of the Church* . . . , pp. 103 ff.

Krauth, C. Port. *The Conservative Reformation and its Theology.* Philadelphia: Lippincott, 1871.

Little, C. H. *Lutheran Confessional Theology.* St. Louis: Concordia, 1943.

Mueller, J. T. "Professional Growth in the Study of the Confessions," *CTM*, IX, 257 ff.

Neve, J. L. "The Faith of Lutheranism," *LCQ*, 1, 75 ff.

———. *Introduction to the Symbolical Books of the Lutheran Church.* Columbus: Wartburg, 1926.

Piepkorn, A. C. "Suggested Principles for a Hermeneutics of the Lutheran Symbols," *CTM*, XXIX, 1 ff.

———. "The Significance of the Lutheran Symbols for Today," *Seminarian* (Concordia Seminary, June, 1954), pp. 32 ff.

Prenter, Regin. "What Does Lutheran Confessional Allegiance Mean Today?" *The Unity of the Church* . . . , pp. 115 ff.

Richard, James W. *The Confessional History of the Lutheran Church.* Philadelphia, 1909.

Sasse, Herman. *Here We Stand.* New York: Harper's, 1938.

———. "The Confessional Problem in Today's World Lutheranism," *The Lutheran Layman* (St. Louis: April 1, 1957), pp. 16 ff.

———. "The Ecumenical Movement and the Lutheran Church," *CTM*, XXXI, 87 ff.

Schmauck, Theo. and G. Benze. *The Confessional Principle.* Philadelphia, 1911.

Vajta, Vilmos. "Lutheranism and Ecumenicity," *Lutheran World*, I, 262 ff.

Wacke, A. G. "What Does Subscription to the Lutheran Confessions Imply?" *Journal of the American Lutheran Conference*, VI, 257 ff.

Walther, C. F. W. "Why Should Our Pastors, Teachers, and Professors Subscribe Unconditionally to the Symbolical Writings of Our Church?" Translated by Alex. Guebert. *CTM*, XVIII, 241 ff.

Greever, W. H. "The Place of Lutheranism in American Protestantism," *LCQ*, 10, 213 ff.

Green, L. C. "Toward an Evangelical Understanding of the Lutheran Confessions," *Lutheran Quarterly* (1957), pp. 234 ff.

Davis, H. G. "What Does Confessional Subscription Involve?" *LCQ*, 13, 360 ff.

Engelder, Theo., W. Arndt, Th. Graebner, F. E. Mayer, eds. "The Ev. Lutheran Church," *Popular Symbolics*. St. Louis: Concordia, 1934.

Mayer, F. E. "The Soteriological Approach to Christian Doctrine," in *The Religious Bodies of America*. St. Louis: Concordia, 1954.

3. STUDIES ON INDIVIDUAL CONFESSIONS, ARTICLES, OR DOCTRINES

Echternach, H. "The Lutheran Doctrine of the *Autopistia* of Scripture," *CTM*, XXIII, 241 ff.

Kramer, F. "*Sacra Scriptura* and *Verbum Dei* in the Lutheran Confessions," *CTM*, XXVI, 81 ff.

Mayer, F. E. "Romanism, Calvinism, and Lutheranism on the Authority of Scripture," *CTM*, VIII, 260 ff.

Nagel, Norman. "The Authority of Scripture," *CTM*, XXVII, 693 ff.

Pelikan, Jaroslav. "Some Word Studies in the Apology," *CTM*, XXIV, 580 ff.

Surburg, Raymond. "The Significance of Luther's hermeneutics for the Protestant Reformation," *CTM*, XXIV, 241 ff.

Davis, H. G. "The Lutheran Conception of the Word of God," *LCQ*, 11, 227 ff.

Dallmann, Wm. "The Augsburg Confession," *CTM*, I, 241 ff.

Graebner, Theo. "*The Story of the Augsburg Confession*. St. Louis: Concordia, 1930.

Jacobs, H. E., ed. *First Free Lutheran Diet in America*, 1877: *Characteristics of the Augsburg Confession*, pp. 206 ff.

Koeberle, A. "Social Problems and the Augsburg Confession," *LCQ*, 18, 258 ff.

Mattes, J. C. "The Augsburg Confession and its Significance to the Church," *LCQ*, 3, 135 ff.

Neve, J. L. *The Augsburg Confession*. Philadelphia: United Luth. Publ. House, 1914.

————. *Story and Significance of the Augsburg Confession on its four-hundredth anniversary*. Burlington: The Lutheran Literary Board, 1930.

Reu, J. M. *The Augsburg Confession. A Collection of Sources with a Historical Introduction*. Chicago: Wartburg, 1930.

Schlink, Ed. "The Breadth of the Church of the Augsburg Confession," *Lutheran World Review*, I, 3, pp. 1 ff.

Tappert, T. G. "The Roman Confutation of the Augsburg Confession," *LCQ*, April, 1931, 147 ff.

"Lutheran Reply to the Confutation," *LCQ*, 5, 36 ff.

Bouman, H. J. A. *The Ecumenical Character of Lutheran Doctrine, Proceedings of the 46th Convention of the Ev. Lutheran Synodical Conference*. St. Louis: Concordia, 1960.

Mueller, J. T. "The Concept of God in Luther and the Lutheran Confessions," *CTM*, XXVI, 1 ff.

Pelikan, J. "The Doctrine of Creation in Lutheran Theology," *CTM*, XXVI, 569 ff.

Spitz, L. W. "The Soteriological Aspects of the Doctrine of the Holy Trinity According to the Lutheran Confessions," *CTM*, XXVI, 161 ff.

Sanders, C. F. "The Challenge of the Trinitarian to the Neo-pagan," *LCQ*, 10, 255 ff.

Franzmann, M. H. "Augustana II, Of Original Sin," *CTM*, XX, 881 ff.

Heim, R. D. "The Doctrine of Original Sin," *LCQ*, 14, 308 ff.

Hanson, H. W. A. "Jesus Christ the Interpreter of God," *LCQ*, 6, 246 ff.

Bouman, H. J. A. "The Doctrine of Justification in the Lutheran Confessions," *CTM*, XXVI, 801 ff.

Petersen, Lorman. "The Doctrine of Justification, the leitmotiv of the Apology of the Augsburg Confession." Thesis. Concordia Seminary, St. Louis, 1940.

Strock, J. R. "On Justification by Faith," *LCQ*, 17, 286 ff.

Buchheimer, L. "De opere Spiritus Sancti (AC V)," *CTM*, XX, 401 ff.

Mayer, F. E. "De ministerio ecclesiastico," *CTM*, XXI, 881 ff.

———. "Significance of the Doctrine of the Church and the Ministry," *CTM*, XI, 19 ff.

Zimmermann, L. M. "The Shepherding of Souls," *LCQ*, 5, 280 ff.

Albert, C. S. "De Nova Obedientia," *Lutheran Quarterly*, XXII, 385 ff.

Herman, S. W. "The New Obedience," *LCQ*, 13, 279 ff.

Bergendoff, C. "The True Unity of the Church," *LCQ*, 12, 257 ff.

Bretscher, P. M. "The Unity of the Church," *CTM*, XXVI, 321 ff.

Mayer, F. E. "The Una Sancta in Lutheran Theology," *CTM*, XVIII, 801 ff.

———. "The Proper Distinction Between Law and Gospel and the Terminology 'Visible and Invisible Church,'" *CTM*, XXV, 177 ff.

Mueller, J. T. "Notes on the 'Satis Est,'" *CTM*, XVIII, 402 ff.

Preus, H. A. *The Communion of Saints*. Minneapolis: Augsburg, 1948.

Piepkorn, A. C. "What the Symbols Have to Say About the Church," *CTM*, XXVI, 721 ff.

Reu, J. M. "Biblical Background of the 7th Article of the Augsburg Confession," *LCQ*, 8, 373 ff.

Beto, George. "The Marburg Colloquy," *CTM*, XVI, 91 ff.

Engelder, Theo. "The Reformed Doctrine of the Lord's Supper," *CTM*, X, 641 ff.

Graebner, Theo. "The Roman Catholic Doctrine of the Lord's Supper," *CTM*, X, 801 ff.

Mueller, J. T. "The Body of Christ in the Holy Supper," *CTM*, IX, 850 ff.

Sasse, Herman. *This is My Body*. Minneapolis: Augsburg, 1959.

Snyder, H. W. "The Lord's Supper," *LCQ*, 9, 288 ff.

Rasmussen, C. C. "Holy Baptism," *LCQ*, 18, 131 ff.

Matser, E. W. "Confession and Repentance in the Light of AC XI and XII," *Journal of the American Lutheran Conference*, 7, 740 ff.

Wickey, Gould. "Christian Confession of Sin and Guidance." *LCQ*, 18, 344 ff.

Davis, H. G. "The Use of the Sacraments," *LCQ*, 16, 115 ff.

Piepkorn, A. C. *What the Symbolical Books of the Lutheran Church Have to Say about Worship and the Sacraments*. St. Louis: Concordia, 1952.

Fischer, M. H. "Civil and Religious Liberty," *LCQ*, 1, 265 ff.

Heick, O. W. "The Doctrine of the Last Things in Lutheran Theology," *LCQ*, 17, 421 ff.

Willkomm, H. "Jesus the Judge of the World," *CTM*, XXV, 257 ff.

Carney, W. H. B. "Of the Cause of Sin," *LCQ*, 3, 261 ff.

Kantonen, T. A. "The Cause of Sin," *Lutheran Quarterly* (1953), pp. 259 ff.

Repass, S. A. "The Causes of Sin," *Lutheran Quarterly*, XIV, 390 ff.

Gaugher, H. L. "Free Will," *Lutheran Quarterly*, XIII, 477 ff.

Grimm, K. J. "The Christian Ideal of Life and Standard of Values," *LCQ*, 7, 217 ff.

Rohnert, W. "Of Faith and Good Works," *Lutheran Quarterly*, 57, 14 ff.

Hoover, H. D. "The Worship of Saints," *LCQ*, 2, 303 ff.

Heintze, R. W. "The Historical Significance of the Formula of Concord," *Theological Monthly* (St. Louis, April, 1928—September, 1929).

Meyer, John E. "Justification in Article III of the Formula of Concord," Thesis. Concordia Seminary, St. Louis, 1944.

Andresen, J. W. *Luther's Small Catechism, 1529-1929*. Rock Island: Augustana, 1929.

Graebner, Theo. *The Story of the Catechism*. St. Louis: Concordia, 1928.

Mueller, J. T. *Luther's Large Catechism*. Burlington: The Lutheran Literary Board, 1929.

Reu, J. M. *Dr. Martin Luther's Small Catechism*. Chicago: Wartburg, 1929.

INDEX OF SUBJECTS

of universal priesthood, 242-245, 250

Sacraments, 180-187
administration by "wicked," 209 f., 234
administration of, 197, 199, 205, 217, 229, 265, 275
contempt of, 214
daily, 145
doctrine of, 182
exclusion, 212 f.
external fellowship of, 209, 217 f.
and faith, 152 f.
hastening to, 136, 143, 180, 305
marks of the church, 199 f., 205-208, 217-220, 223, 231
is ordination a? 245 f.
and proclamation, 199
sign and testimony, 156 f., 277, 310
visible Word, 185
Word and element, 145 f., 155 f., 157
see also Baptism; Confession; Faith; Grace; Lord's Supper; Office, ecclesiastical; Preaching
Sacrifice; see Jesus Christ; Law, ceremonial
Saints
community (fellowship) of, 200, 203 f., 205, 209 f., 211, 215, 217, 221, 222, 225, 253, 284, 285
false, 55, 75, 111, 121
in faith, 104, 132
in Old and New Testament, 69
Scripture, 1-11
authority, 65
autopistia, 10, 16
canon, 4, 9, 16
center of, 27
exposition, 12 f., 29, 297 f.
inspiration, 5, 8, 10, 16
norm of doctrine, 1-11, 25-29, 32, 297
and patristic quotations, 17 f., 171
quoting from, xix, 2, 7, 10, 15, 297-299
Spirit and letter, 30
testament, Old and New, 1, 4, 9, 12, 27, 106 f., 131-134, 273, 298, 311 f.
and tradition of the Fathers, 1-3, 9 f., 17-21, 29

summary of, 6, 13 f., 298 f., 309, 314
whole (entirety of), 52, 132, 311
see also Church; Confession of Faith; Faith; Gospel; Law; Word of God
sin, 40-47
"all works" are, 120, 122
and civil righteousness, 77, 122
concupiscence, 40 f., 44, 119 f., 148, 181, 254
and creation, 38-52, 271 f., 308
. . . , death, and devil, 66, 82, 87, 96, 104, 139, 148, 149, 183, 186, 229, 231, 236, 272, 276
deliberate, 128
faith not with, 105, 106, 117
battle against, 163
forgiveness of, 28, 69, 88, 91, 92, 96, 102, 106, 124, 133 f., 138, 141, 148, 151, 159, 163, 168, 214 f., 271
guilt (debt), 58, 69, 85, 87, 93, 148, 291 f.
knowledge of, 12, 54, 76, 121, 142 f., 195
and Law, 110, 135, 277, 311
mortal sin, 106
obedience "without," 255, 264
impenitent sinners, 212-214
original, 41-49, 52, 59, 75, 84, 87, 148, 194-196
payment for, 68 f., 84-86
punishment of, 82, 102, 261, 291
retaining of, 215, 230
and sinner, 124 f., 142
work of devil, 45-47, 289
see also Confession; Jesus Christ; Man
Son; see God (triune); Jesus Christ
Spirit, Holy
and Baptism, 147-150, 181
and church, 32, 153, 199-205, 209, 211, 216-219, 225
and confession of faith, 15 f., 19-22, 25
creator, 58-60
and faith, 101-104, 289 f.
and flesh, 125, 165
fruits of, 110-115, 127 f., 202
gifts of, 307, 310
and kingdom of Christ, 197 f.
knowledge of God, 28 f., 57, 61, 71
and Law, 71, 77, 120, 129, 133

obstruction of (resistance to), 290-292

renewal, 106-109, 117, 124-126, 273, 286, 287

and Scripture, 5, 8-10

work of, 15 f., 57 f., 102, 105, 114, 150, 178, 225, 290, 292

see also God (triune); Office, ecclesiastical)

State; *see* Office, civil

Summary; *see* Scripture

Temptation (Anfechtung, affliction, attack, trial), 49, 104 f., 108, 118, 140, 182, 187, 211, 295

Testament, Old and New; *see* Church; Faith; Gospel; Law; Scripture

Tradition; *see* Confession of faith; Scripture

Trinity; *see* God (triune)

Two Natures; *see* Jesus Christ

Ubiquity; *see* Jesus Christ

Union; *see* Church

War; *see* Office, civil

Will; *see* God; Man; Regeneration

Word of God

and confession of faith, 16

distinction of Law and Gospel, 91 f., 129-131, 134-138, 141, 275 f., 279

"external," 22, 197 f., 217, 222

and faith, 102, 104

of forgiveness, 92, 102, 107, 125, 212, 273, 288

is Gospel, 139, 201

and man's word, 27 f., 247, 285

mark of the church, 197 f., 199-205, 209, 212, 217-220, 285

and sacrament, 113, 183-187, 218-220, 301

of Scripture, 10, 12, 67, 71, 136, 237

source of knowledge, 52 f., 55, 57, 305

and spiritual and secular government, 229 f., 232 f., 236-243, 246, 247, 251 f., 260, 266

use of, 112

visible, 185

see also Baptism; Gospel; Law; Lord's Supper; Preaching; Scripture

Work; *see* God; Jesus Christ; Redemption; Spirit

Works; *see* Faith; Justification; Law; Man

World

church and, 32, 208, 210, 222, 241, 259, 268

and creation, 38, 308

"before creation of," 288, 293

and devil, 148 f., 182, 195, 209, 289, 294

end of, 279, 282, 283, 285

fallen, 39, 48, 57, 147

history, xviii, 20 f., 27, 59, 178, 278

new, 57, 191, 273

of sin and death, 59, 128, 287 f.